Harvard Contemporary China Series, 14

The Harvard Contemporary China Series is designed to
present new research that deals with present-day issues
against the background of Chinese history and society. The
focus is on interdisciplinary research intended to convey
the significance of the rapidly changing Chinese scene.

Grassroots Political Reform in Contemporary China

Edited by

Elizabeth J. Perry

and

Merle Goldman

Harvard University Press

Cambridge, Massachusetts

London, England   2007

ISBN-13: 978-0-674-02485-4 (cloth : alk. paper)
ISBN-10: 0-674-02485-0 (cloth : alk. paper)
ISBN-13: 978-0-674-02486-1 (paper : alk. paper)
ISBN-10: 0-674-02486-9 (paper : alk. paper)

Cataloging-in-Publication data available from the Library of Congress.

Contents

Acknowledgments

We want to make special acknowledgment of the enormous contributions that Nancy Hearst, the librarian of the Fairbank Center for East Asian Research at Harvard University, has provided in preparing not only this book for publication but also many other books in the Harvard Contemporary China Series. She has checked the notes and sources, helped with the editing, and verified information. We are in great debt to Nancy for her tireless efforts toward ensuring the accuracy of our own work and that of so many of our colleagues. For these reasons, we dedicate this book to Nancy.

We are grateful as well for the financial support we received from the Project for the Study of Political Reform in China at the Fairbank Center, the Harvard-Yenching Institute, the Harvard Asia Center, and the Halpern Foundation. Finally, we thank Wen-Hao Tien, Wilt Idema, and Ron Suleski for their help with the conference from which this book derives.

Elizabeth J. Perry
Merle Goldman

Abbreviations

ACFTU	All-China Federation of Trade Unions
BBS	bulletin board service
CCP	Chinese Communist Party
CID	Common Interest Developments
CWWN	Chinese Working Women Network
ECUPL	East China University of Politics and Law
HR	human resources
ICO	Institute of Contemporary Observation
IRN	International Rivers Network
MoCA	Ministry of Civil Affairs
NFPP	National Forest Protection Program
NGO	nongovernmental organization
NPC	National People's Congress
OLS	ordinary least squares regression
PC	people's congress
PMC	property management company
PRC	People's Republic of China
RC	residents' committee
SLCP	Sloping Land Conservation Program
SMTU	Shanghai Municipal Trade Union
SOE	state-owned enterprise
SUR	seemingly unrelated regression
TAR	Tibetan Autonomous Region
TNC	The Nature Conservancy
TVE	township-village enterprise
VA	village assembly
VC	village committee
VEC	village election committee
VL	village leader
VRA	village representative assembly
WWF	World Wildlife Fund
YWH	*yezhu weiyuanhui* (homeowners' association)

Grassroots Political Reform in Contemporary China

ELIZABETH J. PERRY
MERLE GOLDMAN

1 | Introduction:

Historical Reflections on Grassroots Political Reform in China

At a time when policymakers, media pundits, and political scientists are obsessed with the issue of democratization, any book with the words "political reform" in its title is likely to evoke images of voter registrations, electoral campaigns, and ballot boxes. At the outset, therefore, let us make clear that—although this book includes discussion of local elections—the central focus is not on the prospects for national democratization in China. This volume explores another equally crucial and even more universal aspect of political reform, that of restraining arbitrary and corrupt official behavior and enhancing the accountability of grassroots authorities.

The challenge of curbing malfeasance among lower-level officials poses serious difficulties for all political systems—ancient and modern, democratic and authoritarian alike.[1] China offers an unusually rich site for investigating grassroots political reform, due to its lengthy political history and huge geographical expanse. With thousands of counties and hundreds of thousands of villages under its jurisdiction, the Chinese state for centuries has grappled with the problem of restraining grassroots authorities.[2] In the case of contemporary China, local elections play a role in meeting this challenge, but so too do many other institutions and practices: cadre responsibility systems, budget transparency programs, fiscal reforms, legal aid services, NGO pressures, popular protests, and the media.

China's current grassroots political reforms could actually help forestall rather than facilitate the advance of formal democracy at the national level. Such an outcome is precisely what top-level Chinese leaders desire. They promote basic-level reforms, such as elections for village heads and village committees, to revive the party's local authority in hopes of prolonging the survival of the Communist party-state. Such a policy is not necessarily an unpopular strategy. Deferring progress toward national political reform in favor of dealing with the immediate challenge of curbing corrupt local cadres may be viewed as an acceptable tradeoff by ordinary Chinese citizens, for whom abusive and rapacious local officials pose the more urgent and immediate concern. Preventing one's township party secretary from selling off collective lands without providing proper compensation or punishing a village head who has embezzled school tuition fees, for example, may be of far greater interest than any calls for national elections.

Reforms to improve local governance in order to buttress regime stability are hardly a new feature of Chinese political statecraft. Yet their checkered history reveals the difficulties and dangers involved in trying to preserve a regime through grassroots reforms. Faced with similar problems of widespread corruption and lack of responsiveness by officials to mass demands, China's last imperial dynasty, the Qing, introduced a series of ambitious grassroots reforms during its final decade (1901–1911). Though allowing for only limited suffrage, the late Qing reforms encouraged participation in local self-government in a futile effort to save the monarchical system. The Nationalists, who ruled from 1927 to 1949, also promoted local political reforms in an ill-fated attempt to stem the Communist revolutionary tide. These earlier initiatives, neither of which prevented the fall of the existing political systems, highlight the perils inherent in trying to rescue authoritarian regimes by improving grassroots governance.[3] Yet for anyone looking for signs of Chinese democracy, the failures of these previous experiments offer little evidence that authoritarian-sponsored reforms improve the likelihood of democratization.

Rather than frame our inquiry in terms of prospects for national

democracy, therefore, this volume focuses on the actual impact of reform initiatives on local politics. What measures have been introduced to limit official abuses at the grassroots level? How do citizens
and cadres make use of and respond to these measures? Which
methods enhance or inhibit the provision of public goods? Which
practices undergird or undermine local order?

A local perspective, however, cannot ignore national politics. After all, it is the central authorities who have promoted many of the
grassroots reforms discussed in this volume. In addition, changes
in local state-society relations inevitably have wider repercussions.
Yet whether the contemporary reforms are working to empower or
imperil the party-state remains unclear. Ever since Deng Xiaoping
launched his stunningly successful economic reforms in the late
1970s, China watchers have regularly predicted the advent of major
political transformation, if not regime collapse. With market reforms having produced sustained annual GDP growth rates averaging 9 to 10 percent for the last two decades of the twentieth century,
it was widely assumed that equally momentous political changes
would soon follow. By the early twenty-first century, however, the
People's Republic of China (PRC) had experienced nearly three decades of transformative economic reforms, a period longer than the
Maoist command economy (1957–1978) that preceded it. Moreover,
despite the ever-widening income inequalities and social inequities
that accompanied the economic reforms, China had withstood a series of potentially disruptive top leadership successions without a
major overhaul of the political system.[4] Radical economic change
and political restructuring, it appears, do not necessarily operate in
tandem in contemporary China. Whether or not the current regime
endures much longer, it is worth inquiring into the practices that
make local politics more or less bearable or burdensome for the
hundreds of millions of Chinese who will have lived most, if not all,
of their lives under conditions of partial reform.

The chapters in this volume are all based on substantial fieldwork,
conducted in both rural and urban settings. Taking advantage of
new opportunities for interviews, surveys, and archival research in
villages and cities across China, the authors analyze the challenges
and complexities of ruling a country that is undergoing extraordinary economic and social change. The observations and conclusions

reflect contemporary data and developments, while at the same time evoking striking parallels with previous Chinese experiments in grassroots political reform. Placing current patterns in the historical context raises perplexing questions about the likely trajectory of the post-Mao reforms.

Late Qing Political Reform

From the 1860s until the collapse of the imperial system in 1911, the Qing court sponsored a series of increasingly ambitious reform programs intended to counter the growing threat of foreign imperialism: the Self-Strengthening Movement, followed by the 1898 Hundred Days Reform, and finally the New Policies. While the Self-Strengthening Movement (1860s–1890s) was largely confined to modernization of the industrial and military realms, the Hundred Days Reform (June–September 1898) extended the reformist agenda to the educational, legal, and political arenas. During both of these movements, reformers argued that vibrant local self-government (difang zizhi) was the nation's best defense against foreign domination.[5] Yet only with the New Policies were there serious efforts to implement grassroots political reforms. In the aftermath of the Boxer Uprising (1900), elements of the central government—chastened by the foreign armies' invasion of Beijing—embraced the concept of a thoroughgoing reform initiative that came to include the establishment of elected provincial assemblies, local councils, and other new channels for political participation.

Particularly after Japan's surprising defeat of Russia in 1905, the Chinese imperial court regarded the active promotion of local self-government as an essential step toward invigorating the body politic. Inspired by foreign models of constitutional monarchy and faced with the threat of domestic local elites who had gained considerable powers as a result of the militarization that accompanied the suppression of the mid-nineteenth-century Taiping Rebellion, late Qing reformers endorsed self-government as a key ingredient of national unity. Participation in local governance, it was argued, would improve individual character, curb corruption, and thereby contribute to the overall health of the nation.[6] Elections, with tightly restricted suffrage, were held in 1908–9 for newly established provincial assemblies. The elected assemblymen then agitated for national influence, which resulted in the inauguration of China's first National Assembly in 1910.[7] At the same time that these assemblies were taking shape at the provincial and national levels, other unprecedented developments were occurring at lower levels of the political system. What historian Mark Elvin has described as the "first formally democratic political institution in China"—a city council in the Chinese sections of Shanghai—was founded in 1905.[8] Drawing upon a tradition of guild, charity, and public works activities, the Shanghai city council presided over a "limited welfare state" in which—according to Elvin—political corruption was virtually absent, issues were openly debated at public meetings, and decisions were taken by majority vote.[9]

In 1907 the Shanghai city council—emulating the Tianjin municipal council established earlier that year—expanded voting procedures that extended the franchise to all educated males who had resided in the city for more than five years and who paid more than 10 RMB (*renminbi*) in annual taxes.[10] The city of Guangzhou quickly followed with the formation of an activist Merchant Self-Government Society.[11] In 1909 the emperor issued formal regulations for the establishment of elected local self-government organizations, which were made responsible for overseeing a wide range of critical functions that included education, public health, road repair, welfare, and tax collection.[12] By the time of the 1911 Revolution, some five thousand elected local councils in market towns, townships, and county seats were in operation around the country.[13]

In some cases these grassroots organizations may have built upon and systematized modes of local governance that long predated the introduction of the New Policies. Accounts of "village democracy" date back at least to the mid-nineteenth century. In 1855 the peripatetic Catholic priest abbé Huc reported from his travels across China that "the villages . . . have at their head a mayor . . . who is chosen by universal suffrage."[14] Another foreign observer, writing in 1899, noted that "local affairs are entrusted to village or district councils, and the most worthy person for the office is elected mayor by the suffrages of the community."[15] The missionary Arthur H. Smith, writing on the basis of a deep familiarity with rural China, observed in 1899 that "the management of the village is in the hands of the people themselves. . . . Every Chinese village is a little principality."[16] But Smith was careful to distinguish this situation from "pure democracy," pointing out that the actual village administration rested in the hands of a few headmen whose rise to a position of power often occurred "by a kind of natural selection" rather than through formal elections.[17] Summarizing the "meager data" available on the subject, historian Kung-ch'üan Hsiao concludes that the nineteenth-century Chinese village "was not exactly an autonomous democratic community. Its 'official' or formal leaders . . . were ostensibly nominated by their fellow villagers, but in actual practice they owed their positions more to the pleasure of the 'principal persons' of the neighborhoods than to the free choice of the majority of the inhabitants."[18]

The local councils that emerged in the final decade of the Qing may have drawn some inspiration from earlier electoral practices, limited though they were. The new assemblies, however, differed from previous institutions in that they were officially promoted and regulated by the state. Ironically, this very connection rendered these organizations potentially more politically subversive than their forerunners—whose activities had been confined to the sub-state level. Although little is known about the routine activities of the thousands of local councils that flourished under the New Policies, we do know that they played a significant role in preparing the ground for political revolution. Most council deliberations seem to have revolved around the contentious issue of taxation.[19] The central government charged the new assemblies with not only financing their own operations but also establishing costly new schools, police stations, and other symbols of the modern state. As the elected councilmen and assemblymen increasingly regarded themselves as superior to appointed magistrates and governors, they were more willing to challenge central state authority on the issue of revenues as well as other matters.[20] Consequently, with the increase in taxes occasioned by the New Policies, public anger exploded into large-scale rural resistance that in some areas fed directly into demands for revolutionary change.[21] The 1911 Revolution, which shattered two thousand years of imperial rule, was in large measure fueled by the growing assertion of local autonomy. The swiftness of the dynasty's collapse attested to the strength of the network of self-government associations that had sprung up as a direct product of the New Policies.[22] Grassroots reforms thus hastened the downfall of the Qing dynasty.

Republican China

The collapse of the imperial system in October 1911, and its replacement by a newly proclaimed Republic of China on January 1, 1912, ushered in an extraordinary period of political ferment. Within two years the Chinese electorate numbered in the tens of millions.[23] Continuing the New Policies, the fledgling republican government assigned to local assemblies a wide array of administrative responsibilities, ranging from the oversight of police and militia forces to the provision of public works, especially the construction of new schools. Because these unfunded mandates required substantial expenditures, local officials were increasingly unwilling to share the taxes they collected with higher levels of government. Consequently, in February 1914 the president of the Republic of China, Yuan Shikai, dispensed with the Qing dynasty's local self-government program. The reversal "was cheered by provincial officials who were nettled by local councilors' control over their own jurisdictions and, more important, scarce tax revenues."[24]

Although Yuan Shikai's blanket prohibition of local assemblies temporarily halted experiments in grassroots electoral democracy, it did not resolve the fiscal tug-of-war among administrative levels, as counties and provinces continued to compete for limited revenues.[25] When the counties' decentralized method of tax farming proved effective at capturing revenues, the provinces followed suit.[26] The result was what Prasenjit Duara describes as "state involution"—a situation in which the government's fiscal and administrative growth generated an informal, inefficient, and ultimately uncontrollable "entrepreneurial brokerage" network of tax collectors, middlemen, and local bullies.[27]

When the Nationalists established their new regime in 1927, one of their initial concerns was to revive the concept of local self-government, which Sun Yat-sen had hailed as an essential prerequisite for national unity and strength.[28] Optimistic plans were drafted to implement democratic self-government in all sub-county administrative units by 1934. In those areas where the program was introduced, however, official posts were generally taken over by resident landlords, for whom a local self-government position provided a valuable political shield for one's economic holdings or business deals. Conflicts between government and party agencies over jurisdictions further weakened the Nationalists' reform efforts.[29] The result was hardly the universal democratization of grassroots politics that Sun had envisioned.[30] As the regime's more pressing goals of internal security and central control took precedence, the program was unceremoniously scuttled a year before it was to have been fully implemented.[31]

Aware that success on the battlefield would require at least a modicum of grassroots support, the Nationalist authorities in the 1940s launched another self-government initiative in over a thousand counties and cities. But once again, the councils were captured by local elites who proved far more interested in protecting their own pocketbooks than in providing public goods.[32] Preoccupied with waging war against both the Japanese and the Communists, the Nationalist government never mustered the level of either funding or political commitment required to break the stranglehold of these elites and foster genuinely popular self-government. Instead, state attention was increasingly directed toward security measures such as the *baojia* mutual surveillance system, aimed at identifying and combating the enemy. Although Nationalist directives stressed the compatibility of self-government and mutual security, "in reality the *baojia* system seriously undermined self-governance efforts and eventually replaced the nascent self-government system."[33] When the Nationalists retreated to Taiwan in 1948, not one county in mainland China had attained the level of self-government stipulated by law.[34]

With the Nationalist government stymied in its attempt to implement serious grassroots political reform, hundreds of nongovernmental initiatives sprang up to fill the breach. By one count, "almost 700 distinct organizations devoted to rural work of various sorts" were active during the Nanjing decade.[35] The rural reconstruction programs promoted by intellectual activists such as Tao Xingzhi, Huang Yanpei, Jimmy Yen, Liang Shumin, and others initially focused primarily on the challenge of mass education. Gradually, agricultural modernization, public health, rural industry, and credit and marketing cooperatives also became important elements of the reconstructionist agenda. Even militia reorganization was successfully carried out in some of the experimental village sites.[36] Moreover, Republican-era nongovernmental organizations (NGOs) did not confine their operations to the rural areas. Missionary and quasi-missionary groups, such as the YMCA, the YWCA, and the National Christian Council of China, organized literacy classes, public health programs, and physical education activities targeted at industrial workers and other urban residents.[37] These nongovernmental efforts, however, did not have the capacity to restrain rapacious tax collectors and abusive policemen.

Given the harsh circumstances of wartime China, such quixotic rural and urban nongovernment efforts are sometimes depicted as hopelessly naïve. Yet both the Rural Reconstruction Movement and the YMCA recruited many idealistic young activists who became alienated by the Nationalists' poor record of reform and eventually joined the Communist revolutionaries.

Communist-Sponsored Grassroots Reform

Although the Communists, like their Nationalist rivals, placed high priority on developing a powerful military and security apparatus, they did not discount the critical importance of mass mobilization. From its founding in July 1921 through the establishment of a Communist regime in October 1949, the Chinese Communist Party (CCP) devoted extraordinary attention to organizing workers and peasants. As part of this undertaking, the CCP experimented with a variety of grassroots political institutions. During the period of the First United Front, between the Communists and the Nationalists (1924–1927), when the main focus of the party's efforts was concentrated on the cities, the CCP moved from advocating democratically elected "citizens' representative congresses" (shimin daibiao huiyi) to establishing Bolshevik-style worker "soviets."[38] In the countryside, a similar evolution took place in the early 1930s as peasant associations (nongmin xiehui) were merged into soviet governments.

When the Communists founded their Shaan-gan-ning Soviet following the Long March of 1934–35, they introduced a range of programs intended to foster peasant enthusiasm and support. Much of the rural reconstructionist agenda—mass education, rural industrialization, cooperatives, and the like—was adopted by the CCP at this time. The agenda also included a package of political reforms known collectively as "New Democracy." The cornerstone of this initiative was an election law adopted in May 1937 that expanded voting rights beyond the strict class categories sanctioned by the previous soviet system, providing for "universal direct equal suffrage by secret ballot . . . to everyone who was at least sixteen years of age, regardless of sex, religion, race, financial situation or culture."[39] The Communists encouraged innovative voting methods (e.g., dropping white- or black-colored beans in jars placed behind each candidate) to accommodate the problem of peasant illiteracy while safeguarding the secret ballot. The plan envisaged a four-stage process in which villagers would progress from voting for local township councils all the way up to elections for the border region government. With turnout ranging from 50 to 90 percent of eligible voters, the district elections in the spring of 1937 apparently generated considerable popular interest. Mark Selden describes the electoral process as drawing on familiar rural customs while at the same time introducing a radically new practice—sharp criticism of incumbent officials:

> The pageantry [was] reminiscent of a country festival, which was skillfully utilized to spur popular participation. Balloting climaxed a four-day election meeting in the district seat. After opening-day ceremonies which featured colorful performances by children's groups and mass organizations, the second and third days were devoted to reports and discussion as well as criticism of the government and individual officials. On the final day elections were held.[40]

Although the 1937 campaign was carried out successfully in many districts of the regional government, the progression to voting for the border region council never occurred. Japanese military offensives that summer caused the CCP to scale back its ambitious program. As Selden observes, "Both the enormous organizational energies devoted to the electoral movement and its abandonment in mid-course are characteristic of the mass-movement style of politics, which shunts aside routine procedure and legal niceties."[41] Also typical of mass movement politics was the practice of public criticism, which soon overshadowed elections as Mao's signature method for restraining incumbent officials. Employed during the Yan'an Rectification Campaign (zhengfeng) of 1942–1944, techniques of mass criticism and self-criticism became a central feature of political life in the new People's Republic of China.

The People's Republic of China under Mao

Local government elections continued intermittently under the PRC, with direct voting stipulated for township, town, and urban district congresses, and indirect voting (by the next-lower level of congress) for county, municipal, and provincial congresses.[42] But despite the impressive array of formal powers assigned to these local and regional state assemblies, in fact they generally operated as rubber stamps for higher-level state directives.[43] Moreover, from the early 1960s until the 1980s, people's congress elections were rarely held.[44]

More influential in the lives of most PRC citizens have been substate political activities. Although a national law providing for the election of village committee officials was not promulgated until 1987 (and was not permanently adopted until 1998), village (brigade) and production team elections were held in many parts of rural China during the Maoist era.[45] These afforded some scope for the expression of fundamental peasant interests: "Electing members of one's own group to power ensured better treatment for the group and better protection in conflicts with outsiders."[46] Yet despite the importance of grassroots elections in some locales, their overall impact was severely limited. John Burns concludes that in general, "from 1962 to 1984 village-level elections were neither a reliable nor an effective method for peasants to influence government policy. They were unreliable because they were not institutionalized, and they were ineffective because the elite dominated them."[47]

The "elite" to which Burns refers was of course a very different group from the elite that had prevented the Qing or the Nationalists from effectively implementing their earlier vision of self-government. Not landlords and tax farmers but party secretaries and government cadres were now chiefly responsible for blocking the advance of grassroots governance. Although Mao's China did not seriously promote electoral democracy as a means of dealing with this issue, the problem of unrestrained local officials was of growing concern. From the Rectification Campaign of the Yan'an era through the Cultural Revolution, Mao advocated the mass line and mass criticism as a method for curbing cadre abuses.

After the founding of the PRC, a variety of activities and institutions were officially endorsed as appropriate means for conveying mass concerns and criticisms to higher authorities. These ranged from informal letters to the editor and individual petitions to formally established bureaus of letters and visits. Mass associations such as the Women's Federation, the Federation of Trade Unions, and the Communist Youth League were supposed to protect the interests of their constituencies and transmit their opinions and grievances to higher levels. During mass campaigns, work teams were dispatched to implement designated policies as well as to gauge the grassroots response.

In the early 1950s, movements such as the Three Antis and Five Antis directed mass criticism against urban elites—capitalists and cadres alike.[48] A decade later, in the prelude to the Cultural Revolution known as the Four Cleans Campaign, a more systematized and thoroughgoing mode of criticism led to the public humiliation and purge of millions of rural cadres found guilty of corruption and other abuses.[49] At the same time, however, "sizeable numbers of campaign-weary, stability-seeking Party officials at all levels of the CCP hierarchy sought to routinize and minimize the disruptive effects of the rectification campaign."[50] Disappointment over the party's inability, and in some cases refusal, to police itself during the Four Cleans set the stage for the even more draconian Cultural Revolution (1966–1976). In an effort to purge the party of those who had blocked his orders, Mao "turned to the youth (Red Guards), the Army, and the worker-peasant masses ('revolutionary rebels') of China to carry out the struggle."[51]

In addition to intensifying the practice of mass criticism, which often entailed physical violence as well as public shaming, the Cultural Revolution saw the emergence of new methods for disciplining cadres. May Seventh Cadre Schools were established in remote locations across the countryside to serve as sites for the reeducation of government and party officials. During their stints at these schools (which could last from a few months to several years), inductees were required to engage in manual labor as well as political study and were also expected to accept instruction from local residents. The Cultural Revolution's inauguration of "revolutionary committees," in which representatives from both the masses and the military were supposed to serve alongside party cadres to replace discredited officials at all levels of the political system, was a further attempt to reduce bureaucratism and involve ordinary people in political administration. The use of big-character posters, struggle sessions, worker theory troops, and worker ambassadors represented further channels of popular participation.[52]

Although the Cultural Revolution, especially in its early stage, evoked social conflict bordering on anarchy, it is often portrayed as a period of extreme state orchestration in which popular initiative played little role.[53] Later events indicate, however, that at least some ordinary participants were deeply politicized by the experience. A number of influential leaders in the Democracy Wall Movement (1978–79), who had engaged in mass criticism as Red Guards and then were sent to the countryside to learn from the peasants, when far away from the party and parental supervision engaged in independent political discourse and questioning of authority.[54]

The Post-Mao Reforms

Mindful of the dangers of unleashing popular political potential, Deng Xiaoping and his successors have tried to confine their boldest reform efforts to the economic sphere. Agriculture was swiftly decollectivized, markets and prices were liberalized, foreign trade and investment were welcomed, private entrepreneurship was encouraged, and state-owned enterprises were gradually restructured and privatized. Administrative reforms, such as limiting the tenure of the party general secretary to two five-year terms, were implemented, but fundamental transformation of the political system was rejected. The contrast with Gorbachev's Soviet Union, where glasnost (openness) proceeded hand-in-hand with perestroika (restructuring), could hardly be starker.[55]

The Chinese describe the post-Mao reforms as "socialism with Chinese characteristics," which they define as a market economy in which the Communist party-state remains basically intact. Despite this underlying continuity in political structure, China's grassroots politics—in rural villages and urban residential districts—has experienced significant transformation in recent years. Although some of these changes are the product of conscious top-down state engineering and some a result of the unintended consequences of state policy, others have been generated by bottom-up societal initiatives as well as international influences. The variation both between and within urban and rural areas is enormous, but the general direction points toward a substantial renegotiation of state-society relations at the grassroots level.

The most publicized state-sponsored reforms, the ramifications of which are considered in the chapters in this volume by Richard Levy and John James Kennedy, are the elections for village committees.[56] In a pattern somewhat reminiscent of Jimmy Yen's Rural Reconstruction Movement in the 1930s, the contemporary village elections have attracted a good deal of international notice and support. The Carter Center, the Ford Foundation, the International Republican Institute, and the European Union—to name but a few of those involved—have provided logistical and material assistance in village elections. Political scientists have also devoted considerable attention to studying the village elections, pondering their relationship to economic development and their implications for political participation, interest representation, and state power.[57]

Although elections reportedly have been conducted in over 80 percent of China's villages, it is widely recognized that they are limited as a mode of grassroots self-government. Only a minority of village elections use what might loosely be characterized as "democratic" procedures: open nominations, more than one candidate per position, and provisions for secret balloting. In most cases the Communist Party retains a firm grip on both the nominations and the results. Furthermore, the party's rejection of opposition parties and its restrictions on open campaigning impede public discussion of issues and reduce many elections to perfunctory votes of confidence on officially approved nominees.

A number of other less publicized but possibly equally or more effective state-sponsored grassroots political reforms have also been introduced. These include the village assemblies and village representative assemblies noted in Lily Tsai's chapter, which are intended to encourage villagers' participation in public deliberations; the cadre responsibility and evaluation system discussed in the chapter by John James Kennedy, which is designed to enforce local officials' compliance with higher-level policies; and the budget transparency initiatives described by Richard Levy, which are aimed at combating cadre corruption. Fiscal reforms, treated in the chapters by Kennedy and by Jean Oi and Zhao Shukai, reflect the state's desire to garner peasant support by limiting the taxation demands of township officials. Beijing has eliminated the agricultural tax previously imposed by the central state, but farmers must still pay other local levies. Moreover, since township governments are held responsible for realizing costly educational and developmental goals with dwindling resources, the ongoing conflict over revenues between the center and the localities has ominous overtones familiar to students of the late Qing and Republican periods.[58]

As many of the authors in this volume note, village reform cannot proceed in isolation from township reform. And since townships are required to implement a wide range of unfunded mandates while at the same time being saddled with an unsustainable burden of debt from bloated payrolls and unprofitable rural industries, there have been calls to abolish the township level of government altogether. Such a reform would be a return to the longstanding pre-Communist tradition of the county serving as the lowest rung of the state hierarchy. At the same time, as the chapter by Lianjiang Li explains, experiments to implement township elections have foundered. To date, the party-state has not managed to effect fundamental administrative restructuring, either by eliminating redundant bureaucratic levels and personnel or by separating party and state functions.[59]

Legal reforms represent another critical yet highly constrained area of state innovation in recent years.[60] New institutions such as the workers' legal aid organizations, described by Mary Gallagher, offer officially sanctioned channels for citizens to seek redress for their grievances. The Administrative Litigation Law, introduced in 1989, permits ordinary citizens to sue government officials.[61] At the same time, the promotion and popularization of legal knowledge have also generated unintended consequences, with disgruntled protesters taking to the streets to demand immediate implementation of official laws and regulations. The chapters by Ching Kwan Lee, Yongshun Cai, and Xi Chen highlight the role of "rightful resistance" in fueling disruptive protests by unemployed workers, displaced homeowners, overtaxed farmers, and other aggrieved citizens.[62] These authors also show how state-approved methods of interest articulation (e.g., letters and visits to government agencies and collective petitions) often prepare the ground for more confrontational protests when grievances remain unaddressed.

Grassroots institutions endorsed by the state as a means of channeling and containing the expression of local interests and anger sometimes transgress prescribed boundaries. The homeowners' associations discussed in Benjamin Read's chapter are an example of state-sanctioned organizations whose mobilizing activities have on occasion challenged government control in urban neighborhoods. Conversely, informal institutions that operate without state approval—such as the illegal village temple associations analyzed by Lily Tsai—may actually serve to promote the state's agenda by facilitating the construction of public goods such as rural roads and schools. Ralph Litzinger's chapter indicates that China's opening to the outside world, and the merging of the grievances of local residents with the concerns of foreign countries, have allowed international NGOs operating as grassroots pressure groups to challenge Chinese state policies. These developments in the direction of what one might depict as a nascent civil society expand both the constituency for and the mechanisms of accountability.[63]

Along with a relative increase in freedom of expression and the move of most Chinese media to the market, greater press freedom now exists than in Mao's China. In a number of high-profile cases, detailed in the chapter by Yuezhi Zhao and Sun Wusan, editors and journalists have taken advantage of this opening to publicize the misbehavior of local officials. In some instances, cadres have been severely reprimanded as a result of such publicity. The flood of cases highlighted by the popular television program *Focus Interviews (Jiaodian fangtan)* (which specializes in exposing official malfeasance) and other muckraking outlets indicates the public's belief in the efficacy of media publicity. But as Zhao and Sun caution, the Communist Party still keeps the media on a short leash, limiting their purview to local cases of corruption and punishing maverick editors and journalists.

Thus the picture of grassroots politics that emerges from the chapters in this volume is decidedly mixed. On the one hand, the state has introduced reforms that it expects will improve the performance and accountability of local government officials, reduce corruption, channel public discontent, and maintain stability. On the other hand, mounting pressures on local officials both from the central state (in the form of responsibility contracts, fiscal reforms, and the like) and from their constituents (expressed through elections, protests, media exposure, and NGOs) place grassroots cadres, particularly in places plagued by a paucity of resources and revenues, in an extraordinarily difficult position. There is no evidence that the central government is seriously considering the implementation of thoroughgoing, systemic political reform—multi-party competitive elections, genuine separation of powers, a truly independent judiciary, freedom of the press—as a solution to its dilemmas. The specter of the former Soviet Union and its swift dismemberment in the wake of Gorbachev's bold political reforms still looms large as a negative example in the minds of Chinese leaders.[64] They prefer a more limited and gradual approach that would change only those things needed to encourage economic growth and discourage popular unrest.

Implications of Grassroots Reforms for China's Future

While history does not repeat itself, it may hold lessons for the present. Given the fact that the late Qing's and Nationalists' grassroots reforms did not save those regimes, can we anticipate that a similar fate will befall China's Communist regime? As Samuel Huntington cautioned in 1968: "Reform, it can be argued, may contribute not to political stability but to greater instability and indeed to revolution itself. Reform can be a catalyst for revolution rather than a substitute for it. Historically, it has often been pointed out, great revolutions have followed periods of reform, not periods of stagnation and repression. The very fact that a regime makes reforms and grants concessions encourages demands for still more changes which can easily snowball into a revolutionary movement."[65] After several decades of reform, both the Qing and the Nationalists were toppled by revolutionary movements. Will China's contemporary reforms help trigger a revolutionary reaction as well? It is impossible to answer this question with certainty, not least because China's post-Mao Communist party-state, unlike earlier Chinese regimes, to date has been able to deliver economically. Despite mounting inequalities and inequities, the post-Mao market reforms in fact have provided tangible benefits to most of the population. This is in stark contrast to Gorbachev's Soviet Union, where the standard of living for the majority of the population plummeted.[66] Consequently, China's Communist party-state enjoys a degree of legitimacy—or at least public toleration—that the former Soviet party-state was unable to retain.

Nevertheless, as is clear from the chapters in this volume, grassroots reforms in contemporary China have unleashed certain centrifugal tendencies, encouraging some local authorities to disregard directives from the central government.[67] Even more worrisome to leaders in Beijing, if they take seriously the lessons of their country's history, is that the reforms have not proved fully effective in restraining abusive officials and rapacious elites, who have reemerged with the loosening of party controls under the market reforms. In the event of an economic downturn, pervasive corruption and predation could again prove to be the Achilles' heel of an authoritarian Chinese state.

The various grassroots reforms described in this volume provide more popular oversight than did the dictatorial controls of the Mao era. Still unclear, however, is whether their cumulative impact will serve to strengthen the present Communist regime or pave the road toward revolution as happened to the Qing and the Nationalists. The Hu Jintao leadership is a technocratic elite, composed overwhelmingly of pragmatic engineers who seek to "'manage' political reforms in a controlled way. . . . Social stability . . . ranks at the top of their agenda."[68] Still, as seen across several successive governments in the Soviet Union in the 1970s and 1980s, technological expertise may postpone a regime's demise, but in the end it cannot save a political system that is out of sync with dynamic economic and social changes occurring at the grassroots level.

Of course, violent revolution is not the only route through which the Chinese political system might be fundamentally reconstituted. Systemic political reform, stimulated in part by successful grassroots electoral experiments, is not without precedent in other polities, including post-Confucian societies, among them South Korea and Taiwan.[69] Successful reform, however, is even harder to accomplish than revolution because of the extraordinary political skill that it requires.[70]

China scholars are divided in their assessment of the effectiveness and adaptability of the current PRC regime. Some point to the government's difficulties in eradicating the rampant corruption and increasing inequalities that have accompanied the market reforms, stressing variously the ineffectiveness of existing institutions and the need for greater central state capacity to deal with these urgent issues.[71] Others highlight the state's recentralization of power in the post–Jiang Zemin era and its determination to curb corruption through new regulatory institutions, tax relief, and ideological indoctrination.[72] Regardless of whether in the long run China's grassroots reforms serve to prolong dictatorial rule, propel dramatic revolution, or even promote comprehensive political reform, the outcome will hinge as much upon the skills of the central leadership as upon developments at the grassroots level. In the meantime, the reforms are reconfiguring local politics in surprising and significant ways. The chapters that follow illuminate these important ongoing changes in China's state-society relations while leaving open the question of their long-term impact.

RICHARD LEVY

2 | Village Elections, Transparency, and Anticorruption:
Henan and Guangdong Provinces

Village self-government and, in particular, village elections, village-level transparency, and associated anticorruption efforts continue to be an area of experimentation in China, as well as a topic of increasing focus among both Chinese and Western scholars. Critical questions abound: What are the purposes of village self-government and village elections? Are they designed to increase democracy for its own sake, or are they a means to an end for reducing the central government's costs in the countryside, constraining the power of local officials, combating corruption, and increasing party legitimacy and overall stability in the rural areas? To what extent are the goals being achieved? How democratic are the elections and the wider self-government processes, and how are they to be assessed—that is, what is democracy? In what types of villages, and under what conditions, do potentially democratic elements flourish or wane? How do they affect the ability of different elite and mass groups and strata to expand their own power or to constrain that of their competitors? To what extent are village self-government and village elections likely to contribute to a transformation of China's political, economic, and social institutions? Will there be elections and self-government at higher levels as part of a movement toward increasing citizenship? If these processes do contribute to a significant transformation, how would this come about and to whose benefit?

Many scholars in China and the West have dealt with these questions in considerable depth.[1] Building on this foundation, this chapter focuses on: (1) recent developments in village self-government and village elections, with an emphasis on how these have developed in Guangdong and Henan;[2] (2) how and why village self-government and village elections have become a means for a new, more economically based rural elite to challenge the older, more politically based village elite and the means by which the older political elite are meeting this challenge;[3] (3) the degree to which village self-government and village elections have been effective in combating corruption at the village level, particularly in light of the increasing frequency and scope of vote-buying in these elections (including both *lapiao*, literally "pulling votes," or using improper methods such as small gifts and free meals to attract voters, and, more significantly, *huixuan*, buying votes or bribing voters); and finally (4) the degree to which items 2 and 3 are linked, that is, how and why corruption in village self-government and vote-buying in village elections are related to the entry of the rural economic elite into the village power structure.

This research draws on a wide review of written materials on village self-government and village elections, a series of formal and informal interviews with over sixty individuals in Guangdong and videos of two elections between October 2001 and March 2002, interviews with village leaders, including party secretaries and members of village committees (VC), in five villages in Xinmi city, Henan province, in January 2004, further interviews with village officials in Xinmi in April 2005, as well as interviews and ongoing exchanges with numerous experts.

Guangdong was chosen because of its coastal location and the high level of economic development in many of its coastal areas, my existing ties with scholars in Guangdong, and my ability to speak Cantonese. Xinmi city was chosen as a contrast because it is at least somewhat representative of central China and a middle level of economic development and because Chinese colleagues with whom I have had lengthy cooperative relationships had studied Xinmi in depth.[4]

The development of village self-government and village elections has been a complex and contradictory process. It includes struggles between and within the central, provincial, and local-level government and party authorities, particularly between the townships and villages, as suggested by the struggles over nomination procedures in Guangdong, efforts to prohibit VC candidates from promising not to collect taxes, and contention over township audits of village books. Because provinces are responsible for developing their own laws to implement village elections, while lower levels implement their own regulations, contradictory laws and regulations have frequently developed, making accurate generalizations quite difficult.[5]

Although both Guangdong and Henan held elections in 2001–2002, Henan's elections were in the fourth round, whereas Guangdong's elections were only in the second round. Largely because of Guangdong's focus on rapid economic development and the perceived negative influence that village self-government might have, VC elections in Guangdong were initiated some ten years later than those in many other areas in China.[6] Because Guangdong had maintained a strict regime of management districts (*guanliqu*) until they were converted to village committees in 1998–99, there seems to have been little variation in the route taken from management district to village committee, although the degree of township interference in village elections did vary and provoked varying degrees of resistance.[7] By contrast, interviews in Xinmi city suggest that with the elimination of the communes, party control nearly collapsed in some villages, and village government was not functional. Taxes were not collected consistently or on time, and village projects, such as irrigation and road repair, were not undertaken due to lack of funding. As a result, in two of the Xinmi villages, in advance of provincial authorization (in 1986 and 1994, respectively), party secretaries organized representative local organizations in which the representatives voted on individual projects, thus facilitating the collection of funds for the projects. It is unclear how widespread such practices were, but a sprout of spontaneous village self-government was clearly beginning. Though in both cases the party secretary initiated this self-government, it nonetheless gave both local governance and the party additional legitimacy and provided a stronger basis for the subsequent development of a more meaningful village self-government movement.

Although it is not possible to deal with election mechanisms fully here, villages in Guangdong, particularly more affluent villages, seemed to pay somewhat more attention to procedural aspects of village elections, that is, the method of selecting the village election committee (VEC), the definition of a villager, the use of proxies *(weituopiao)*, methods of filling in ballots for illiterate voters, mobile voting boxes *(liudong piaoxiang)*, vote counting, the specifics of the voter registration process, secret ballots and secret voting booths, as well as funding for the elections. The reasons for this are unclear, but possible explanations include the greater resources available in more developed villages and the greater stress placed on such issues by the provincial leadership (perhaps due to Guangdong's ability to learn from provinces that had begun elections earlier). This greater emphasis is evident in Guangdong's regulations for village elections and the greater resources allocated for these elections by both the Guangdong provincial government and the Guangdong villages themselves.[8]

Election Outcomes, the Party, and Competitiveness

In elections held in the early years of the twenty-first century, both Guangdong and Henan followed a number of national trends, but clear differences between the two existed, as can be seen in Table 2.1.[9] Although both reported turnout rates higher than the national average, Guangdong's rate was noticeably higher than Henan's, perhaps in part because of the greater number of village enterprises and assets in many Guangdong villages and the use of stipends for voters in various parts of Guangdong.[10] In 2005, three villages in Xinmi city had an average turnout rate of 84.4 percent, though in the village with the highest rate, nearly 50 percent of the votes cast were proxy ballots. In addition, although in 2004 village officials seemed surprised by the notion of voter stipends, pens (valued at 0.8 RMB), detergent, and cash (5 RMB) were distributed in three of the elections.

One clear and significant difference is Guangdong's higher degree of party control of VCs. This is reflected by the percentage of party members on the VCs, which is noticeably higher than both the national average and Henan's rate, and the highest rate of village leaders who are also party secretaries in China.[11] Although

Table 2.1 National village election results, 2001–2002

	Round of election[a]	Date of election	Elections successfully completed (%)	Elections completed on first round (%)	Turnout rate (%)	Elections in which VL was elected (%)	VLs who are female (%)	Party members on VC (%)	Incumbents re-elected to VC (%)	Incumbent VLs re-elected (%)	VLs who are party members (%)	VLs who are party secretaries[g] (%)	VC members who are women (%)	VCs with female members[h] (%)
Guangdong[b]	1	1998–99	98.1	77.5	96.1	97.1		65.0	79.7			50.9	16.4	81.1
Guangdong	2	2001–2	98.1		96.0	99.9		80.0	74.0	65.0		67.0		
Henan[c]	3	1999	97.4[d]	88.3[d]	88.3									
Henan	4	2001–2	98.0	92.5	90.1	97.5		55.5	66.5	61.8	81.0	8.1	16.1	67.5
Anhui	5	2002	98.9				1.6	64.7	65.2				22.0	
Beijing	5	2001	99.1	76.2	92.5	99.9		68.2		40.3	78.6	30.6	23.8	81.1
Chongqing	5	2001–2	100.0	89.3	80.8	97.4	2.8	49.2	59.0	64.3	73.3	1.8	24.0	
Dalian	7	2001	99.4	85.2	68.0	96.0	2.9	81.1	78.0	78.0	89.8	56.4	25.1	98.1
Gansu	4	2001–2	94.0		85.7				65.8				15.1	66.6
Guangxi		2002	99.7		96.3	99.8		68.4					15.7	76.0
Guizhou	5	2001–2	99.5		89.7	100.0	1.5			58.5	51.3			
Hainan	3	2002	99.9	85.6	95.5	99.4	1.9	78.3		55.5	91.0	63.0	18.7	84.5
Heilongjiang	6	2002	54.6		80.0									

Province												
Hunan	5	2002	99.3	91.5				72.5	81.6			29.4	95.8
Inner Mongolia	4	2000	78.6	90.0			48.1	58.7				18.6	82.6
Jiangsu	6	2001–2	94.9	95.8	99.5				59.1	89.1	15.0		
Jilin	5	2001	99.8	92.0		1.0	62.9		63.0	73.0	13.0	20.2	90.9
Liaoning	7	2001	99.9	83.3	99.3		62.0			21.9		24.2	96.7
Ningbo[e]	6	2002	97.9	96.6	103.3		61.2	47.6	48.2	66.0		14.9	47.4
Ningxia	5	2001–2	97.5	87.3	97.4			71.0	48.0			19.0	68.1
Qingdao	7		99.7	91.0	96.2	0.8	68.6		52.7	76.5	28.1	8.1	24.5
Qinghai	5	2001–2	100.0	87.0			49.3	31.2				15.8	77.9
Shaanxi[f]	Trial	2002–3	99.8	87.0	100.0	0.7	51.1		64.4	65.4		5.9	23.7
Shandong	7	2001–2	99.0	91.4	100.2		71.4				68.0	9.1	30.4
Shanghai	7	2002	73.0	90.0									
Sichuan	5	2001–2	98.1	93.5	100.7	3.7	51.3		59.7	75.4			
Tianjin	4	2000	99.7	86.0	75.1		59.0			83.3			
Xinjiang	5	2001–2	84.1		91.8	2.5	41.4			60.1		24.1	105.3
Zhejiang	6	2002	96.9	98.0			50.0			58.0			
Average[j]			95.6	89.4	97.4	1.9	61.1	62.7	60.0	70.9	35.1	18.4	71.6

Note: VC = village committee; VL = village leader.

a. Most data are drawn from reports at the November 2001 Ningbo meeting. No data are available for Fujian, Hebei, Yunnan, Jiangxi, Hubei, Tibet, and Shanxi, either because no data were submitted or because elections were not yet complete. The data provided were not uniform across provinces, leading to some minor inconsistencies in the ways in which the data in this table were calculated.

b. Data for the first round of elections in Guangdong are from "Guangdongsheng lixun gongzuo qingkuang zongjibiao" (Summary Chart on the Situation in the Changeover Work [From Management Districts to Village Committees] in Guangdong Province), in Minzhengbu jiceng zhengquan he shequ jianshesi nongcunchu, *1999 niandu nongcun jiceng minzhu zhengzhi jianshe ziliao huibian* (Collected Materials on Democratic Construction of Basic-Level Rural Democracy in 1999) (Beijing, 2000), pp. 606–607. Li Jiangtao et al., *Minzhu de genji: Guangdong nongcun jiceng minzhu jianshe shixian* (The Basis of Democracy: The Practice of Building Grassroots-Level Rural Democracy in Guangdong) (Guangzhou: Guangdong renmin chubanshe, 2002), p. 46, cites party members as composing 78.4 percent of VC members.

Table 2.1 (continued)

c. Data for the 1999 round of elections in Henan are from "1999 nian Henansheng cunmin weiyuanhui huanjie xuanju qingkuang zongjibiao" (Statistical Totals of 1999 Henan Village Election Situation), on the Ministry of Civil Affairs Web site, www.chinarural.org/readnews.asp?newsid=[E0C84495-E0B1–11D6-A7FF-009027DDFA1E] and www.chinarural.org/readnews.asp?newsid=[E0C84497-E0B1–11D6-A7FF-009027DDFA1E] (accessed May 2002). Since the totals for the makeup of the VCs prior to 1999 do not correspond to the city-by-city numbers provided, and all the data for Zhengzhou in 1999 vary from the prior election by a factor of plus or minus 18, these data are too dubious to be included here.

d. Since, however, only 46,731 of 48,335 villages elected village committees, the percentage of total villages completing the election on the first round is 85.4.

e. Ningbo also provided data for a test site in Yishan Xian: 95.9% (elections successfully completed); 95.74% (elections in which village leader was elected); 64.57% (party members on VC); 51.11% (village leaders who are party members); 98.0% (village leaders who are party secretaries).

f. Data based on test sites elections in three *xian* in August–September 2002.

g. This column may understate party influence because there are no data for party vice secretaries who are village leaders.

h. This was calculated by dividing the total number of women elected by the total number of VCs. Thus, to the extent that some VCs included more than one woman, the figures overstate the number of VCs with female members.

i. The averages exclude the data for the prior rounds of elections in Guangdong and Henan.

no definitive reason for this can be provided, there are two likely contributing factors. First, Guangdong's recruitment of elected non-party village leaders into the party is probably the key factor in explaining this high degree of overlap. Second, the continuing efforts by the Guangdong Organization Department (vis-à-vis the Civil Affairs Department) to assert its power over the elections and the efforts of township governments and party organizations to maintain control of the VCs are also likely to have influenced this outcome. In Henan, by contrast, the more spontaneous beginnings of the village self-government movement and the greater number of small entrepreneurs on the VCs who have not been systematically recruited into the party may help explain the higher number of nonparty local leaders. In addition, the lesser value of village enterprises and the fact that the elections are in their fourth round may reduce the incentives for township interference.

Although neither Guangdong nor Henan provides meaningful statistical data on this topic, competitiveness is another confusing and controversial element in these elections. Western analysts have proposed various hypotheses about the conditions under which such elections are competitive.[12] Anecdotal information about Guangdong's 2001–2002 elections raises questions about the degree of competitiveness there. In the 1999 elections, Henan reported that 79 percent of villages had competitive elections for village leader (VL), of which 90.1 percent had more candidates than positions for village leader, vice leader, and committee members.[13] In 2001–2002, in 47,935 successful elections, 342,487 candidates were nominated for a total of 209,430 VC positions, with a total of 197,779 elected.[14] This suggests that the system of having more candidates than positions for each post may have been relatively uniformly implemented, though it says nothing about the degree of competitiveness among the various candidates.

Somewhat more insight into the competitiveness of elections can be garnered from the interviews in villages in Xinmi city. In at least three of the villages in the 2002 elections, the winning candidate for VL received over 70 percent of the votes, and in another village the party secretary was unable even to remember the name of the losing VL candidate. The 70 percent figure, however, does not always signify a lack of competitiveness. In Village 1, the VL for the first three terms, who had excellent relations with the party secretary, died suddenly near the end of his third term. The township leadership wanted the village party vice secretary to be the next VL, but many villagers did not trust him, so they encouraged the candidacy of the deceased VL's younger brother, a successful businessman not living in the village. Although he was initially hesitant to run for the position,[15] in the process of making his candidacy known, he and his supporters invited a number of villagers to lunches and distributed small gifts. He was subsequently elected with some 70 percent of the vote, and, after some initial friction with the party secretary, the two developed a better working relationship. (The VL, however, was not reelected in 2005 because of the villagers' resentment of his arbitrary leadership methods and allegations of "economic problems.") Elections for vice VL in Villages 2 and 3 seemed to be somewhat more competitive than the VL elections in that no candidate for vice VL received more than the required 50 percent of the vote. With a tendency to be lax about certain electoral procedures, neither village held a supplementary election to fill these positions. In one village the position was left unfilled, while in the other an individual was hired to fulfill the responsibilities of the position although that person was not a member of the VC. In 2005 only one of five elections was truly competitive. In another village, however, after protests from villagers, the primary election was rerun when the party secretary, who was running for VL, withdrew.

Where there was more competition for VL in 2002, it frequently seemed to be linked to "unhealthy tendencies." For example, some had criticized the free meals and small gifts that were distributed in Village 1 as vote-buying. In Village 3, though the VL eventually received 76 percent of the vote, the election was postponed for six months because of allegations of "economic problems" against the prior VL and the party secretary. In Xinmi, in another village in Chengguan township, the winning candidate for VL, who was a successful mine owner, had made promises that cost him some 300,000 RMB in free seeds for villagers, supplies for the VC office and the schools, and a free cable TV hookup for every village family.[16] Although these situations were well known locally, in no case did municipal authorities intervene.

Women on Village Committees

Every province's regulations on village elections address the issue of electing women to the VCs. Henan is one of five provinces that requires one woman on each VC, whereas other provinces call for "an appropriate" number of women.[17] Some controversial efforts have been made in the direction of affirmative action. In some villages in Guangdong, for example, when no woman was elected, the village leadership replaced the male victor who had garnered the fewest votes with a female candidate, even though this procedure was considered to be improper.[18]

Despite such regulations and new practices, the general outcome of this round of elections seems similar to past results. Where data have been reported, only 1.9 percent of village leaders (VLs) are women, 18.4 percent of VC members are women, and some 71.6 percent of VCs have female members.[19] For the most part, when women are elected, they are assigned to "women's work," for instance, family planning and Women's Federation projects. Although there do not seem to be clear data to support it, numerous Chinese analysts have suggested that women may have been better represented in appointed village governments than on elected VCs.

There are conflicting reasons for such results as well as controversial suggestions for ways to increase female representation. On the one hand, recent economic developments have led many men (and a number of women) to leave inland villages for jobs along the coast. This has resulted in a higher proportion of women in many villages, and higher female representation on VCs would be a logical consequence. On the other hand, the downsizing of many VCs to as few as three members would likely decrease female representation unless remedial steps are taken.[20]

But many old and new factors make it difficult for women to be elected.[21] These include the generally lower status of women, which in turn means that they are less likely to gain a significant position on the VC and to be able to realize the goals of their supporters, thus undermining their credibility as candidates.[22] Cultural inhibitions make it harder for women to attend meetings and give speeches, and frequently male backing is required for a female candidate. Many women are not aware that they are eligible to be elected to VCs. Also, they lose their rights in a given village when they marry outside that village (despite guarantees to the contrary), and they are generally unknown in the new village. Finally, women are increasingly competing against a largely male group of entrepreneurs. Thus for meaningful progress to be made, it is likely that measures will have to be taken to address not only the problem of getting women on the ballot but also the deeper issues relating to culture and power in the countryside.[23]

The Rise of Entrepreneurs

A more controversial but less clearly defined issue is the rise of the entrepreneurial strata *(nengren)* at the village level.[24] The key question is why village self-government, and village elections in particular, have become a means for a new rural economic elite to challenge the old political village leadership elite, and how the older political elite is meeting this challenge.

There is a clear tendency toward growing representation of entrepreneurs on VCs. In a number of provinces and municipalities such representation is increasingly viewed as desirable. Individuals are promoted who possess "two strengths" *(shuangqiang)*, that is, the ability to do well in both party work and business.[25] Although Guangdong did not provide any data on the second round of elections, in the first round 10,343 VC members (9.5 percent) and 28 percent of village leaders and vice leaders were *nengren*, though this result was seemingly concentrated in more economically advanced areas.[26] Henan's data are vaguer, stating only that 53.8 percent of those elected in the recent elections were "experienced in management" and that in Shayang city 38.9 percent of those elected had the "two strengths." Interviews with village leaders in Xinmi, however, revealed a larger percentage of party secretaries and VC members who were entrepreneurs.

The issues of entrepreneur participation in and leadership of village self-government and entrepreneur recruitment into the party are of great significance both because they reflect the combination of struggle and cooperation between this new, more economically based elite and the older, more politically based elite and because they reveal what classes or class strata will be in control of these important organizations. In light of the increasing efforts by the government and party to recruit entrepreneurs into both the VCs and the party, it is not surprising that, despite cases of corruption and arbitrary leadership by *nengren* VLs, particularly in Guangdong, most analyses of leadership by entrepreneurs are largely uncritical.[27] Generally, this is based on the belief that these entrepreneurs are motivated to work for the undifferentiated non-zero-sum public good rather than to accumulate wealth and power and, implicitly, that they operate as individuals rather than as an increasingly cohesive class.

Several factors may help explain the different patterns of leadership in different areas of Guangdong and Henan. On the one hand, because of the abovementioned fear that elections might undermine rapid economic development, village elections began later in Guangdong than in other provinces. This suggests that entrepreneurs would remain more on the political sidelines in Guangdong, except to the extent that party secretaries had become entrepreneurs or entrepreneurs had become party secretaries. It also suggests that in Guangdong's coastal areas, where there was greater access to wealth and investment, there may have been a greater ability to maintain collective enterprises in different forms, for instance, the collectively owned development corporations of developed villages such as Wanfeng and collectively owned resources in other urban villages in Guangdong. On the other hand, because the election process began earlier in Henan, and because there were fewer resources available and less ability to attract outside investment, small-scale entrepreneurs were more likely to rise to informal leadership positions in the villages and to join the VCs earlier than in Guangdong.

More significant are the structural factors which help account for the rise of the entrepreneurial strata and their participation in the VCs. With the introduction of tax reforms, many township governments and village committees have been unable to meet their obligations. Several of the villages in Henan were six months to a year behind in paying their cadres. This is not surprising in light of the tripling of the number of cadres nationally since the 1980s. To meet these obligations, local governments frequently become predatory

organs focused primarily on their own survival rather than on providing services. The victims of this predatory behavior are the villages, which have to borrow to pay taxes. This increases their debt
and forces villages to sell their assets to pay cadres, thus further encouraging the privatization of the countryside. At the same time,
many villages have failed in their efforts to develop their own enterprises, resulting in both privatization of village firms and efforts (often organized at the township level) to attract outside investment.[28]
Consequently, because the state no longer balances public interests
in the villages, private interests and private interest groups have become more important.[29]

The virtual bankruptcy of local government combines with the increasing wealth and prestige of the entrepreneurial elite to create
and reinforce in numerous ways the tendency for entrepreneurs increasingly to dominate rural economic and political structures. Several village leaders in Henan referred to the increasing reliance of
the VC on private enterprises following the tax reform. Since villages
often cannot pay their cadres, it becomes more difficult for individuals without independent sources of income to be cadres.[30] In 2004
most of the cadres in the various villages in Xinmi were entrepreneurs (with the exception of Villages 2 and 3, which had the stron-
gest collective economies). In Village 1 the accountant was able to
continue in his post only by relying on loans from the VL members
who were entrepreneurs. In another village in Guankou township,
the VL abandoned his position and went to the township to work as
a truck driver in order to support himself. Moreover, as villages have
fewer and fewer resources, the VCs (and voters) increasingly come
to rely on the entrepreneurs' resources to meet their obligations,
thus further strengthening the political position of the entrepreneurs.

Along with numerous Western scholars, many Chinese analysts see
the participation of entrepreneurs in village (and perhaps higher-
level) elections as an inevitable result of economic development,
which will contribute to the development of democracy by undermining the unitary power system represented by the party-state (although usually no mention is made of alternate sources of power for
non-elites).[31] The dominant perception of the entrepreneurs by officials and analysts alike is to present them as selfless skilled individuals working for the good of the community and able to provide the

skills and resources that will allow others in the village, and the village as a whole, to prosper, thus signifying the degree to which the Maoist notion of class analysis has been discarded. This is the same picture of themselves that the entrepreneurs on the VCs in Henan forcefully presented and is seemingly accepted by many villagers.[32] The small size and multigenerational nature of Chinese villages do give a certain degree of credibility to local entrepreneurs' claims to be concerned primarily with helping the village (and/or clan) and establishing a good personal reputation.

Nevertheless, in wealthier areas in China, winning village elections, according to Qiao Xinsheng, a professor of law at Zhongnan University of Economics and Law in Wuhan, can be a means of gaining control of huge amounts of assets, thus making vote-buying cost-efficient.[33] Reading between the lines of the claims of entrepreneurial village leaders in Henan reveals that they are also developing social capital, through increased credibility and links with township and municipal government and party officials, which can result in business and political opportunities. Simultaneously, they are building linkages in the political and economic structure as their relatives take positions in the government and in party township, county, and municipal structures.[34] Such tendencies could well be part of the process of the creation of a self-conscious class.

Democratic Supervision in Village Self-Government

One premise of village elections and the wider village self-government movement is that elections and democratic supervision (of which transparency is an element) will reduce corruption and increase the legitimacy of the party while also providing information about village management and fiscal affairs to the villagers. These procedures, it is assumed, will better allow the villagers to elect honest cadres and reject, or remove, corrupt ones.

Corruption is widely acknowledged to pose a significant threat to the legitimacy of the party and state and to the development of the Chinese economy.[35] This has been highlighted by the allegation of large-scale corruption at the county level, combined with cover-ups by higher-level officials, such as Huang Jingao, the party secretary of Lianjiang county, Fujian, in August 2004.[36]

An understanding of how corruption is defined and perceived in

China must precede any meaningful evaluation of corruption and anticorruption. Although the definition of corruption is constantly in a state of flux as a result of the rapidly changing economic structure and is itself an arena of substantial political struggle involving significant stakes, Chinese law defines corruption as economic crimes committed by public officials. This definition virtually excludes private entrepreneurs and bribe-payers, although their acts frequently are categorized as "unhealthy practices" *(buzhengzhi feng)* and/or economic crimes, and thus significantly narrows the range of activities that need to be countered.[37]

In order to reduce corruption and give villagers a better understanding of political and fiscal affairs before, during, and between elections, new measures have been developed to increase transparency, improve fiscal and accounting practices, and allow the recall of officials. As long as they are implemented fairly and thoroughly, and are not influenced by corruption or protection networks among cadres, many of these practices and structures could effectively contribute to reducing corruption at the village level.

Village-Level Corruption

Village-level corruption is frequently very different from higher-level corruption. Higher-level corruption often involves large amounts of money in unsecured loans; large-scale embezzlement; bribes for preferential access to materials, markets, and/or decisions about allocation of government resources; cadre participation in smuggling; and so forth. By contrast, in large part because of the more limited scale of villages and village economies (except for some of the more economically advanced villages in places such as Guangdong), village-level corruption usually is more personalistic and cadre-initiated rather than entrepreneur-initiated, and far smaller in both scale and scope. Nevertheless, as entrepreneurs enter the village leadership ranks, this has begun to change. Such village-level corruption most often involves using public funds for private purposes, for instance, lavish meals, entertainment, and personal use of cell phones, cars, and motorcycles; preferential treatment for cadres, relatives, and bribe-payers in allocation of land and village contracts, loans from banking cooperatives, permits for housing, handling of family planning issues, and access to the military; as well as embezzlement and falsification of payments from higher-level authorities.

Recently a new phenomenon, certainly not unique to China, has aroused considerable dispute about whether it should be considered corruption, bribery, an "unhealthy practice," or even a positive development. Vote-buying, which ranges from distributing cigarettes, small gifts, and free meals to directly paying for votes and/or making promises to do certain things for the village or villagers using private funds, has become increasingly widespread, facilitated by the lack of any transparency requirements for campaign financing. Although small-scale vote-buying may be more a process of building personal and social bonds than an economic exchange, large-scale vote-buying is increasingly considered an unhealthy practice.

In the now famous case in Laoyaotou village in Shanxi, for example, Wang, the winning candidate for VL, initially promised to pay voters, who had an average annual income of 1,000 RMB, 200 RMB each if he were elected. By the time of the election, competition had pushed the price up to 2,000 RMB per vote, totaling some 2 million RMB (U.S. $230,000).[38] Once elected, he indeed paid each villager 1,800 RMB. The runners-up spent approximately 145,000 RMB (U.S. $17,530) for the office of vice leader. Despite some debate over whether or not this was bribery (since the benefits were given to all voters, not just supporters), Wang lost his position at the end of 2003, when the Discipline Department of Hejin city ruled that the election was at least tainted with bribery, if not a sheer case of bribery, and thus invalid. In Xinmi such practices were not infrequent, as evidenced by the incidents in Village 1 and Chengguan township mentioned earlier.

The evaluation of such practices varies widely in China. On the one hand, a March 2004 circular from the Ministry of Civil Affairs, in the context of calling for increased party leadership over village elections, defined all vote-targeted actions involving money, goods, or other forms of payment, transacted either by candidates themselves or through their agents, as bribery. The ministry demanded that effective measures be taken to stop such practices and announced that elections won via vote-buying would be declared void.[39] On the other hand, a leading researcher on corruption takes a more benign view, arguing that vote-buying is a form of corruption that signifies the development of a modern economy and that makes elections more competitive. Another leading researcher on village elections, speaking anonymously, though acknowledging that bribery in elections can undermine the villagers' faith in the electoral process, argues that by demonstrating that the elections are important enough for candidates to invest large sums to bribe voters, "bribery is a training course for democracy." If everyone involved in small-scale vote-buying were arrested, he claims, 99 percent of all elections would be invalid.[40]

Why has this practice developed so rapidly in recent years? One reason is the ability of local officials to control meaningful collective resources (where such exist) and/or to build social capital. Another factor is the wide range of local village regulations allowing non-villagers with higher levels of education, more likely but not necessarily the children of the newly rich, and large investors, who by definition are wealthy entrepreneurs, to run for village office. But the most significant factor seems to be the recent increase in the number of *nengren*, entrepreneurs and capitalists, interested in running for election and wealthy enough to engage in vote-buying while receiving the party's endorsement as village leaders and party members.

Zhejiang has attempted to address this problem concretely by developing a detailed list for distinguishing between valid election promises and vote-buying. Valid promises must be made in public electoral speeches; any money promised must be given for a public purpose or to a public organization; promises must be posted in public places (with the approval of the VEC); and candidates must respond to questions about such promises in public ways organized by the VEC. (The rules also prohibit threats, violence, excessively expensive gifts or use of large amounts of money to buy votes, smearing other candidates, giving gifts to individuals or making promises to pay taxes for them, and making other illegal or false promises.) This set of rules, however, is premised on an understanding of vote-buying which itself is based on two unclear criteria: (1) whether the actions have negative consequences for voters and the election, and (2) the scale of the activities.[41]

Many officials and analysts recognize that there is no unambiguous definition of vote-buying or any clear designation of a particular organization or agency charged with investigating or prosecuting such cases,[42] particularly since many national and provincial laws dealing with electoral violations do not cover village elections.[43] When vote-buyers are caught, weak laws, unclear definitions, and protection umbrellas often make punishment impossible. Although individuals engaging in vote-buying may have their candidacies canceled in some provinces, if they win, they cannot be prevented from taking office, or at least they could not until the March 2004 Ministry of Civil Affairs circular was promulgated. Nonetheless, if an election is invalidated because of vote-buying, the vote-buying candidates cannot necessarily be excluded from the runoff election, which frequently requires only 33 percent of the vote to win. In short, the weaknesses of such laws give a decided advantage, if not a structural incentive, to those able to engage in vote-buying.

There seems to be no obvious solution to this problem. Some analysts and officials have suggested very concrete steps, such as guaranteeing that secret voting actually takes place in order to increase the cost of vote-buying, and requiring that in cases where elections are invalidated because of vote-buying, the vote-buyer must pay the costs of the supplementary election (which, ironically, only *nengren* can afford to pay). There is no evidence, however, that these suggestions have been codified into law.[44] At a more structural and controversial level, Qiao Xinsheng of Zhongnan University, recognizing that the ability to control villages' collective resources makes vote-buying cost-effective, suggests that one way to reduce vote-buying would be to remove these assets from the control of the VC, thus leading to further privatization of the countryside.[45] Another highly unlikely alternative suggested by some Chinese analysts is to assign these village assets to the township, which would allow for the reduction of some inter-village inequalities.[46]

Transparency and Democratic Management

Both transparency *(touming)* and "making village affairs public" *(cunwu gongkai)* represent a new lexicon in the Chinese discourse on village self-government and democracy which not only is used by authorities and regulations at all levels but also is integrated into the lives of villagers by the new displays of transparency and praise of transparency by authorities at various levels.

Efforts to control corruption have produced a large number of laws and regulations and training materials at all levels, as well as widely varying degrees of implementation within and between provinces.[47] Although Henan's regulations require that a wide range of data be published at least quarterly, the responsibility for this is implicitly left to the VC itself.[48] Though neither the national government nor most provinces require the establishment of specific committees for transparency or fiscal oversight work, such practices are encouraged. But Guangdong's laws and regulations do call for establishing various organizations, such as elected financial management committees *(licai xiaozu)* and transparency supervision committees *(gongkai jiandu xiaozu)* at the village levels, to increase democratic management and supervision.

In Guangdong, financial management committees are supposed to review and publicize fiscal affairs and/or approve spending requests prior to the disbursement of funds. Transparency supervision committees were authorized in July 2001. While being responsible for oversight of the village transparency system, they also have responsibilities similar to those of the financial management committee, that is, at least semiannual publication of an extremely wide range of materials, which in many other provinces is required of the VC itself. The materials to be publicized include, among others, the program for village economic and social development; the annual VC work plan and data regarding its execution; the annual fiscal plan; all income, expenses, debits and liabilities, and collective assets, including land; specifics of collective contracts *(chengbao)*, including public tenders, income, and expenses of the village collective economy; data on fundraising and construction projects; the requisition of collectively owned land; disaster and general relief spending; supplementary government funding; all fees which make up the peasants' burden; cadre compensation; applications, permission for, and use of residential plots; family planning; and so forth.[49] Although many villages publish these materials, it seems virtually impossible for all villages, particularly poorer ones, to publish everything in a timely manner. For example, the civil affairs director of moderately economically developed Boluo county noted that, at the time of the first election, 20–30 percent of the villages did their transparency work well, 60 percent satisfactorily, and 10–20 percent poorly. Inadequate performance was linked to limited capacity and frequently meant that an insufficient level of detail was published, that is, data were pro forma, and/or materials were published late or not at all. Anecdotal information on the second round of Guangdong elections, however, suggests improved performance in economically advanced villages as well as continuing problems in less developed villages.

A review of transparency in several villages in Guangdong and Henan is quite instructive. Although wealthier urban villages in Guangdong, such as Wanfeng and several villages in Dongguan, had established financial management and/or transparency supervision committees, in 2004 and 2005 in the less economically developed villages in Henan (and likely in Guangdong as well), implementation was more irregular. Though village officials in Henan never referred to transparency supervision committees, financial management committees did exist in different forms. Village 1 had a village *licai xiaozu*. Village 3 had a village *licai xiaozu* composed of four people with a good understanding of economics (excluding the village accountant). (The *licai xiaozu* was part of the rules committee [*yishihui*] of the village representative assembly [VRA].) Village 4, by contrast, had *licai xiaozu* at the team but not the village level, and Village 5 did not have a *licai xiaozu,* but did have a seven-person directors' team *(lishi xiaozu)* of the village assembly (VA), composed of old cadres and the village accountant, which supervised expenditures of projects approved by the VRA.

The frequency and quality of transparency postings vary considerably, though it is still unclear how many villagers actually read the posted materials. In Guangdong's nationally famous Wanfeng village, a bulletin board outside the VC office shows each VC member's monthly expenses for entertainment, cell phones, gasoline, and parking, as well as quarterly reports on total village expenditures. But in Team 3, although accounts were posted, the figures were vaguer than required by law and, as a result, were of limited value in combating corruption. Moreover, the Wanfeng Stock Corporation, which administered much of the village's collective economy and wealth, was not subject to these same transparency laws, even though its books were managed and audited by a firm of professional accountants.

In Longyan village in Humen township in Dongguan, the entire wall outside the VC office was covered with relatively detailed fiscal reports and statements covering housing, public debt, insurance for the elderly, basic construction investment, and accounting of *chengbao*, as well as a village cadre pay chart, which showed a monthly base pay of 1,600–1,800 RMB plus incentive pay of up to 13,000 RMB per month. In addition, a picture of each fixed asset, that is, buildings and cars, owned by the VC was posted, along with date of purchase, price, use, and (for buildings) square footage.

The most astounding case of transparency in Guangdong occurred in Minle village, Xiqiao district, in the "Information City" of Nanhai.[50] Minle village has been highlighted as a model of transparency in the press and in visits by Jiang Zemin and Zhu Rongji in the fall of 2001, although it is far from representative of China or even Guangdong.

Under a municipality-wide plan to link all 250 villages electronically, place a computer in every household, and provide universal computer training starting in elementary school (a viable strategy only in such wealthy places as Nanhai, with a 1999 per capita income of 6,741 RMB), Minle has established a computerized village management system. An astonishingly wide range of data—including the structure, membership, and responsibilities of the party and village committees; VC goals, work plans, and accomplishments; data on population and housing; status of *chengbao;* various village and some team fiscal reports; and numerous national laws, procedures, and forms for undertaking tasks such as applying for permits to construct housing—are available to villagers through an Intranet (for home computers) and a regularly functioning computer in the VC office lobby, which also makes the information available to visitors.[51] Some of these materials are also posted in hard copy in the lobby of the VC office.

Cadres and publications in Minle constantly highlight the system's scientific management aspects, arguing that making such precise and up-to-date information (which is entered daily) accessible to village cadres will increase managerial efficiency. Simultaneously, simply making the data available to the villagers was said to enhance their role in the democratic management and supervision of village affairs and thus help reduce corruption, although no concrete examples of this were cited. Numerous interviews with village and township cadres suggest, however, that this system is used more to publicize already-made decisions rather than to facilitate village input into decision making.

In the villages visited in Henan, the range of practices also varied widely, although no village had a computerized system, and no computers were visible in the VC offices. The best transparency work was done in the richest village, Village 3, which had a large courtyard-wide multicolored transparency bulletin board that posted not only the village regulations *(cungui minyue)* but also monthly income and expenditures, the farmers' tax obligations (including the recent agricultural surtax) on a team-by-team (rather than individual) basis, family planning and housing application information, prices for electricity, relief income and expenses (although the data were, not surprisingly, far less extensive than those on Minle's computerized system), as well as a section for economic development and culture *(wenming)*, including song lyrics describing a list of virtues *(daode)*.

In 2004 Village 1 also had a courtyard-wide bulletin board, which was considerably smaller than the one at Village 3, with permanent categories for different types of income and expenses, to be filled in by hand on a regular basis. According to the party secretary, data on such factors as elections, income and expenditures, family planning and penalties, standards for cadres, cadre goals, and pension data were all posted regularly. Although the bulletin board did in fact show the membership of the two committees, as well as the village regulations and family planning regulations, numerous categories that would have been helpful to combat corruption (e.g., membership of the *licai xiaozu*, monthly expenses, housing applications, electricity prices, collective *chengbao*, and relief income and expenses) were all blank when I visited in 2005. Several panels of the board had fallen down and had not been repaired.

The party secretary of Village 4 stated that monthly village and team analyses as well as quarterly team reports were developed and posted, although the one team bulletin board that I observed was blank. In Village 1 data are posted not at set intervals but only when something important occurs, leaving the transparency blackboard available for games and scribbling in the interim. This was also the case in Village 4.

Although transparency in itself is a meaningful step forward in developing democracy and most likely has had a deterrent effect on many cadres, numerous structural obstacles stand in the way, preventing actually existing transparency from achieving many of its goals, at least in the short term. First, many villages, especially those in poorer areas, simply do not have the resources to publicize the long lists of required data, even if they have the capacity to collect the data. Second, the degree of detail necessary to prevent or even detect corruption is frequently far more than what is required to be published. Third, given that those involved in the corruption would most likely be preparing the public data, it is expected that where corruption does occur, much of the data is late, vague, or inaccurate, as has often been reported to be the case. Moreover, even when villagers can read and understand the data, they do not necessarily have the knowledge necessary to winnow out the key information (in potential information-overload situations, as in Minle village) or to perceive the data manipulation that frequently facilitates corruption. Finally, the unwillingness of many cadres at the township and village levels to acknowledge corruption in their domains, either because they are part of the protection network or simply because acknowledging corruption would be a black mark on their records, also undermines the effectiveness of such transparency efforts.

Accounting Practices

Accounting practices (including both general accounting and pre-election audits) which could, at least theoretically, improve democratic supervision by preventing or uncovering corruption and waste are very controversial and vary widely across provinces. Much of the controversy centers on whether audits must be done prior to elections, whether the village or the township will conduct ongoing audits, who will conduct such audits and under what conditions, and how these audits affect the very notion of village self-government.

Few provinces require pre-election audits.[52] Although Guangdong's regulations do not require such audits, officials in Guangdong's Civil Affairs Department argue that elections cannot be held without a prior audit of the existing VC. One analyst of Guangdong's elections claims that every village in the province did conduct such an audit prior to the 2002 elections, though this claim is disputed elsewhere.[53] None of the village leaders interviewed in Henan mentioned pre-election audits in either 2004 or 2005.

In many areas the township plays a significant role in auditing village finances. Numerous village leaders in Guangdong and Henan stated that their accounts were audited annually by the township, and in Henan specifically by the Agricultural Economy Management Bureau *(zhen nongye jingji guanliju)*. Not surprisingly, economically more developed Guangdong has more regulations and requirements on these issues, even if they are not uniformly enforced across the province. Many new accounting practices and recent laws and regulations require audits, frequently by township authorities.[54] For example, although the new fiscal management regulations in Guangzhou's Tianhe district left responsibility for rural village fiscal management in village hands, they required a broad range of both systemic and cash flow reforms. The systemic reforms included (1) professional management departments responsible for establishing and implementing a fiscal management system, organizing training of fiscal personnel, executing various fiscal reviews, and investigating and prosecuting fiscal problems; (2) a fiscal personal responsibility system; (3) set qualifications for fiscal personnel; and (4) maintenance of signed contracts and other records. Cash flow reforms included (1) a division of responsibilities between cashiers and accountants; (2) limits on cash advances and on various expenses; (3) eight conditions which must be met before cash is disbursed; and (4) documentation of all expenses.[55] These regulations certainly cannot be considered representative of other villages, particularly those in remote areas, nor is the degree to which they have been implemented known. Nevertheless, such fiscal management measures would put in place ex ante and in-process supervision, as opposed to the ex post facto supervision of audits. Thus they might prevent corruption, perhaps even through democratic supervision, rather than making villagers wait passively as external higher organizations try, frequently unsuccessfully, either to recover stolen funds or to repay villagers for excess levies which they had already paid. These proposals thus represent a significant move in the direction suggested by many anticorruption experts for reducing corruption and villager passivity at the local levels.

In 1999 Humen township in Dongguan developed a preventive system called the "linked teams accounting assignment system" *(lianzu kuaiji weipaizhi)*. Under this system, township-organized hiring committees, composed of representatives of various groups (including women), would hire an accountant for each village on the basis of his or her skills. Accountants for teams, most frequently with one accountant responsible for several teams, would also be selected on a competitive basis by the township but would be hired by the villages. Through the sharing of team accountants, the number of cadres would be decreased and the villagers' burden reduced. The required training of the more skilled accountants and increased use of computers also allowed for a reduction in the number of accountants and improved publication of data. Some villagers did not understand the new system, however, and were unwilling to give the assigned accountant access to the accounts, while other accountants, being from outside the village, were unwilling to confront local cadres when they discovered financial problems.[56] Subsequently, Dongguan established a system of "village finances administered by the township" *(cun caizheng guan)*, under which the township sets up an accounting center which collectively manages the financial systems for all villages through an interconnected computer system. Under this system, the village makes spending decisions in which the township cannot intervene, but the township makes payments and manages cash flow and the overall record keeping.

Such systems have been criticized for undermining the very notion of village self-government by strengthening the power of the township vis-à-vis the village, which can lead to abuse of village funds by the township and result in villages being forced into corruption to meet the demands of the township.[57] It is also unlikely that such a system would be able to detect the types of tax evasion and linked payoffs noted, for example, by Jonathan Unger in Guangdong.[58]

Weaknesses in Village-Level Anticorruption Work

Numerous factors continue to undermine the anticorruption effectiveness of village elections. The continuing if not increasingly high degree of overlap between village party leadership and the VCs undermines checks and balances at this level. Few if any of the organs providing supervision of the VCs are adequately funded, truly independent, villager-run, and/or endowed with meaningful enforcement powers. Although village transparency is carried out in varying degrees, anticorruption protests and complaints are rarely publicized in the media. Low educational levels and illiteracy place limits on villagers' knowledge of their rights under the various electoral laws and on the effectiveness of many transparency regulations and displays. Also, systemic anticorruption training for village cadres is limited.

In addition, there is a lack of clarity regarding many aspects of anticorruption. Continually changing institutional and structural arrangements as well as definitions of both corruption and the very line between public and private affairs frequently make it difficult to distinguish reform from corruption. There is also an absence of legal precision on village-level corruption, and the obligations of village officials as well as the organs responsible for dealing with this corruption and the relevant punishment. Finally, the difficulty and infrequency of removing corrupt officials *(bamian)* put further limits on village anticorruption efforts.[59]

Given the variations in village self-government between and within provinces, it is extremely difficult to make any sweeping generalizations. Nonetheless, it is clear that the Chinese party-state has invested significant resources in the village self-government movement. Although this has had an overall effect of legitimizing the discourse of voting and self-government and providing a possibility for the concepts and institutions of self-government to move up to the townships, and perhaps even beyond, many factors will influence how this develops, not the least of which is the degree to which villagers perceive these elections as relevant, meaningful, and legitimate. Not surprisingly, this discourse itself is continually changing as a result of its own contradictions and pressures from old and new actors in the system. Perhaps most symbolic of these contradictions is the fact that village elections, which were put forward in significant part to help increase transparency and combat corruption, have spawned their own form of corruption in vote-buying.

Many elements of democratic elections and village self-government are becoming increasingly institutionalized, though with wide variations and many contradictions. Neither the voting per se nor the practices that have been put into effect, however, are necessarily the equivalent of local-level democracy. Furthermore, continuing efforts by contending and overlapping old and new elites to gain ground in China's emerging social formation tend to undermine many of the democratic aspects, at least for the non-elite. Whereas in the past the party monopoly on power undermined the likelihood of checks and balances at various levels, and continuing efforts by the party to maintain its "leadership" of the village self-government movement threaten the same, the recent increase in the number of entrepreneurs entering village self-government could well create new obstacles and conflicts of interest as entrepreneurs cum village leaders seek control of public resources for private gain. This also clearly creates an uneven playing field where some entrepreneurs have access to official power while competitors or average citizens do not. Altogether, these tendencies may contribute to the development of a Chinese form of bureaucratic crony capitalism.[60]

The institutionalization of village self-government tends to obscure numerous key issues, such as increasing polarization, the formation of new class strata and/or classes, the absence of nationwide nonparty organizations, and China's increasing integration into the global economy. It is precisely the ways in which elections have reinforced both the changing makeup of village-level leadership (the increasing entry of entrepreneurs) and the changing structure of the village-level economy (the decreasing reliance on the collective economy) that are critical to the future relationships among the village self-government movement, village-level corruption, and the changing makeup of China's rural political-economic structure.

The increasing number of entrepreneurs in village leadership positions, including entrepreneurs who win such positions, entrepreneurs who are recruited into the party, and party secretaries who have become entrepreneurs, is not an incidental or unexpected development. Rather, it results from and contributes to (1) changes in China's economic structure which allow and encourage not only the emergence of entrepreneurs but also corruption and the not infrequent interaction between the two; (2) changes in party policy which welcome entrepreneurs and present them as benefactors of society as a whole, and as individuals imbued with a spirit of noblesse oblige;

(3) changes in tax policies which make it increasingly difficult for non-entrepreneurs to hold village positions and make villages more dependent on contributions from entrepreneurs; and (4) growing linkages among entrepreneurs and officials at the village and township levels. This leads to a situation, noted by numerous analysts, in which the older, more politically based and the newer, more economically based elites are engaged in a complex struggle to dominate and/or co-opt each other. These changes suggest that there will be continuing struggle and additional contradictions in relation to both village self-government and anticorruption measures, perhaps resulting in further integration of the elites while continuing to exclude ordinary villagers.

Given the slow increase in the competitiveness of village elections, and the slow progress in establishing transparency and fighting corruption, the ability of any existing elite in China today to maintain a stable situation in the countryside is questionable. Moreover, China's entry into the World Trade Organization (WTO) could significantly transform rural landownership patterns and lead to even greater out-migration of the rural population, further undermining village power. The likelihood, however, that an open struggle within the elites could activate the masses against either or both of them provides an additional and very significant incentive for the elites to proceed with mutual co-optation rather than a divisive contest for clear dominance.

These conflicts decrease the likelihood that present methods of village self-government will significantly reduce village-level corruption.[61] The party-state's ambivalent approach to defining and combating vote-buying (largely by entrepreneurs) in village elections further reflects and reinforces the types of limits on dealing with both new and old forms of village-level corruption. Thus although China's village self-government movement contains sprouts of democracy and anticorruption measures that may well begin to grow, however slowly, into township elections, they can flourish only with support from increasingly higher levels of the political leadership and only within a wider political, economic, and social context that is conducive to real democratization. It is unclear whether the higher levels of leadership are committed to such changes.

JOHN JAMES KENNEDY

3 | The Implementation of Village Elections and Tax-for-Fee Reform in Rural Northwest China

Since the early 1990s, reports of rural unrest over excessive taxation and mistreatment at the hands of local cadres have caught the attention of national leaders in China as well as foreign observers. These reports suggest that local cadres are out of control and that there are limited mechanisms for villagers to monitor cadre behavior. The question is whether or not the central government has the political capacity to control local cadres at the county and township levels and to introduce institutions that also allow villagers to check local leaders. Faced with the prospect of increasing rural unrest, national leaders attempted the implementation of two policy solutions: reducing villagers' taxes and fees, and establishing village self-government and local elections.

Taxes and fees in rural China are referred to as villagers' burdens; in some areas they can reach upward to as much as 35–40 percent of the villagers' income.[1] In an attempt to reduce villagers' burdens and control local cadres, the central government issued the Regulation Concerning Peasants' Fees and Labor (1991), which limits fees and apportionments to 5 percent of the villagers' net income the previous year. In 2000 the central government introduced a tax-for-fee reform in several provinces in another attempt to reduce villagers' burdens.

The Organic Law of Village Committees, promulgated

in 1987, permits villagers to monitor local cadres and allows villagers to elect a leader and from five to seven members of the village committee. Eleven years later, in an attempt to reassert the central government's commitment to village elections, amendments to the Organic Law included the provision of open (villager) nominations of candidates and noninterference by township officials.

Despite these reform efforts, since 2000 there have been reports of excessive taxation well beyond the 5 percent threshold and an uneven implementation of the 1998 Organic Law. Why do these problems still persist? Does the central government lack the political capacity to implement reforms at the local level? Or does the central government lack the commitment to fully implement a burden reduction and village elections?

Successful political reforms within an authoritarian regime, such as introducing local elections and limiting the predatory practices of grassroots government officials, require a central government with the political capacity to influence the behavior of local administrators. One of the defining characteristics of any regime is the political capacity to implement desired policies.[2] This means having effective political institutions that elicit compliance and consent.[3] Compliance must be garnered from both the citizens and the civil service. Coercive measures and the prolonged use of physical force reflect a loss of political power and, hence, capacity, because it indicates a deterioration in the relationship between the rulers, their agents, and the ruled.[4] More important, the continued lack of compliance on the part of local officials erodes the political legitimacy of the central government. For example, Edgar Kiser and Xiaoxi Tong demonstrate that in China during the late nineteenth century, the excessive taxation and the coercive methods used by local officials to collect taxes reflected the weak political capacity of the Qing central administration, which was unable to control the behavior of these grassroots officials.[5] Decades of rural exploitation at the hands of uncontrollable local officials contributed to the erosion of political legitimacy and to the eventual collapse of the Qing dynasty.

Throughout the 1990s, cadre behavior at the township and village levels contributed to excessive burdens and uneven implementation of village elections. Scholars have offered two explanations for this behavior. One explanation highlights the weak political capacity on the part of the central government to monitor local cadres.[6] A second explanation focuses on the political incentives of the local cadres and selective policy implementation.[7] Thomas Bernstein and Lü Xiaobo argue that because the township governments were largely left on their own to fund essential services in the 1990s, local cadres had to resort to the collection of fees and apportionments on households in order to generate revenues.[8] These burdens were heaviest in the poorer agriculture-dependent communities in the central and western regions, which lacked the revenue-generating township and village enterprises found in the wealthier coastal provinces.

Central government attempts to reduce villagers' burdens failed because it was impossible to monitor township and village cadres. According to these authors, "the central state lacked the capacity to enforce its preferences or to put in place a fair rural tax system."[9] In addition, while the local administrative staff at the township level was growing and becoming more invasive in the social and economic affairs of village communities, the central government was becoming increasingly "weak" in protecting villagers, disciplining local cadres, and effectively implementing policies.[10] Bernstein and Lü suggest that the solution to the problem is not more aggressive central government attempts to monitor village cadres from above but rather surveillance from below through local elections.[11]

Kevin O'Brien and Lianjiang Li point out that higher authorities at the county and municipal levels can influence the behavior of local cadres.[12] They argue, however, that grassroots cadres are responding to officials just one administrative level above them rather than to central government directives. The mechanisms that these higher authorities use to control lower-level cadres are the one-level-down management system *(xiaguan yiji)* and the cadre exchange system *(ganbu jiaoliu tizhi)*.

In the one-level-down management system, officials at each level have the authority to appoint their own subordinates.[13] For example, a county official can appoint the township party secretary or the government head without seeking approval from higher authorities at the municipal or provincial levels.[14] The implication is that promotion or reassignment depends on the ability of the subordinate to carry out the policies of his or her immediate superior.

The cadre exchange system promotes leading cadres (the party secretary or the government head) by transferring them every three to six years depending on the locality. The rationale behind the cadre exchange is to reduce localism by limiting leading cadres to a short fixed term of office so that they have little time to develop local networks.[15] The system can have a strong influence on the leading cadres' orientation of accountability. On the one hand, if a township party secretary or government head does not fulfill his or her policy obligations to the county government after a fixed time, he or she may receive a lateral transfer to another township. On the other hand, leading cadres who successfully complete their policy obligations may be promoted to the county government. Under this system, the orientation of accountability leads upward to authorities one administrative level above, rather than downward toward the ordinary villagers.[16]

This combination of one-level-down management and the cadre exchange system is characterized by tight control over immediate subordinates, which leads to selective policy implementation. Subordinates selectively implement the policies that can enhance their positions while ignoring policies that have little influence over promotion or transfer. O'Brien and Li make an important distinction between popular and unpopular policies, showing how higher authorities use these measures to evaluate local cadres. Popular policies can be burden reductions, such as the 5 percent regulation or the Organic Law, whereas unpopular policies include revenue collection and birth control. O'Brien and Li argue that the unpopular policies are more quantifiable than the popular policies.[17] For instance, revenue collection is a straightforward measure that superiors can use to gauge the performance of subordinates, whereas implementation of the burden reduction and the Organic Law are more difficult to measure and thus may not count as much toward promotion. The key point for O'Brien and Li is that subordinates will conform to what is being measured.

O'Brien and Li propose that an effective way to reduce villagers' burdens is to allow greater participation in the selection of village cadres.[18] When villagers can elect their village committee members and select the final candidates before the election, the ability of residents to monitor local cadres is enhanced. Elections with villager nominations can influence cadre behavior such that elected village cadres will become as accountable to their villager constituents as they are to the township government. Similarly, Bernstein and Lü point out that although elected village cadres are still obligated to collect taxes and fees and carry out the birth control policy, villages that hold open elections tend to enjoy more transparent tax systems and lower village fees.[19]

Both O'Brien and Li and Bernstein and Lü conducted their field research in the mid-1990s, when the central government did not prioritize the reduction of villagers' burdens, and both sets of authors come to the same conclusion: the only way to reduce these burdens is from the bottom up. In the 1990s there was no evidence that the central government had the desire or the political capacity to reduce villagers' burdens. The consensus regarding local taxes and fees was that the high level of villager burdens was due to decentralization and an inability of the central authorities to monitor local cadres. Thus if the central government lacks the political capacity to control local cadres from the top down, then the logical argument is that there needs to be a mechanism to monitor local cadres from the bottom up.

While village elections provide residents with a mechanism to monitor village cadres from the bottom up, the Organic Law of 1998 first must be fully implemented from the top down before villagers can use this institution. For the central government, the continuous monitoring of local cadres is a daunting and costly task, especially at the village level. The intent of the Organic Law is to shift the costs of long-term monitoring of local cadres from the higher authorities to the villagers. At least in the short term, however, the higher authorities must apply top-down pressure to ensure the full implementation of the Organic Law. Nevertheless, earlier studies present a paradox. On the one hand, scholars suggest that the central government lacks the capacity to control local cadres below the county level. On the other hand, these scholars recommend village elections as an effective means of monitoring village cadres. Yet if the central government does not have the capacity to control local cadres, then how can the center enforce the Organic Law? Township officials rely on village cadres to carry out unpopular policies that are crucial for promotion. Therefore, unless township leaders have an incentive to implement the Organic Law that elects these village cadres, they will continue to resist electoral reforms fiercely.

Selective policy implementation may also explain how the central government *can* implement desired policies at the local level. Maria Edin suggests that the reason why popular policies such as burden reductions are not implemented is that the central government does not consider these to be top policy priorities.[20] She contends that the central government does have the political capacity to control local cadres and to implement high priority policies selectively. This does not mean that all central policies can be carried out at all times, but rather that the central government càn implement important policies at the village level. The center is able to carry out these policy priorities through political campaigns. This type of implementation can be effective, but the political commitment of the center must be high due to the time and effort it takes to sustain such a campaign. Family planning, for example, is maintained through a succession of political campaigns in which the center exerts policy pressure down to the village level. A tremendous amount of time and effort is needed to implement priority policies. This means that the center has to be selective in deciding which policy is to be prioritized and when the campaigns should begin. The mechanism for the campaign-style policy push is based on performance contracts and specific targets.

Policy priorities are spelled out in performance contracts between superiors and their subordinates. The contracts specify targets that need to be fulfilled by leading cadres for a positive evaluation and possible promotion. Policy obligations such as quotas on birthrates or the amount of revenues collected are considered "hard" targets and are typically the priority policies that higher authorities use to evaluate leading cadres. The subordinates have little room to maneuver when it comes to implementation of these targets. Many of these hard targets have "veto power," which means that although fulfilling these targets does not guarantee a good evaluation, failure to meet the targets will result in censure. Burden reductions and village elections, by contrast, are considered "soft" targets. These policies are "less important" than hard targets, allowing subordinates more flexibility when it comes to implementation. As O'Brien and Li suggest, popular policies are typically soft targets, whereas unpopular policies tend to be hard targets.[21]

Although Edin uses selective policy implementation to show the relationship between cadre management, cadre promotion, and economic growth, she proposes that the central government has the capacity to carry out priority policies selectively whether they are unpopular or popular.[22] If this is the case, then it is possible for soft targets to become hard. In other words, once the central authorities decide that a popular policy is important enough, it can become a top priority. Nevertheless, without some evidence that the central government can enforce popular policies, it is difficult to argue that the central authorities have the political capacity to implement all kinds of top priority policies.

In this chapter I test the selective policy hypothesis to determine whether or not the central government has the political capacity to carry out popular policies. I examine the implementation of the 2000 tax-for-fee reform *(shuifei gaige)* and the Organic Law of Village Committees (1998) in Shaanxi province. In 2000, Shaanxi officials announced that they would carry out the "Three Guarantees" *(sange jiebao):* alleviate *(jianqing),* standardize *(guifan),* and stabilize *(wending).*[23] The goal was to alleviate villagers' burdens, standardize the tax-and-fee system, and stabilize the countryside. In 2003, reaffirming the commitment to tax-for-fee reform, the party secretary of Shaanxi, Li Jianguo, said, "After land reform and the introduction of the household responsibility system, the tax-for-fee reform is the greatest central policy to protect villagers' interests and stabilize the countryside."[24] In addition, the Shaanxi government expressed its commitment to improving the quality of village elections by enforcing the 1998 Shaanxi Province Public Village Affairs and Democratic Management Provisional Measures *(Shaanxisheng cunwu gongkai, minzhu guanli zanxing banfa).* This provincial regulation reflects the central government's amendments to the Organic Law of Village Committees, specifically the notion of villager nominations and a transparent tax system. A third round of village elections occurred in 1999, and a fourth round took place in 2002. Both the "Three Guarantees" and the "Democratic Management" regulations were implemented in earnest between 2001 and 2002; the first priority was tax reform, followed by improvement of the village elections.[25]

Using a unique panel data set collected in eighteen villages from three different counties in November 2000 and June 2004, I show that popular policies, such as burden reductions and village elections, can be implemented at the township level when higher authorities at the provincial and county levels make these policies a priority.[26] Data analysis from the 2000 survey suggests that the tax reform and the democratic management regulations were not enforced because other policies such as revenue collection and birth control were higher policy priorities at that time. Data analysis from the 2004 survey of the same villages, however, reveals a dramatic reduction in villagers' burdens and clear improvements in the quality of village elections regarding the nomination of candidates and the competitiveness of elections.

To illustrate these findings, I outline the basic logic of my approach. I first focus on the one-level-down management system and the cadre exchange system to see how these institutions influence cadre behavior and the implementation of priority policies. In the second section I examine the implementation of the tax-for-fee reform by comparing the overall burdens for villagers in 2000 and 2004. All the villages in the sample experienced a significant reduction in villager burdens. The third section examines differences between the village elections in 1999 and 2002. The greatest variation in village elections involved the method of nominating candidates: whether by township government, village party branch, or villager nomination. Between the 2000 and 2004 surveys, some villages improved the quality of their elections while others remained unchanged. In the final section I discuss the differences among counties, including in terms of the cadre exchange system, implications of selective policy implementation, and finally the need for greater commitment on the part of the central government to carrying out political reforms.

Selective Policy Hypothesis

O'Brien and Li's argument that hard targets (unpopular polices) are more quantifiable and easier to measure than soft targets (popular policies) seemed to hold for the 1990s. Yet burden reductions and village elections can in fact be measured.[27] If soft targets become hard, then higher authorities will find measures to evaluate their subordinates.[28] For example, in the 2004 survey, the township leading cadres whom my Chinese colleagues and I interviewed stated that the county government sent officials to check on township revenues and to interview several village accountants to ensure implementation of burden reduction policies. Village elections can also be monitored to confirm that the township officials and the village party branch do not manipulate the nomination and election processes. The hardening of previously soft policies, however, does not necessarily mean that unpopular policies, such as revenue collection and birth control, become less important; rather the priority list may be expanded for the subordinates (that is, their jobs may become even more difficult).

I assume that township leading cadres conform to what is being measured and that, given the opportunity, they will manipulate village elections and avoid significant reductions in villager burdens. I do not suggest that township officials are inherently nondemocratic; nevertheless, these cadres have a very difficult job in that the authority to select village cadres and collect revenues can be an important factor in fulfilling their performance contracts.[29] The township leading cadres are responsible for the fulfillment of hard targets, especially tax collection and birth control, but the village cadres actually implement these policies by dealing with villagers on a face-to-face basis. The Organic Law of Village Committees reduces the authority of the township party secretary and government head to select compliant village cadres. If the Organic Law is fully implemented so that villagers nominate candidates and elect the committee members and the village leader, the township officials will have no idea who they will be dealing with until after the election. In order to reduce the level of uncertainty in the selection of village cadres, township officials, given the opportunity, will interfere in the elections by controlling the nomination process. Therefore, I assume that without pressure from the county government to implement the 1998 Organic Law fully, the township leading cadres will continue to manipulate the village elections.

In order to determine whether or not burden reductions have become priority policies (hard targets), and whether or not the central government has the political capacity to implement popular policies, I examine the reduction of taxes and fees as a percentage of the villagers' income. The tax rate and the annual amount of villagers' household burdens are measured as a percentage of their annual household income. This is a direct measure of the villagers' estimate of burdens and income as well as the village accountant's estimate.[30] In 2000 and 2002 the central government and the Shaanxi provincial leaders made a very public commitment to the reduction of villagers' burdens. This was not the first time provincial leaders had announced an intention to reduce villagers' burdens. The only way to determine whether or not significant pressure from above (in prioritizing the tax reforms) is actually occurring is through a direct measurement of villagers' tax rates. If they have decreased, then we can assume that the tax-for-fee reform is being implemented.

I argue that the level of outside interference from either the village party branch or the township government will determine the quality of the village elections. The most common method of manipulating the outcome of village elections is through the nomination process.[31] The nomination process can vary greatly within a single province or county and even within a township. Although there are a number of variations and types of nomination processes, the three general types are villager, party branch, and township nomination of candidates.[32] Villager nomination of candidates is the most democratic of the three methods. The "open sea" nomination process is conducted in an open assembly where individuals or groups of five or ten villagers select the candidates. This is the method prescribed in the 1998 Organic Law. Although both of the other two methods are considered undemocratic, the village party branch selection of candidates tends to be much closer to villager preferences than are township nominations.[33] The village party branch nomination is done by the party secretary and two or three deputy party secretaries who are members of the village community. Thus their selection of candidates may reflect at least a portion of villagers' preferences. By contrast, the township government nomination process means that the final selection of candidates is conducted outside the village, and most or all members of the village community are left out of the final selection process.[34] Thus the quality of elections is measured as either high (villager nomination), medium (party branch nomination), or low (township nomination).[35] If the Organic Law has become a priority policy, then we would expect an improvement in the quality of village elections from 2000 to 2004.

Finally, I explore the administrative influence over the implementation of the tax-for-fee reform and the Organic Law. At what level of the political system do we observe the full implementation of these reforms? For instance, a variation in the reduction of the villagers' burdens between the townships within a county indicates that the township leading cadres are making the final decision to implement the reform, whereas a variation at the county level implies that county leading cadres are making the final decision. Finally, a lack of variation across counties would suggest that the policy push is coming from the provincial or national level.

Tax-for-Fee Reform

Throughout the 1990s and the early years of the twenty-first century, the Shaanxi provincial government announced the need to reduce villagers' burdens (taxes and fees). In the late 1980s and early 1990s the problem was in the form of excessive village fees *(tiliu)* and township fees *(tongchou)*. Taxes are formal state charges, whereas village and township fees are informal local charges. The list of fees and taxes can be long. One example from an accountant questionnaire in 2000 lists six different fees and two types of taxes (see Table 3.1). The village fees include payments to support the family members of revolutionary martyrs, village militia, family planning, and electricity. In the Shaanxi sample, the two main taxes were the agricultural tax and the specialty tax. The agricultural tax is proportional to the village's annual grain output. The specialty tax is levied on non-grain agricultural products, such as vegetables, fruits, and tobacco. In the three sample counties, the specialty tax is associated with cash crops, that is, fruits and vegetables. In 2000 the collection of agricultural and specialty taxes constituted hard targets that township leading cadres needed to fulfill in order to ensure their own promotions. In Table 3.1 the specialty tax constitutes 45 percent of total taxes and fees, making it the largest single item. Another measure of the villagers' burdens is taxes and fees as a percentage of the villagers' estimated household income. The village example (Table 3.1) uses the village accountant's estimate of the villagers' household income, with total taxes making up 21 percent and total fees 16 percent of the villagers' income. As I have noted, however, according to the Regulation Concerning Peasants' Fees and Labor (1991), village fees should not exceed 5 percent of villagers' annual income.

Table 3.1 Average fees and taxes for a single household in one sample
village in 2000

	Amount in RMB
Village and township fees (tiliu and tongchou)	
Road fee *(daolu)*	80
Militia *(minbing)*	32
Family members of revolutionary martyrs *(youfu)*	12
Family planning *(jisheng)*	40
Education *(jiaoyu)*	100
Electricity *(dianfei)*	300
Taxes	
Agricultural tax *(nongye)*	160
Specialty tax *(techan)*	600
Total	1,324
Accountant's estimate of villagers' average household income	3,600
Total burdens as a percentage of villagers' average household income	37%

Note: The sample village is coded 612. It is the number 2 village from Township 1 in County 6.

The tax rate within villages is also uneven. For many poorer households within a village, fees constitute the bulk of their burden. These poor families cannot afford to invest in greenhouses or fruit orchards, and therefore they grow mostly grain crops. While they do not pay the specialty tax, village fees are nevertheless a very expensive proposition. For example, in Table 3.1 the poorer villagers reported an estimated annual household income of 1,500 RMB. Because these households do not grow cash crops, the agricultural tax constitutes only 11 percent of their income, but the village fees make up a whopping 37 percent of their annual income. Under the previous system, the poorest families had the highest rates of fees.[36]

In the three sample counties the tax-for-fee reform eliminated the long list of village and township fees and drastically reduced the overall tax-fee rate for rural residents. In most villages the specialty tax was reduced or completely eliminated as a formal tax. In 2000, according to the accountants' estimates, the mean specialty tax per household was 607 RMB and ranged from 200 to 980 RMB. In 2004 none of the accountants surveyed reported collection of specialty taxes. The agricultural tax, by contrast, increased from a mean of 80 RMB per household (or 20 RMB per capita) in 2000 to 256 RMB per household (or 64 RMB per capita) in 2004. This reflected the purpose of the tax-for-fee reform, which was to simplify the tax system and eliminate village fees. Despite the increase in the agricultural tax, the total burden as a percentage of the villagers' household income declined dramatically from 2000 to 2004 (see Table 3.2). The reduction in villagers' burdens is essentially the same across all six townships and all three counties. The lack of variation among townships and counties reflects a uniform implementation of the tax-for-fee reform from the top down. It also demonstrates that at least the provincial government has the capacity to implement priority policies down to the village level.[37]

Village Elections

Local elections allow residents to monitor village cadres; but for the Organic Law to be effective, it needs to be fully implemented. Compliance with the Organic Law means that villagers must be permitted to nominate candidates openly, and the number of candidates must exceed the number of positions available (i.e., elections must be competitive). Although over 80 percent of the villages in rural China have conducted competitive elections, the types of nomination processes vary widely throughout the country.[38] One of the reasons for this variation is that control over the nomination process is the most common method of manipulating village elections.[39] If the township government selects two individuals to run for village leader in a competitive election, the township has its candidate in office no matter who wins the election. If, however, the villagers themselves nominate the candidates, the final selection of the village leaders is more uncertain, especially for the township officials. In counties where the Organic Law is fully implemented (e.g., County 5), township government heads and party secretaries whom we interviewed complained that the villagers do not know how to select "qualified" candidates, and in the end the township government is left dealing with inept

Table 3.2 Changes in the tax rate as a percentage of reported household income from 2000 to 2004 (in RMB)

	County 3		County 5		County 6	
	T31	T32	T51	T52[a]	T61	T62[b]
Villager estimate of household burdens						
2000	794	702	1,234	1,800	1,340	1,054
2004	369	503	740	486	441	436
Burdens as a % of household income						
2000	10%	12%	20%	31%	43%	21%
2004	4%	7%	8%	7%	13%	10%
Accountant's estimate of household burdens						
2000	561	592	835	825	802	825
2004	493	403	660	512	341	290
Burdens as a % of household income						
2000	16%	17%	14%	10%	27%	20%
2004	7%	10%	9%	5%	12%	6%

a. Missing a village in 2000.
b. Missing a village in 2000 and 2004.

village leaders.[40] It is not surprising that township leading cadres are not satisfied with some of the villagers' leadership choices and even less pleased with their own lack of influence over candidate selection. What is surprising is that the Organic Law can be fully implemented despite the obvious reluctance of township leading cadres.

This section examines the changes that occurred between the 1999 and 2002 village elections and the variation in village elections across townships and counties. Table 3.3 provides a general distribution of the village nomination process and illustrates the difference between the 1999 and 2002 village elections. The most striking finding is that in 2002, five out of the original sixteen sample villages experienced a change in nomination process. The quality of the electoral institutions improved in all but one village. Moreover, the type of nomination process reflected the level of village autonomy with

Table 3.3 Candidate nomination type by township in 2004 and 2000 (villages)

| | County 3 | | | | County 5 | | | | County 6 | | | |
| | T31 | | T32 | | T51 | | T52 | | T61 | | T62 | |
	2004	(2000)	2004	(2000)	2004	(2000)	2004	(2000)	2004	(2000)	2004	(2000)
Village assembly	3	(1)	2	(2)	3	(3)	3	(2)	0	(0)	0	(0)
Party branch	0	(2)	1	(0)	0	(0)	0	(0)	1	(2)	1	(0)
Township government	0	(0)	0	(1)	0	(0)	0	(0)	2	(0)	1	(1)
Appointment	0	(0)	0	(0)	0	(0)	0	(0)	0	(1)	0	(1)
Total villages	3	(3)	3	(3)	3	(3)	3	(2)	3	(3)	2	(2)

Note: The village election types are based on the 2002 (2004 survey) and the 1999 (2000 survey) elections; in 2000, sixteen villages were sampled, and in 2004, seventeen villages were sampled (the same sixteen plus one).

respect to the township government. In villages where the township government controls the nomination process, the village committees have relatively weak authority to govern, and villagers have few mechanisms to monitor or influence cadre behavior. By contrast, in villages with an open nomination process the committees are relatively strong, and the villagers have a number of legal methods to monitor cadres. In fact, in some of these villages, villagers use techniques to check cadre behavior that go beyond the intent of the Organic Law. Finally, I find a strong variation in the quality of elections across counties, suggesting that the Organic Law is not as rigorously enforced as the tax-for-fee reform.

The general trend within the sample is that the quality of elections, as measured by the type of nomination process, gradually improved from the 1999 to the 2002 elections. One unexpected observation is that the nomination process tended to evolve gradually from low (township government nomination) to medium (village party branch nomination) and from medium to high (villager nomination). The election process seemed to progress in stages rather than in sudden leaps from low to high. For example, in Township 61 (T61), a village that had previously not experienced elections in 1999 (i.e., all leaders were appointed) held competitive elections for the first time in 2002, but the township controlled the nomination process. In Township 31 (T31), two villages whose elections previously had been subject to party branch nominations adopted the "open sea" method in the 2002 election, whereby villagers nominated the candidates in an open assembly. A village in Township 32 underwent a transition from township control over the nomination process in 1999 to village party branch nomination in 2002.

This evolutionary development of village elections seems to have resulted from both top-down and bottom-up pressures for change. For example, in County 3, interviews with the village party secretaries and township cadres in T31 reveal that bottom-up pressure from villagers for a more open nomination process was constant. In the 1996 and 1999 elections, though the party branches selected the official candidates on the ballot, villagers could also write in the names of their favored candidates. Before 2002 the village party secretary could choose to accept or reject the write-in candidates without permission or interference from higher authorities. Nevertheless, in the

2002 election pressure from the county government was brought to bear on township government to allow villagers formal control over the candidate selection process. Two months before the election, responding to county government demands, the township officials informed the village party branches that they must implement an "open sea" nomination process. So while the villagers had pushed the limits of the party branch nomination process by writing in the names of their desired candidates, real institutional change did not come about until the township officials ordered the implementation of village assembly nominations.

Change in the other township (T32) in County 3 from township to party branch nomination was the result of a bargain between township officials, the village party secretary, and the wealthiest families in the village. Although the village is coded as having a party branch nomination, the actual process of candidate selection occurs within an election committee made up of the party branch and the wealthiest households. In fact, the makeup of the election committee reflects the close relationship between the village entrepreneurs (*nengren*) and the village party branch. This is similar to Richard Levy's argument in this volume that participation by wealthy village entrepreneurs is growing. But whereas Levy finds that the entrepreneurs are in competition with the village party branch, this case shows greater collusion between the two groups.

All the farmland in the village is collectively owned and managed by the village committee. Since there is limited arable land, in order to maintain a fair distribution the land may be redistributed every five to ten years to adjust for demographic changes such as births, deaths, and marriages. Yet a number of families have invested heavily in greenhouses (semi-permanent structures built on arable land). This can be a considerable investment for farmers. Therefore, it is in the interest of the wealthy families to maintain the status quo regarding land distribution. Given the amount of revenue from the specialty tax collected from these families, it is also in the interest of the township government not to redistribute the land. Nevertheless, in 2002 the township government was asked by the county authorities to "reduce the level of interference" in village elections, and a new election committee was formed to oversee the election process and make the final selection of candidates. Although this met with the satisfaction of the party branch and the wealthy families, the vast majority of villagers surveyed reported that the 2002 election was "very unfair."[41]

In County 6 none of the villages surveyed in 2000 or 2004 reported having a villager nomination process, and the township government directly controlled the nomination process in most of the villages. An interview with the head of the township agriculture department in T61 revealed that about two months before the election she and several deputy government heads had surveyed the villages and met with the village party branch to determine a list of possible candidates. Once the "survey" was completed and the list for each village compiled, the township officials selected the "appropriate" candidates. Then they drew up a list of the final candidates and printed the ballots for each village. This is different from the party branch nomination process, in which the village party secretary writes up an initial list and then sends it up to the township government for approval. Although the party branch nomination process may be closer to the villagers' preferences, the township leading cadres can change the nomination process from party branch nomination to township nomination. One of the villages in T61 regressed from a party branch to a township nomination process because the township government sought greater control over the village committee and the party branch. In the 2002 election the incumbent village leader was the township government's top choice, but he lost the election. Thereafter, the township party branch simply removed the village party secretary and installed the previous village leader as the new village party secretary.

Interference in village elections is one way in which township officials have weakened the village governing bodies in order to manage village affairs more closely. Another way is by micromanaging or not allowing village bodies the authority they need to govern. One clear example is from a village in T61 involving two neighbors and a stolen goat. A man stole a goat from his neighbor, who reported the crime to the village committee. The committee then sent three members to evaluate the accusation. They determined that the goat had indeed been stolen and sold to someone outside the village. The village committee instructed the accused to pay a fine of 200 RMB (the market price of the goat) to the victim. The accused, however, instead took his case to the township government. The township public security officials ruled that the village committee did not have the authority to fine the accused, and the matter remained unsettled. Thus the village committees lack the authority to resolve basic village disputes.

An example from County 6 demonstrates the limited influence of the village committees when the township government weakens the authority of the village cadres. The township nomination process indicates a broader interference in the affairs of village governance from above and exacerbates the lack of village autonomy and influence from below. In the 2000 survey, villagers in County 6 expressed a strong dissatisfaction with the election process that persisted in 2004. This dissatisfaction seems to stem both from an inability to replace village cadres and from the lack of power of elected cadres to perform even the most basic functions, such as mediating conflicts among villagers. Under these conditions, villagers' legal options for representation and local political participation are limited. There have been no reports, however, of large or small rural demonstrations in the county, and the township officials interviewed expressed no major complaints about villagers or village committees. In fact, the township officials in County 6 insisted that the tax-for-fee reform has contributed much to the stability of the rural areas within the county, and that villagers are more concerned with the level of burdens than with the method of electing village committee members. This may be true, but it also reflects the fact that in County 6 implementation of the tax-for-fee reform has a much higher priority for the township leading cadres than full implementation of the Organic Law.

Whereas in County 6 the tax-for-fee reform is a higher priority than the Organic Law, the township leading cadres in County 5 rate both policies as high on the policy priority list. County 5 has the highest-quality elections in the sample, with every village in both the 2000 and 2004 surveys reporting villager nominations. Nevertheless, despite the fact that the Organic Law has been fully implemented, there is still variation among villages in the use of the Organic Law to monitor cadres and resolve lineage disputes.

One of the most striking differences between Counties 5 and 6 involves the attitudes of the township leading cadres and the village respondents toward the elections and the elected leaders. Unlike the leading cadres in County 6, township officials in County 5 complained bitterly about the open election process and the elected village leaders. The township party secretary in T51 expressed concern about how villages with a history of lineage conflict could manage village elections. He stated that "the villagers are tricked into nominating and voting for individuals who make grand promises during the campaign but then represent only their own family's or clan's interests once in power."[42] The result is that village elections can exacerbate lineage divisions within a village. In one village with over 800 households, for example, the dominant lineage, named Liu, has over 200 households, and the second-largest lineage, named Li, has 150 households. Another five families ranging from 40 to 80 households each also live in the village. Before 1999 the township government appointed the village leadership by alternating the party secretary and the leader between a Liu and a Li. In 1999 village elections and the open nomination process were introduced to the village. The representative for the Liu lineage campaigned for equal redistribution of land and lower village fees. He won the election, but during his term he allowed small redistributions of land that favored the Liu family, and he also enforced the birth control regulations unevenly. In 2002 the Li candidate made campaign promises similar to those that the Liu representative had made three years before, and the Li candidate won the election. Upon taking office, however, Li used his position for the betterment of his own lineage, and the Liu clan began preparing for the next election.

There are other examples within the same township in which villagers have taken advantage of elections to create a balance among lineages within the committee. Whereas villagers may be satisfied with the election process and outcome, the township leading cadres tend to be frustrated with the results. For example, the township party secretary in T51 stated that "villagers will nominate and elect inefficient leaders in order to preserve a lineage balance among village cadres within the village committee."[43] Unlike the village in the previous example, this village has three large lineages of relatively equal size. The three family names are Li, Meng, and Men, and the three most important positions in the village are divided among them. The party secretary is Li, the accountant is Men, and the village leader is Meng. Although the village party members and the township party branch control the selection of the party secretary, the villagers have the authority to nominate the village leader and the accountant. For village committee elections, the candidates are selected in order to maintain a balance among the three families within the committee. According to the villager respondents, the arrangement is quite satisfactory, but the township party secretary complained that many members on the committee are useless and make his job more difficult.

Despite the reservations of the township party secretary, these examples demonstrate that the village election process can mitigate differences among lineages within a single village and eventually become an accepted village political institution. In the first example, the Liu candidate won the election in 1999, but the Li candidate won in 2002. In the first election, the loser (Li) accepted defeat and waited for the next election to gain influence over village affairs. In 2002 Liu accepted defeat and began to plan for the next election. According to democratic theorists, one indicator that elections have become an accepted institution among local elites is that losers accept defeat because they believe that they have a fair chance of winning the next election.[44] Moreover, in this particular village neither lineage can win the election on its own. Both need to enlist the support of other, smaller lineages in order to capture enough votes to win the election. In this case, the lineages adapted to the village elections. In the second example, the three relatively equal lineages used the open nomination process to create a mutually acceptable arrangement. Although the outcome is not entirely democratic, because the lineages make choices about the composition of the village committee before the election, the villager nomination process does provide residents with an opportunity to make this choice. In the end, it is the villagers and their lineage leaders who decide how best to maintain a balance within the village.

In villages that held open nominations in the 1999 and 2002 elections, the most notable development was the use of political pamphlets (*chuandan*), both before the election as well as after, to recall elected leaders. In the 2000 survey, villagers and elected cadres reported that in the 1999 elections the campaign process was limited to short verbal explanations during the mass assembly. Disagreements about candidates and village committee members were usually confined to the mahjong tables and storefront benches. Before and after the 2002 election, however, a number of villagers began using printed and photocopied handbills to present their cases and to win support from the village community. For example, in one village in Township 32 a handbill openly criticizing the incumbent village leader was circulated throughout the village just before the election. The accusations were related to education, health care, village investments, and uneven implementation of birth control policies. After providing a list of problems that had occurred over the past three years, the author asked, "Do you still want this kind of village management?" The author then made a plea for the "masses to elect a new village leader." The handbill did not mention names and was signed simply from a "village party member and farmer." The incumbent village leader addressed the issues raised in the handbill during the final days before the 2002 election, and then won the election.

A handbill can also be used to recall an existing village leader between election cycles. The Organic Law allows villagers to launch a petition for the recall of a village leader or committee members at a mass assembly. In order to attempt a recall, the concerned villagers must first drum up support from the community and possibly the township government. For example, in Township 52 a group of village activists started a campaign to recall the village leader before the next election in 2005. The activists distributed a handbill accusing the leader of misappropriating village funds that were to be used to repair the village elementary school. A larger group of villagers armed with the handbill also complained to the township government. According to the village leader, the accusations were groundless. Nevertheless, he said that he was so upset that the township leading cadres took the villagers' accusation seriously that he resigned. This occurred in April 2004, and in June the village was still without a village leader.

Although there are numerous reports of villagers across China using handbills and big-character posters to make their cases known either to the local community or to the higher authorities, it is unclear how the quality of village elections influences this type of political behavior.[45] In the 2004 sample, the use of handbills as a method of openly criticizing local cadres was limited to villages with high-qual-

ity elections. This suggests that when the Organic Law is fully implemented, villagers not only accept the election process as a method of
monitoring cadres but also use the process for openly expressing political grievances.

The Differences among Counties

In the 2004 sample, implementation of the tax-for-fee reform was
uniform across all six townships and three counties, whereas the Organic Law was unevenly implemented and varied by county. This suggests that the tax-for-fee reform was a top-priority policy or a hard
target for county leading cadres, and the Organic Law was considered a soft target. The one-level-down management system implies
that hard targets are nonnegotiable, and promotion depends on
fulfilling these targets. But at each level the municipal or county
leading cadres can decide to make soft targets hard if they believe it
is a policy worth implementing. This reinforces the argument of
O'Brien and Li, who suggest that soft targets are subject to the personal decisions of leading cadres. This may explain the difference
between Counties 5 and 6 regarding implementation of the Organic Law.

A more systematic explanation of the difference between Counties
5 and 6 (as well as County 3) is based on local economic conditions
and the cadre exchange system. County 6 (C6) is the poorest county
in the sample. The mean family income for 2004 was 4,388 RMB, as
opposed to 9,048 RMB in C5 and 9,600 RMB in C3.[46] The annual
family income in C3 and C5 is more than twice the annual income in
C6. The income disparities among counties also existed in the 2000
survey. The differences are due to land, agriculture, and distance to
the major metropolitan centers. Counties 3 and 5 have relatively flat
arable land, and the county economic development plan in the early
1990s hinged on the fruit orchards (apples and pears). In addition,
their close proximity to major metropolitan centers makes it easier for villagers to find off-farm labor opportunities (short-term labor migration). These two factors have had a significant influence
on the rising incomes in these counties; by national standards the
household income in C3 and C5 is just above the middle-income
level.[47] County 6 is in a more remote region with less arable land and

farther away from the major metropolitan center. There was little industrial or agricultural development in the 1990s. As a result, the income level in this county was closer to the low-income category by national standards. According to Tianjian Shi, economic development at the county level has an influence on the quality of village elections in China.[48] He finds a concave relationship between economic development (measured as county per capita income) and village elections, such that low- and high-income counties had poor-quality elections, while middle-income counties had better-quality village elections. This may be one explanation for the differences among counties. In this case, however, it is both the economic conditions of the county and the cadre exchange system that seem to have had an influence on the quality of village elections.

The frequency and type of cadre rotation vary greatly between C6 and the other two counties. In C3 and C5 the county party secretaries are rotated every three to four years, and the township party secretaries are rotated every five to six years. The main reason for this practice is to reduce localism, especially at the township and county levels.[49] The rotation of cadres in C6 is very different, however. The township cadres are rotated every three to four years, while the county party secretary had remained in office for over twelve years (since 1992). Moreover, before he was county party secretary, he was the county government head for over ten years. As a result, C6 presents an unusual case regarding the tenure of a county leader.

The poor economic conditions in C6 also meant that the county party secretary had no incentive to implement the village election law vigorously, because the main source of revenue was the collection of taxes and fees.[50] The township cadres needed to maintain their authority to select compliant village committee members and ensure revenue collection. Nevertheless, despite his relative autonomy and entrenched local power, the county party secretary was still obligated to give in to increased pressure from the provincial authorities and fully implement the tax-for-fee reform.[51] Thus within the county the tax reform is considered a hard target while the village elections remain soft.

Leading cadres in Counties 5 (C5) and 3 (C3) have a greater incentive to implement village elections due to a higher level of economic development in the townships, more frequent rotations, and pressure from municipal and provincial governments. The diverse revenue sources from local industry and rural residents relaxed some of the pressure to collect all the revenue directly from the villagers. This also reduced the need for direct township control over village committee members. Moreover, the request for county leading cadres to implement the Organic Law was based on the notion that village autonomy and local elections may contribute to a more stable relationship between township government and villagers. In fact, Jean C. Oi and Daniel Kelliher suggest that political stability was the original intent of the Organic Law.[52] A county party secretary may strictly enforce the Organic Law as evidence to higher-level authorities that he or she is serious about maintaining stability within the county. For example, in late 1998, following implementation of the Shaanxi Province Public Village Affairs and Democratic Management Provisional Measures, the county party secretary in C5 made the village elections a hard target, and in 2001 he was promoted to the municipal government.[53] Thus social stability is the top priority, and the tax-for-fee reform and the Organic Law are viewed as means to this end. Social stability may not guarantee the promotion of a county or a township leading cadre, but instability will ensure that such leaders do not receive a promotion.

The data suggest that once the elections are fully implemented, it is difficult to revert to semi-open elections or no elections. Although there is an example of a reversion from party branch to township nominations in C6, it is clear that none of the villages with an open nomination process (i.e., fully implemented village elections) in C3 and C5 reverted to party branch or township nominations. The open nomination process, competitive elections, campaigns, and formal public criticisms of village cadres have become accepted modes of political expression in these villages. One reason for the continued development of the local election process is that while the initial institution requires top-down pressure to be fully implemented in the village, the continual maintenance of these practices depends on pressure from the bottom up. This does not mean that county or township leading cadres may not have a change of heart and decide to disregard the Organic Law. The example in County 6 shows that the quality of elections can regress. Yet villages that hold open nominations and enjoy relative autonomy from the township government for a period of time tend to develop democratic practices, such as the use of handbills, which go beyond the requirements of the Organic Law.

The findings concerning the central government's political capacity to carry out both popular and unpopular policies in rural China support Edin's contention that the central government can selectively implement priority policies.[54] Moreover, policy priorities can change, and soft targets can become hard. This suggests that the reason why researchers throughout the 1990s observed little or no reduction in villager burdens and an uneven implementation of village elections is that the central leadership did not consider these policies important. Moreover, given the one-level-down management system and their short-term positions, leading cadres would do whatever it took to fulfill their performance contracts, including manipulating village elections and using coercive methods to collect taxes and fees. The differences among previous scholarly explanations (stressing weak state capacity and local and national selective policy implementation) may be more temporal than theoretical. Although the central government announced strong intentions to reduce villager burdens and enforce the Organic Law, in the 1990s there was scant evidence that these policies were being implemented in the countryside. The survey data from 2000 show high villager burdens and uneven implementation of the Organic Law within counties. Without the comparative survey conducted in June 2004, it would have been impossible to test the selective policy hypothesis.

The next step is to examine the timing and the length of time whereby the central government can sustain a policy push. Although the central government can selectively implement priority policies, this does not mean that the central government will always have the capacity to implement the desired policies; nor can the central government implement all priority policies at once. The evidence demonstrates that relatively immediate enforcement of a priority policy, whether popular or unpopular, can be achieved, but this does not mean that the central government can sustain indefinitely the pressure to enforce priority policies selectively. In fact, as enforcement of the birth control policy suggests, the center may force a campaign-type policy that reaches even the most remote villages, but like the tension in a rubber band, the pressure cannot be maintained for too long by the central and provincial governments and must eventually retract.[55]

Therefore, can the central government sustain the top-down pressure needed to enforce the tax-for-fee reforms? Continuation of the tax-for-fee reforms may first require greater enforcement of the Organic Law. Findings support the view that, when fully implemented, the Organic Law allows villagers to monitor cadres and reduce excessive burdens. The pressure needed to sustain the tax-for-fee reforms must come from both the top down and the bottom up. Village elections provide a mechanism for pressure from below. Higher authorities can measure burden reductions, but monitoring lower-level cadres is costly in terms of both time and effort. Village elections shift the monitoring costs from the central government to the villagers. Without village elections, the central government may not have the capacity to maintain the policy pressure needed to continue to reduce villager burdens. Thus attaching a higher policy priority to the tax-for-fee reform than the Organic Law may be putting the cart before the horse.

JEAN C. OI
ZHAO SHUKAI

4 | Fiscal Crisis in China's Townships:
Causes and Consequences

Many township governments across China are in debt. They cannot pay their bills and cannot get loans because their credit is exhausted. Wages are owed to both local leaders and regular office staff. Some cadres complain that they have not been paid for over a year. A 2000 Ministry of Agriculture study states that villages are burdened by an average debt of 170,000 RMB. The same study finds that townships have an average debt of 2.98 million RMB, which is more than the total annual revenue of some townships. A State Council study of three provinces estimates township debt to be much higher, averaging 10 million RMB. No one seems to know the exact size of the debt. More is known about the causes of the debt, but the issue is complex and varies not only by region but also over time. Some townships have been able to escape this problem, but others have not. Why is this so? What is the cause of these fiscal problems? Is it simply that townships have become synonymous with corruption and an uncontrolled growth of bureaucracy? Or are there deeper systemic problems of funding and governance at the grassroots that trace back to China's piecemeal reform?

Budget shortfalls are a common problem in many countries, but unlike American local governments, for example, townships and villages in China do not have the option of legally increasing taxes or selling bonds. These instruments are the purview of the central government. At the same time, unlike local officials in Russia, township officials in China are not pleading for bailouts from the central authorities.[1] Rather, they usually try to hide the fact that they cannot collect enough revenue. What is the political logic that drives the behavior of China's township officials in what would appear to be a fiscal crisis? Is this another case of politics as usual in China's transitional system? What are the political consequences for peasant-state relations and grassroots governance?

The findings in this chapter are based on data collected from twenty townships in fifteen counties located in ten provinces.[2] We begin with a brief examination of the structure of township finance, which will help explain why some townships have developed such heavy debt while others remain solvent. The amount, sources, and consequences of the debt will be examined in later sections.

Structure of Township Finance

Beginning in the mid-1980s, townships became a level of finance when China adopted the "eating in separate kitchens" fiscal reforms.[3] Despite later changes, including the 1994 fiscal reforms, the basic principles governing revenue sharing have remained fairly constant. A township has quotas for tax revenues that are shared with the upper levels; it collects and turns over all revenues that are designated as central taxes, and it keeps those revenues designated as local taxes. With these revenues it must balance its own books. In the twenty townships studied, nineteen used a system called "divided tax contracting, balancing one's own accounts" (*fenshui baogan, ziqiu pingheng*). In this system, the township tax revenue is first sent up to the county; the county then returns funds to the township according to set rules.[4]

Sources of Revenue

The determining characteristic of township finances is the source of its revenues. Up until 1994 these were divided into within-budget and extra-budgetary revenues.[5] The most important within-budget revenues were the four agriculture-related taxes,[6] some portion of the local industrial commercial tax (sales and income tax), and a small portion of the national industrial commercial tax (the value added and the enterprise income tax). The most important extra-budgetary revenues included the original township unified levy *(tongchou)*, administrative fees such as the village house fee *(zhaijidi shouxufei)*, fines such as for those who exceed the family planning limits, and special funds from different agencies.

After the implementation of the tax-for-fee reform *(shuifei gaige)*,[7] the existing agricultural taxes and surcharges were abolished and replaced with just two taxes on peasant households: a reformulated agricultural tax and a surcharge on the new agricultural tax. Instead of paying a village retained fee *(tiliu)* and a township unified levy *(tongchou)*, a land contract fee, and various other ad hoc surcharges, peasant households are assessed only one tax, either the agricultural or special agricultural products tax, and its associated surcharge.[8] In 2005 the central government took a further step and announced that by the end of 2006, peasants would no longer have to pay the newly adjusted agricultural tax or surcharge. The majority of peasants in China now are totally free from these taxes and fees.[9]

We have long suspected that areas dependent primarily on agriculture are more likely to be in poor financial shape, while those that engage in rural industry are better off.[10] In our twenty-township study we indeed found that finances are still in good shape where townships have successful rural industry or are able to attract outside investment, whether foreign or domestic. Revenues continue to flow in, and there are funds to pay township expenses and provide public goods. In such townships the *shuifei gaige* policy has had relatively little impact.

Given that the impact of the tax-for-fee reform obviously would differ depending on the income streams, let us first delineate the sources of revenue in our sample. As Table 4.1 shows, our sample consists of relatively less well off townships, where revenues are 3 million RMB or less. Only in two townships do taxes from industry and commerce constitute more than 50 percent of total revenues. It is therefore possible that our findings will overstate the degree of fiscal crisis in the countryside.

Although we can generalize about the most lucrative sources of revenue, caution should be used in predicting financial conditions from the structure of the economy. Research across twenty townships, as well as results from earlier survey data, suggest that en-

Table 4.1 Composition of fiscal income

	Total fiscal income (million RMB)				
Range	<1	1–2	2–3	7–9	10 or >
Number of townships	3	6	7	2	2
	Agricultural tax as percentage of total (%)				
Range	<10	10–20	30–50	50–70	70 or >
Number of townships	1	3	4	4	3
	Industrial commercial tax as percentage of total (%)				
Range	<10	10–20	30–50	70–80	90 or >
Number of townships	1	1	5	1	1

gaging in rural industry is insufficient to determine revenues.[11] Trajectories of development may not be linear. Some villages and townships never took off in industrialization, while others initially took off but then at some point crashed and burned, spiraling into heavy debt from the failed rural enterprises. As later sections will document, our twenty-township study is full of such examples. Borrowing to develop rural industry is one of the most frequent sources of debt.

The Size of Township Debt

There is no authoritative figure for the amount of debt carried by townships across China. Even if we knew the precise amount, it would be of only limited use. More useful is a disaggregated picture that shows the variation across different townships. We could then explore why some townships have more debt than others. This is where our study is able to provide some preliminary insights.

Given our selection bias toward agricultural areas, as expected, we found a prevalence of debt in our sample. Of the twenty townships studied, only four had no debt. Of the remaining sixteen townships,

Table 4.2 Size of township debt

RMB	Number of townships
Less than 1 million	5
1–3 million	3
3–5 million	3
5–7 million	3
More than 8 million	2

ten reported that their debt had a direct impact on their work, with four townships noting a serious impact. The debt in the sixteen townships totaled 56 million RMB, which averages out to 2.8 million RMB of debt per township, a figure that is very close to the Ministry of Agriculture estimate. Comparing this average debt to the income of our townships, we see that in almost half of the townships the debt is larger than their total average annual income. Table 4.2 shows the number of townships and their range of debt. We see that more than half of our sample had debt of at least 1 million RMB.

If we look at specific cases, certain patterns emerge that lend support to our hypothesis about the importance of the sources of revenue and whether the revenue needs to be shared with upper levels. The richest of the twenty townships in our study is in Zhejiang, with a total population of 45,000 and revenue of 47 million RMB in 2002. Of this amount, only 17 million RMB was within-budget revenues, and 30 million RMB was extra-budgetary income that did not have to be shared with the upper levels. Moreover, of that revenue, 10 million RMB was from land use, which would have been unaffected by the cuts mandated by the *feigaishui* policy. In stark contrast, the poorest township in our sample, in Ningxia, had a population of 10,000 people and revenue of only 130,000 RMB, all of which had to be shared with higher levels. The township received a subsidy of 630,000 RMB but was still short 500,000 RMB. In this poor township the implementation of the tax-for-fee reform effectively eliminated extra-budgetary revenues because the locality had no nonagricultural revenue-generating projects. In a township in Hunan, also with a population of 10,000, total revenues were 570,000 RMB. Not all taxes had to be sent to upper levels, however. The upper levels provided a fiscal transfer of 160,000 RMB, which gave the township a total revenue of 730,000 RMB. These cases suggest that the fiscal situation in townships varies greatly depending on their fiscal contracts, whether they receive fiscal transfers, and their own sources of revenue, that is, whether revenues have to be shared. The degree of the variation is suggested by the finding that the "miscellaneous" (*qita*) category of revenue in the richest township in our sample was four times the total revenue of the poorest township.

Reasons for Township Financial Troubles

The reasons why townships have encountered financial crises can be examined from a number of different angles. One way is to look at costs; a second is to look at revenues; and a third is to look at the source of debts, that is, the reasons why funds are borrowed and not repaid. The situation in China's townships requires that we examine all three of these elements.

Increasing Expenditures

One reason for growing township debt is simply that expenditures are increasing. Township expenditures fall into two major categories: basic operating costs—personnel and administration—which include wages and basic administrative expenditures; and costs for public goods and services. Locals refer to the first category as "food money" (*chifande qian*), that is, for the basic survival of local government; the latter is called "project" or "work money" (*banshide qian*).

Growth in the first category—basic operating costs—is the reason why the growth of township bureaucracy since the mid-1980s has become so notorious. An ever-increasing wage bill obviously comes with this expansion. This has occurred in spite of the center's efforts to merge townships, cut allocations, and lay off cadres. The number of personnel that the townships are actually supporting is difficult to ascertain. If one asks townships about the number of bureaucratic positions (*bianzhi*) they have for which offices, officials will provide numbers in accordance with their allocations. But these numbers are unrevealing. The *bianzhi* for different offices may have nothing to do with what the person in that *bianzhi* actually does. Most important, the *bianzhi* does not include those people paid by the township but outside of the official allotment. Furthermore, there are payees who have no real jobs.

It should be noted that the enlargement of the township bureaucracy is not entirely the fault of local governments. Up until a few years ago, townships (as well as counties) were required to take in new graduates annually assigned to them under the unified allocation system.[12] For example, one county in Hebei had to take in five or six new cadres each year, regardless of need or skills.[13]

Although it is beyond the scope of this chapter to examine in detail the expansion of the township bureaucracy, we can say that basic operating costs are a major township expense, which inevitably leads to debt unless the townships can continue to increase their income accordingly. Moreover, we also found that the wage bill and basic expenditures fail to vary with the size or wealth of a township as much as one might expect. All townships, even the very poorest, feel compelled to host guests, subscribe to newspapers and journals, and maintain a fleet of cars. While we might conclude that this is a good example of waste and corruption, from the perspective of local cadres who are subject to a promotion system that still requires showing proper political behavior *(biaoxian)*—in this case, adherence to upper-level directions—this is anything but wasteful. Local officials say that they would much prefer to spend their limited funds on other expenses, but they cannot. Having the newspapers and journals in the township offices when upper-level officials come to visit shows that the township respects and reads what the upper levels write in the specialized publications issued by bureaus and ministries. The same goes for hosting visiting dignitaries: these are necessary signs of respect. One could argue that some of these expenditures yield more enjoyment for local officials than others, but all are seen to be a part of doing business. The inflexibility of certain costs means that the wage and administrative expense bill is likely to be a greater source of debt in poorer townships because they have a smaller base from which to draw funds. We found that in the less well off townships the wage bill and essential administrative costs *(chifande qian)* constituted between 50 and 70 percent of expenditures. In townships that owed three or four months' back wages to their personnel, the wage bill amounted to more than 80 percent of total expenditures.

Reduced Township Revenue: Tax-for-Fee Reform

With rising expenditures, revenues must keep pace. Unfortunately for townships, although the tax-for-fee policy relieved peasant burdens, it also eliminated the key way for townships to raise revenues.

The tax-for-fee policy marked a major departure by the state in its response to the peasant burden problem.[14] Unlike earlier directives that simply urged local officials to keep fees in check, this policy closed off those channels. To ensure that cadres could not manipulate the new system by padding the quotas that households had to pay, in some provinces each household was sent a letter explaining the new tax system. To ensure that peasants actually received and read the letter, peasants had to sign an agreement that stated how much their household would pay for the tax and surcharge.

So far the tax-for-fee policy evidently has reduced peasant burdens.[15] In the eighteen townships in our sample that had implemented the policy, peasant payments to township and village authorities had been substantially reduced. In one village peasant burdens had been cut by 38 percent over the previous year.[16] In another village the new policy resulted in a 40 percent drop compared to the previous year.[17] Our findings are in line with a 2002 State Administration for Taxation report that indicates an average 31 percent reduction in the per capita tax burden in Anhui, 30 percent in Jiangsu, and over 25 percent in the other pilot areas.[18] A State Council research report indicates that after the expansion of the *shuifei gaige* policy to sixteen provinces in 2002, in the first half of the year the per capita spending on taxes and fees nationwide decreased by 3.9 percent.[19] According to a 2004 National Bureau of Statistics report, peasant burdens averaged 11.5 RMB per person, which was a 27.2 percent decrease from 2003. The agricultural tax alone decreased by 11.3 percent from 2003.[20]

Nevertheless, this well-intentioned policy has created more problems than it has solved for many local levels of administration, precisely at a time when more, not less, revenue is needed by townships.

The tax-for-fee reform cuts peasant burdens, but it also reduces village and township revenues by an equal amount, with no reliable means to replace them. Under the *shuifei gaige* policy, the new agricultural tax is designated for the township, whereas the surcharge on the agricultural tax is earmarked for the village. Yet neither amount equals the earlier fees that villages or townships collected. As a result, some local governments have been pushed over the edge and left in deficit. More than a few areas are unable to pay their expenses, including cadre salaries. Of the twenty townships studied, only seven had sufficient funds to pay their personnel on time, and five were able to pay salaries, but behind schedule. Seven other townships could pay some salaries on time, but only a portion of each of the salaries owed.[21] Some paid salaries, but only two or three times a year instead of monthly. Many townships owed two to three months' back pay to their staff. In some recent cases townships owed as much as twenty months' back wages to their employees; some cadres complained that they had not been paid for as long as two years. Such problems extended to the villages. In one township the tax-for-fee system cut village revenues by 2 million RMB. This meant that six of its thirty-four villages were unable to pay their village cadre salaries; another five to six villages scraped by and barely covered their village cadre salaries but had no money left for any other expenditures.

Localities are expected to make up for the lost revenue through increased economic development. In some areas where there are relatively abundant development possibilities, especially those areas near cities and convenient for large factories to set up subsidiary plants, the goal is feasible. Some villages, for example, have already earned more in a year than they lost with the policy change. Some richer villages never depended on the *tiliu,* and some villages were even able to pay the *tiliu* for the peasants, but these types of villages are in the minority.

The difficulty is in those areas that lack easy development opportunities. In such areas it seems likely that local authorities will find other ways of squeezing out the needed additional revenues unless the central authorities can compensate for their loss. The syndrome that Jean Oi describes elsewhere, where cuts in one type of surcharge drove increases in another, will reemerge to increase peasant burdens again.[22] Anticipating such problems, central authorities have limited additional peasant levies to 15 RMB per person per year, even if the village as a whole decides to go forward with a project and raise additional funds. Again, this is good for the peasants, but it does little to solve the fiscal problems for rural administration.

In a concession to the localities, the center started a program of fiscal transfers (*zhuanyi zhifu*) as an explicit substitute for the loss of revenues from the tax-for-fee reform. The abolition of the new agricultural tax and associated surcharge in 2006 have made these transfers a necessity.[23]

The center allocates monies to provinces, which then funnel funds to counties and eventually to townships, which will then use the money to help their villages and to supplement their own revenues. The central state thus provides a fiscal safety net, as it did when implementing its 1980s fiscal reforms, to stem political opposition from the localities.[24] These fiscal transfers are intended to compensate for the revenue shortfalls and allow localities to meet basic expenditures.[25] For example, one county received more than 39 million RMB for its thirty townships, approximately half of which was used to subsidize villages.[26]

Although monies are being provided by the center, interviews suggest that the overall impact of the fiscal transfers seems to be limited, especially with regard to solving the problem of local debt. The problem is twofold. First, township officials complain that some of this money never reaches its intended target.[27] One township had no direct access to its share because the county held and allocated the funds. In another township, funds were sent directly to the villages, with the township receiving nothing. Second, the transfer amounts are often insufficient to cover even the lost revenues and current expenditures. Part of the problem, of course, is that under the old system, in practice, the revenues collected were much larger than the officially allowed exactions, both for the agricultural tax and for the fees.[28] In areas where there was profitable industry, that industry would make up the shortfall; otherwise the locality would have to find other ways to make up the difference. In poor areas such as the three townships in our study that did receive a transfer, the amounts were minimal and did little to relieve the debt. At most the funds provided a small supplement to pay some salaries.

Waves of Debt

The tax-for-fee reform policy alone fails to explain the fiscal crisis that exists in large parts of the countryside. This policy merely exacerbated an existing problem. Many townships and villages were already in debt. Consequently, any further reduction in revenues easily pushed them into crisis.

Local officials identify different stages and causes of debt since the reforms began. Most if not all of this debt can be traced to the pressures placed on cadres who still must operate in a mobilizational bureaucratic system where meeting upper-level quotas and directives is the only route to job security and promotion. This includes debt derived from borrowing to establish township and village enterprises, to meet educational standards and quotas, to develop agriculture, and to invest in basic infrastructure *(jichu sheshi touzi)*. It also includes borrowing to make up for shortfalls in tax revenues, to undertake individual fundraising *(siren jizikuan)*, to invest in projects to attract business *(zhaoshang yinzi peitao gongcheng)*, and to pay back wages to cadres *(tuoqian ganbu gongzi)*. In addition, rural credit associations collapsed.

Table 4.3 shows the amounts of each type of debt. In the townships we studied, three types of debt constituted the largest amount of the total. Tied for first place were funds borrowed to reach centrally mandated educational quotas[29] and funds borrowed to pay the debts of the rural credit associations;[30] tied for second place were debts from infrastructural projects and borrowing to pay owed wages and personal loans; the third-largest source of debts was funds to develop TVEs. Though debts from TVE development and investment in infrastructure projects were not necessarily the largest in terms of the size of debt, they were among the most common sources of debt.

Although we are able to attach some numbers to existing debt and disaggregate different types of debt, in some places local officials claim that they have no idea of their total township arrears. Such an assertion may be questioned, but it is indeed plausible, given the frequency with which local-level officials are rotated. Furthermore, this debt has been accumulated since the beginning of the reforms by different agencies and individuals, including officials and non-officials. For example, the debt from the development of TVEs was

Table 4.3 Structure of township debt

Source of debt	Number of townships with this type of debt	Approximate total (10,000 RMB)	As approximate percentage of total debt
TVEs	6	700	12
Investment in infrastructural projects	6	850	15
Meeting education quotas	5	960	17
Debt of rural credit cooperatives	5	930	17
Wages owed and debt to individuals	3	820	15
Routine expenditures	3	550	10
Interest payments on loans	2	530	9
Making up owed taxes	1	280	5

Note: TVE = Township-village enterprise.

accrued mostly in the late 1980s to the early 1990s. The debt from the rural credit associations occurred mostly during the early 1990s, while the debt from education was mainly from the mid- to late 1990s. Since 2000 or so the causes of the debt have continued to change. Instead of their debt arising from TVEs, universal education, and credit associations, townships now borrow primarily to keep themselves going and to pay for routine expenditures and public works. In addition, localities are spending simply to service their old debt. One township, for example, accumulated a new debt of 250,000 RMB to pay off its rural credit association's debt.

One of our most unexpected findings is that peasant failure to pay taxes and fees is a source of township and village debt. Townships and villages must make up for shortfalls in tax collection when individual villages or peasants fail to pay. Local officials report that in recent years peasants increasingly have refused to pay taxes and fees, even after the reductions mandated by the tax-for-fee policy. We do not know just how widespread this phenomenon is, but a number of townships mentioned this as a problem. Officials in the Ministry of Civil Affairs, which has major responsibility for overseeing village governance, also have acknowledged such problems.[31] In our sample, townships like the two in Zhejiang where the collective paid the various village (tiliu) and township (tongchou) fees had no problem with owed taxes. In the remaining eighteen townships, however, we found nine in which the number of peasants who owed taxes and fees had increased. In two townships officials reported that more than 60 percent of the peasants owed taxes and fees. Still, there were another nine townships where tax collection was about the same or slightly better than in the past. Overall, in our sample about 10 to 20 percent of peasant households owed taxes and/or fees.

Some township officials noted that the *shuifei gaige* policy, and the announced abolition of the agricultural tax within five years,[32] only exacerbated the situation: peasants continually failed to pay taxes, thinking that they would soon be forgiven. Some officials attribute these acts of defiance to "the low cultural level of the peasantry" and their lack of understanding of the importance and necessity of paying taxes. A few township leaders more bluntly identified some peasants who refused to pay as "troublemakers" (dingzihu).[33]

We cannot say with any confidence at this point why some peasants paid their taxes and others did not. We did observe, however, that in areas where peasants owed taxes and fees, trust between cadres and peasants seems to be lacking, with peasants often expressing ill feelings toward township and village cadres. These also seem to be areas where there has been an increase in the number of peasants who migrate out to work, so more land is lying fallow, or where there has been an increase in the number of outsiders migrating in to work. More systematic research is needed to see whether these patterns hold in a broader sample of cases.

Local officials complain that central-level policies are hampering their tax recovery efforts because of prohibitions against going after peasants to collect old tax debt. We are unaware of any specific regulations to that effect. Apparently the concern for stability and the need to prevent peasants from petitioning and presenting grievances to the upper levels may in practice cause officials to feel con-

strained in the way they deal with the peasants. In the cadre responsibility system, any black mark on the record of local officials can
negate (yipiao foujue) all other achievements, thus heightening the
constraints on how they deal with the peasants. Township officials
complained that townships can do little except live with the nonpayment and find other ways to meet their quotas. Whether this is really
the case, we do not know on the basis of our current research. Local
officials elaborating on their predicament say that the situation is becoming worse. They say that those peasants who have been paying
their taxes and fees increasingly question whether they too should
stop. If their neighbors are getting away with not paying, why should
they comply? Some may feel that paying on time simply means that
they are losing out (chikui).

Fudging the Fiscal Crisis: Ad Hoc Strategies for Political Survival

Localities are expected to make up for lost revenues by developing
their economies and increasing long-term revenues so that they can
move beyond dependence on the ad hoc fees and fiscal transfers.
Success in economic development is the key to political success. Sustainable economic development, however, is not always possible.
While many localities may not be able to develop their economies
rapidly enough to meet the current fiscal crisis, the need at least
to appear to be engaged in economic development has generated
a range of strategies designed to allow them to survive the current fiscal difficulties and to get through their annual cadre evaluations.[34] As the following sections will detail, the long-standing "cat-
and-mouse games" that localities play with the upper levels in an
effort to maintain the façade of compliance are continuing, while
cadres are using land grabs to raise revenues.[35]

Hiding Excess Personnel

One obvious way for townships to deal with the fiscal crisis would be
to cut the number of people on the public payroll. The upper levels
have attempted many times to streamline township bureaucracy. Beginning in the mid- to late 1990s, large numbers of townships were
merged to cut administrative costs. Some reductions may have come

about as a result of such mergers. Other reductions, however, may have been in name only. According to some county and township officials, the newly formed townships were too large to manage effectively. As a result, the newly merged townships subdivided the management of villages under their jurisdiction and strengthened their subordinate organizations to carry out much of the detailed work of monitoring. Personnel were assigned to oversee the new substations and implement the more stringent control mechanisms in the reorganized townships. Some townships have gone so far as to hold and disburse village funds to tighten control.[36]

The upper levels have instituted graduated, automatically enforced cuts in the money allocated by the county for township payrolls in a new attempt to reduce personnel—a further indication that earlier efforts were less than successful. For example, in Hebei, starting in 2002, as one township official explained, the county began to cut one third of the township wage bill each year for three successive years. Yet even with such draconian measures, in China's current context he still found it almost impossible to lay off cadres.

Just as it was difficult to dismiss workers in China's state-owned enterprises (SOEs), the problem for township leaders is more than economic.[37] The calculus is firmly rooted in the way local officials are evaluated by their superiors at the upper levels. In this specific instance, local officials fear protests and demonstrations by laid-off cadres. We have examples in which a township cut personnel only to have them put back on the payroll after they went to the upper levels to protest *(shangfang)*. Township officials have learned that it may be less costly to ignore directives to cut personnel, keep people on the payrolls, and have deficits than to have disgruntled laid-off officials going to the upper levels to protest.

In the face of such constraints, some townships have started to offer lucrative economic incentives to persuade surplus personnel to leave voluntarily. The offer is to accept a severance package now or be left with nothing later. In the meantime, when personnel refuse to leave, some local officials openly admit that they are concealing these individuals on their employment rolls while appearing to abide by the upper level's order to cut personnel. They remove them from the *bianzhi* rolls and pay them with other monies, or owe them, as the case may be.

Borrowing to Pay Off Debt

Townships, like other governments, can borrow legally and openly to service their debt in a transparent manner. But there are also examples of township officials borrowing to cover their failure to fulfill their assigned tax quotas. In contrast to the Russian case, Chinese local officials, even in relatively poor townships, try to mask rather than advertise their fiscal woes to obtain fiscal transfers or subsidies. Because they wish to keep their jobs, the last thing local cadres want is to make the upper levels aware of their debt problem. The exceptions are those townships that already are designated poverty townships and therefore are exempt from tax quotas, or those that receive special subsidies precisely because they have already been determined to be too poor to pay taxes.

Sometimes the borrowing is a short-term strategy to accommodate the bureaucratic process that requires townships to submit taxes to the county before remittances are sent back down to the localities. One township in 2002, for example, had a tax quota of 2 million RMB. It had reported to the upper levels revenue projections of 4.89 million RMB, but it actually collected only about 790,000 RMB in taxes. It thus borrowed over 1 million RMB from the savings cooperative to pay the upper levels. Then, after the county sent back its remittance, the township repaid the cooperative. In this case, once the county remitted the funds, the township was back in the black. In other cases, however, townships borrow to meet tax quotas, but no revenues are sent back, thus resulting in their falling further into debt.

Individual Cadre Borrowing to Pay Off Collective Debt

A related but distinct strategy from borrowing by a township or village is individual borrowing to pay off collective, township, or village debt. This is called "making up the tax revenues" *(dianshui)*. It is sometimes undertaken by tax collectors who fail to meet the assigned collection quota; at other times it is undertaken by leading local officials. We found various examples in a number of townships as well as villages. The party secretary in one township said that starting in the late 1990s, this practice of borrowing to make up the difference between what a locality could collect and what it owed to the upper levels was quite common. He reported that in the two years since coming to the township, he had already borrowed 200,000 RMB to cover its debt. The party secretary stressed that he had to take out a personal loan, because if he had tried to borrow in the name of the township, the loan would have been denied.[38]

This practice of personal borrowing to pay collective debt reflects the extraordinary degree to which the fiscal crisis has affected some localities. Debt has become such a problem that the credit of township or village government is no longer sufficient to secure a loan. Individuals are thus taking on debt for the government. Part of the reason may also lie in the stricter regulations instituted in the 1980s and 1990s, when local government agencies, such as the township economic commission, acted as guarantors for township and village enterprise loans. When enterprises failed, there was no one for the banks to hold responsible, because the government agencies are not considered economic actors. In the example just cited, the party secretary who took out the two loans said that if he were to be transferred, he would still be liable for repaying the loan.

What local officials do not openly say is that these loans, which may be a political necessity for the township, also may serve as an economic opportunity for the individual local cadre. He can charge the township a high interest rate and make a profit from the transaction. Moreover, the cadre's risk in taking out a personal loan for the township is somewhat mitigated because he would be in a position to determine the priority of repayment. Only if the official is transferred would there be problems.[39]

Poaching Taxes

Some townships engage in an ingenious practice that essentially hijacks or poaches (maishui) tax payments from nearby localities. In order to understand how this works, one must first know that under Chinese law an individual or a business can pay its owed taxes anywhere as long as a receipt is issued indicating payment. A locality will lure a business into paying its owed taxes to that locality rather than to the locality in which the business is located. The incentive for the business is the poacher township's offer to accept less than what is officially owed, with a promise to issue a receipt for the full amount due. For example, if the owed tax is 10,000 RMB, the township may be satisfied if only 9,000 RMB is paid. A receipt will be given to the taxpayer for the full 10,000 RMB. The township official who explained the practice realized that it was wrong and ultimately would harm the state's interest but saw no other way to meet his quota.[40]

This strategy costs the township but is still a profitable endeavor. At least five townships in our sample engaged in this type of activity to increase their revenues in order to meet mandatory tax quotas. One township official explained that his township was assigned a local industrial commercial tax of 320,000 RMB, even though it had only about 60,000 RMB in income. To make up the difference, the township hijacked taxes from other localities. To facilitate this strategy, recipient townships usually need the cooperation of a friendly tax official from a neighboring township to help identify who owes how much in taxes in order to approach a possible participant in the scheme.

Using Land as a Source of Revenue

The center sided with the peasants in adopting the *shuifei gaige* policy to relieve their burdens, but because this policy effectively limits the amount that peasants must pay in taxes and fees, townships have had to turn to other means of finding additional revenue. In the past, local officials changed from increasing *tiliu* and *tongchou* to increasing other local surcharges. With those channels also effectively blocked, local officials are now trying to control the remaining sources of current and future revenue. One such tactic is to take over land belonging to villages and their peasants, often with questionable compensation.

In our interviews, some of the most animated discussions and heated venting of frustrations toward township cadres had to do with land—what the peasants refer to as land seizures without compensation, whether it be for roads or for development. In some localities, village cadres have turned to land rentals or sales to generate revenue. Villagers have stopped farming, and leaders are renting out the land for commercial development and industrial use. In these villages, village officials then use that income to provide peasants with a higher stable income than they were receiving from farming. This is a strategy used as early as the 1980s in places such as Shenzhen. But in other villages, villagers see their land taken away with little compensation.[41] Even in the 1990s in relatively undeveloped areas such as Yunnan, local officials sold village land without giving due and sufficient compensation to the peasants whose land was being sold.[42] Most of the time the township sells the land it takes, but in some places where the fiscal situation has deteriorated to a point where township cadres have little or nothing in the way of regular salaries, and presumably where there is no booming land market, the township officials farm the appropriate land on a semi-commercial basis as a source of revenue to pay themselves.

More research needs to be done on this topic, but the large number of recent reports of cadre abuse with regard to land suggests that this is a growing problem.[43] There have been numerous reports of peasant unrest. Numbers released by the Ministry of Public Security indicate that there were 87,000 "public order disturbances" in 2005.[44] These were not all land related, but in a speech in January 2006, Premier Wen Jiabao called illegal land seizures a "historic error" that could threaten national stability.[45]

The press has reported on a number of high-profile cases of peasant protests, including incidents of violence that resulted in deaths and beatings. It is beyond the scope of this chapter to explore this topic fully, but several examples are illustrative. One case occurred in Shengyou in Hebei province, about 220 kilometers southwest of Beijing, where six peasants were killed in June 2005 in a fight with thugs who were said to have been hired by local authorities—the culmination of a drawn-out fight that began in 2003.[46] Another case occurred in Huaxi village outside Hangzhou, where in 2005 violent demonstrations broke out after failure to resolve a land dispute that had started in 2001.[47]

The Political Consequences of the Fiscal Crisis

Although the fiscal situation is dire in a growing number of localities, politics goes on as usual. After more than two decades of reform and movement away from central planning, local officials in China's countryside maintain the façade of compliance with upper levels.

They dutifully respond to orders to cut personnel from their pay-rolls, but this is done only on the books, by moving the personnel from one category to another. Local officials comply with upper-level orders when they must, but they do what they need to do to sur-vive the rest of the time. As local officials explained, there is no way to do everything that the upper levels demand. Over time, they fig-ure out what the upper levels most want implemented and strive to meet those targets. Maintaining stability and preventing peasants from lodging complaints is one such target. The penalty is much greater when those targets are not met than when debt accumulates or salaries are not paid. Other guidelines may or may not be fol-lowed, depending on local preferences. There is a significant degree of autonomy, in spite of limits on local revenues.

One of our most striking findings involves the risks and debts that local cadres shoulder to keep their jobs, even in the face of the mounting fiscal crisis. Such actions might suggest that China's local officials are uncommonly devoted—willing to do almost anything to secure sufficient funds to keep township government going, in-cluding taking out personal loans and poaching another township's taxes. Such an altruistic interpretation, however, is tempered by our finding that although cadres take risks to help their townships, this can also offer individual local cadres an opportunity to profit from such transactions. Moreover, such responses by local cadres to the fiscal crisis reveal that they still see a career in government as their best chance for success. Local officials are willing to take out loans because they want to meet their assigned tax quotas so they can keep their jobs and do well on their annual cadre evaluations. This sug-gests that there is more reward to being a local official than salary alone. Once a cadre is secure, there are still a multitude of strategies to get ahead and get along in a system in which the perks of office still outweigh the costs, even in townships where there is a fiscal cri-sis.[48] Thus, overall, the Chinese Communist Party (CCP) can take comfort in knowing that local officials still have a vested interest in keeping the current system going. Furthermore, in all the localities that we visited, those cadres who were waiting to be paid seemed confident that the CCP in the end would come through and pay them.[49] In this sense, the fiscal crisis has yet to create a political crisis within the cadre ranks at the grassroots. Nevertheless, this is a fragile situation.

Some local officials complain that the cuts in fiscal and political resources have "hollowed out" township administration, leaving it nothing more than "fake government." The various policies implemented by the central state to reduce peasant burdens and improve peasant-state relations have left many townships in a very precarious position. The abolition of the agricultural tax has exacerbated their fiscal situation, and so far the transfer system has yet to fill the revenue gap or the needs of grassroots governance. One can speculate on the impact of township elections.

As we have stressed, there is tremendous variation in the resources and wealth of townships and villages across China's countryside. This variation is naturally mirrored in the services that are provided in these different localities and thus in the quality of governance. Some townships and villages are serving their peasants well. A large and evidently growing number, however, are providing nothing in terms of public goods, or even worse, they are trying to squeeze funds from the peasants in whatever ways they can.

The real political cost of the fiscal crisis may be the longer-term effect on peasant-state relations, more specifically, the legitimacy of local government. The fiscal crisis has created a situation whereby township officials more than ever before are consumed by the need to survive—to find enough revenue to stay alive (*chifande qian*). In the context of the new fiscal policies and the recent cuts from the *shuifei gaige*, this means that most of the revenue raised by township cadres will go toward nothing more than supporting themselves. No wonder peasants in poor areas increasingly see townships as useless. These negative feelings are fueled by the illegal land appropriations by townships that seek to control what is likely to become the most important new source of wealth in China's countryside. This has become the most contentious issue in rural China, one that even the top leaders admit has the potential to threaten political stability.

Township government is now at a crossroads. There has been discussion of abolishing townships as a level of government. That is something unlikely to occur in the immediate future. In the meantime, and certainly if the center decides to keep the township as a level of government, the center must resolve the institutional disjunctures that are a legacy of China's piecemeal reforms. The center cannot simply let townships wither away due to lack of resources. But township governance must be based on a stable economic base.

Governmental and economic reforms need to be brought into balance for there to be effective township governance. The role and resources of townships need to be redefined to fit China's new political economy. For now, as some township officials readily admit, "they manage everything, but manage nothing well."

5 | Direct Township Elections

Democratic theorists argue that the fundamental principles of democracy include fair competition among elites
and free popular participation.[1] Seen in this light, any institutional reform that enhances elite competition and ex-
pands popular participation can contribute to democratization. It is perhaps for this reason that observers and
analysts of China's political reforms have been so atten-
tive to the possibility of extending direct elections from
the village to the township level, especially after the first
direct election of a township head was held in Buyun,
Sichuan province, in December 1998.[2] Although the experiment with direct township elections was soon called
off by Beijing, which ruled that direct election of township government heads "does not accord with the Constitution and the Organic Law of Local People's Congresses
and Local People's Governments," it left behind two important legacies.[3] First, Guangdong's application to conduct
such an experiment prompted Li Peng, then chairman of
the National People's Congress, to state that alternative
procedures for selecting candidates could be explored.[4]
Taking advantage of this opening, local leaders in Sichuan,
Jiangsu, Henan, and Hubei quickly carried out experiments with "open selection" *(gongxuan)*—a reform that
lowers the entry barrier for elites to compete and enlarges
the selectorate—at the township level and even at the

county level in Jiangsu.[5] Second, direct township elections have become a barometer that outside observers (domestic and foreign) use to assess the Chinese leaders' commitment to democratic reform. In March 2000, for instance, when Premier Zhu Rongji was asked whether he would support the extension of direct elections beyond the village level, he responded that he would like to see such an extension "as soon as possible."[6] In 2003, after an unauthorized election was aborted in Pingba town by county authorities in Chongqing, some analysts raised doubts about Hu Jintao's credentials as a political reformer.[7]

Researchers have examined the background, process, and design of the Buyun election and a lesser-known direct election in Nancheng township, Qingshen county, Sichuan.[8] Baogang He and Youxing Lang argue that the Buyun election was designed to strengthen the party's authority rather than to weaken it.[9] Joseph Cheng suggests that bottom-up pressure to improve cadre accountability and the party's failure to curb corruption might encourage future Chinese leaders to develop more interest in political reforms such as direct township elections.[10] I have noted that Jiang Zemin's pledge to expand grassroots democracy at the Fifteenth Party Congress created a discursive opening for ambitious local leaders to pioneer political reforms.[11] Tony Saich and Xuedong Yang highlight the important roles played by resourceful and strong-willed local leaders in initiating direct township elections, suggesting, however, that competition among ambitious cadres in different localities might diminish the lasting power of most institutional innovations.[12]

Scholars have also examined villagers' attitudes toward direct township elections. Cai Dingjian, for instance, argues that the level of economic development has no correlation with villagers' attitudes toward direct township elections. He finds that the key predictor of whether ordinary villagers supported such elections was whether they had a chance to learn more about them through practice.[13] Using a survey conducted in 1997–98, I have noted that villagers who were economically better off, who were less satisfied with the performance of township officials, and who were politically more assertive were more likely to believe that township heads should be directly elected.[14]

Scholars, however, have yet to examine systematically how township officials themselves look at direct township elections. Field observations already indicate sharply differing attitudes among township officials. In the aborted Pingba township election, for instance, we see two extreme positions. The township party secretary risked his career to push forward the election, while the township government head agreed at first to keep quiet, but ultimately sought to sabotage the reform because of fear of losing out to an unexpectedly serious contender.[15] Other township officials took positions somewhere between these two extremes. Buyun township officials, for example, were fully cooperative when the county leadership decided to carry out the reform.[16] Similarly, some township officials in Henan indicated that they would volunteer to take the lead in experimenting with township elections if the party center were to decide to go ahead with them.[17] Also, a township head in Anhui announced in front of dozens of other township officials that he wished to have direct elections so that he could escape the predicament of having either to disobey his demanding county superiors or to alienate his constituents.[18] By contrast, a number of township officials whom I interviewed in Fujian, Hebei, and Jiangxi agreed that direct elections should be a long-term goal, but they insisted that their immediate introduction would destabilize the countryside.[19]

This chapter addresses the factors that affect township officials' attitudes toward direct township elections and how township officials respond to the prospect of this reform. Using a 2003–2004 survey, I identify three representative views held by township officials about direct township elections: (1) a "conservative" view that township heads should not be directly elected; (2) a "moderate reformist" view that township heads should be directly elected but the conditions for holding such elections are not yet ripe; and (3) a "radical reformist" view that township heads should be directly elected and that such elections can be conducted right away. Multivariate regression analyses show that (1) incumbent township party secretaries and government heads tend to be less supportive of direct elections than their deputies and staff; (2) township officials who believe that the reform is in accord with the constitution tend to agree that it should be instituted; (3) township officials who are unhappy with the current cadre management system and regard direct elections as a more transparent and fair alternative are more likely to agree that direct township elections should and can be introduced immediately; (4) support for the immediate initiation of the reform is also correlated with township officials' assessments of the adequacy of the economic development, the ability of villagers to elect township heads, and the potential impact of holding direct elections. On the basis of these empirical findings, I argue that if they are introduced by Beijing, direct township elections are likely to encounter resistance from incumbent township leaders and their patrons at the county level. I also argue that a largely instrumentalist rationale for political reforms places reformers in a strategically poor position because electoral reforms are unlikely to generate tangible payoffs in the short term.

Township Government and Its Reforms

Rebuilt after the dissolution of the commune system in 1982, township (xiang) and town (zhen) government is the lowest level in the Chinese governmental hierarchy.[20] In 2003 there were 38,000 townships and towns, of which 19,600 were towns.[21] (Towns are generally more urbanized and industrialized than townships. For simplicity, I use "township" to refer to both townships and towns.) On average, each township had about 26,000 residents and eighteen villages.[22] Townships are governed by a township party committee and a township government. Leaders of these two institutions, however, are chosen in different ways. The township party secretary is appointed by the county party committee, but according to articles 98 and 101 of the constitution (adopted in 1982, amended in 1988, 1993, and 2004) and the Organic Law of Local People's Congresses and Local People's Governments (1979, revised in 1982, 1986, and 1995), the head and deputy heads of the township government should be elected by township people's congress deputies, who in turn are to be directly elected every three years by residents of the township.[23] In reality, though, township heads are always preselected by the county party committee and its organization department, and the congress election is little more than a formality.[24]

Discussions of reforming township government started almost immediately after the townships were reinstituted. As "street-level bureaucrats," township officials must carry out a wide range of tasks assigned by officials at the county level, most of which, unfortunately, are hugely unpopular. For instance, they must collect taxes and fees, enforce the birth control policy, and carry out mandatory cremation of the deceased.[25] In the mid-1990s, because the 1994 tax reform drained the revenue base of many county governments, township officials in those places had to impose illegal fees on farmers so that they could get paid, and they increasingly relied on the use of coercion to collect such fees.[26] As might be expected, townships in many places have become the most hated level of government. Villagers often blame township officials for increasing peasant burdens and using excessive force. They have engaged in spirited protests and have sometimes rioted against abusive township officials.[27] Excessive township extractions have provoked so many protests that even the central leaders and the official news media have sometimes publicly criticized township officials for arbitrary imposition of fees.[28]

In an attempt to ease tensions between township officials and villagers, two reforms have been experimented with. In the mid-1980s, officials at the Ministry of Civil Affairs (MoCA) drew up an administrative reform to strengthen township governments by making the county government devolve some of its powers to the township, especially the power to appoint directors of key agencies of township government, such as the police station and tax office. If the township government were to become full-fledged rather than badly fragmented, MoCA officials believed, it would be more capable of resisting unlawful orders from the county and would garner popular support by providing public goods, such as paved roads and irrigation facilities. Under the auspices of the MoCA, a number of experiments were conducted in Shandong and Hebei, all of which failed because the county governments in question simply refused to devolve any of their power.[29]

By the late 1980s and early 1990s, the problem of many township officials ruling like "local emperors" (tu huangdi) had worsened to such an extent that senior party leaders such as Peng Zhen began to worry that peasants might soon attack rural cadres "with their shoulder poles."[30] Many Chinese policy analysts came to believe that the township government had become the weakest link in the structure of power. They worried that township officials would sooner or later "drive the peasantry into rebellion." It was against this backdrop that a few senior leaders and policy researchers in Beijing began to consider introducing direct elections of township heads. Just as village elections might stop village cadres from acting like local emperors, they argued, direct township elections might do the same for township heads. They also suggested that popular elections would enable township heads to resist unreasonable and unlawful demands from county governments. In 1990 Peng Zhen instructed the MoCA, which had drafted the Organic Law of Village Committees (1987, revised 1998), to draw up a law that would initiate direct township elections. As late as 1994 MoCA officials had hoped that the law would be enacted by 1996.[31] Owing to the conservative backlash in the post-1989 era, however, the promised legislation never materialized.

Electoral reforms of township government were initiated in 1998 by a number of reform-minded local leaders, who were apparently encouraged by the pledge of the Fifteenth Party Congress to "extend the scope of democracy at the grassroots level."[32] By the end of 2004, six significant reforms had been experimented with in at least nine provinces. By far the most widespread reform is "open selection," which allows selected citizens to participate in the screening of candidates for township head by casting a "vote of recommendation." "Open selection" has been adopted in much of Sichuan and in a number of counties in Guangxi, Henan, Hubei, and Jiangsu.[33] Compared with "open selection," two short-lived reforms introduced more electoral competition and popular participation into the selection of township heads. "The three-round-two-ballot system" (san lun liang piao zhi) involved popular recommendation of candidates and a primary participated in by villager representatives. This system was adopted in Dapeng town, Shenzhen, in January 1999 but was quietly terminated three years later.[34] Similarly, "the two-ballot system" (liang piao zhi) allowed all villagers to cast a popular vote of confidence on whether the incumbent township head, party secretary, and chairman of the people's congress were eligible for reelection, but this was implemented only once, in Zhuoli town, Shanxi, in April 1999.[35] As for building "inner-party democracy," the direct election of township party secretaries by all resident party members was tried in Pinchang county, Sichuan, in 2002 and again in Luxi county, Yunnan, in August 2004; the direct election of township party congress delegates was adopted in Yingjing county and Yucheng district of Ya'an municipality in Sichuan in December 2002.[36]

Among the six electoral reforms, the direct election of township heads has attracted the most interest and attention, primarily because it is considered a possible starting point for a bottom-up democratic restructuring of the Chinese state. Unlike partial reforms such as "open selection," the "three-round-two-ballot" system, and the "two-ballot" system, direct township elections are less susceptible to manipulation. Also, unlike the election of township party secretaries and party congress delegates, direct elections of township heads do not preclude from participation villagers who are not party members. Moreover, reform-minded leaders and scholars seem to share the vision that direct township elections may help prepare the way to introduce direct election of government leaders at the county and even higher levels of government.[37] Direct township elections are also more resilient than many observers would expect. After more than five years with no word of successful experiments since 1999, news emerged that seven townships in Shiping county, Yunnan, had held direct elections of township heads in April 2004.[38]

Data

The data on which the following analysis is based come from a survey conducted in 2003–2004 in Anhui, Fujian, Guangdong, Hunan, Liaoning, and Shandong provinces. Primary survey sites were provincial and city party schools, where respondents were undergoing political training. Altogether, 844 questionnaires were distributed and collected, 136 of which were dropped from the analysis because the respondents skipped more than a quarter of the questions.

Due to political constraints, the requirements of probability sampling were compromised to avoid attracting unwanted attention. Since no strict probability sampling procedure was enforced, the data set obtained from the survey is not representative of township officials in the six provinces. Consequently, it cannot be inferred with certainty whether the observed patterns hold true for all township officials in these six provinces, let alone in all of rural China. The goal was to generate hypotheses to be tested in future research. Definitive conclusions about the issues discussed in this chapter cannot be drawn until national probability samples of township officials are available.[39]

Desirability and Feasibility of Direct Township Elections

The dependent variable was measured with the question: "Should the leaders of the following levels of government be elected directly by voters through the method of one-person one-vote?"[40] Respondents were asked to indicate their attitudes toward direct election of (1) "town and township government heads," (2) "county government heads," (3) "city mayors," (4) "provincial governors," and (5) "the state chairman," by choosing one of three alternative positions.[41] With regard to township heads, 21.5 percent of 708 respondents chose "should not," 43.6 percent chose "should but at present it is not feasible," 28.7 percent chose "should and can be conducted right now," and 6.2 percent skipped the question.[42]

There are two issues here. First, is the reform desirable? Second, if it is desirable, is the reform feasible, and can it be implemented right away? To simplify the analysis, two pairs of contrasting positions were set up: the view that township heads should not be directly elected is called "conservative," and the view that township heads should be directly elected, either now or when conditions are ripe, is placed in the "reformist" category. Within the "reformist" category, the view that direct township elections at present are infeasible is characterized as "moderate," in contrast to the "radical" view that they can be carried out right away.

The analysis is done in two steps. First, the factors affecting township officials' choice between the "conservative" and "reformist" positions are explained. Then the factors affecting the reformists' choice between the "moderate" and "radical" positions are explained. Both steps include the same set of predictors (i.e., independent variables) in logistic regression models. The results are summarized in Table 5.1.

The Insignificance of Demographic Predictors

All demographic predictors included in the model turn out to be statistically insignificant, suggesting that the attitude of township officials toward direct elections is correlated primarily with their career considerations and political values. Still, a number of patterns are worth noting. First, contrary to expectation, younger respon-

Table 5.1 Logistic regressions predicting township officials' choice between "conservative" and "reformist" and between "moderate" and "radical" positions regarding direct township elections

	Conservative vs. Reformist[a]	Moderate vs. Radical[b]
Gender (female = 0, male = 1)	−0.031	0.179
	(0.345)	(0.370)
Age (from younger to older)	0.291	0.106
	(0.172)	(0.167)
College education (no = 0, yes = 1)	0.055	0.126
	(0.377)	(0.174)
Township party secretary or township head (no = 0, yes = 1)	−0.720**	−0.753*
	(0.277)	(0.327)
Constitutionality (negative = 1, ambivalent = 2, positive = 3)	0.461**	0.121
	(0.186)	(0.233)
Direct election violates the principle that the party manages cadres (no = 0, yes = 1)	−0.119	0.247
	(0.260)	(0.286)
Township officials are slaves of county leaders (no = 0, yes = 1)	0.978***	0.462†
	(0.272)	(0.266)
Current cadre selection system is not transparent and fair (no = 0, yes = 1)	0.199	1.385***
	(0.273)	(0.368)
Election helps overcome buying and selling of offices (no = 0, yes = 1)	0.492†	0.734†
	(0.272)	(0.392)
Economic development level is inadequate (no = 0, yes = 1)	−0.322	−1.429***
	(0.279)	(0.270)
Farmers are capable of electing township head (no = 0, yes = 1)	0.307	0.813**
	(0.272)	(0.273)
Direct township election is useful (most negative = 1, most positive = 12)	0.091	0.123†
	(0.068)	(0.075)
Constant	−1.851*	−4.218***
	(0.922)	(1.042)
Observations	508	394
Nagelkerke R^2	0.192	0.367

†$p ≤ .10$ *$p ≤ .05$ **$p ≤ .01$ ***$p ≤ .001$.
a. "Conservative" is coded as "0"; "reformist" is coded as "1."
b. "Moderate" is coded as "0"; "radical" is coded as "1."

dents were not significantly more pro-reform than their older colleagues. Controlling for the effects of other predictors, age has no significant impact on the respondents' choice between the "conservative" and "reformist" positions, nor does it have an impact on their choice between the "moderate" and "radical" positions. In fact, bivariate analysis shows that the oldest group of respondents (those between the ages of fifty-one and sixty) was more favorable toward direct elections. This is indicated by the positive correlation coefficients of the variable "age" in Table 5.1. Perhaps officials who are close to the mandatory retirement age see direct elections as an opportunity rather than as a risk. In most provinces, township party secretaries and government heads are required to step down at age fifty-five, though the official retirement age is sixty. So incumbents in the oldest group may hope to stay in their positions by winning an election, and older deputies may see elections as their last, best chance to move up.

A similarly counterintuitive finding emerges in regard to education.[43] Bivariate analysis shows that township officials with a college education were less likely to agree that township heads should be popularly elected. This is indicated by the negative coefficient of the variable "college education" in the column "conservative vs. reformist" in Table 5.1. More specifically, 87.1 percent of the 101 respondents without a college education found the reform desirable, while 75.4 percent of 549 officials with a college education thought the same. One possible explanation is that officials with a college education are more likely to be non-natives, so they may be less confident about winning the support of local voters. In the Buyun election, the regional origins of the candidates became a campaign issue. A local candidate repeatedly stressed that he was from Buyun, suggesting that a non-local township head would not put the interests of the local populace above his career. In response, the outsider vowed not to seek "political achievements" (zhengji) by increasing the tax burden and promised to give up his "official cap" (guan mao) without any hesitation if he had to choose between keeping it or siding with his constituents.[44]

Gender is also not significant in predicting the respondents' attitudes toward direct township elections. One might suspect that women would be less enthusiastic about direct elections because they are often beneficiaries of the party's efforts to reserve some positions for women in order to maintain a "reasonable" *(heli)* gender ratio among government leaders. Moreover, due to cultural influences, women might feel less comfortable about campaigning for public office. In the Buyun election, for example, despite strong encouragement from the district party secretary, who happened to be a woman, only four of the fifteen nominees were women, and none of them survived the primary.[45] Nevertheless, this research indicates that, other things being equal, females are only slightly less supportive of direct township elections than males.

Assessments of Desirability

Three findings emerge in regard to the township officials' assessments of the reform's desirability. First, incumbent party secretaries and government heads were less supportive of direct elections than their deputies and staff. Other things being equal, compared to deputy heads, secretaries, and staff members in the sample, incumbent party secretaries and government heads were more than two times more likely to choose the "conservative" position over the "reformist" position (odds ratio = 2.055).[46] The impact of this predictor remains highly significant ($p < .01$), controlling for the effects of eleven other determinants in the model.

That incumbent township leaders are less supportive of direct elections is hardly surprising, since direct elections may mean little gain and considerable risk. In the Pingba case, the incumbent township head did not openly oppose the election in the beginning because he was confident of winning. But after a local school principal, at the urging of a democracy activist from Beijing, began to campaign vigorously and showed strong signs of winning, the township head panicked. He reported the scheduled election to the county leaders, making it impossible for the county, which had learned about the election but had declined to intervene, to retain the option of claiming credit if things turned out well and evading responsibility if things went wrong.[47]

For most township party secretaries, township elections also present more risk than opportunity. Although the reform does not apply to them, and they do not face the danger of being defeated at the polls, township party secretaries might be challenged or defied by popularly elected township heads. Given what happened after village elections in many places, such a concern is well justified. Many popularly elected village heads challenged the authority of village party secretaries on the grounds that the latter did not have a popular mandate.[48] Such a scenario could play out at the township level as well. Consequently, party secretaries in the sample were very concerned about upholding the authority of village party secretaries versus village committee directors; 91.6 percent of 155 party secretaries thought that popularly elected village committee directors should obey the leadership of village party secretaries. In contrast, 76.7 percent of 416 respondents who were not township party secretaries held such an opinion. The difference is statistically significant ($p <$ .001). In fact, the key architect of the Buyun election was so concerned about the possible tension between popular election and hierarchical appointment that she intentionally appointed a weak-willed party secretary in Buyun, informing him that his job was to assist rather than lead the popularly elected township head.[49]

The second finding also suggests that the attitudes of township officials toward township elections are based on career considerations. In response to the statement "Township officials are slaves of county leaders," 5.5 percent of the 708 respondents strongly disagreed and 52.3 percent disagreed;[50] 30.2 percent agreed and 6.4 percent strongly agreed; and 5.6 percent skipped the question. Those who agreed or strongly agreed that township leaders were very weak compared to county leaders were significantly more likely than those who disagreed or strongly disagreed to choose the "reformist" position over the "conservative" position.

That over 35 percent of the respondents had a negative view of county leaders is not entirely a surprise. For years, township officials have borne most of the blame for increasing peasant burdens, manipulating village elections, and using undue coercion against villagers, despite the fact that they were often doing the bidding of their superiors at the county level.[51] As a result, many township officials have complained, in private, of being used like "cannon fodder" (paohui), being "hatchet men" (dashou), or being treated like "slaves" (nuli) by county leaders.[52] A township party secretary in Hebei, for instance, complained that "township cadres like me are prostitutes, more precisely, old prostitutes. We must do whatever county leaders ask us to do, and we have absolutely no right to disagree."[53] Some township leaders have become so disgusted with being caught in the crossfire between often lawbreaking county leaders and villagers who vigorously use the law to defend their rights that they have quit their positions.[54] For such officials, direct township elections may offer a preferred alternative because they would empower them to say no to the county leaders' unlawful demands. As shown earlier, this survey reveals that strong dissatisfaction with the demands of county leadership helps explain why some township officials find direct elections desirable.

Still, the attitudes of township officials toward the desirability of township elections are not entirely based on their career experiences and considerations. The survey reveals that their judgment on the constitutionality of the reform had a significant impact on their attitudes. The 1998 Buyun election triggered a debate over the constitutionality of direct township elections. Critics argued that such elections were unconstitutional, while advocates insisted that they accorded with the constitutional spirit that all powers belong to the people.[55]

When presented with both sides of the debate, the majority of surveyed township officials saw no problem with the constitutionality of the reform. Of the 708 respondents, 6.2 percent strongly disagreed and 57.5 percent disagreed with the statement that "direct election of township government heads violates the constitution";[56] 22.6 percent agreed and 1.3 percent strongly agreed; and 12.3 percent skipped the question. As for the counterargument that "direct election of township government heads accords with the constitutional spirit that all powers belong to the people,"[57] 2.0 percent strongly disagreed and 26.7 percent disagreed; 54.8 percent agreed and 4.4 percent strongly agreed; and 12.1 percent declined to answer.[58]

When these two indicators were combined into a three-level scale called "constitutionality," it turned out that 9.3 percent of 708 respondents were "negative" about the reform's constitutionality, in that they agreed that direct township elections violated the constitution and did not accord with the "constitutional spirit"; 33.2 percent were "ambivalent" in that they agreed that it accorded with either the constitution or the "constitutional spirit";[59] 44.1 percent were "positive" in that they agreed that the reform accorded with both the constitution and the "constitutional spirit"; and 3.4 percent skipped one or both questions.

That over 60 percent of the respondents did not think that direct township elections were inconsistent with the constitution (article 101) could be due to their lack of knowledge about the constitution. Still, the judgment of township officials about the constitutionality of direct township elections had a significant effect on their attitudes toward the reform's desirability. Other things being equal, the more positive one was about the constitutionality of direct township elections, the more likely one was to agree that township heads should be popularly elected. These results suggest that although many township officials do not actually know what is in the constitution, they may oppose locally initiated reforms on the grounds that they do not accord with the constitution, contending, like a commentary in the *Legal Daily* in 1999, that "democracy must not overstep the law."[60]

In addition to the apparent tension between upholding the rule of law and pushing forward political reforms, there is a more fundamental tension between introducing democratic elections and continuing the party's monopoly over cadre management.[61] With regard to village elections, conservatives typically invoke the principle that "the party manages cadres" *(dang guan ganbu)* in order to assert that popularly elected directors of village committees must accept the leadership of appointed village party secretaries. They have also used the principle to reject suggestions that direct elections should be held at the township level.[62] According to conservatives, what is most urgently needed at the grassroots is to strengthen the party's grip on power. To introduce popular elections of township government heads will do just the opposite. This deeply rooted suspicion of popular elections was evident in Jiang Zemin's comment on the Buyun election: "Those who ran the election either did not understand China or had ulterior motives *(bie you yongxin)*."[63]

By contrast, those who seek to introduce electoral reforms have attempted to reinterpret the principle that the party manages cadres. For example, Zhang Jinming, the key architect of the Buyun election, argues that "managing cadres" should not mean imposing cadres on the people. Rather, it means that the party trains cadres and allows the people they serve to choose the most qualified. She compares the management of cadres to that of the economy. In the era of the planned economy, she argues, the party tightly controlled every aspect of the economy, and therefore only poor-quality products were available to the people. As a result, she explains, the party undermined its own authority. Although in the post-Mao era the party still is in charge of the national economy, it is more effective in that it allows the market to do its job. What is needed with the management of cadres, according to Zhang, is to improve the management of cadres by introducing a market mechanism so that the party's candidates can compete with one another and the beneficiaries can decide which candidates best serve their interests. She insists that there is no conflict between direct elections and maintaining party leadership because holding direct elections is the most effective way to improve and strengthen party leadership.[64] Even some retired old revolutionaries have begun to embrace the idea of introducing electoral competition into cadre selection in order to contain corruption and fortify the party's leadership. A former head of the Organization Department of the Guangzhou City Party Committee, for example, argued that since the party no longer faced serious external threats and the older generation of party leaders was retiring, the party should depend on competitive elections to ensure its long-term health. Without open competition, he pointed out, officials in the party's Organization Department, most of whom have "shed neither blood nor sweat for the party and have no faith in communism," are likely to take bribes and make little effort to "distinguish the paddies from the weeds" or to "distinguish the thousand-*li* horses from inferior horses."[65]

Quite remarkably, this rather liberal interpretation has attracted considerable support from township officials. Among 708 respondents, 4.5 percent strongly disagreed and 58.3 percent disagreed with the statement that "direct elections violate the principle that the party manages cadres";[66] 27.7 percent agreed and 1.7 percent strongly agreed; and 7.8 percent declined to answer. Moreover, only 1.1 percent strongly disagreed and 16.8 percent disagreed with the statement that "the essence of the party's management of cadres is that the party trains cadres and allows the people to choose";[67] 61.6 percent agreed and 11.9 percent strongly agreed; and 8.6 percent skipped the question. More interestingly, multivariate analysis shows that the attitude of township officials toward whether direct elections violate the principle that the party manages cadres is not a significant predictor of their attitudes toward direct elections. This finding suggests that even conservative township officials may no longer find it sensible to oppose direct elections by invoking that Leninist principle.

Thus township officials' choice between the "conservative" and "reformist" positions is determined primarily by their current positions, their views on the constitutionality of the reform, and their experience with superiors at the county level. Among the three predictors, experience with county leaders turns out to be most powerful (standardized logit = 0.233), followed by current position (standardized logit = 0.162) and opinion about the constitutionality of the reform (standardized logit = 0.148).

Considerations of Feasibility

Desirability is closely related to feasibility. Since some township officials may not wish to appear too conservative politically by opposing direct township elections, they may express the moderate position even though they are truly conservative. Therefore, we may learn just as much, if not more, about township officials' real attitudes toward direct township elections by examining those factors that affect their choice between the moderate and radical positions.

As shown in Table 5.1, seven predictors have a significant impact on the respondents' choice. As explained earlier, incumbent township party secretaries and government heads were less likely to agree to hold direct township elections immediately. Other things being equal, compared to deputy secretaries and deputy heads, incumbent secretaries and government heads were more than twice as likely to be moderate rather than radical (odds ratio = 2.124). In addition, those who were upset about the domineering treatment by county leaders were more likely to support the immediate introduction of the reform. Other things being equal, compared to those who strongly disagreed or disagreed that "township officials are slaves of county leaders," those who agreed or strongly agreed were nearly twice as likely to be radical rather than moderate (odds ratio = 1.587).

Five other predictors affect the township officials' choice between the moderate and radical positions. First, those who regarded direct elections as more transparent and fair than the current cadre selection system were more likely to agree to hold direct elections immediately. Two indicators pick up this result. On the first question, 1.4 percent of 708 respondents strongly disagreed and 20.3 percent disagreed that "the current cadre selection system lacks transparency and fairness";[68] 53.2 percent agreed and 19.4 percent strongly agreed; and 5.6 percent did not answer the question. Those who were critical of the current system were more likely to be radical. On the second question, 2.0 percent strongly disagreed and 19.2 percent disagreed that "direct elections can help overcome the problem of buying and selling offices";[69] 59.3 percent agreed and 9.0 percent strongly agreed; and 0.5 percent skipped the question. Again, as one would expect, those who found direct elections a helpful check on widespread corruption in cadre selection and promotion were more likely to take the radical position.

In addition to career considerations, township officials based their choice between the moderate and radical positions on their understanding of the preconditions needed for direct township elections and the consequences of holding such elections. In this respect, many respondents accepted the official position laid down by Beijing. As we know, Chinese leaders often cite three factors to defuse pressure for extending direct elections to townships: the low economic development level, the low educational level of the rural population, and the need to maintain social stability and develop the economy. Premier Wen Jiabao, for instance, suggested in 2003 that China's economy was still too underdeveloped and much of the population was too poorly educated to extend direct elections to townships.[70] This argument implies that if direct elections for government leaders were to be introduced prematurely, they would have a negative impact on the economy, social stability, and the party's leadership.

The survey revealed that many respondents apparently believed what the central leadership told them. Of 708 respondents, 3.1 percent strongly disagreed and 28.0 percent disagreed that "the level of economic development is not high enough, the conditions for direct election of township government heads are not ripe";[71] 51.8 percent agreed and 4.8 percent strongly agreed; and 12.3 skipped the question. Those who agreed or strongly agreed were significantly less likely to think that direct township elections could be held at the present time. Similarly, 4.7 percent strongly disagreed and 41.5 percent disagreed that "farmers have the capability to directly elect township government heads";[72] 37.3 percent agreed and 4.8 percent strongly agreed; and 11.7 percent skipped the question. Again, those who lacked confidence in the ability of farmers to elect township leaders were significantly less likely to be radical.

It is worth noting that respondents' assessments of the level of economic development and farmers' ability to elect township leaders had little relevance to where they worked, despite the fact that the six provinces where the survey was conducted were quite different in degree of economic development. Furthermore, respondents from all six provinces were about evenly divided in their assessments of farmers' ability to elect township heads. The lack of correlation between township officials' judgments and the existing reality (whatever it is) suggests that the level of economic development and farmers' "ability" (nengli) or "quality" (suzhi) can easily be turned into pretexts for resisting democratic reform.

Respondents were also divided in their assessments of the possible impact of direct elections. First, of the 708 respondents, 3.5 percent strongly disagreed and 37.1 percent disagreed that "direct township elections will facilitate economic development";[73] 42.2 percent agreed and 3.0 percent strongly agreed; and 14.1 percent skipped the question. Second, 2.7 percent strongly disagreed and 33.3 percent disagreed that "direct township elections will help combat corruption";[74] 46.0 percent agreed and 4.9 percent strongly agreed; and 13.0 percent skipped the question. Third, 2.1 percent strongly disagreed and 33.9 percent disagreed that "direct township elections will facilitate the strengthening of party leadership";[75] 44.9 percent agreed and 4.5 percent strongly agreed; and 14.5 percent skipped the question. Last, 1.3 percent strongly disagreed and 32.1 percent disagreed that "direct township elections will facilitate the construction of the rule of law";[76] 48.6 percent agreed and 4.5 percent strongly agreed; and 13.6 percent skipped the question.

To simplify the analysis and, more important, to avoid the problem of multicollinearity that would arise when two or more highly correlated variables are included as separate predictors in a regression model, four indicators were used to construct a simple summation index that measures the respondents' attitude toward the possible impact of direct township elections (Cronbach's alpha = 0.84), which ranges from "most negative" to "most positive."[77] Other things being equal, the more positive one was about the possible impact of direct township elections, the more likely it was that one would support their immediate introduction.

As to which of the seven significant predictors carries the most weight for township officials in assessing the feasibility of direct township elections, concerns about the level of economic development is the most powerful predictor (standardized logit = 0.301), followed by whether respondents agreed that the current cadre selection system lacks transparency and fairness (standardized logit = 0.245). The other five predictors have roughly equal weights.

Discussion and Analysis

This research helps explain the dynamics of introducing direct township elections in three ways. First, the fact that conservative respondents did not invoke the principle that "the party manages cadres" in order to defend their opposition may indicate that the idea of popular election of government leaders has gained some currency on the ideological front. If this is the case, conservatives may increasingly be forced to reject demands for political reform on grounds of abiding by the constitution and upholding the rule of law. At the same time, reformers may have to abandon the strategy of initiating changes on the ground before changing the law, which they used so effectively in pushing forward the economic reforms. In other words, future political reforms are more likely to be introduced through constitutional and legal amendments than without such amendments.

Second, the finding that township officials' attitudes toward township elections were based primarily on career considerations suggests that such a reform can be imposed only from above. Incumbent township leaders lack the incentive to do so, while deputy township leaders lack the authority to do so. This finding also suggests that if Beijing decides to promote such a reform, it most likely will run into resistance from sitting township secretaries and government heads and their patrons at the county level. Although no accurate data are available, it is agreed that the problem of "buying and selling offices" is very widespread and severe.[78] If incumbent township leaders have indeed bought their positions, they are unlikely to give them away without a fight before their investments have paid off. Similarly, if county leaders have bought their positions, they will not readily give up the chance to reap profits from their investments.

Finally, this research suggests that instrumental considerations will continue to be a prominent factor in the Chinese debate over political reform.[79] For reformers, this implies a strategic disadvantage, because political reforms are unlikely to generate tangible payoffs within a short period of time. In fact, they may initially expose more problems than they resolve. Instrumentalism, however, may not work against reformers in the long term. If they can somehow convince policy makers in Beijing that electoral competition can help root out the least competent and most corrupt officials, produce more capable cadres, and even clean up the thoroughly corrupt cadre management system, they might make direct township elections a more attractive notion to even the most conservative elements in the leadership.

6 | The Struggle for Village Public Goods Provision:

Informal Institutions of Accountability in Rural China

People everywhere struggle to make sure that the state provides schools for their children, roads to bring their goods to market, and safe water to drink. Villagers in China are no exception. Why are some Chinese villagers more successful than others at holding village officials accountable for providing these basic public goods and services? Many studies have underscored the importance of democratic village elections and bureaucratic cadre evaluations. But analysis of a unique combination of original survey data and in-depth case studies gathered during twenty months of fieldwork gives no indication that well-implemented election procedures or top-down institutions of bureaucratic supervision have any major effects on how village governments perform in terms of providing public services.[1]

Instead, these data show that what does have an important effect are a village's social institutions. Even when formal democratic and bureaucratic institutions of accountability are weak, government officials can be subject to unofficial rules and norms that establish and enforce their public obligations. These informal institutions of accountability can be provided by solidary groups—social groups based not only on common interests but also on shared obligations—which encompass everyone in the village and incorporate the participation of village officials.

In rural China these groups often take the form of village temple organizations or village-wide lineage groups. Where these groups exist, villages are more likely to have better public goods provision than villages without these solidary groups, all other things being equal.

The provision of public goods and services at the village level is a huge problem in China. Because of fiscal decentralization, village governments are almost completely on their own when it comes to financing village roads, drainage systems, irrigation works, sanitation and trash disposal services, primary school facilities, and community recreational facilities. Not only are subsidies from higher levels of government minimal, but also by the time any such funds make their way down to the village, each level of government above has had a chance to siphon off a share. Village governments rarely have the resources to supply all of the public services for which they are responsible. Most villages lack successful enterprises or a significant tax base. A small percentage of villages have industrialized sufficiently to provide generous levels of infrastructure and welfare services, but decentralization still gives officials in these villages strong incentives to divert funds away from public services and into further "productive" investments that can increase their future revenues.

Not surprisingly, many villages in China have poor public goods provision. But there are some places where public goods provision is surprisingly good. Even more surprisingly, these villages are not always the ones with high levels of economic growth and industrialization. Wealth does not guarantee good governance or public goods provision. So what factors lead to good governance? In the next section I evaluate the impact of formal bureaucratic and democratic institutions on the performance of village governments and find that these formal institutions have very limited effects. I then evaluate the impact of informal institutions of accountability and find that rules and norms established by solidary community groups can enable citizens and officials to hold each other responsible for their duties to the village community. Using quantitative data collected in a survey of 316 villages from four provinces in 2001, I show that solidary community institutions have a significant positive effect on village public goods provision. I then use a structured comparison of "most similar" and "most different" case studies to corroborate these findings and to illustrate in greater detail the causal mechanisms through which informal institutions of accountability operate. In conclusion, I discuss some of the implications that reliance on informal institutions of accountability may have for local governance and state capacity.

Formal Accountability

When looking at how state officials are held accountable for their behavior, political scientists tend to look first within the state's formal organization of institutions such as electoral procedures, bureaucratic regulations, and official codes of conduct. These formal institutions regulate government and keep officials from abusing their power. In general, they fall into two broad categories: top-down bureaucratic institutions and bottom-up democratic institutions. Bureaucratic institutions enable higher-level officials in the state to supervise lower-level officials and to make sure they are doing their jobs. Democratic institutions enable citizens to elect officials whom they believe to be responsive and responsible and to vote these officials out of office when their expectations are not met.

Formal Top-Down Institutions of Accountability at the Village Level

State elites in China have two sets of formal top-down institutions they can use to secure compliance from village officials: village party organizations and the cadre responsibility system. For the portion of village officials in the village party branch, higher-level party officials can, in theory, elicit compliance by controlling appointments and activating organizational norms that emphasize corporate identity and party loyalty, which have been inculcated through selective recruitment and regular indoctrination or "study" *(xuexi)* meetings.[2] Since central party directives have repeatedly highlighted the importance of rural public goods provision, we might expect villages in which the elected village head is also a party member to have a better record of public goods provision than villages in which the elected head is not a party member. We might also expect villages where a higher percentage of officials on the elected village committee are party members to have better public goods provision than villages where a lower percentage of village officials are party members.

The cadre responsibility system is also intended to guarantee that village officials meet certain policy targets and performance standards set by higher levels. In the cadre responsibility system, leading officials at each level of government sign performance contracts or "cadre responsibility commissions" with the leading officials at the next-higher level. These contracts specify targets and responsibilities that local officials are expected to meet. At the village level, failure to meet these targets usually results in a lower salary or bonus. Specific performance targets vary across localities, but if the cadre responsibility commission is an effective institution for holding village officials accountable, it seems reasonable to expect villages where officials sign contracts that mandate public goods provision to have better public goods provision than villages where officials do not sign such contracts.

Democratic Bottom-Up Institutions of Accountability at the Village Level

In 1987, hoping to arrest the downward slide of village government performance, the central government passed the Organic Law of Village Committees, giving villagers the opportunity to elect village officials and establish a number of democratic institutions for village governance. Theories of democracy argue that governments should be more responsive to citizen demands when citizens have the power to vote individuals in and out of office. Voting procedures help ensure that citizens can really elect the people they would like to elect. The use of secret ballots, carefully regulated use of proxy voting, ballot boxes resistant to tampering, public vote counting: all of these institutions help to ensure that voters will not be coerced into voting for a candidate they do not support and that their choices will be accurately represented and reported. The pre-election process is also important. Even when electoral procedures seem free and fair, sometimes the real decisions are made behind the scenes before election day. Free competition requires institutions which ensure that incumbent officials permit their opponents to run for office and which prevent unfair intervention by incumbents or higher-level officials in the nomination of candidates. Ideally, independent third parties enforce electoral regulations and monitor the electoral process.

In some places in rural China grassroots democratic reforms have also established popular assemblies composed of representatives selected or elected by villagers. Elections, after all, occur infrequently. Popular assemblies increase the opportunities for engaging larger portions of the population in the political process and for assessing governmental performance. We would therefore expect that villages where these democratic institutions are better implemented would be more likely to have better public goods provision than villages where these democratic institutions are less well implemented.

Findings from the Survey

Contrary to these expectations, survey data indicate that bureaucratic and democratic institutions have limited effects on the performance of village governments and village public goods provision. These data come from a survey I conducted in 2001 of 316 villages randomly sampled from eight counties in four provinces: Shanxi, Hebei, Jiangxi, and Fujian. These four provinces were chosen to reflect regional differences between North and South China, and differences in economic development between coastal and interior provinces. Within each province, two counties were selected to vary in pilot county status for village democratic reforms but to have similar economic and geographic characteristics.[3]

Measurement

To measure public goods provision, I used the per capita village government expenditure for public projects for 2000 as well as objective measures of specific public goods: the existence of paved village roads and paved village paths, the proportion of village classrooms usable in rainy weather, the newness of the village school building, and the availability of running water. Villages varied widely in their provision of public goods and services (Table 6.1). Half of the villages in the survey had paved roads; half did not. Half had running water, and half did not. Per capita investment in villages within just one standard deviation of the mean varies from 0 to over 250 RMB. Substantial variability also characterized other measures of public goods provision.

Table 6.1 Descriptive statistics on village public goods provision outcomes (standard deviation reported in parentheses)

Mean total village government expenditure on public projects per capita in 2000	67 RMB	(192)
Percentage of villages with paved roads	50%	(50)
Percentage of villages with paved paths	13%	(33)
Mean percentage of classrooms unusable in rain	11%	(29)
Average age of school building	27 years	(18)
Percentage of villages with running water	47%	(50)

Table 6.2 Descriptive statistics on party-state bureaucratic institutions of accountability (standard deviation reported in parentheses)

Percentage of villages with bureaucratic targets for public projects	44	(50)
Percentage of villages where village head is party member	69	(46)
Mean percentage of village officials with party membership	74	(19)

As indicators for the strength of top-down party and state institutions for holding village officials accountable, I looked at whether or not the village head is a party member; the percentage of village officials who are party members; and whether or not village officials sign a performance contract that has targets for public goods provision (Table 6.2).

In order to evaluate the overall degree to which democratic reforms have been implemented in a village, I constructed an index out of a battery of questions on the pre-election process, voting procedures, and villagers' representative assemblies, using the conventional technique of principal components analysis to weight each indicator. Tables 6.3 through 6.5 summarize the data on the implementation of these different types of democratic institutions. To measure the implementation of pre-election democratic institutions, the survey asked questions about nine types of interference in the

Table 6.3 Descriptive statistics on pre-election institutions
(standard deviation reported in parentheses)

Percentage of villages reporting:

No interference in determination of primary candidates by		
Township government	95	(21)
Village party branch	85	(36)
Incumbent village committee	90	(30)
No interference in determination of final candidates by		
Township government	82	(39)
Village party branch	90	(29)
Incumbent village committee	97	(17)
No interference in selection of election oversight committee by		
Township government	87	(33)
Village party branch	68	(47)
Incumbent village committee	92	(27)

pre-election process (Table 6.3). To evaluate the actual voting process, the survey asked whether villages implemented seven basic voting procedures to guarantee free and fair elections; the percentage of villages implementing each procedure is reported in Table 6.4.

The survey also evaluated villages for seven of the most common institutions structuring village representative assemblies (VRAs). In Table 6.5 we can see that most villages have not fully implemented a village representative assembly. While formal powers to oversee village finance are a common VRA institution, competitive elections for village representatives using a secret ballot are not. Fewer than half of the villages reported that village representatives had the power to recall the village head, and only 13 percent reported that the VRA had opposed a decision made by the village officials in the past year.

Control Variables

To identify the effects of bureaucratic and democratic institutions accurately, we must also control for a number of other factors that

Table 6.4 Descriptive statistics on voting institutions
(standard deviation reported in parentheses)

Percentage of villages reporting:

*Immediate announcement of election results	99	(11)
*Contested election	98	(14)
*Public vote count	87	(33)
*Secret ballot booth	77	(42)
Campaign speeches	54	(50)
*Regulated proxy voting	40	(49)
Fixed ballot boxes	30	(46)

Note: Criteria with asterisks indicate voting procedures mandated by the 1998 revised Organic Law.

Table 6.5 Descriptive statistics on implementation of VRA institutions
(standard deviation reported in parentheses)

Percentage of villages reporting:

Existence of a VRA	94	(24)
Measures of VRA institutions		
Competition for VRA seats	37	(48)
Elections with secret ballot for VRA seats	25	(44)
Formal regulation on when VRA is convened	21	(41)
Formal power to recall village head	45	(50)
Formal power to inspect village expenditures	91	(29)
Formal power to audit village accounts	85	(35)
VRA veto of village government decision in the last year	13	(34)

Note: VRA = village representative assembly.

may also have an effect on village public goods provision. This analysis holds three sets of variables constant (Table 6.6). As mentioned earlier, the survey controlled for variation in the level of economic development and the amount of resources available to the village government by including 1997 income per capita, 1997 village government assets, and 1997 village government tax revenue per capita. The second set consisted of geographic and demographic controls. Distance from the county seat, village terrain, number of natural villages, and village population were included to control for variation in demand for specific public goods as well as for variation in costs

Table 6.6 Descriptive statistics on control variables

	Mean	(Standard deviation)
Economic controls		
1997 income per capita (RMB)	1,481	(1,130)
1997 village govt. assets (RMB)	42,644	(393,067)
1997 village tax revenue per capita (RMB)	22	(27)
Geographical controls		
County dummies	—	—
Distance from county seat (km)	26	(21)
Village terrain (1 = flat, 0 = not flat)	0.36	(0.48)
Number of natural villages	3.9	(4.53)
Village population	1,240	(981)
Social controls		
Surname fragmentation index	0.5	(0.26)
Existence of a temple manager	0.14	(0.36)
Existence of a village-wide lineage group	0.07	(0.26)

for comparable goods.[4] A third set of variables was included to control for variation in village social institutions. These included a measure of potential social fragmentation as reflected by the number of surname groups in the village, the existence of village temple institutions, and the existence of village-wide lineage institutions.[5] In the next section these variables become the main explanatory variables of interest, but for now I include them as controls in order to identify the effects of democratic and bureaucratic institutions.

The Impact of Bureaucratic Institutions

Findings from these data indicate that neither the party membership of the village head nor the percentage of village officials with party membership had a notable effect on village public goods provision. (Estimated effects were produced using the seemingly unrelated regression method. Details on the statistical analyses used in this chapter are included in the endnotes.)[6] Village head party membership did not have a substantively interesting or statistically significant effect on any of the six public goods provision outcomes, regardless of which control variables are included or excluded in the analysis.[7] Nor did levels of party membership among village officials have any substantively interesting or statistically significant effects on any of the public goods provision outcomes.[8]

Performance contracts had different effects on different public goods provision outcomes. In general, the magnitude of these effects was modest. The estimated effect of bureaucratic control as measured by performance contracts was negative for three out of six outcomes (roads, paths, and running water) and positive for three outcomes (investment, usable classrooms, and age of school building). When I controlled for all economic, geographic, demographic, and social factors, only the negative effect on roads and the positive effect on classrooms remained statistically significant, although the estimated positive effect on investment is also worth noting.[9] To give a substantive idea of the size of these effects, I calculate what public goods provision is like in the average village where officials did not sign contracts and in the average village where officials did sign contracts (the average village being one that possesses the average characteristics of the surveyed villages in the sense that all control variables are set at their means). In sum, performance contracts may have a large impact on government investment in public projects, but this increase in investment is not accompanied by similarly large increases in the provision of actual public goods and services. When officials in an average village signed performance contracts, investment rose from 57 RMB to 88 RMB (the mean for the sample was 67 RMB), but the mean percentage of usable classrooms rose only 7 percent from 87 to 94 percent.[10]

In other words, performance contracts may be associated with higher government investment, but they are not associated with substantially higher-quality village public goods. One possible explanation is that performance contracts stress quantifiable measures of village government performance, which encourages village officials to spend more on public projects (ostensibly) but fails to ensure that these additional expenditures translate into higher-quality public goods and services.

The Impact of Democratic Institutions

There is also no evidence to indicate that democratic institutions as measured by a composite index of pre-election institutions, voting procedures, and village representative assemblies had any sizable or statistically significant impact on village government public goods provision.[11] This was true regardless of which control variables were included or excluded, or whether the effect was estimated by means of seemingly unrelated regression or two-stage least squares estimation using pilot county status as an instrument to deal with possible endogeneity.[12]

The implementation of democratic institutions as measured by a composite index of three categories of democratic institutions does not have a clearly discernible effect on village public goods provision outcomes. It is possible, however, that one of these categories does have an effect that is being masked by the inclusion of the other categories in the index. I thus evaluate the impact of each category of democratic institutions individually. But even when the index measuring the implementation of democratic institutions is broken down into three separate measures of pre-election institutions, voting procedures, and village representative assembly institutions, none of these has a major impact on any of the villages' public goods provision. Among the three different categories of democratic institutions and the six different public goods provision outcomes, the most noteworthy causal impact is that of voting institutions on investment. Even this effect, however, is relatively small. Per capita investment increased only 12 RMB on average when the average village moved from relatively poor implementation of voting institutions (scoring in the twenty-fifth percentile) to relatively good implementation of voting institutions (scoring in the seventy-fifth percentile).[13] Moreover, 25 percent of the time, per capita investment actually decreased when the average village moved from poor to good implementation. All other estimated effects were even weaker.

These findings suggest that just because formal institutions of accountability exist does not mean that they will be effective or that people will use them. Are villagers in China then doomed to poor village roads, schools, and infrastructure? Not necessarily. Although in general, rural public goods provision leaves much to be desired, both case studies and survey data show that there are also many villages in which officials do the best they can with the resources they have to organize public projects for rebuilding schools, paving roads, and installing running water. These officials provide public services even though they have nothing to fear from village elections or sanctions applied by the township government. The question is: Why do these village officials bother?

Informal Institutions of Accountability

The answer lies in a community's social institutions. In places such as rural China where formal state institutions fail to make sure that government officials fulfill their public responsibilities, governmental performance may still be good when local officials feel obligated to do what their religious institutions, ethnic groups, or civic groups expect them to do. Solidary groups such as village temple organizations and village-wide lineage groups in rural China acquire the moral authority to define group obligations by demonstrating persuasively that they are motivated by moral considerations and are "uncontaminated by self-interest." Such groups are not limited to the Chinese context. In the United States, for example, Rhys Williams and N. J. Demerath have found that churches and other religious organizations often enjoy a political advantage because they have sources of moral authority that interest groups and political parties cannot access.[14] In both China and the United States, where people commonly associate politics with special interests and personal gain, moral authority can be an important source of political power. Groups such as community churches and solidary village-wide lineages that demonstrate their commitment to the good of the entire community can acquire enough moral standing to define and enforce norms requiring citizens and officials to contribute to the collective good.

During the pre-Communist period in China, solidary village-wide lineages and temple groups were integral elements of local power structures.[15] The imperial state extended only as far down as the county, so there was no formal village government for these groups to hold accountable for public goods provision. But in many places temple and lineage groups themselves took responsibility for grassroots governance and the provision of local public goods and services. After 1949 the Communist state embarked on a systematic program to destroy these kinds of communal groups and replace them with formal party and state structures reaching all the way down to the village. Since the beginning of the reforms in the late 1970s, however, these solidary groups have reemerged all over the country-side. Most focus on organizing community activities and rituals that add to the prestige and local reputation of the village community, which in turn benefits the reputation of each individual in the village. These activities range from traditional rituals of respect for village guardian deities and village ancestors to village basketball tournaments, welfare assistance, and the mediation of village disputes. By increasing the value of the community to its members, these institutions invoke norms of indebtedness that obligate individuals to repay their debts to the village community. Such moral obligations need not be romanticized as traditional values or virtues that rural communities have succeeded in preserving. As with cooperation within the rural Indonesian communities studied by Clifford Geertz, these obligations are "founded on a very lively sense of the mutual value to the participants of such cooperation, not on a general ethic of the unity of all men or on an organic view of society."[16]

By establishing moral standing as a political resource, solidary groups strengthen the incentives of government officials to fulfill their community obligations. Because they prescribe the ways in which people should act in order to maintain and improve their moral standing, solidary institutions enable those who exhibit exemplary behavior—citizens or officials—to acquire moral authority in the community. Citizens who have high moral standing can use it to hold officials accountable for their actions. Officials who acquire moral standing can use it to elicit compliance with state policies from citizens or to secure the help of community leaders in carrying out state tasks, giving them strong incentives to fulfill their obligations to the public. Solidary institutions can thus facilitate the creation of mutual accountability and compliance.

When the state's credibility with citizens is low, the opportunities for acquiring moral authority provided by solidary institutions can be invaluable. Once citizens view the state with suspicion, it can be very difficult to convince them otherwise. Solidary group leaders can vouch for government officials and act as their "guarantors." They can also provide ways for citizens and officials to have "test interactions."[17] Solidary activities such as community festivals and lineage hall reconstruction projects allow people to practice making and fulfilling agreements when they do not have an enormous amount at stake. They also allow people to develop a common language for communicating their intentions. A solidary activity such as a ritual for paying respect to common ancestors can be a forum for signaling one's intentions and helping others to interpret one's motivations. Village officials who participate consistently in village community rituals and activities can earn the trust and respect of villagers. Those who choose not to participate, or who work in villages where such activities do not exist, cannot.

Findings from the Survey

Here I look at two types of solidary institutions: village-wide temple institutions and village-wide lineage institutions. Findings from the survey data indicate that both types of solidary institutions have a significant positive effect on village governmental public goods provision, even after controlling for economic development, geographic and demographic factors, and the implementation of the formal bureaucratic and democratic institutions discussed in the previous section.

Village Temple Institutions

In this chapter I use the existence of a formal temple manager to measure the existence of active temple institutions in a village.[18] Village temple groups vary widely in their level of institutionalization. In some villages, temple activities are impromptu affairs that are not regularly organized. In other villages, a temple manager, sometimes overseeing a temple council, organizes temple and community activities. Temple managers may be expected to do a variety of things: collect donations from villagers for temple activities, oversee and publicize the temple's accounts, organize religious rituals and non-religious community activities, supervise temple reconstruction projects, or mediate village disputes. In the survey, 14 percent of the villages reported the existence of a temple manager (see Table 6.6).

Analysis of the survey data indicates that villages with strong temple institutions were substantially more likely to enjoy higher levels of village government investment in public projects as well as better roads, paths, classrooms, school buildings, and running water. The estimated relationship between village public goods provision and village temple institutional strength as measured by the existence of a temple manager was positive and statistically significant (in the sense that we can reject the null hypothesis that temple institutions have no effect on the six public goods provision outcomes).[19] These results were similar regardless of which geographic, demographic, economic, and institutional controls were included and whether the effect was estimated by seemingly unrelated regression or two-stage least squares instrumental variables estimation.[20]

To give a sense of how much impact temple institutions, as measured by the existence of a temple manager, have on public goods provision, we can compare the mean level or likelihood of provision of different public goods in an average village with a temple manager to that in an average village without a temple manager. In an average village, the mean per capita investment almost doubles from 63 RMB to 124 RMB when there is a temple manager. There is some uncertainty around these estimates, but the fact that the provision of actual public goods and services also increases in villages when there is a temple manager gives us more confidence that the effect of temple institutions on village public goods provision is indeed positive. The mean probability of finding running water in an average village, for example, increases from 46 percent to 61 percent with a temple manager, and the mean percentage of finding classrooms usable in rain increases from 88 percent to 100 percent.[21]

Village-Wide Lineage Institutions

Like village temple institutions, village lineage institutions inculcate a sense of collective duty and community obligations. In order for lineage institutions to act as informal institutions of accountability, however, the collective or community in question must be the village, not a sub-village lineage group. (It is important to note that lineage groups are not the same as surname groups. A single-surname village can have multiple lineage groups, for example, groups referred to as *fang*.) As an indicator for village-wide lineage institutions, I use a dichotomous variable coded 1 when a village has one and only one active ancestral hall with spirit tablets and 0 otherwise.

The existence of an ancestral hall is the clearest and most easily observed indication of organized kinship activities. Out of the 316 villages in the survey, 32 percent reported that they had at least one ancestral hall. The mere existence of an ancestral hall building, however, does not guarantee active lineage institutions. Many villages stopped using their ancestral halls for ritual activities during the Cultural Revolution and never reinstituted kinship practices. The halls are still standing but are not used for lineage activities. In order to measure consistently active lineage institutions, I look at whether the village reports the existence of an ancestral hall with spirit tablets (*paiwei*). Ancestral halls with spirit tablets indicate that people gather at the hall to pay their respects collectively on important holidays. Among the surveyed villages, 14 percent reported ancestral halls with spirit tablets; 7 percent of the villages reported having only a single ancestral hall with spirit tablets, whereas 7 percent reported multiple ancestral halls with spirit tablets (see Table 6.6). As with the measure used for temple institutionalization, this measure sets quite a high bar for the existence of organized village-wide lineage institutions.

Analysis of the data suggests that villages with village-wide solidary lineage institutions were indeed more likely to enjoy substantially higher village government investment, paved roads, paved paths, newer schools, and running water. This finding holds regardless of what control variables were included or excluded or whether the effect was estimated by means of seemingly unrelated regression or two-stage least squares instrumental variables estimation.[22]

How much of a positive impact do solidary village-wide lineage institutions have? Again, we can compare the mean level or likelihood of different public goods in an average village with village-wide lineage institutions as measured by a single functioning lineage hall to that in an average village without village-wide lineage institutions. The difference in per capita investment between villages with solidary lineage institutions and villages without solidary lineage institutions is considerable. The mean per capita investment for an average village with solidary village-wide lineage institutions is 153 RMB, more than double that of an average village without solidary lineage institutions. There is some uncertainty about these estimates, but again, the fact that village-wide lineage institutions have positive effects on a variety of other measures of public goods provision makes us more confident that this positive effect is real. For the estimated difference in the probability of paved roads, for example, the level of uncertainty is quite low. The probability of paved roads in the average village with solidary village-wide lineage institutions is 84 percent, whereas the probability in an average village without solidary lineage institutions is only 50 percent. Solidary village-wide lineage institutions also have a positive effect on the probability of running water, although this effect is somewhat smaller than the effects on roads and investment.[23]

Data from the survey clearly suggest that solidary village-wide community institutions have a significant positive effect on village government performance and public goods provision. But how do we know that they have this effect because they make moral authority a political resource and institute a system of informal accountability? The next section uses structured comparisons of "most similar" cases and "most different" cases to corroborate the statistical findings and to illustrate the causal processes more concretely. These case studies further clarify the importance of solidary institutions and moral obligation in village governance.

Structured Comparative Analysis: "Most Similar" and "Most Different" Cases

In this section we look at case studies of four villages, two in Jiangxi province and two in Fujian province. Using a series of structured comparisons between "most similar" cases and "most different" cases, this analysis corroborates the statistical findings and illustrates the causal processes more concretely, further clarifying the importance of moral authority and informal institutions of accountability in village governance. Table 6.7 compares the four village cases along key dimensions and shows how the cases are paired into "most similar" and "most different" comparisons.

In each province, the two village case studies are very similar to each other yet vary a great deal in terms of how well their village governments provide public goods and services. The first two cases, High Mountain and Li Settlement, are located seven kilometers apart in a mountainous area of Jiangxi province. Both are poor and

Table 6.7 Comparing villages with and without village-wide solidary groups

	Most similar cases Different public goods provision		Most similar cases Different public goods provision	
	High Mountain Village	Li Settlement	West Gate Village	Three Fork Village
Income per capita (RMB)	1,100	1,200	6,712	~6,000 (est.)
Public funds	Low	Low	High	High
Implementation of democratic reforms	Poor	Poor	Good	Good
Distance from county seat	Distant	Distant	Close	Close
Geographical location	Inland Jiangxi province in South China	Inland Jiangxi province in South China	Coastal Fujian province in South China	Coastal Fujian province in South China
Village social institutions				
Village-wide solidary group	No	Yes: Village-wide lineage	Yes: Village-wide temple and lineage group	No
Public goods outcomes				
Government investment in public goods and services	Low	Modest but regular	High	Low
Quality of village public goods and services	Poor	Good	Good	Poor

Most different cases: Same public goods provision

agricultural. Neither village has well-implemented democratic reforms or bureaucratic institutions to hold village officials accountable for their actions. Yet public goods provision is very different in the two villages. Officials in High Mountain embezzle money from public coffers and do their best to avoid spending money on public goods and services for villagers. Officials in Li Settlement are the exact opposite: they do the best they can with the scarce resources they have to organize and fund village public projects. The two villages also differ in another critical dimension. Li Settlement has a solidary village-wide lineage group, and virtually all the households in the village participate in collective lineage activities. High Mountain, by contrast, lacks any sort of solidary group—lineage or otherwise. In short, all potentially explanatory variables are held constant in these two cases except for their social institutions. The fact that public goods provision also varies between these two cases suggests that differences between village social institutions have an effect on village governmental performance.

The second and third cases—Li Settlement in Jiangxi and West Gate in Fujian—constitute a comparison between "most different" cases. In most ways, the two villages could not be more different from each other. As noted, Li Settlement is poor and is located in the interior of the country, far from any prosperous areas. West Gate is wealthy and is located in the suburbs of a special economic zone in coastal Fujian. In Li Settlement village democratic reforms have made little headway. By contrast, villagers in West Gate vote for village officials using secret ballots in competitive primary and final elections and even listen to campaign speeches from candidates. In most ways the two villages are polar opposites. Yet they are remarkably similar in two aspects: both have vibrant village-wide solidary groups in which village officials participate, and both enjoy relatively responsible village government provision of public goods. In other words, all the factors that might affect village public goods provision vary except for the existence of village-wide solidary institutions, thus supporting the argument that villages with solidary groups experience better governance and public goods provision.

The third and fourth cases—West Gate and Three Fork—are neighboring villages located in Fujian province. Like the two villages in Jiangxi, they constitute "most similar" cases. Both are located in a wealthy suburb of the Xiamen Special Economic Zone. Both hold model village elections. In fact, one of their neighbors, Houpu village, was selected as an observation site for an American election observation group from the International Republican Institute in 2000.[24] These villages do not lack for bureaucratic or democratic accountability. Yet only West Gate enjoys good governance and public goods provision. In Three Fork, village officials fail to organize any public projects. Conflicts between lineage groups that subdivide the village have paralyzed village government, and the implementation of election institutions has only exacerbated the situation. Again, since these two cases are similar in so many ways, the differences in their social institutions seem to be an important factor in explaining the differences in their public goods provision.

Case 1. High Mountain Village: No Public Goods Provision

In the winter, villagers in High Mountain, a poor agricultural village in southern Jiangxi province, have to get off their bicycles and drag them through the village's muddy lanes. High Mountain's per capita income in 1999 of about 1,100 RMB (approximately U.S. $138), was only around half of the national average of 2,210 RMB (about U.S. $276) for that year. Residents rely on income from farming and from the remittances of family members working in Guangdong. High Mountain's village government possesses few public assets. The village has not developed any industrial enterprises, and the only source of government revenue is from village levies *(tiliu)*. Like many villages in China that have not industrialized, High Mountain has been liquidating village assets to pay for government expenditures, and villagers believe that officials have pocketed much of the money from these fire sales.

Democratic reforms required by the central government are poorly implemented in High Mountain. Election ballots are not counted publicly. Although candidates are ostensibly nominated by households, higher-level officials rig the elections by getting elderly illiterate villagers to submit nominations. As one villager noted, township officials select people to be village officials on the basis of whether they dare *(gan)* to fine their neighbors by entering their houses and confiscating their belongings.

Not surprisingly, villagers have repeatedly registered complaints with higher levels about the behavior of village officials. In 2000, between fifty and one hundred villagers went to protest at the township and county government offices because their estimates of village expenditures differed from the tables reported by village officials by about 30,000 RMB. Villagers stressed that this was a village-wide *(quan cun)* effort, not just that of a particular lineage group. The only public project that village officials in High Mountain organized in the past few years was the rebuilding of the village school, which they were compelled to do by the county government. Otherwise, there is little in the way of public services in High Mountain.

Case 2. Li Settlement: Solidary Lineage Institutions

Located just seven kilometers away from High Mountain, Li Settlement has very similar geographical, socioeconomic, and institutional conditions. Neither village has industrialized, nor does either have much in the way of public assets. Village elections are poorly implemented in both places. Two differences, however, are immediately visible. First, the road leading from the main road into Li Settlement and its fields is wide enough for two cars, and it is well paved. Second, the immense village auditorium in the center of Li Settlement has been transformed into a village lineage hall used by all of the residents of the village.

The key difference between High Mountain and Li Settlement lies in the social organization of the two communities. High Mountain lacks any sort of solidary community institutions. In contrast, Li Settlement has an active village-wide lineage organization. Like many single-surname villages, Li Settlement had had six different sublineages *(fang)*, but divisions among the sub-lineage groups have been flexible and blurry.[25] Different *fang* are in the habit of sharing the same ancestral hall. Over the past century, when political conditions permitted, members of the first, second, and third *fang* visited the ancestral hall at the north end of the village to pay their respects, while members of the fourth, fifth, and sixth *fang* visited the ancestral hall at the south end of the village. In 1998, however, village officials and villagers renovated the village auditorium into a lineage hall that incorporated all of the *fang* and created a new, unified spirit tablet to represent the deceased elders of the village as a whole. Another wooden tablet, embossed in gold, implores the common ancestors of the village-wide lineage to bestow prosperity as well as wisdom and government positions on their descendants.

By working for the good of the lineage and fulfilling lineage obligations, village officials were able to increase their moral standing in the village. Instead of constructing a new office building, as officials in High Mountain did, Li Settlement officials chose to conserve public funds and work out of their houses instead. They used their own personal connections with township and county officials of the same lineage to secure a bank loan of 90,000 RMB to pave the main village road running up from the provincial asphalt road into the village's forests on the mountainside. After starting construction on the road, they then organized a lineage banquet on the first day of the lunar calendar. Villagers were invited to a simple meal of noodles and a general community meeting to reinforce lineage solidarity. Village officials hung red banners at the front of the auditorium with the messages: "Eat together." "Don't forget your brothers and sisters." "Help take care of one another." By activating lineage norms of obligation among the villagers, officials collected over 20,000 RMB to begin repaying the bank loan for the road. Officials raised another 60,000 RMB from nearby township enterprises and from profits from the sale of lumber from the village's forests. A fundraising banquet the following year provided sufficient voluntary contributions to pay back the rest of the loan.

Even though Li Settlement's officials were not chosen through free and fair elections, the moral authority they have earned by working for the good of the lineage and organizing public projects helps them carry out state tasks. In general, villagers comply with birth control quotas and state tax collection. When village officials fined three couples who violated the family planning policy, villagers did not fault them for enforcing what is generally an unpopular policy. The moral standing that Li Settlement's officials earn by upholding solidary lineage institutions is an important resource for them since they have little access to economic or coercive resources from higher levels of the state. Lineage norms reward and obligate both officials and villagers to contribute to public goods provision. This arrangement, however, works only as long as the officials themselves continue to act in accordance with the norms of the solidary lineage group.

Case 3. West Gate Village: Solidary Lineage and Temple Institutions

In most ways, West Gate Village is the polar opposite of Li Settlement. Located in the Xiamen Special Economic Zone in coastal Fujian province, West Gate is highly industrialized and far wealthier than Li Settlement. In 2000 the per capita income was almost 7,000 RMB, more than three times the national average. West Gate's village government also enjoys annual revenue of around 1 million RMB. Unlike Li Settlement, West Gate and other villages in the township are subject to an annual performance evaluation by the township government, the criteria for which are set out in the village charter, which is itself required to be revised every three years, with the revisions approved by villagers and the township government.

But as in Li Settlement, all-inclusive village-wide solidary institutions in West Gate reinforce community identity and obligation. In 1985 an initial group of villagers decided to renovate a village storehouse to serve as an ancestral hall for the Wu lineage. They organized a community lineage council to oversee the project and other lineage activities. Over time, the lineage council developed into an all-inclusive village community organization that arranges both temple and lineage activities. When the council decided to construct a new Wu ancestral hall in 1996, even households with other surnames contributed to the project without solicitation. Wu families make up only about 80 percent of the village households, but the council estimates that 99 percent of the village ultimately contributed to the construction of the hall, because even families with other surnames felt an obligation to pay back the Wu lineage group for allowing them to move into the village many generations ago.

Over time, the lineage basis of the group has faded. The council now emphasizes membership in the village community, and it has turned its attention to rebuilding the village temples. In 2000 the council renovated the village Guandi temple.[26] A commemorative plaque honoring the villagers who initiated the re-creation of the village community council in the early 1980s is placed not in the Wu lineage hall—the first big project—but in the village Guandi temple.

Rebuilding a village's temples is a central part of maintaining its reputation and "face." Several villagers complained during interviews that the council should be starting to think about renovating the village temple for the goddess Mazu, another folk deity protecting the village, because visitors would see that it was old and rundown.

In addition to protecting village face, the village community council sets an example for the village government through its governance institutions and transparent financial practices. Though the state has encouraged local officials to publicize local government revenues and expenditures since the early 1990s, the success of these efforts is debatable. In West Gate, however, the village community council makes the council's accounts and receipts freely available to public scrutiny at any time and documents and posts the amount of each donation and the name of the donor. Such meticulous financial management establishes an ideal to which villagers naturally compare the performance of village officials.

It would be wrong, however, to characterize the village community council as subverting the village government's authority. Both village officials and council members see their objectives as complementary, so much so that in 1996, when the district government directed all its villages to set up senior citizens' associations, village officials and council members agreed to call the community council the village's senior citizens' association and to help shield the council from state censure. In addition, two glass-framed certificates in the village temple identify it as a branch of the village's family planning committee. Both villagers and officials say that these certificates are just "propaganda"—in this case, propaganda created jointly by villagers and local state agents and aimed at higher levels of the state.

Village officials recognize that collaborating with the council allows them to leverage the council's moral authority to achieve state objectives. The temple council helps mobilize villagers for assemblies convened by the village government. When the village government wanted to construct a drainage channel for nearby factories, it encountered strong villager resistance, since the channel would have to run through the fields of numerous households. These households refused to cooperate with the village government until council members accompanied village officials to visit each household. When officials invoked the authority of the state, villagers refused to comply. But when council members with moral standing told them it was the right thing to do, villagers felt obligated to comply.

Providing help to the village government allows the temple council to propose needed public projects and to pressure the village government to organize them. Numerous villagers reported that the village government agreed to pave a road or make repairs on the village primary school only after the temple council had taken the lead *(dai tou)* by collecting donations from villagers to get the project off the ground and then talking the village government into funding the rest.

In West Gate the performance of the village government and the authority of village officials have benefited from collaboration with the village temple council. The community council's power to give input about village policies and to hold officials accountable for public goods provision has been institutionalized. Even when the specific individuals holding positions in the village government change, village officials, regardless of who they are, make it a point to ask temple council members for advice in dealing with village issues. Community council members, for their part, also make suggestions and give criticisms even when unsolicited. West Gate's council head is on good terms with both the current village head and the previous village head. During the 2000 elections both came to chat with the council head, who told the current village head that he needed to make a public commitment to improving the village economy in order to get elected and advised the previous village head to address rampant gossip among villagers about corruption during his previous term in the bidding for village government construction projects. In short, the community council in West Gate ensures that village officials and villagers have common expectations, enables village officials to use moral authority to secure compliance from villagers, and allows villagers to hold the government accountable for public goods provision.

Case 4. Three Fork Village: Divisive Sub-village Lineage Institutions

Located next to West Gate, Three Fork has almost identical geographical, socioeconomic, and political conditions. Relative to other areas in rural China, both villages have very high levels of economic development. Village elections and bureaucratic institutions for performance evaluations are well implemented in both places. But unlike the system of mutual obligation that characterizes relations between officials and villagers in West Gate, in one area of Three Fork villagers have accused officials of discrimination and have tried to secede from the rest of the village. In contrast to the solidary community institutions that unify West Gate, sub-village lineage institutions divide the village of Three Fork into Sun lineage members and non-Suns. Despite the fact that Three Fork's officials are democratically elected in well-implemented elections, villagers in the Sun lineage complain that village officials (who are not members of the Sun lineage) favor other neighborhoods in their allocation of village resources and fail to provide their neighborhood with public services and economic opportunities. Tensions have run high, and numerous fistfights have broken out between Suns and non-Suns.

As with the first two case studies—High Mountain and Li Settlement—major differences in village social institutions distinguish Three Fork Village from West Gate. In West Gate, the dominant Wu lineage group has expanded to incorporate non-Wus and has evolved into a community organization. In Three Fork, the Sun lineage group represents a minority group in the village, but it is particularly tight-knit because the Sun ancestral hall is a focal point for a larger Sun lineage organization that extends beyond Three Fork to include members in more than a dozen villages scattered across the county-level districts of Huli, Tongan, and Jimei. In the early 1980s a few Sun elders from one village in Jimei started contacting Sun elders in different villages around the area. Eventually, a group of elders proposed rebuilding two ancestral "temples" *(zu miao)* honoring their ancestral patriarch and matriarch. As with the Wus in West Gate, the Suns set up a temple reconstruction committee *(chongjian weiyuanhui)*. The hall for the lineage's founding patriarch was built first, near the purported site of his grave in Three Fork Village. Sun elders in Three Fork supervise the ancestral hall's ritual activities and maintenance. The rebuilding committee evolved into a permanent committee of twenty elders, one or two from each village in the area with a large number of Suns. This committee meets once or twice a year to plan activities and ceremonies on the major holidays when lineage members are supposed to congregate at the ancestral hall in Three Fork. Sun elders in Three Fork hold leadership positions in the lineage committee.

Although Sun lineage institutions do not improve the performance of Three Fork's village government, they do in some sense substitute for the village government by taking over its responsibility for providing social services to lineage members. The Sun lineage committee provides welfare assistance to lineage members who are sick or impoverished. Lineage members report that roads, school repairs, and even the new public toilets in their neighborhood have been organized and funded by the lineage group, not the village government.

After several years of constant conflict, in 2000 the township government sent down work teams to canvas every household in Three Fork and to meet with the elders of various village groups to discuss the possibility of dividing the village into two new administrative villages. Ultimately, the township officials decided that it would be impossible to agree on how to split up the village's factory buildings, land, and collective debts and announced that most residents did not want to split up the village. By the end of 2000, township officials had succeeded in subduing overt clashes, but it was unclear how long the uneasy peace could be maintained. As with Li Settlement in Jiangxi, we see in Three Fork that lineage institutions can be important resources for political mobilization; but when these institutions are not village-wide and solidary, they may actually have a negative impact on village governance.

Table 6.8 summarizes the findings from these four case studies. Neither wealth, nor performance contracts, nor the existence of village elections correlates with the quality of public goods provision. The two Fujian villages, West Gate and Three Fork, rank high in all these respects, but village governance in Three Fork is in shambles. Economic development and formal accountability are weak in both of the Jiangxi villages, Li Settlement and High Mountain, yet officials in Li Settlement still organize major village public projects. The two villages that enjoy good governance and public goods provision— West Gate and Li Settlement—are the two villages with solidary community institutions. Although the specific solidary activities and practices that people in these two villages organize may be different—West Gate organizes a variety of temple, lineage, and recre-

Table 6.8 Accounting for variation in public goods provision

Solidary community institutions?	Wealth? Performance contracts?	Implementation of elections?
	Yes	No
Yes	**Fujian—West Gate Village** *Good* **public goods provision**	**Jiangxi—Li Settlement** *Good* **public goods provision**
No	Fujian—Three Fork Village *Poor* public goods provision	Jiangxi—High Mountain Village *Poor* public goods provision

ational activities, whereas Li Settlement focuses on lineages—solidary groups in both villages uphold standards of duty to the community and use moral authority to enforce these standards.

The Limitations of Formal Accountability

By and large, formal bureaucratic and democratic institutions fail to hold village officials accountable for public goods provision. Why might this be? Further research is needed, but part of the answer is that in order for these institutions to be effective at sanctioning officials for poor performance and public goods provision, village officials have to care about potential dismissal or being voted out of office. But in many places (though not all), the rewards of holding office are either low or short term. In poorer places, the wages associated with being a village official are theoretically a strong incentive. Yet it is in these same places that local governments are the most likely to be in debt and the least likely to have sufficient funds to pay wages either on time or at all. In wealthier places, officials' privileged access to networks and resources may make holding office attractive to local businessmen or would-be entrepreneurs. But it is in these same places that the opportunity costs of being an official are likely to be highest. Once these connections are made, it is often more beneficial for businessmen to step down from office. Private entrepreneurs who had held office often complained that their time and energy were divided and that their income and business interests suffered while they were in office. As one village head in western Fujian commented, "When a village cadre's personal [i.e., business] and public responsibilities conflict, they choose the personal interest." In this village, the last two village heads had quit in the middle of their terms to return to running their bamboo bead–making factories. The current village head, whom the township government asked to fill in when the previous one quit, said that he constantly joked with villagers about the likelihood that he would finish his term before going back to running his highly lucrative medicinal herb shop in the township seat.

Another possible motivation for holding office might be the prospect of controlling public funds. It is true that some villages enjoy a steady source of rental income or revenue. In these villages, officials may indeed have a strong incentive to hold on to their positions. But these places are increasingly rare. In most places officials find either that they need to use most of the village government revenue to service huge debts, or that it is in their interest to embezzle whatever they plan to embezzle within one term. Both villagers and township and county officials reported that it was much harder to hold people responsible for financial mismanagement after they stepped down from office.

In the few places where officials do have strong motivations to stay in office, democratic and bureaucratic institutions of accountability for public goods provision are still weak. For bureaucratic institutions such as performance contracts, the problem is that higher-level officials often lack incentives to monitor village officials. Two factors in particular discourage township governments from ensuring that village officials provide public goods and services. First, policymakers at the top prioritize economic development and industrialization and do not reward grassroots officials for providing public services conscientiously. Second, fiscal decentralization gives local officials strong incentives to invest in industrialization and maximize their revenue flow, which means minimizing the resources they spend on public services as well as the resources spent on making sure that local officials below them invest in public services at their level.[27] Township governments often economize on time and money by monitoring only those villages that are significant to them in terms of economic growth and the generation of tax revenue. As one former township party secretary explained: "Village officials get targets, like how much grain their village has to produce, but if they don't reach the target, the township just meets with them and tells them to do better next year. It doesn't affect their wages. They only get a little over 100 RMB a month anyway."

Recent research on rural China has devoted a vast amount of attention to the implementation of elections and other village democratic reforms. The assumption is that elections have an important and usually positive effect on village governance. Further research still needs to be done in order to assess the impact of elections and democratic reforms over a longer time frame. But analysis of both quantitative and qualitative data in this study indicates that the implementation of elections and village democratic reforms have not had a significant impact on village governmental accountability for public goods provision. This finding holds for villages that have both democratic institutions and solidary groups as well as for villages that have only democratic institutions.[28]

One of the key problems for democratic institutions such as elections and village representative assemblies is that it is difficult for villagers to distinguish between village officials who fail to provide public goods because there is no money in the village coffers and village officials who fail to provide goods because they are bad officials. Numerous policies mandate financial transparency, and numerous experiments have been carried out with public budgeting and open accounts systems, but in most places (at least when this study was conducted in 2001), villagers felt that these reforms had had little effect. Neither villagers nor higher-level officials found it easy to obtain information on village public finance that they could be certain was accurate. Villagers often protest to township and county levels about fiscal mismanagement, but in many cases, audits by higher levels provide little evidence. (In fact, one village reported that protests resulted only in the county's sealing [feng] the village accounts.) In some cases, fiscal mismanagement by village officials was not discovered until new people took office and found that the previous set of officials had run up large debts or that the village accounts did not make sense. In one village, when villagers protested at higher levels, those officials told them that they had no power over ex-officials (*meiyou quanli chuli*). In short, one of the key lessons from rural China is that elections do not automatically mean democratic accountability. Many other supplementary institutions that, ironically, have to be implemented from above are needed. In order to make elections work properly, the state, as Dali Yang and Fubing Su argue, must establish independent electoral commissions, independent accounting offices, and independent statistical agencies.[29]

Implications for Local Governance and State Capacity

Formal bureaucratic and democratic institutions implemented by the state have had little effect on enhancing the accountability and performance of village officials; but village social institutions—specifically those in which village officials participate actively and which provide a common framework of moral obligations for the entire village community—have enabled villagers to hold village officials accountable for their performance. Such institutions are enforced in part through coercive social sanctions such as criticism, shaming, and social exclusion; but the most important sanction is to deny officials access to the moral authority and social networks of community solidary groups. In environments such as China where formal state institutions and the rule of law are weak, informal social institutions that incorporate participation from both state and social actors can have an enormous impact on local governance.

Informal institutions are often equated with the pursuit of private interest. In China informal clientelist norms have enabled non-elites to subvert formal state regulations and elicit special favors from officials.[30] So-called *guanxi* networks have provided "a mechanism for people to collude for private gain by abusing the power entrusted to agents of the state."[31] This chapter demonstrates, however, that certain types of informal institutions can facilitate the pursuit of public interest. These findings are consistent with other studies which argue that informal institutions and social networks can enhance governmental performance and complement the state's formal institutions. David Wank has contended that *guanxi* practice does not have to be a particularistic strategy. He finds that local government bureaus may develop localistic networks with private firms and informal institutions that support these firms.[32] Pittman Potter has argued that *guanxi* relations can complement rather than hinder China's legal reforms.[33]

An informal institutional approach also helps illuminate "everyday forms of governance." Recent studies of governance in rural China have tended to focus on the dramatic and highly visible rather than on the mundane, everyday interactions between citizens and the state. Over the last ten years or so, scholars of rural China have taken advantage of new opportunities for data collection and have produced empirically rich studies of village democratic reforms, popular protest, and rural industrialization. But what about everyday village politics and the day-to-day operation of village governments? How do citizens make village officials respond to their needs and demands quickly and consistently? When do citizens comply with state policies and when do they ignore state policies? We need a better understanding of the rules and norms structuring the daily give-and-take between citizens and officials on ordinary issues, such as repairing a hole in the roof of the village school, as well as larger issues, such as coping with pollution from a nearby factory or negotiating land rights.

Writ large, these questions have major implications for issues of state capacity. Strong states are strong not simply because they have the power to enforce their demands, but because they also have the ability to secure societal cooperation with these demands.[34] Informal institutions supplied by social groups can create a system of mutual cooperation and accountability between citizens and the state, but each side has to want something from the other. Local officials who care little about implementing state policies have no reason to participate in an informal system of mutual accountability; and when the state has little to offer citizens—as is the case with so many local governments in arrears—there is always a danger that citizens will simply establish their own system of nongovernmental governance, using solidary institutions to substitute for, rather than to support, the state.

7 | Inadvertent Political Reform via Private Associations:

Assessing Homeowners' Groups in New Neighborhoods

Logically, there are dozens of ways in which constraints can be placed on state officials in order to limit their latitude for arbitrary and socially deleterious action. One type lies in modifications to the institutional environment within the state. This category would include reforms that strengthen oversight and hierarchical discipline; apply clearer standards by which to assess performance; regularize procedures for things such as procurement and contracts; or heighten horizontal accountability to courts or legislatures. A second form imposes checks from outside standard structures and subjects officials to election, recall, or perhaps merely evaluation by the public or by a group of peers or assessors.[1]

This chapter considers yet another type of reform that may impose constraints on officials through mechanisms outside the state itself: establishing or strengthening private associations.[2] The forming of organizations outside of state control holds the potential to constrain state officials by enabling members to express their collective interests more loudly and resist government encroachment more powerfully than would otherwise be the case.

Political theory, particularly the recent wave of scholarship on civil society, commonly ascribes such capabilities to associations. As a review of this work indicates, however, the actual behavior of private associations is complex. Researchers working on many parts of the world have turned toward examining specific kinds of associations and critically assessing the political roles they play and the internal practices they follow. In China, associations are just as varied and multifaceted as they are elsewhere; but conditions there make it especially difficult for membership organizations to achieve the strength and independence that are needed to exert real pressure on the state. Moreover, it cannot be assumed that in their stance toward and dealings with government they behave the same as groups elsewhere. Careful empirical analysis is thus called for.

This chapter looks at the peculiar case of the homeowners' associations *(yezhu weiyuanhui,* hereafter YWH) that began emerging in recent years in new neighborhoods. The latter term refers to residential developments built (for the most part) since the end of the 1980s, containing commercial housing *(shangpinfang)* in which maintenance, security, utilities, and such are handled in an integrated fashion by a property management company (PMC).[3] Like other forms of organization that lie outside the immediate managerial authority and payroll of the state, these groups have aroused controversy within China and are looked at with suspicion by some officials. At the same time, the YWH are distinct from other such organizations in that they received explicit authorization by national-level policy beginning in 1994. Though their emergence in some form was no doubt inevitable regardless of the state's stance, the YWH were encouraged by the Ministry of Construction and other agencies that saw them as a way to regularize market relationships in the realm of property ownership, development, and management.

No state agency overtly identifies homeowners' groups as a form of grassroots political reform. In actual practice, however, the YWH do have political implications. The most robust of the associations act aggressively to defend members' interests against both state and private adversaries. In stark contrast to longstanding patterns in which constituencies of many kinds of workers, entrepreneurs, and others are represented through government-run organizations, the YWH can be highly autonomous bodies with which the state and other interlocutors have no choice but to deal and negotiate. They constitute a new model for private associations in the PRC as well as an attractive laboratory for activists who have ambitions for far-reaching political change.

At the same time, not all the YWH exhibit such qualities. Many if not most of them are dominated by the powerful firms that they are intended to hire and supervise. They can be thwarted by local officials who block their approval and deny them legal standing. Some become the creatures of a small clique of homeowners who make decisions in the name of others without their assent.

The purpose of this chapter is to evaluate these organizations and the extent to which they constitute a form of political reform, a check on state power. It also aims to explain the forces that shape these groups into a diverse array of outcomes. The conclusion of the chapter is that although potent and democratically run associations are currently in the minority, it appears that they are becoming more numerous and hence a more important constraint on local government.

This study primarily draws upon fieldwork conducted in 1999, 2000, 2003, and 2004. I interviewed homeowner organizers in twenty-two new neighborhoods in Beijing, Shanghai, and Guangzhou. Valuable information also came from separate interviews with municipal officials in all three cities, as well as conversations with several Chinese researchers who are studying this phenomenon. A wealth of Chinese newspaper and newsmagazine accounts provided insight as well.

The chapter begins by reviewing theories of voluntary associations and drawing from them three expectations about the kinds of organizations that have the most strength vis-à-vis local governments. It briefly reviews studies of homeowners' groups in other countries, and then discusses the origins of those groups in China and the policies that are intended to shape them. The next section notes the features of the grassroots-level political setting that affect the homeowners' groups and their organizational properties. The chapter then presents a typology of the YWH. It concludes with observations about associations as a variety of political reform in China.

Theories of Associations

Theorists of civil society, defined as a sphere of voluntary associations situated between state, market, and family, have consistently identified these associations as bulwarks against government abuse. Widely differentiated regional, occupational, ethnic, and religious groups serve as the basis for the limitation of state power, hence for the control of the state by society, according to Samuel Huntington.[4] Larry Diamond writes that civil society works in such a way as to monitor and restrain the exercise of power by democratic states and to democratize authoritarian states.[5] According to Michael Walzer, civil society "challenges state power," and "confronted with an over-bearing state, citizens, who are also members, will struggle to make room for autonomous associations and market relationships."[6] This capacity for resistance is, of course, why states with the greatest ambitions for radical social transformation tend to do away with membership organizations that are beyond their control.[7]

The idea that civil society organizations express demands to the state and resist its incursions is only one of a number of salutary properties that theorists attribute to them. These associations are also said to inculcate virtuous civic habits of tolerance and participation, build interpersonal ties of trust and reciprocity, recruit political leaders, and cross-cut otherwise destabilizing lines of social conflict. Of these many claims, the state restraint argument is probably among the better supported and more generalizable, as it makes fewer assumptions about groups' internal workings.

But not all voluntary organizations behave in the same ways. Indeed, a lively countercurrent within the civil society literature points out how certain groups can be detrimental to democracy and the public interest.[8] A sensible step forward in this research agenda has been to create distinctions among different varieties of organizations and empirically determine what role they play, rather than to assume that everything from trade unions to churches to secret societies has the same political properties.[9] These attempts to disaggregate the world of groups generate several expectations about the political significance of private associations in authoritarian political settings. Their importance for reform, there is reason to believe, will be positively related to three principal characteristics.

The first factor is the group's internal democracy. Groups will be better able to restrain state power if they follow internal institutions that keep the organization responsive to its rank and file. This includes things like fair elections for leadership, meetings and records that are open to the membership, and decision-making practices that allow everyone's voice to be heard. There are counterexamples. Even a hierarchically governed, autocratic association could stand up against or exert influence on the state. Examples might include secret societies or highly regimented political organizations.[10] Nevertheless, groups in which leaders are not accountable will generally have less significance for political reform. Internal democracy should make leadership less susceptible to being co-opted by the government or other outside actors. It should bolster the leaders' moral standing when they claim to speak on behalf of their constituents. And it should enhance their ability to mobilize their members to engage in collective action.[11]

The second factor is the group's external autonomy. Organizations that are strongly beholden to other entities will be less able to contribute to political reform. This does not mean that an association must be free from all institutionalized links with state actors. Indeed, regularized channels of contact with the government could allow associations to make themselves heard in ways that have a good chance of getting the officials' attention. Still, if groups do not have the latitude to establish their own leadership, manage their own affairs, set their own agendas, and determine their own positions on important issues and act on them, but instead take their cues (or orders) from external bodies, their ability to effect reform will be limited. This is true whether the external organizations in question are themselves part of the state or are non-state actors such as firms.[12]

The third factor is the group's representational authority. Organizations must be empowered to speak on behalf of their constituencies, and be acknowledged as such. Without this, external bodies will not feel obliged to listen to the group. Members themselves may be uncertain of the association's standing, and there may even be more than one association competing for the same mandate.

China scholars have paid considerable attention to associations generally, and in particular have debated the concept of civil society.[13] Some observe that, empirically, there were relatively few examples of independent organizations to be found as of the mid-1990s.[14] Some cast doubt on the idea that civil society will be an important source of political change in China.[15] In particular, the notion that the newly wealthy (especially entrepreneurs or businesspeople) will form representative organizations outside the state's control has been called into question, although some find mixed evidence.[16] With wholly or mostly autonomous grassroots groups beginning to emerge in significant numbers—for instance, in the fields of environmental protection, women's and workers' rights, and the AIDS epidemic—the relevance of these groups seems ripe for reassessment. A further strand of discussion has centered on whether concepts derived from Western terms like "civil society" are appropriate yardsticks for measuring associations that are rooted in the Chinese cultural milieu, which may (for example) favor kinship-based groups and state-society relationships much more complex than a simple dichotomy.[17] Here, too, a logical response is to delve into empirical analysis, evaluating organizations not in terms of how well they conform to Western-derived definitions but rather in terms of how they achieve important outcomes.

In analyzing China's YWH it is appropriate to bear in mind accounts of roughly comparable homeowners' organizations elsewhere. A number of researchers have posed the question of how associations in U.S. Common Interest Developments (CIDs) stack up as democratic, self-governing bodies. Some of these studies are harshly critical. Evan McKenzie's *Privatopia* alleges that American CIDs practice an anemic form of politics featuring low rates of participation and revolving narrowly around the defense of property values.[18] Similar themes can be detected in other countries as well. For instance, Teresa Caldeira's study of São Paulo paints a dark portrait of internal governance in the gated communities to which crime-fearing residents retreat.[19] Others, however, find homeowners' groups to be laudable examples of local democracy and civic association, or at least find the criticism to be overstated.[20] Moreover, supporters, skeptics, and others seem to agree that homeowners' groups do engage in vocal political action directed at local governments, especially when their interests are threatened.[21]

Overview of Empirics

Other researchers and I have written preliminary analyses of China's homeowners' movement elsewhere.[22] The process by which the YWH came into existence is intrinsically interesting and complex, and raises as yet unresolved questions as to the motives of key actors within the state. Less opaque are the general contours of housing reform, the backdrop against which the new organizations emerged, as well as the national policies that support them. Here I present only a capsule version of these events and documents, sufficient to make the grassroots-level analysis clear.

The system of housing administration created after the establishment of the People's Republic featured what might be called a two-track system for the management and distribution of urban homes. On one level, work units *(danwei)* oversaw apartment blocks that were occupied by their staff and dependents; investment in new housing was concentrated in these buildings, which were often located within the confines of the unit's facilities. On another level, housing offices *(fangguansuo)* reporting to city housing bureaus managed all other homes, particularly residential areas built prior to the revolution. Private ownership was minimized within this system, and property rights were diluted. *Danwei* members did not own their unit-provided homes; rather, they were conditionally granted the privilege of using them. The *fangguansuo,* meanwhile, aggressively appropriated and redistributed older domiciles in such a way that by the end of the Cultural Revolution, only a small fraction of urban households owned homes, and even in those cases, ownership often was no more than nominal.[23]

In the late 1980s housing policy began to take a far-reaching new turn, although it was not until the mid- to late 1990s that these changes swept through cities on a massive scale, and they still remain incomplete today. The reforms fell into three general categories. Work-unit homes were sold off to their occupants, usually at below-market rates. Large segments of older housing areas began to undergo demolition and redevelopment. And construction of new homes began to be de-linked from the *danwei.* Although work units sometimes continue to help their employees afford places to live, for the most part new housing is not created on behalf of work units; rather it is built by commercial developers. Whether households acquire this housing at market rates or at subsidized prices, not only do they own these newer homes, but also their employers have little or nothing to do with how the neighborhoods are run.

With *danwei* and their logistics departments getting out of the housing administration business, the Ministry of Construction began articulating a market-based approach to the management of newly built neighborhoods. Professional PMCs would run these developments (known in Hong Kong, the evident inspiration for the policies, as estates). The management companies would be selected and hired by the owners themselves. In order to choose and monitor these service providers, homeowners would form what came to be called owners' committees *(yezhu weiyuanhui)*, but were initially called residential neighborhood management committees *(zhuzhai xiaoqu guanli weiyuanhui)*.

The Ministry of Construction first announced national policies for this practice in a March 23, 1994, document titled "Methods for Managing New Urban Residential Neighborhoods."[24] These policies were updated in the Property Management Regulations issued by the State Council on June 8, 2003.[25] The 1994 rules called for management committees to be formed, consisting of elected representatives of the residential neighborhoods' property owners and occupants. The groups were afforded a list of four rights *(quanli):*

1. Establish a management charter and represent the owners and occupants within the residential neighborhood, upholding the legal rights and interests of the property owners and occupants;
2. Decide on the hiring or rehiring of a property management company;
3. Discuss and review the annual management plan drawn up by the property management company, along with major measures in the neighborhood's management service;
4. Inspect and oversee the implementation of every aspect of management work and the carrying out of the rules and regulations.

The 2003 policy is a longer and more complex document. It emphasizes the rights of the owners *(yezhu)* themselves, but especially of the *yezhu dahui,* which refers to the full body of homeowners taken as a collective entity. It spells out a set of ten specific rights enjoyed by owners, as well as the powers of the *yezhu dahui.* The homeowners' committee is defined as the executive body of the *yezhu dahui,* and it possesses responsibilities *(zhize)* rather than rights.

In theory, homeowners' groups did not emerge in an organizational vacuum, of course. According to article 111 of the State Constitution and the 1989 Residents' Committee Organic Law, neighborhoods should already include mass organizations that, ostensibly, serve the interests of those who live there.[26] The network of Residents' Committees (RCs), numbering nearly eighty thousand nationwide, has undergone extensive repackaging and state investment since the early 1990s under the rubric of community construction (*shequ jianshe*).[27] Rhetoric notwithstanding, the new RCs remain firmly under the control of the street offices and higher levels of urban authority, and all but a smattering of RC elections contain only trace elements of democracy. Instead, the community reforms aim to make the state's neighborhood-level liaisons more efficient, better educated, and prepared to cope more skillfully with contemporary administrative challenges. The simultaneous emergence of the YWH and the rebuilding of RCs has raised the question of what the relationship between the two should be.

State policy never regarded the YWH as a type of political reform, and in some ways has tried to limit the authority of the owners' groups. Both the 1994 and the 2003 policies make efforts to restrict the powers of the *yezhu weiyuanhui* to the hiring and firing of a management company. The 2003 version particularly emphasizes strictures on the YWH, reiterating in several places its subordination to higher government authorities as well as to the Residents' Committee (an organization that is not mentioned in the 1994 document). The YWH, however, is also to be restrained by ensuring its accountability to the owners and to the *yezhu dahui*. Thus accountability for the YWH is to be accomplished in part by empowering the owners as a whole, not merely by tightening top-down controls on the YWH.

As important as these national policies have been, their actual implementation has been left up to city and provincial governments. Cities develop their own practical guidelines, basing them on the national documents but fleshing them out with things like specific procedures by which the YWH are to be established and elections held. City governments further delegate authority over the homeowners' groups to the district or sub-district level.

This has led to a complex process whereby, in each new housing development, the development (or nondevelopment) of a homeowners' group has been shaped by three factors, each representing a competing set of interests. The first is the organizational efforts of the homeowners themselves. Owners in some neighborhoods have banded together and mobilized powerful and sustained campaigns to establish a YWH and exercise its legally mandated powers. In many other cases, homeowners have been unable to mount such efforts. The second is the attitude of city officials. In most but not all situations, municipal cadres have taken a dim view of homeowners' groups, both because they have economic stakes in the development companies that are the homeowners' adversaries and because they are chary of groups outside their control. The third is the stance of developers and property management companies. Very rarely do these firms encourage the development of powerful homeowners' associations, but they employ a range of strategies in dealing with their customers' demands, from guarded cooperation to stalling tactics to co-optation to physical intimation and violence. Variation in these three factors has produced a spectrum of different outcomes at the neighborhood level, to be discussed later in this chapter.

These forces, moreover, have evolved in a dynamic fashion. City governments initially retarded the development of the YWH by denying approvals to most associations except for toothless committees controlled by the developers. Yet over time, this stance has changed, most dramatically in Shanghai. Housing authorities in Shanghai switched to an approach in which the YWH were actively encouraged, but their formation was to be carried out through a closely state-guided process. By the end of 2003, 4,756 homeowners' committees had been established in Shanghai, an order of magnitude greater than the figures for other cities.[28] As of the summer of 2004, the Beijing city government appeared also to be adjusting its institutions to lessen resistance to the YWH.[29]

As noted earlier, the 2003 State Council document reiterated national policy, emphasizing the central government's determination to bring homeowners' groups into existence, but also modified the national government's approach to one that aimed to place constraints on the organizations. Just as important have been the dynamic factors operating outside the state. Organizers of early homeowners' groups have loudly publicized their successes, coaching other homeowners on the finer points of laws and tactics. They have been boosted by Web sites that provide popular forums for discussion and for comparing notes. The media have also played an active role, providing increasing coverage of the homeowners' movement and spotlighting particularly conflict-ridden neighborhoods.

The Micropolitical Setting

The characteristics of homeowners' committees in urban China are strongly conditioned by features of the structural setting in which they are formed. Some of these structural features are common to homeowners' groups everywhere, but most are particular to developing-world and post-socialist environments, or perhaps specific to China.

First is the high degree of neighborhood-by-neighborhood idiosyncrasy in the functioning of homeowners' groups. This is a general feature of many phenomena in China.[30] To be sure, no two neighborhoods or condominiums in any country are exactly alike. But in the United States, for instance, homeowners' groups are often created through the repeated application of standardized legal documents.[31] In China, particularity is manifested in (1) approval from state authorities, which is given on a case-by-case basis; (2) relationships between residents and authorities or between developers and authorities, which vary; (3) the degree to which residents are aggrieved by fraud and abuses on the part of the developer, problems that are pervasive in the construction industry; and (4) the developer's stance in responding to homeowner efforts to form an association. Consequently, the power dynamic and organizational status of a given neighborhood can be entirely different from that of a development just down the road.

Second, there are the high costs of organizing. Regulations concerning the YWH require that at least half the owners assent to the creation of a homeowners' association and to enact major decisions, a hurdle that is difficult to overcome, especially if this requires that they all be personally present at a meeting. Mobilizing the participation of hundreds or even thousands of households demands a major effort from the YWH organizers: planning meetings, circulating announcements, and often going from home to home knocking on doors. Organizers also must gather information about the neighborhood and negotiate with the developer, management company, and government offices. Sometimes those who take the lead in home-owner activity even face violent retribution at the hands of thugs hired by the developer. Thus the scale, breadth, demands, and risks of this activity make it a costly endeavor, certainly relative to many other forms of private association.

Third are the high stakes involved. Upon formation of a YWH, one of the first items on the agenda is to resolve what are called leg-acy matters *(yiliu wenti)*, problems left over from the homes' con-struction and sale, often involving what amount to gross breaches of contract. Moreover, property management itself is big business, and a company's right to manage a neighborhood and to charge fees to residents is valuable. In addition to the management fees them-selves, companies charge for items like parking; they sometimes col-lect fees for water and electricity on behalf of public utilities; and they parlay their management authority into monopoly provision of things such as home redecoration services, repairs, plumbing, and so forth. Finally, the YWH will seek control over the significant sums accumulated in maintenance funds that otherwise lie at the man-agers' disposal. In short, it is not only that homeowners' groups in China are concerned with matters in which large quantities of money hang in the balance,[32] but also that these are struggles be-tween owners and firms over major liabilities, assets, and conces-sions.

Fourth is the problematic legal environment. In First World set-tings, homeowners' relationships to one another are often defined as much by contracts as by an organization or association. Indeed, a tendency to enforce rules by recourse to the court system is often subject to criticism or ridicule. In China as well, it is quite com-mon for homeowners to attempt to settle disputes by hiring lawyers. China's legal environment, however, is such that courts are rarely the final word in these disputes, but merely the site of one or more skir-mishes in ongoing struggles.[33]

Fifth is the far greater power of the developers relative to most homeowners. Of course, property developers are known around the world for establishing close, symbiotic relationships with city govern-ments, which result in nearly unstoppable policy tendencies cap-tured in the concept of the urban growth machine.[34] In China the machine is especially sturdy. Development firms are often themselves part of the city government, and their power is particularly unconstrained.

Typology of Outcomes

Because they vary so widely, it is impossible to describe the nature of actually existing YWH without breaking them down into a typology.[35] The following discussion refers to Table 7.1. It distinguishes six categories of homeowners' groups according to how they measure up along the criteria established earlier: internal democracy, external autonomy (which tend to co-vary), and representational authority.[36] Examples from field research are given for certain types in order to convey a concrete sense of the character of these organizations.

Many neighborhoods that are eligible to establish YWH remain without them, and thus fall into the first category in the left-hand column, "nonexistent." In some of these situations, the lethal combination of discouragement by property developers and management companies, together with indifference from or active stifling by local officials, leaves neighborhoods with no YWH at all. The homeowners' committee sometimes languishes in an unending state of preparation (*choubei*), with officials claiming that it lacks the proper prerequisites. Alternatively, matters pertaining to property management may be overseen by the Residents' Committee or simply by the developer or the property management company.

In other situations, a "puppet" YWH is established that nominally represents the homeowners but in fact merely fronts for the developer or PMC. These companies choose from a wide assortment of methods that can enable them to control the association. Often, they are able to take control of the mechanics of YWH elections, for instance, distributing and collecting ballots. They can ensure that residents with personal ties to the companies are elected. Developers commonly attempt to buy off homeowner organizers in various ways. Local government is often overtly or covertly complicit in maintaining these unaccountable YWH by failing to intervene or by helping to oversee elections that are rigged.

Puppet YWH typically exhibit the features of organizations that are embarrassed by their dubious legitimacy. These groups operate

Table 7.1 *Yezhu weiyuanhui* (YWH) typology

Internal democracy, external autonomy	Representational authority	
	No	Yes
No	*Nonexistent.* The establishment of the YWH is blocked by the developer and/or local officials.	*Puppet/noblesse oblige.* In both of these subtypes, a YWH is officially recognized, but the organization is dominated by the developer. "Puppets" are wholly unaccountable to owners, while relatively benign developers sometimes foster "noblesse oblige" committees, willing to respond to at least some homeowner demands.
Partial	*Riven.* Homeowners form factionalized proto-organizations.	*State-facilitated.* A YWH is formed through a closely state-guided process that affords at least some accountability and representation. National policy has aimed for this; local implementation in Shanghai has moved in a direction favoring these outcomes.
Yes	*Uncredentialed.* Seen in some cases where relatively unified homeowners' movements organize yet are denied official standing.	*Fully empowered.* Achieved by a relatively small but highly visible number of YWH through a combination of vigorous organizing and fortuitous circumstances. Sometimes difficult to sustain in the long term.

quietly. Meetings are poorly publicized, sometimes to the point of being held in secret. These meetings may in fact be chaired by an employee of the developer or PMC. The members of the homeowners' committee are not readily identifiable by the residents, let alone easy to contact.

The "noblesse oblige" YWH is a variant of the developer-dominated category. In some neighborhoods, developers take the approach of co-opting the homeowners' association by keeping it under control, as in the puppet cases. But in this situation, the developer or PMC also enables the committee to act as a conduit for input and complaints by owners, and satisfies some of the demands that are expressed via this channel. Thus the YWH at least makes gestures toward representing homeowners' interests, while remaining basically toothless and inert as a forum for deliberation or meaningful participation on the part of the owners.

"Fully empowered" groups contrast most sharply with the inanimate (or nonexistent) YWH in the first category in the right-hand column of Table 7.1. As of the summer of 2004, cities such as Beijing and Shanghai each had at least several dozen YWH that managed to establish themselves as representative organizations free from domination by either government agencies or the companies that they are meant to oversee. These committees came into existence through several different processes. In some cases, the groups were among the first YWH to form in a city, and were treated with tolerance by local officials, who were more hostile to groups that emerged later. In other cases, developers imposed a puppet group that received state approval, only to be subverted from within by dissident homeowners. Some neighborhoods are fortunate enough to be the home of residents with deep *guanxi* with city-level leaders who can intervene against obstructionist housing bureaus. In yet other cases, exceptionally dynamic and convincing leaders took charge of the YWH organizational process, and local officials were talked into approving their well-run associations.

Constructed in the mid-1990s, D. Apartments is a relatively small set of buildings located in a section of Beijing that lies between the second and third Ring Roads. The developer-installed management company had promised buyers that it would help them set up a YWH but never did so. Residents took the initiative to organize on their own out of frustration with high management and electricity fees, being asked to pay for an entire winter's heat up front, disputes over the actual square footage of the apartments, and suspected embezzlement by the managers. Activists alleged that the PMC put up big-character posters criticizing them, harassed them, and obliquely threatened violence against them and their children.

A small group of organizers held an open meeting of the owners and obtained the assent of a majority for the forming of a YWH. The district authorities, however, initially refused to authorize their committee. It was only after the husband of one of the organizers, a ranking official at a powerful state-owned enterprise, threatened to deploy his formidable political connections against the obstructionists in the district that approval was forthcoming. The owners promptly sacked the PMC, though they were unable to stop it from sabotaging equipment and accounts before it left the premises, and replaced it with a much more pliant Hong Kong firm. Subsequently, the main YWH activists became part of a small network of successful organizers who extended advice and encouragement to counterparts in other neighborhoods.

In fully empowered cases, the YWH asserts strong control over the management company. Some groups have fired their PMC and hired a new one several times over. Others choose to retain the original service provider but negotiate with it from a position of strength. It must be mentioned that not all such groups maintain a strong commitment to internal democratic mechanisms. Some YWH, for example, are initially formed through an election, but neglect to hold subsequent rounds of elections every two or three years as stipulated by local policy. Others are more conscientious in maintaining accountability through elections and open meetings.

The "riven" and "uncredentialed" categories constitute inchoate forms of homeowners' groups. In these situations, the owners have not been able to achieve the official recognition that would authorize them to represent the homeowners and to negotiate on their behalf. This can be because a developer-dominated YWH is already in place, or because local officials are blocking the group's formal establishment. Owners are nonetheless able in these cases to undertake and sustain a significant degree of organization.

In some instances, uncredentialed groups are well established, orderly, acknowledged by the homeowners, and open to their input. A suburban Beijing development of approximately seven hundred homes provides an example of this type. Residents began moving into W. Woods around 1997, and the next year they began holding meetings to prepare for the formation of a YWH. An eleven-person committee was duly elected at a meeting attended by two thirds of the owners. The district housing office, however, refused to approve this body. (Neighborhood activists fervently believe this to be the result of bribery by the privately owned development company.) The elected committee in some respects functioned like an authorized YWH, serving as a focal point for homeowners' deliberations about various conflicts with the developer and ideas for improving the neighborhood. By withholding fees, owners were able to win concessions from the PMC on utility rates. The committee even successfully stood for reelection in 2002. As of the summer of 2003, however, the YWH was still operating without state approval, meaning that it had no official stamp, could not collect dues from residents or maintain a bank account, and had limited leverage in negotiating with the neighborhood managers.

In other instances, riven organization is more attenuated, taking the form of loose networks or congeries of homeowners, sometimes locked in conflict with other factions.[37] One development of around three hundred units in a suburban county of Beijing, S. Gardens, exemplifies the way in which internal strife, together with other pressures and challenges, can leave a neighborhood without representation. A small group of owners led a rights-upholding *(weiquan)* movement against the housing developer, collecting voluntary contributions from their neighbors to pay for legal fees and a large protest banner. The other owners, however, blamed the movement leaders after the lawsuit failed. The initial activists went on to establish a YWH through what their critics felt were slipshod and secretive procedures. Various groups of residents traded rancorous accusations in person, on bulletin boards, and on Web sites. The YWH incumbents resigned collectively to protest what they saw as the ingratitude of their neighbors, and nothing was done to replace them. The PMC hired by the homeowners' committee proved incompetent, but the residents' mutual hostility was such that no one believed that a consensus could be reached to do anything about it.

Uncredentialed and riven groups, lacking official recognition, suffer from a disadvantage in their negotiations with developers and their dealings with the state (including lawsuits, which they may not have standing to file). At the same time, they are sometimes able to function with a surprising degree of effectiveness. Such groups agitate to be allowed formally to establish a YWH or to democratize one that was created without owner participation. At times they challenge the developer or the PMC on specific substantive matters, for instance, fee scales, quality of service, or shuttle buses to and from the neighborhood. Some actively maintain lobbying efforts directed at government officials, media outlets, and People's Congress deputies.

As discussed earlier, local governments, particularly in Shanghai, have turned from blocking the creation of YWH to encouraging their establishment through a process in which state officials are actively involved. This can lead to state-facilitated associations that are not creatures of the developer or puppets of the authorities but also are less than fully democratic. Elections, for example, may involve a round of open nominations but also a vetting cycle in which homeowner leaders who are not to the government's liking can be removed from the slate of candidates. Sometimes the candidate nomination process is such that the number of candidates is equal to or only slightly larger than the number of seats on the YWH. Sometimes votes are conducted by circulating clipboards door-to-door rather than by convening actual meetings.

These are, of course, some of the same mechanisms that are regularly used to take the democracy out of elections for institutions such as People's Congresses or, at the neighborhood level, Residents' Committees. Still, state management of homeowners' elections does not always lead to unaccountable YWH that do not speak up for the owners. On the contrary, state-facilitated groups can be aggressive in promoting owners' interests and responsive to their suggestions and demands. Government structuring of YWH elections, when done so as to provide all residents with the opportunity to participate, can also give the resulting association extra legitimacy. This contrasts with situations in which owners hold votes at small meetings that they themselves organize, which then are called into question by other owners who feel left out of the process.

H. Village, a neighborhood of around 1,200 apartments on the west edge of Shanghai, illustrates the fact that government involvement in the formation of a YWH need not result in an ineffective or unrepresentative committee. The leader of this homeowners' group was appointed in 2003 through an indirect election in which the electorate comprised about thirty-five owners' representatives who had been chosen by the district authorities together with the Residents' Committee and the developer, and in which there were no opposing candidates. The YWH chairman was a retired official from a major Shanghai enterprise who had specialized in party organization. Belying his apparatchik background and the scarcely democratic fashion in which he was selected, this man proved to be a vocal and committed spokesperson for his constituents. He convened open meetings and methodically polled residents to determine their priorities and favored course of action on a list of neighborhood problems. He aggressively sought recompense through the courts for a tax error and a land use dispute that aggrieved the owners. At one point, he explained in an interview, the developer came to his door to try to persuade him to abandon these lawsuits. "I said to him: I'm facing 1,200 other homeowners. If I withdraw the lawsuits, my windows will be broken. And I told him not to visit me at home anymore."

If the foregoing categories go some distance toward capturing the variation in China's homeowners' organizations, in what proportion are these several types then found? To answer this question in any precise way poses several problems. First, as yet there are no surveys available that comprehensively sample the universe of eligible neighborhoods, either nationwide or within a specific city. Moreover, the situation is evolving rapidly as state policies shift, individual neighborhoods change, new developments rise, and older types of housing become qualified to form YWH. All that can be said with confidence is that so far, nonexistent or puppet groups constitute the majority, while fully empowered committees are modest in number. A substantial number of housing developments are engrossed in the external and internal struggles that characterize the riven and uncredentialed types, while the growing number of state-facilitated organizations represents one possible way of resolving otherwise intractable conflicts.[38]

Mechanisms of Reform

Having drawn a sketch of the empirical status of homeowners' groups and pointed out features of the legal and political contexts that shape their development and variation, this chapter can now discuss the mechanisms through which these groups contribute to political reform.

First, it is worth pointing out that, even before any consideration of homeowners' organizations themselves, the broader context of urban housing reform lends itself to a shrinkage of certain aspects of state power. This reform favors or even itself constitutes political reform, in that trends toward more and more private housing and market-based distribution of housing rights leave officials without the same levers of control that they once wielded. This does not mean that the state has removed itself from the process of housing provision. Needless to say, state authority and resources are deeply involved in the murky real estate deals that pave the way for new housing projects, as well as in the sale of subsidized housing. Although the attitude of officials remains important to the fate of homeowners' groups, the rapid move to privatized housing meant for many urbanites an end to their dependence on their work units or their housing offices. And, as mentioned earlier, the turn to professionalized, market-based property management puts the state at one step's remove from direct control over residential areas. Some of the management companies are state-owned, while many are descended from earlier *fangguansuo,* and they tend to oblige the authorities as necessary. Nevertheless, they are businesses whose first purpose is to make money, not to serve as an arm of government.

Homeowners in the new neighborhoods are not the only people seeking to exercise land rights in China, nor are they the only claimants toward whom the state has made gestures of support.[39] But although the state has issued laws and policies about other forms of land or housing, no new form of organization has been authorized in these cases to allow those whose property rights are at risk to band together and protect their claims. In effect, the message is that for older neighborhoods, property claims often must give way to the redevelopment imperative; but once people purchase or otherwise acquire a spot in newly built (or rebuilt) neighborhoods, they can put a higher degree of faith in the solidity and breadth of their ownership rights. This resonates with a longstanding theme of the post-Mao era: those who weather the transition from the pre-reform system and prosper in the competitive new environment of the marketized economy will be allowed to enjoy the fruits of their efforts unmolested.

Turning to the homeowners' associations themselves, we have seen that so far, most of these groups are of types (nonexistent, puppet, and noblesse oblige) that do little to further political reform. Indeed, it could be argued that they set back the reform by perpetuating patterns of behind-the-scenes state collusion with economic actors. But focusing too closely on the nonexistent or developer-controlled cases would be misleading, for two reasons. First, these YWH seem unlikely to remain prevalent, given the shift in city-level implementation regimes. Second, it would neglect the changes that the more active and democratic homeowners' groups have already brought about.

Although at first blush the YWH seem to pertain more to regularizing market relationships and reining in abuses by developers and management firms than to restraining the state, it must be emphasized that the two are intimately linked. Impositions on the interests of property holders by firms often take the form of collaboration with state actors, or are carried out at the behest of the latter. For example, state agencies commonly pressure developers to give or sell them the use of office space or empty land within housing developments. These are often areas that have been designated for other purposes such as parks, recreational facilities, day care centers, or the like. Thus empowering homeowners' groups to defend claims to such neighborhood space places constraints both on the firms and on government.

As pointed out earlier, national policies contain ambiguities on the scope of the rights enjoyed by owners and their organizations. The 2003 policy deliberately deemphasizes open-ended rights and interests and indicates that owners' groups are to confine themselves to overseeing matters relating directly to property management. Still, even though their legal mandate is limited and they are supposed to be subordinated to state authority, in fact they become a venue that homeowners expect will be used to uphold their interests more generally. Once formally established, or in some cases even be-fore obtaining official approval, the YWH become organizations that the state has to negotiate with or to take into account in a variety of contexts, whether it wishes to or not.

Nor do the YWH merely negotiate with the state in a passive way. To the contrary, they actively lobby officials at many levels in efforts to get the state to give them what they want. In situations where the YWH have not received approval, homeowner representatives com-monly approach the housing authorities to demand official authori-zation. They call for the redress of all kinds of defects in the con-struction of their homes. They ask the state to clear up irregularities in the issuance of property deeds.[40] In formerly rural areas not con-nected to urban-quality utility networks, they demand a more reli-able electricity supply. They protest construction projects such as roads or other buildings that infringe on their peace and quiet, green space, and sunlight or are otherwise noisome.

These forms of lobbying are not unique to homeowners, of course. Individuals and groups of all kinds avail themselves of letters and vis-its *(xinfang)* channels.[41] Nor are homeowners unique in appealing to the authorities to follow through on the government's own policies and commitments, à la rightful resistance.[42] Especially pronounced in the case of the homeowners, however, are the resources that back up these appeals. Not only are owners of homes in new neighbor-hoods relatively affluent compared to urban society as a whole, but also YWH leaders generally have skills, experience, and contacts that help make their voices heard. These include prestige (for instance, when committees are led by retired military officers or professors), connections within city government or the media, legal training, or entrepreneurial experience in opening doors and getting things done. If YWH leaders themselves lack some of these useful qualities and skills, they often enlist the help of others living in the neighbor-hood who do possess them. Homeowners thus are particularly volu-ble in taking their demands to the doorsteps of state agencies.

All of the foregoing is in addition to the second-order effects of the YWH, the ways in which they may contribute to other kinds of political reform beyond the neighborhoods themselves. As we have seen, these organizations operate in quite disparate ways, with some dancing to the developer's tune and others mired in internecine squabbles. But they also can be a venue in which homeowners take part in democratic practices as they endeavor to run the neighborhood in a way that they perceive as fair. Whether this means the kind of indirect participation seen in Shanghai's H. Village or the big meetings and balloting seen in D. Apartments and W. Woods, it contrasts with the nondemocratic ways RCs have been selected and managed since their inception in the early 1950s.

The homeowners' groups, in a surprising number of cases, attract leaders who have a proclivity to take on social causes and express a long-term desire for more sweeping political reform.[43] Presumably this is because these organizations offer both a cause to fight for and a venue that is relatively safe from the harsher forms of state repression. Running a homeowners' group, or struggling to establish one, provides them with organizational experience that could well translate into future efforts in the service of other reform causes. YWH activists apply their leadership skills in other political arenas, as seen in their prominence among independent candidates for People's Congresses (PC). In the Beijing PC elections of late 2003, six out of about two dozen independent would-be candidates were homeowner organizers.[44] Of four independent candidates who managed to persist through the government weed-out process to be elected to local PCs in Beijing and Shenzhen, one was a YWH leader.[45]

Just like village- or firm-level institutions, the YWH pose the challenge of understanding change as it plays out in a large number of geographically dispersed cases. Analysis at this stage is limited by the lack of systematically acquired data from representative samples. Moreover, the YWH themselves, for the most part, are still in a larva-like early stage of development. Nonetheless, it is possible to hazard some conclusions about how these institutions contribute to political reform.

The endorsement of YWH by the central government is in some respects a surprising initiative. There are other possible ways the Ministry of Construction could have chosen to deal with the problem of providing property management services to new neighborhoods. Some of these alternative routes could have been far more statist and might even have extended the scope of action (and corruption) for state cadres. Authority over property management contracts could have been assigned to parts of the housing bureaucracy, or to local government agencies like the street offices. Rather than being composed entirely of owners, the YWH could have been set up as advisory committees composed mostly of local officials. Thus the YWH represent a novel way of thinking about how to address problems of governance.

Second, the YWH are distinct from other kinds of grassroots organizations. Their purposes are first and foremost economic, and membership and representation are based on property ownership rather than citizenship. Unlike, for instance, NGOs that fight AIDS or environmental abuse, they are committed not to the public interest but to the private interests of collections of individuals, even though, as mentioned earlier, quite a few of the most active homeowner organizers see their efforts as contributing to broader political goals. Yet precisely because of their ostensibly economic, market-supporting nature, they were legitimized in national-level policy during the Jiang Zemin era, a time of wariness toward many other kinds of reform. Moreover, if their treatment were someday to be applied to other types of economic groups, such as workers, farmers, or entrepreneurs, it could mean a considerable shift in patterns of interest representation.

As we have seen, the state has played a mixed and changing role in establishing these novel forms of association. The central government has strenuously promoted them, while also aiming to limit their powers. Local authorities initially dragged their heels and made it difficult for representative groups to establish themselves, but they gradually turned toward approaches that manage the development of homeowner-elected YWH rather than stifling them entirely. Surprisingly, one might conclude that in high-stakes settings like these, local associations are better served by a certain kind of "hands-on" state fostering rather than a "hands-off" attitude that leaves the homeowners entirely to their own devices. Given the power asymmetries between homeowners and developers, the unreliability of the legal system, and the barriers to collective action, state support of the organizational process can help promote the formation of accountable groups rather than developer-dominated ones.

The kind of political reform that the more active forms of YWH suggest is evolutionary and subtle rather than sudden and dramatic.

Assuming (and this is by no means certain) that homeowners gradually manage to assert more and more control over the associations that are established in their names and through them speak out on their own behalf, the corollary will be a state that is more and more willing to tolerate, listen to, and negotiate with self-organized constituencies. Although the earliest YWH emerged disproportionately in the higher-priced commodity housing estates, professional property management is becoming more and more widespread, thus bringing the model of homeowners' committees to a far broader set of neighborhoods, including older and less wealthy ones. The groups have become focal points drawing the attention of consumer, community, and even political activists, and they may play a broader role as testing grounds for democratic self-governance practices and training centers for politicians.

Ironically, we can predict that the further reform develops in other aspects of the political system, the less exceptional and significant the homeowners' groups will become. If district- or city-level People's Congress elections were opened up to free competition among any and all candidates, for example, YWH elections would no longer seem so notable. If autonomous unions were allowed to organize themselves at will, the YWH would not appear such a remarkable mode of interest articulation. But this is not to say that they would have no importance whatsoever. Instead, they would merely take their place as one among many types of local association, defending their pieces of turf and concrete, quietly adding to the density of non-state forces that government cadres must take into account.

8 | Civil Resistance and Rule of Law in China:
The Defense of Homeowners' Rights

Rule of law is a concept open to interpretation, but "virtually all definitions of rule of law agree on the importance of law's function to set limits to the exercise of private and state power."[1] Yet restraining state power is not easy even in democracies, not to mention in authoritarian regimes where citizens lack important weapons—notably, elections and a free press—to restrain state actors. Research on legal development in authoritarian regimes points to insurmountable internal or external pressures that force a government to restrain its power. For example, in Poland in the late 1980s, the internally divided and substantially weakened Polish Communist Party was no longer able to control effectively the growth and strength of the opposition movement.[2] Negotiations between the Communists and the Solidarity-led opposition resulted in changes to the Polish judiciary that in time came to resemble its West European counterparts.[3] External pressure may also contribute to legal development. Although progress toward judicial independence in Japan was limited before the end of World War II, after the war the American Occupation authorities instructed the Japanese government in reforming the legal system. As Laifan Lin points out, "After reform of the judicial system, judicial independence had basically been established both in system and in practice."[4]

Insurmountable internal opposition or external pressure, however, may not always be necessary for legal development. In China, the party-state dominates the legal system, but this does not mean that progress toward rule of law is unlikely in the regime.[5] An important component of the rule of law is the presence of clear and stable laws that are seen by citizens as legitimate.[6] China has made a number of efforts to strengthen legal institutions by enacting or revising laws to constrain the power of state agencies. In 1997 the Chinese Communist Party announced that "Chinese governance will be adopted according to law and will be constructed as a socialist country of rule of law"; in 1999 this statement was included as an amendment to the constitution.[7] Given the political system in China, it is unrealistic to expect rule of law to be achieved in the near future, but there have been definite signs of progress.[8]

What incentive does the Chinese party-state have to restrain state power and move toward rule of law? Current explanations of legal development in China tend to focus on economic development, suggesting that an emerging market economy necessitates the establishment of a legal system that guides and protects economic transactions.[9] While the importance of a market economy is beyond dispute, this is not a sufficient explanation of China's progress toward rule of law. The interaction between officials and citizens is not limited to the economic arena. In this chapter I show that, in state-citizen interactions, one important reason for the government to limit its power has to do with concerns over both legitimacy and social stability. Since the existing legal channels are limited in their effectiveness, citizens may resort to civil resistance that causes social disruptions. Moreover, when citizen resistance becomes widespread, it may generate empathy and support from other members of society, thereby challenging the legitimacy of the government.

This research is based on the case of Chinese homeowners' defense of their homes. Due to the privatization of public housing and the development of the real estate market in China, about 70 percent of urban households owned their homes by the early years of the twenty-first century. Although a home is the most important asset for most families, some urban residents have been required to relocate without receiving reasonable compensation for their home. To protect their homes, homeowners have staged persistent resistance. By exploring citizens' defense of their vital interests against state and business actors, this chapter demonstrates that civil resistance, though often difficult, has forced the government to limit its power and to respect citizens' rights by revising existing laws and regulations and enacting new ones.

Land Use and Conflicts in Urban China

In the post-Mao era, land use has become a conflict-ridden issue in both rural and urban areas. In rural China, conflicts arising from land use have become the leading source of social unrest after the tax reform that has significantly reduced peasants' financial burdens since 2000. According to a research group at the Chinese Academy of Social Sciences, of the 62,450 messages sent by citizens to a central media organization in the first half of 2004, about 36 percent concerned rural issues. Complaints related to rural land use accounted for 69 percent of the messages about rural issues. The research group's survey of 632 peasants who submitted petitions to Beijing in 2003 found that 73 percent complained about rural land use. Of its record of 130 mass confrontations between peasants and police in 2004, about 67 percent were over land use.[10] Peasants resist because their basic interests are often ignored by land users, including governments, state agencies, and business actors.[11]

Similarly, in urban China land use, mainly in the form of city construction and urban renewal, has provoked numerous instances of social unrest because homeowners' interests are often violated by state or business actors. Since the late 1980s, many urban residents have had their homes relocated due to urban renewal or city construction. For example, the homes of 820,000 people from 260,000 households in Beijing were reallocated between 1991 and 2000. In Shanghai at least 2.5 million people from 850,000 households have been relocated since the early 1990s. Residents are usually compensated by one of three methods if their homes are demolished for urban renewal or city construction: (1) they are provided homes elsewhere; (2) they are provided new homes in their original neighborhoods after the construction is completed; or (3) they receive cash compensation instead of a new home. Before the early 1990s, the first two modes were more commonly used, and residents' interests were largely accommodated.[12]

Since the mid-1990s, however, urban renewal and city construction have become a nightmare for some residents. In addition to bringing personal benefits to government officials, such as kickbacks from developers, urban renewal and city construction are now regarded as achievements of local governments and their leaders.[13] Most local governments have a special organization in charge of urban renewal and city construction. A typical practice is to form a leadership group that includes local leaders and officials from government agencies in charge of city construction, land management, economic planning, urban planning, tax collection, forestry and park management, and water and electricity supply, among others. It may also include representatives of banks.[14]

Although local officials have a large stake in city construction and urban renewal, a common problem they face is a shortage of funds, that has led to two changes that have significantly affected the welfare of urban residents. First, compensation is now mostly made in cash payments instead of new homes because cash payments cost less. For example, in Beijing in the 1980s residents were often able to return to their original districts after urban renewal was completed. Compensation in the form of new homes at that time was based on the condition of the old homes and family size. The government increasingly regarded this mode of allocation as a financial burden. In 1998 the municipal government stipulated that compensation would be based on the floor area of an existing home instead of family size, and compensation would be made in cash. The directive gave government agencies the power to carry out compulsory demolition if residents refused to move.[15]

Second, business actors are increasingly playing an unprecedented role in urban renewal and city construction. Because of their financial difficulties, local governments have often sought to attract business actors by lowering land prices and simplifying the transfer of land use rights. In exchange, the developer will undertake construction projects that should have been borne by the government. In a typical situation, the government leases a piece of land to a developer who will develop the land by putting up commercial buildings. The profit made from the construction projects will be used to cover compensation of the homeowners as well as other expenditures. Since this mode of urban development benefits both the government and the developer, it has become widespread in China. A former mayor of Shanghai admitted that without this mode of land lease, urban renewal in the city could have taken one hundred years instead of ten. It was estimated that up to the year 2000, land lease attracted 100 billion RMB in investment in infrastructure construction in Shanghai. For this reason, the municipal government sometimes allows developers to use the land for urban renewal at no charge.[16]

These policy changes, however, no longer benefit the residents who live in the old neighborhoods. As new buildings are often much more expensive than the old ones, business actors have little incentive to allow former residents to return to the new neighborhood after it is completed, unless the residents are willing to pay an extra sum on top of the compensation they receive. In most cases, business actors simply provide cash compensation to sever relations with the former homeowners in order to prevent disputes. But the cash compensation is often too little for the homeowners to afford new homes in the original neighborhood or nearby.[17] In Shanghai, for example, the homes of about 120,000 families were demolished in 2002, and the majority of these families could not afford to buy new homes in the city.[18] One reason for the limited compensation is the government's unfavorable regulations regarding compensation. Another reason is that the organization that assesses the housing prices is designated by the government agency in charge of housing demolition or by the developer, so the result is often biased against the homeowners.[19]

The inadequate compensation limits the homeowners' choices. Some old neighborhoods are shantytowns with tiny, cramped houses, where three generations may squeeze into a single room. When these families have to leave, few of them can afford to buy a new flat in the same area. They are typically allocated bigger homes in outlying districts. Still other families reside in undersized units, or parts of their old homes without city permission, so these are not included in the compensation package. As a result, many receive negligible reimbursement, barely enough for a decent home even in the outlying suburbs. The Ministry of Construction has repeatedly urged local governments to build cheap homes for rental by low-income residents, but such instructions have been ignored by local governments.[20]

Homeowners also face other problems if they move elsewhere. One is the loss of the employment opportunities associated with the former neighborhood. Some old neighborhoods are located in business areas, and residents may lease rooms for income; others maintain retail businesses in their own houses or in the neighborhood. If these homeowners are required to leave, many of them cannot afford to buy homes within the city and have to settle in the suburbs, incurring a loss of employment. Some homeowners have fallen into poverty because of housing relocations.[21] In addition, welfare benefits provided to poverty-stricken families in cities are often distributed by the residents' committee of a neighborhood. Thus leaving the neighborhood may also result in a loss of these welfare benefits. Furthermore, residents will face the problem of their children's education if they move elsewhere, especially to the outlying suburbs. Schools in the cities are often better than those in the countryside or in the suburbs in terms of facilities and teachers' qualifications. Sometimes homeowners may resettle in suburbs with no schools nearby. All these factors make residents reluctant to move, but they often have no choice because of their weak position in relation to that of the government and the business actors.

An Unbalanced Triangle

In urban China land is owned by the state. After 1988 the Chinese government began to commercialize land use by separating land-ownership from land use rights. In theory, homeowners are entitled to land use rights for up to seventy years after they buy their home. Yet the government has the authority to reclaim the land before the land use rights expire if (1) the land is to be used for the public interest; (2) the transfer goes through legal procedures; and (3) reasonable compensation is provided. This implies that if the land is to be used for commercial purposes, it should be a civil matter between the homeowner and the developer, based on the terms of the agreement between the parties.[22]

Nevertheless, as mentioned earlier, because local governments and officials have a stake in city construction and urban renewal, they often intervene in favor of the business actors. They do so by extending their power in housing demolition for public projects to demolition for commercial construction projects. In 2001 the State Council issued a directive to prevent resistance by residents from threatening the construction of public projects. This directive is ambiguous about the homeowners' land use rights but grants enormous powers to the government and its agencies. First, it denies citizens the right to bargain with the government. According to the directive, if there is a dispute between a homeowner and the party responsible for the housing demolition, the dispute will be judged by the government or its agency in charge of housing demolition. It is surprising if the verdict favors the homeowner.

Second, the directive denies citizens the legal right to protect their homes. In theory, a homeowner may file a lawsuit if he or she refuses to accept the verdict issued by the government or its agency. Yet article 16 of the directive stipulates that if the party responsible for the demolition has provided compensation as specified in the verdict of the government or its agency, it can demolish the home *before* the court makes a judgment. This regulation renders it meaningless to sue the government. Article 17 further stipulates that if the homeowner refuses to move before the deadline, the local government or its agency may require compulsory demolition, or request the court to do so.[23]

The directive of the State Council became the basis for local governments to make similar regulations to deal with homeowners. According to the State Council directive, if a party applies for a license for housing demolition, it needs the approval of the land management bureau. If the land is to be used for commercial purposes, according to the Land Law, the bureau cannot issue approval without a prior agreement between the business actors and the homeowners on the transfer of the land use rights. To sidestep these regulations, business actors often request that the government grant them land use rights in the name of constructing public projects. As a result, the public interest has been very broadly defined by local governments, and commercial projects are commonly treated as public projects. It is estimated that 80 percent of the housing demolition is carried out not for the construction of public projects but for commercial purposes.[24] Homeowners' rights are thus frequently violated. Given local governments' regulations, as long as the developer provides compensation in accordance with the verdict of the government or its agency, it can ask the government or apply to the court for compulsory demolition. As one lawyer explained: "Real estate companies often sue homeowners and apply to the court for compulsory enforcement. The courts would rule in their favor for sure."[25] In addition, the government may help developers by pulling down the homes or arresting those who resist. It may also cut off the supply of water, electricity, and gas to the homes.[26]

Resistance of the Weak

Despite China's authoritarian regime, there is space for political participation.[27] Yet such space may actually increase tensions between the state and citizens, because while it allows citizens to take action, it is inadequate and may force citizens to take steps beyond the government's limits. In rural China, peasants who have lost their farmland without reasonable compensation have staged various modes of resistance, ranging from lawsuits to protests and demonstrations. This is also true for homeowners in urban areas. Although government policies discriminate against homeowners, the latter are still able to cite relevant articles in the constitution, the General Principles of Civil Law, the Administrative Litigation Law, and other stipulations to fight against the government and the business actors. But without an autonomous judiciary, the use of legal channels in China is not effective.[28] Alternatively, homeowners have resorted to nonlegal channels, such as appeals to state authorities, protests, sit-in demonstrations, or even deadly confrontations.[29] Their resistance indicates both the possibility and difficulty of defending rights in this authoritarian regime.

Suing Government Agencies

Since its enactment in 1990, the Administrative Litigation Law has been increasingly used by Chinese citizens to defend their interests against state actors. Despite the difficulties, its increased use indicates the rise of citizens' awareness of their rights. Within ten years the courts judged 573,000 administrative litigations; of these, the plaintiffs won over 40 percent. Dozens of ministries at the national level, not to mention local governments, have been sued.[30] Not surprisingly, those government agencies responsible for land management and city construction are in the top three among agencies that have been most frequently sued in recent years.[31] In Zhejiang province, legal disputes concerning urban renewal, housing demolition and allocation, city planning, and other issues related to housing account for one fourth of the total number of administrative litigations in the province.[32]

In Beijing, city construction has expanded rapidly due to economic development. Conflicts between homeowners and government agencies or business actors are common. A vice mayor of Beijing once admitted that city construction and housing demolition were the leading sources of conflict in the city.[33] In one district, homeowners filed thirty-three collective lawsuits between 1995 and 2000. In June 1995 more than six hundred people in a neighborhood in the district filed a lawsuit against the land and housing management bureau of the district for housing demolition. Initially they filed the lawsuit with an intermediate court, but the court refused to accept the case. They then took the case to the high court, but they were again rejected. The residents, however, did not give up. In February 2000 seven homeowners, on behalf of 10,357 residents, filed a "10,000-person lawsuit" against the land resources and housing management bureau of Beijing municipality in an intermediate court in Beijing. The suit claimed that the government did not have the right to allow the developer to use the homeowners' land for commercial purposes. But the municipal government had enacted regulations to simplify the procedures for land use in order to attract businesses. In China, government regulations can serve as the basis for the courts to make a judgment, thereby increasing the difficulties homeowners face in suing the government or business actors. Although the court accepted the case, it did not put it on file for trial.[34]

In another high-profile case in Shanghai, a large number of homeowners sued the land management bureau for violating their rights by leasing the land to a developer. In May 2002 the land management bureau of Jing'an district in Shanghai signed a land use contract with a company owned by a well-known businessman, Zhou Zhengyi, who was said to be the richest man in Shanghai. According to the contract, 2,159 households in that district would have to relocate. Conflicts arose when the homeowners and the developer failed to reach an agreement on the home relocation. Many homeowners hoped to have apartments in the original district after the new homes were completed, but the developer ruled out this possibility. Despite the homeowners' objections, some homes were demolished by force. The 2,159 households then sued the land management bureau in May 2002, requiring that it revoke permission to demolish their homes. Not surprisingly, in 2002 the homeowners lost their lawsuit.[35]

There are several obstacles to suing government agencies in China. First, because the courts lack autonomy, they may be prevented from accepting certain cases, such as those involving housing demolition. In Beijing and elsewhere, for example, the high court promulgated regulations that prevent the courts from accepting lawsuits concerning housing demolition.[36] Second, although lawyers are often crucial in helping citizens sue the government or its agencies, lawyers lack an incentive to take on administrative litigation because of the risks involved in confronting state agencies.[37] In the Shanghai case just presented, a lawyer who provided legal advice to the homeowners was arrested and sentenced to three years in prison on charges that he had revealed "national secrets" to foreigners.[38] To avoid offending government agencies, some law firms prohibit their lawyers from representing clients in such cases. For example, a law firm in Shanghai announced that "to protect the reputation and rights of this law firm and its lawyers, lawsuits involving administrative litigation and housing demolition will be accepted only with the approval of a meeting of the law firm partners."[39]

Non-legal Modes of Resistance

The limited effectiveness of the legal system encourages homeowners to adopt other modes of resistance, such as protests and appeals. Homeowners can proceed in either of two ways when resorting to non-legal channels. One is to confront the developer and prevent it from carrying out the demolition before an agreement is reached. The other is to generate pressure on the local government that has authority over developers, housing demolition authorities, and legal departments. For example, lodging complaints with higher-level authorities is an important mode of resistance in China.[40] Between Jan-

Table 8.1 Average monthly petitions to the National Complaints Bureau regarding housing demolition

Year	Letters	Petitions in person	Number of people making petitions
2001	710	147	432
2002	1,126	173	583
2003[a]	1,455	184	670

Source: Compiled from Wang Hongliang, "Kaishi bei guifan de chaiqian xingwei" (Beginning Regulated Housing Demolition), *Sanlian shenghuo zhoukan* (Sanlian Life Weekly), January 19, 2004.

a. Between January and August 2003.

uary and August 2002 the Ministry of Construction received 4,820 letters of complaint, 28 percent of which focused on housing demolition. Among the 1,730 visits received by the ministry, about 70 percent focused on housing demolition.[41] In 2002 about seven thousand people approached the National Complaints Bureau to complain about housing demolitions (see Table 8.1).

Homeowners often combine different modes of resistance in order to increase their chances of success. Since individual resistance is often ineffective, a more forceful way is for homeowners to organize collective action to resist business actors and to seek the help of state agencies. In some places, in order to prevent developers from destroying their homes, homeowners organize themselves day and night in patrol squads to monitor the people entering their neighborhood. In a neighborhood in Nanjing, homeowners adopted a unified approach by refusing to respond to the unreasonable demand of the developer to move elsewhere or to negotiate with the developer individually. Homeowners elected representatives to deal with the developer; these representatives tried to seek help from the municipal people's congress and the municipal political consultative conference, and negotiated with the officials from the housing demolition authorities. They also appealed to the Ministry of Construction, the provincial complaints bureau, the standing committee of the provincial people's congress, and the provincial construction bureau. Collective action made it more difficult for the developer to violate the homeowners' rights arbitrarily.[42]

Although homeowners usually do not wish to take violent action against the government and business actors, they will take such action if they believe that it is the only way to protect their homes.[43] In Shandong province, collective resistance to housing demolition is one of the main sources of social unrest.[44] In Beijing it is not rare for residents to take to the streets and block traffic or blockade government compounds. For example, on April 26, 2003, about three hundred residents protested against compulsory housing demolition. Some of them complained that "when Beijing won the bid for the 2008 Olympic Games, our housing became a problem. Now it is a disaster."[45] In Shanghai in 2003 a number of protests against housing demolition occurred, and hundreds of protesters were detained. On May 1, 132 people protesting against housing demolition were detained. Some residents shouted, "SARS is horrible, but compulsory housing demolition is worse!" On June 17 another thirty-five residents protesting against housing demolition were detained.[46]

Leading collective actions can be risky as well as costly, however. Citing various pretexts, some developers may increase the compensation for most homeowners but not for the leaders of the collective actions.[47] The solidarity among homeowners should also not be overestimated. Owing to factors such as differences in the location of apartments, floor area, access to sunlight, and expenditures on housing renovations and decorations, homeowners receive different amounts of compensation. Therefore their incentives to resist vary.[48] When the developer or government agencies cut off water or electricity, continually disturb homeowners, or buy them off, some homeowners are more willing than others to leave. Under these circumstances, individual action is more common than collective action. Yet sustaining individual resistance against a developer is not easy. Some homeowners refuse to leave despite the many difficulties created by the developer. This mode of resistance, however, can be costly. Homeowners must continuously guard their homes, using either strong people who can resist threats or old people who might be easily hurt in confrontations to deter the developers. Any relaxation can provide the developers with an opportunity to demolish their home.[49]

When the developer or the government agency in charge of housing demolition loses patience, individual resistance becomes difficult to sustain because the developer may resort not only to harassment but to force as well. Some homeowners have lost their lives because their health failed to withstand the pressures and anxieties arising from resistance against housing demolition. For example, in 2003, due to a construction project that demolished a Beijing neighborhood, at least six residents died when the continual threats and harassment by those carrying out the demolition triggered fatal illnesses.[50] At other times, developers may use outright force. For example, on the night of September 19, 2003, half a dozen people broke into a house in a district of Beijing, where they tied up the family members, who had been asleep, moved them outside, and then pulled down their house. Two days later, on September 21, a similar event occurred in another district in Beijing. In the early morning dozens of peasants hired by a real estate company forced more than twenty people from thirteen households to move out, and then they demolished their homes, even wounding some residents.[51]

Some homeowners have lost their lives while actively resisting developers or government agencies. A number have died in violent confrontations; others have died because they believed that only by threatening to commit suicide or by sacrificing their lives would their families have a chance to receive sufficient compensation for a new home. Such events are not common, but they do indicate the seriousness of the problems arising from compulsory housing demolition and the lack of legitimacy on the part of both the government and business actors. High-profile suicides in Nanjing and Beijing have led the central government and society at large to pay serious attention to the issue of housing demolition.

In May 2003 a developer in Nanjing contracted for a piece of land in a business district to build commercial buildings. The more than 1,500 households in the neighborhood were required to move elsewhere. Many homeowners were reluctant to leave because the neighborhood was in the downtown area, and because the amount of compensation they were offered was based on criteria promulgated by the government in 1998, despite the sharp increase in housing prices since then. Some homeowners also earned their livelihood by leasing rooms or engaging in retail businesses in the neighborhood.[52] As elsewhere, the city government had based its regulations on the directive of the State Council, giving itself the power to carry

out compulsory demolition in the name of advancing public projects. Although most residents eventually moved out, by late August
2003 about ten families still refused to leave. One morning, when
Weng, the head of one of these families, was negotiating with the
housing demolition office, the office deployed people to pull down
his home. When Weng saw what had happened, he returned to the
office and doused himself with gasoline. He then got into a heated
argument with the office personnel and set himself on fire. Weng
died fifteen days later.[53]

Not long after Weng's suicide, two similar cases occurred in Beijing.
On September 15, 2003, a resident from a county in Anhui province
attempted to burn himself to death in Tiananmen Square beneath
the portrait of Mao Zedong in protest against the local government's
forcible resettlement of his family. Security officers rushed to his assistance and the man was saved, suffering only minor burns.[54] Ten
days later, on September 25, a thirty-five-year-old resident of a district
in Beijing set himself ablaze in a desperate attempt to avoid eviction
as a property developer burst into his home to evict him and his family. He suffered serious burns on his body.[55] The Ministry of Construction revealed that conflicts arising from housing demolition resulted in twenty-six deaths and sixteen injuries from January to July
2002.[56]

The State's Responses

The success of the weak in resisting the powerful is highly condi-
tional. To a large extent, the power of the weak lies in continual
and widespread resistance that not only undermines the regime's
legitimacy but also points to a possibility of persistent or better-
organized resistance if their interests continue to be ignored. In the
case of housing demolition, homeowners' resistance eventually attracted the attention of the central government not only because of
the scope and frequency of such resistance but also because of the
empathy it generated in the society, along with the popular resentment toward government policies.

The numerous appeals put direct pressure on the government.
The widespread resentment of the fate of unfortunate homeowners
and their sympathizers also translates into pressure on the govern-

ment through the media and Internet disclosures. News of Weng's tragedy soon spread on-line even though the local media were prohibited from reporting the case. As expected, the event aroused unreserved empathy for the victims and widespread criticism of the local government and the developer. The pressure on the central government was reflected in the fact that the State Council not only sent several teams to a number of cities to investigate the situation of housing demolition but also in September 2003 issued a directive titled "An Urgent Notification on Taking Housing Demolition Seriously to Maintain Social Stability." The State Council admitted that there had been an increase in disputes, including deadly confrontations and collective appeals arising from housing demolition. It attributed the conflicts to a failure to compensate or relocate residents and the inappropriate working style of government agencies: "These events have affected the social order and stability. Leaders of the State Council have taken this issue very seriously and have given important instructions. They require local governments and departments concerned to attend to the people's interests, act in accordance with the law, and take the issue of housing demolition seriously in order to maintain social stability."[57] The pressure eventually prompted governments at both the central and local levels, together with the courts, to take a number of steps—revising unreasonable rules, issuing new rules, and strengthening enforcement—to address the problems arising from housing demolition.

Restraining Government and Business Actors

As many of the chapters in this volume note, a priority of the central government is social stability. The State Council directive regarding housing demolition emphasizes that local governments should ensure social development while preventing collective actions from disrupting social stability. According to the directive, "Prompt and legal measures should be taken to deal with the minority of the people who take advantage of housing demolition to make serious trouble or to organize concerted action and threaten social order." It also stipulates, "If a large number of collective appeals are due to the work of government agencies, the leaders or persons concerned should be punished." Although the directive warns that the media and the Internet should not report mistakes and problems in demolition so as to avoid instigating social instability, it also states that social stability cannot always be achieved through repression. The directive stresses that citizens' interests, especially those of low-income families, must be respected. It stipulates that if there are disputes over compensation between homeowners and the parties responsible for demolition, compulsory demolition should be carried out only after arbitration.

At the end of 2003 the Ministry of Construction issued two directives that took effect in 2004.[58] One directive addresses the problems associated with compensation assessment. It stipulates that the assessment of home prices should take a number of factors into account: compensation for relocation, cost of temporary residences, losses caused by demolishing nonresidential housing, and expenditures incurred for the renovation and decoration of the homes to be demolished, among others. It also stipulates the procedure for addressing disputes over the assessment between the housing demolition party and the homeowners. In addition, the government should publicize the market values of houses each year, to be used as reference points for assessing the value of the houses that are to be demolished.

The other directive stipulates the documents needed for administrative judgments made by the authority in charge of housing demolition as well as the procedure for arriving at judgments. It specifies the conditions for compulsory housing demolition, emphasizing that such demolition must be decided upon by the collective leadership of the authority in charge of demolition. In addition, the housing demolition party is required to provide seven types of documents and to hold a public hearing before compulsory demolition can take place. The housing demolition party is prohibited from issuing threats, stopping the supply of water, electricity, gas, or heat, and carrying out compulsory demolition of its own accord. In China, the importance of promulgating these directives lies in the fact that they also serve as the legal basis for the courts to make judgments.

At the local levels, the government also promulgated regulations to accommodate the interests of homeowners. First, housing demolition cannot be carried out until compensation is made. Stopping the supply of water and electricity or employing the police in housing demolition is not allowed.[59] Second, local governments and business actors must address the problems faced by homeowners who, after receiving compensation, cannot afford to buy even the most inexpensive home.[60] Third, information regarding various aspects of demolition should be made known to the public. Government authorities in charge of housing demolition need to provide channels for citizens to voice their concerns and problems and must respond to those problems.[61]

In Beijing the municipal government issued an urgent directive in September 2003 regulating that compulsory demolition should cease during National Day and during the Third Session of the Sixteenth Party Congress. If there was any instance of ruthless demolition, the license of the demolition company would be revoked. The land and housing management bureau of Beijing also issued an urgent notice warning that eviction and demolition companies could risk losing their licenses if they resorted to abuse, threats, or deceit to pressure residents to move. The bureau made public a telephone number and Web site through which residents could lodge their complaints. In October 2003 the government of Beijing municipality revoked the licenses of thirteen demolition companies that had violated the law and regulations.[62]

In Nanjing the city and provincial governments were under serious pressure after Weng's suicide was disclosed. They adopted a number of measures to accommodate homeowners' interests in order to improve their image and maintain social stability. As in many other places, housing demolition was slowed and then halted in the city beginning in September 2003. Weng's family not only was provided with an apartment but also was offered a large sum in compensation.[63] The provincial government issued a directive in October 2003 stipulating that homeowners had the right to choose the mode of compensation and should not be forced to accept cash, that low-income families should be provided with options to buy or rent modest apartments, and that compulsory demolition must strictly adhere to legal procedures. The Nanjing city government canceled forty-nine construction projects that would have involved the demolition of 20,320 homes. It also revised its previous directive on housing demolition by increasing the amount of compensation and specifying the procedures for demolition. To accommodate the basic interests of low-income families, the new directive regulates the minimum compensation that would be sufficient to buy a small apartment in the city. The city government also was to build inexpensive apartments that low-income households could buy or rent.[64]

Response of the Courts

In housing demolition, homeowners' chances of winning their cases are "like those of winning a lottery."[65] Yet this does not imply that the courts do not feel pressure from the citizens. The courts may be caught between the government's demands and the citizens' requests, since there are articles in the laws, including the constitution and the criminal law, that grant citizens legal protection. Citizens' use of relevant laws sometimes embarrasses both the government and the courts. For example, in July 2003, 116 citizens in Hangzhou, capital city of Zhejiang province, sent a request to the Standing Committee of the National People's Congress (NPC) for a constitutional review of the local government's regulations on housing demolition. Similarly, in Nanjing in August 2003, some homeowners collectively appealed to the NPC Standing Committee for a constitutional review of the city government's directive regarding housing demolition.

In March 2003 the intermediate court of Hangzhou issued a notification titled "On the Acceptance of Lawsuits Regarding Housing Demolition." The notification states that grassroots courts should not accept lawsuits that apply for compulsory demolition if the homeowners have not yet reached an agreement with the party responsible for the demolition. The high court of Zhejiang province issued a similar directive in June. Homeowners' resistance was a direct reason, and perhaps the most important reason, for the promulgation of these directives. A judge in Hangzhou admitted that the directive of the intermediate court was to "regulate housing demolition and give citizens some rights." Resistance from homeowners and their lawyers made it increasingly difficult for the courts to ignore the homeowners' interests. A grassroots court once reported to an intermediate court that the debate over housing demolition was becoming intense. Some homeowners and their lawyers cited relevant articles in the constitution in court, and the judges did not know how to deal with such situations. Against this background, another event became a direct reason for the issuance of the directive by the intermediate court. In early 2003, when a grassroots court in Hangzhou adjudicated compulsory enforcement of housing demolition, it triggered a violent conflict with homeowners, resulting in the death of some residents. Faced with pressure from citizens, the intermediate court issued a directive that discouraged courts from rendering verdicts on compulsory demolition. Thereafter, there was a reduction in the number of compulsory housing demolitions.[66]

The numerous conflicts arising from housing demolition and citizen resentment against the courts' unconditional support for government agencies also generated pressure on the Supreme Court. In early 2003 the Supreme Court established a task force to review the directive issued in 2001 by the State Council. In October 2003 the Supreme Court distributed a draft to the provincial high courts on the ways courts should handle housing demolition issues.[67] The draft attempted to address the main concerns of the homeowners, although the impact it intended to make should not be exaggerated. First, it urges courts to accept administrative litigation if homeowners have followed the conflict resolution procedures. More specifically, if a homeowner refuses to accept an offer of compensation by the housing demolition party, he or she first has to apply to the relevant government agencies for arbitration. If the homeowner refuses to accept the relocation plan after arbitration, he or she can file a lawsuit, and the court must then accept the case as a civil dispute. If homeowners do not accept the compensation offered by the government agencies in charge of housing demolition, their lawsuits must be accepted as administrative litigation.

Second, the draft limits the power of government agencies to carry out compulsory demolition. Unlike the State Council directive discussed earlier, the Supreme Court's draft states that the court will not approve compulsory housing demolition before a case is judged, with the few exceptions being where state interests would be endangered if no compulsory action were taken. Third, the Supreme Court specifies rules for compensating homeowners. It regulates that when issuing compensation, local governments should take into account the location of the house, its usage, and its floor area. If compensation is made in cash, the price (per square meter) should not be less than 90 percent of the price of existing homes in the same area at the time when the demolition is being carried out. The city government should regulate the minimum compensation. If such compensation is still insufficient for the homeowner to buy a home, the government should provide an inexpensive rental home.[68]

After receiving the Supreme Court draft, local courts made similar regulations. In Jiangsu province, for example, the provincial high court finished its draft in September 2003. Like the draft of the Supreme Court, it not only allows homeowners to sue government agencies but also includes items to protect homeowners' rights. First, it regulates the qualifications of the organizations that can assess the value of the homes to be demolished. If the two parties fail to agree on an assessment, they can apply to the court for a new assessment. Second, if the compensated amount is less than 90 percent of the price of an existing house in the same area at the time when the housing is being demolished, it should be deemed inadequate. If the homeowners are to be provided housing as compensation, the availability of such housing should be proved before the demolition takes place. Third, the courts can no longer actively participate in compulsory demolition. If homeowners believe that the government is organizing illegal compulsory demolition, they can file an administrative litigation.[69]

It would be unrealistic to expect that these measures will address all the problems faced by homeowners. Indeed, conflicts between homeowners and the government or business actors have recurred in urban China. The government's position on compulsory housing demolition in public projects seems to be unchallengeable. Moreover, the definition of "public interest projects" remains vague. These new policies, however, point to the significance of citizen resistance in contributing to China's progress toward rule of law. They also serve as legitimate bases for citizen resistance. Some local officials report that housing demolition is now extremely difficult to carry out without providing a reasonable amount of compensation to the homeowners.[70]

This analysis has explored the rationale for the Chinese government to limit its power and move to rule of law in state-citizen interactions through the example of housing demolition. It finds that the Chinese government is willing to restrain its power and respect citizens' rights when it is in the government's own interest to do so. Maintaining social stability is one of the top priorities of the Chinese government at both the central and local levels. A violation of citizens' rights by government and business actors inevitably invites citizen resistance. In the case of housing demolition, as local governments often take the side of business actors, citizens' interests are sacrificed. Yet the citizens' stake in their homes is often too great for them to give it up. As a result, housing demolition without reasonable compensation has become a thorny issue that has provoked resistance.

In relation to government and business actors, homeowners are weak. The laws that are supposed to protect citizens are ineffective, and those stipulations made and enforced by governments at the central and local levels ignore their interests. This means that homeowners cannot stage effective resistance by using legal channels. Consequently, homeowners have employed a range of non-legal modes of resistance, including protests, petitions, and deadly confrontations. The resistance of the weak is effective when it becomes so widespread that it threatens social stability. Under these circumstances, the Chinese government has an incentive "to get the struggles off the streets and into the courts" or to "make the revolution before the people do."[71]

Yet even more than issues such as peasant burdens, undercompensated housing demolition captures widespread attention because it cuts across political, social, and economic status in urban China. With the aid of the media and the Internet, violations of homeowners' rights cause widespread resentment, undermining the legitimacy of the government. As a result, governments at the central and local levels finally revised their stipulations by accommodating homeowners' interests. Citizen resentment and resistance also generated pressure on the courts to revise rules regarding the acceptance of administrative litigations filed by homeowners.

The case of housing demolition reveals both the difficulty and the possibility of progress toward rule of law in China. The difficulty lies in the fact that rule of law may be in conflict with other vital interests of the government. When such conflicts arise, the credibility of the law is sacrificed, suggesting that progress toward rule of law in China is not a smooth process. Yet development toward the rule of law is also difficult to reverse. The possibility of progress is reflected in the fact that the government will restrain itself when society generates sufficient pressure, which is likely to grow in China as an emerging market economy and privatization enhance the people's awareness of their rights.

9 | "Hope for Protection and Hopeless Choices":
Labor Legal Aid in the PRC

Teacher Lu nearly shook as she described the workers who searched her out at the legal aid center where she worked. "They come here with hope for protection, but they are always presented with hopeless choices." She was depressed after another case had just been lost, or more precisely first won in judgment, then lost in implementation. "What's the point of legal aid if this is the result? It's too much trouble and too little success. Nowadays it's impossible to fight against companies, and the government does the companies' bidding anyway." She talked about quitting, but continued to go to work and advocate tirelessly for the losers in the economic reform.

At the time Teacher Lu had worked in labor legal aid for more than four years, after retiring from one of Shanghai's largest shipbuilding state-owned enterprises (SOEs). The vicissitudes and disappointments of her own career had led her to identify with the stream of workers who waited patiently for a chance to speak with her each day. As a young woman, she was sent to the far northeast, along the Sino-Soviet border, during the latter half of the Cultural Revolution. She found stability and prestige upon her return to Shanghai in the early 1980s when she was placed in an SOE doing party and trade union work. Along with other leading female cadres from across the city, she was chosen for additional education and legal training at Fudan University's School of Law in the late 1980s, and she rose through the ranks at her company as the importance of the legal system grew. When the pace of restructuring of SOEs quickened in the late 1990s, she was not spared, however, and she was forced out, taking the early retirement that most middle-aged female employees are offered in any failing enterprise. But she was not yet fifty years old and wanted to continue to use her legal training. She began staffing a hotline at Fudan University on women's legal issues, then moved a few years later to a full-time legal staff position at the Labor Law Service Center for Workers at East China University of Politics and Law. When she spoke the words I have quoted, she appeared exhausted and haggard, visibly thinner than in the early pictures of her on the legal aid center's Web site and in promotional material. Her own physical and mental state personified the general state of legal aid in 2004: fragile but dynamic, overwhelmed but enthusiastic.

That year marked the official tenth anniversary of legal aid in China. In 1994 the minister of justice had formally recommended that China establish a system of legal aid.[1] Within ten years, legal aid organizations developed rapidly under the jurisdiction of the Ministry of Justice, at the law schools of many universities, and under the direction of the mass organizations, including the All-China Federation of Trade Unions and the Women's Federation. The mission of legal aid is to offer legal advice and services to weak or vulnerable groups (*ruoshi qunti*) in Chinese society, usually defined as including the handicapped, women, juveniles, the elderly, the poor, and laid-off, unemployed, and migrant workers. Some legal aid advocates also include those regularly subject to social discrimination, among them those with AIDS and other chronic diseases. In these ten years, and in concert with rapid social and economic change, legal aid has gone from merely "helping the poor to upholding justice and human rights."[2]

Although the development of legal aid has been state-supported and state-led, the coexistence of at least three different systems of legal aid organizations has allowed for a certain degree of flexibility and variation in the structure and implementation of legal aid programs.[3] In addition to protecting vulnerable groups, other important goals of legal aid, as expressed both by the state and by legal aid activists, include reducing social contradictions and ensuring social stability.[4] While in practice there is often tension between these goals of protection and stability, the development of legal aid is an example of political reform through which the state expects to control both the arbitrary power of officials and the power of China's new economic elite. The promotion of legal aid is only one part of a larger political reform project to build up the rule of law.[5]

The legal aid system for workers has been a critical focus of the legal aid project since the 1990s, when labor relations in China began to undergo rapid and destabilizing changes, including the end of lifetime employment in the public sectors and the large-scale movement of rural residents to industrial employment in the cities. An understanding of both the achievements and the problems of legal aid for workers reveals not only the specific challenges of providing legal assistance to a disadvantaged group, but also the more general difficulty of grafting democratic institutions onto an authoritarian political system.[6] Rather than serving as safety valves or control channels for dealing with social contradictions and disputes, labor legal aid institutions promise more than they can achieve and raise expectations before smashing them. Consequently, they expose some of the systemic problems of capitalism within an authoritarian political system. Rather than mitigating the social contradictions of China's rapid but unequal growth, the development of legal aid highlights the barriers to justice for workers across the whole spectrum of China's diverse, dynamic economy.[7] It is the difficulty of maintaining the long-term coexistence of democratic institutions, such as legal aid, within an authoritarian context that leads to increased pressure for an expansion of civil and political rights in China.

Whether one studies how authoritarian regimes sustain themselves through the adoption of legitimating institutions or how authoritarian regimes implode after selectively adopting institutions that are then used against them, the Chinese case is not well integrated, sometimes barely even mentioned, in the debate on the nature of modern authoritarianism. The literature on the adaptation of democratic institutions by authoritarian regimes focuses almost exclusively on the use of elections. This is a debate from which China is excluded, because its electoral systems do not rise to the level of even limited competition beyond the village level.[8] Yet given the significant changes in other aspects of China's political environment, including legal aid, media liberalization, and the development of social organizations, China's case of sustained authoritarianism with some liberalizing changes on the margins deserves more attention. As Larry Diamond notes, "Every step toward political liberalization matters, both for the prospects of a transition to democracy and for the quality of political life as it is daily experienced by abused and aggrieved citizens."[9]

This chapter briefly examines the various types of legal aid that have evolved to serve citizens with labor- or employment-related problems, including the general legal aid offered through the Ministry of Justice system and the specialized legal aid offered through China's official trade union. It then provides an in-depth analysis of the largest university legal aid center for workers in the country. As a university center, it is a specialized center for labor and employment law, sharing some of the characteristics of legal aid offered through the trade union system. There are two major problems for the sustainable development of this type of legal aid: the economics of labor legal aid within a legal profession that does not reward altruism and the level of political suspicion directed at groups that offer help to workers.

The final section focuses on how the legal aid process affects the legal consciousness of recipients, providing a sense of "informed disenchantment," a critical stage in the development of legal consciousness. Although it is common to talk of the rise in legal consciousness in China over the past twenty-some years, the notion of an ever-increasing movement from low to high consciousness misrepresents the actual experience of coming into contact with, learning about, and using the law. This is a complex process of going from high expectations for the law to low evaluations of the legal process and one's chances of success in it.[10]

Informed disenchantment differs from simple disenchantment or cynicism because participation in legal aid, whatever the end result, is an empowering experience. It not only imparts knowledge about laws, regulations, collection of evidence, and legal procedure, but also gives recipients an understanding of the pervasiveness of corruption, the power of capital, the weakness of judges, and the ineptitude of labor arbitrators. To go through the dispute process with a busy, harried paid lawyer is different from being shepherded through the process by someone who explains it and provides insider information about why, despite your win and the court order, the decision is not implemented. Informed disenchantment encompasses both high levels of legal knowledge and a sharp focus on protecting one's legal rights with a negative opinion and adversarial position vis-à-vis legal institutions.

The emergence of more knowledgeable yet disenchanted citizens is not a goal of China's introduction of the rule of law beginning in the 1990s. It is considered a political reform that offers the promise of political modernization without the loss of political power by the ruling party. Its adoption is touted as improving governance, giving access to justice for weak groups, guaranteeing transparency, restraining the arbitrary use of state power, and providing due process. Although in practice these goals often are not met, it is the practice of the rule of law, as people make use of the law to suit their own needs, that reveals other effects unintended by the state.[11] Informed disenchantment of workers as they seek legal aid is not limited to legal aid. It appears when authoritarian regimes attempt to adopt some democratic institutions not as a process of democratization or liberalization but as a means of maintaining social stability and ensuring their hold on power; these institutions then become a new source of instability because they promise what they cannot deliver and educate as they disappoint.

The bulk of the data come from interviews conducted in Shanghai from September 2003 to December 2004 with legal aid recipients, legal aid volunteers, legal aid lawyers, government officials, members of the legal profession, and enterprise managers. Fifty in-depth semistructured interviews were conducted with legal aid recipients whose cases had been picked up by a Shanghai legal aid center for workers.[12] Interviews were also conducted with other models of labor legal aid in other cities and at trade unions.[13]

Legal aid in Shanghai is better funded and more developed than in many other cities. The center where I conducted interviews and the center at the Shanghai Municipal Trade Union (SMTU) are both well known nationally for their representation of key cases and general high level of activism. As in a number of other large cities, such as Beijing, Shenzhen, and Guangzhou, Shanghai's media also do a good job of covering labor issues and highlighting certain cases. Shanghai legal aid can take advantage of a large number of legal professionals, though Shanghai's booming economy creates competition for the attention of good lawyers. Moreover, Shanghai's reputation as a relatively open and international city creates a good atmosphere for legal aid, most of which, outside of the branches of the Bureau of Justice, is dependent on foreign funding for its existence. Shanghai is neither the "head of the dragon" (which assumes that eventually all places will come to look like Shanghai), nor is it completely different from other cities along China's coast that are increasingly wealthy, well integrated into the global economy, and facing the contradictions of rapid economic growth.

The Development of Legal Aid

Experiments with legal aid in China began in the early 1990s with the establishment of legal aid centers at Xi'an's Northwestern University of Politics and Law and at Wuhan University in Hubei province.[14] These developments were followed in 1994 with an announcement by China's minister of justice that China would develop a legal aid system to fit its national conditions. In 1996 the Ministry of Justice began to experiment with legal aid in a number of large cities, including Beijing, Tianjin, Shanghai, and Guangzhou. This experiment was expanded in 1998 with a general call for all provinces and all localities to the county level to establish legal aid organizations under their jurisdictions. This government-run legal aid program is the centerpiece of the government's plan.

In Shanghai the legal aid centers under the jurisdiction of the justice bureau are mainly places for consultations and introductions to practicing lawyers. They are staffed by lawyers on a rotating basis who offer free consultations to applicants. The centers represent a limited number of cases. There are, however, several significant barriers to legal aid both for the general population and for workers specifically.[15] The first barrier is the scarcity of lawyers willing to take on legal aid cases. From their establishment in 1997 to 1999, government legal aid centers in Shanghai took on 2,205 criminal cases and 1,189 civil cases, while offering 69,793 consultations. The number of consultations far outweighs the number of cases actually accepted for representation (though not every person who consults with legal aid needs representation). According to one researcher, the ability of Shanghai legal aid centers to take on cases is far from meeting the demand; lawyers average only one to two cases per year.[16] This inability to satisfy demand is reflected in interviews with workers who tried to use government legal aid when disputes arose.[17] One woman, for example, reported calling up Zhabei district's legal aid only to be told that free consultation did not exist, and the Huangpu district office never answered the phone (26). Another worker was given free consultation at Xuhui district legal aid office but was told by the lawyer that a second round of advice required a fee and would take place at his law office (24).

Shanghai also has strict regulations that limit legal aid to the truly impoverished. Although this hurts the general population, workers in particular almost never qualify for government legal aid unless they have already been laid off or unemployed for a significant period of time (in which case the time limit for bringing a labor dispute would have expired). Pudong New District Legal Aid Center accepts cases only if the recipients have proof of their status as *dibao* (minimum-income guarantee) recipients or as an "impoverished" family; both of these categories require an average monthly salary below 290 RMB, which is less than half the minimum wage.[18] Although many workers receiving the minimum wage cannot afford paid legal representation, they also do not qualify for government legal aid. In Shanghai, lawyers' rates for labor disputes generally start at 5,000 RMB and go up from there, nearly eight times the monthly minimum wage.

Government-run legal aid centers also do not offer specialized legal aid for employment and labor issues. Consequently, some workers who seek government legal aid on labor issues question whether legal aid workers or consulting lawyers are knowledgeable enough about labor laws to win their cases. Given the lack of relevant knowledge, the government centers are likely to transfer cases on labor law to the trade union legal aid centers, which are able to offer specialized advice (interview, July 26, 2004). Therefore, government legal aid, though by far the largest and most extensive legal aid program in China, does not figure prominently in providing legal aid for workers. For free consultation on labor issues, workers are more likely to use the well-advertised and better-staffed hotline at the Shanghai labor bureau, which fields on average ten thousand calls per week.[19] These calls include consultations and reports of enterprise infractions. Many legal aid recipients report using this hotline as a starting point to learn about their legal rights.

In addition to government legal aid, workers with employment disputes in Shanghai have other options: the trade union legal aid system and the university legal aid system. Relative to other areas, both of these systems are well developed in Shanghai. The trade union legal aid center has thirty-five branch offices at the district and industrial trade union level, in addition to a main office at the Shanghai Municipal Trade Union. There are also at least two university legal aid centers that offer labor legal aid, with one center specializing in the protection of women workers' rights.

Trade Union Legal Aid

The development of trade union legal aid is one of the new missions of the All-China Federation of Trade Unions (ACFTU), the government-sanctioned trade union organization. Trade union legal aid staff hope that by concentrating on district, industrial, and local-level legal aid, the trade unions will be able to gain more power vis-à-vis enterprises and more respect from workers. By the end of 2002, trade unions in thirteen provinces had established trade union–run legal aid offices, including 475 branch offices. Shanghai alone has nearly 8 percent of all the branch offices in China. Nationwide, there are 2,298 full- and part-time workers in these offices, though only 8.5 percent have either lawyer credentials or legal worker qualifications. From 2000 until the end of 2002 these centers accepted 178,000 consultations, 14,000 cases for mediation or out-of-court settlement, and 4,168 cases for arbitration or litigation.[20] In other words, out of the 473,943 labor disputes that went to arbitration from 2000 to 2002, trade union legal aid assisted workers 0.8 percent of the time. This abysmally low figure indicates the limits of trade union legal aid.

The SMTU Legal Aid Center was the first legal aid center in the country to be established under the jurisdiction of a trade union. As one of the national showcases for trade union legal aid, the SMTU

204 | Mary E. Gallagher

Legal Aid Center is far above the national average in terms of the number of workers aided and in the number of cases accepted for representation. From its establishment in August 1997 to 2003 the SMTU Legal Aid Center offered legal assistance to 80,000 workers, including 4,558 cases of out-of-court settlement or mediation and 1,596 cases accepted for arbitration and/or litigation.[21] Although the difficulties it faces are less severe than those in other areas, it still experiences the perennial problems of a trade union that lacks independence from the party-state and has a weak or nonexistent presence within enterprises. Trade union legal aid also faces specific problems related to the ability to attract, develop, and retain skilled legal staff.

As a mass organization under the leadership and direction of the Chinese Communist Party, the ACFTU and its local branches must stay within certain boundaries in their attempts to represent and aid workers. In terms of legal aid, these restrictions are manifested in a number of ways. First, the trade union must emphasize out-of-court mediation and settlement. Legal avenues are a last resort, when all other attempts at negotiation and mediation have failed. The trade union often collaborates with the local labor bureau and the justice bureau to achieve results through mediation in accordance with the government's own recent policy of increased support and encouragement of mediation instead of the more adversarial processes of arbitration and litigation. The government's renewed emphasis on mediation since 2000 is in reaction to the overwhelming societal response to increased legalization of labor relations in the 1990s, which led to annual increases of arbitrated labor disputes of more than 40 percent. Since mediation does not require the assignment of blame, government officials hope that a return to mediation as a central mode of resolution will lessen somewhat the sharp contradictions that emerge during labor disputes, especially during collective disputes caused by SOE restructuring. Prior to the passage of the Regulations on the Resolution of Labor Disputes in 1993, enterprise-level mediation was the main mode of dispute resolution, with over 90 percent of recorded disputes resolved through mediation. By 2000, however, enterprise mediation resolved only about 39 percent of the total number of disputes. The new type of mediation as practiced in Shanghai by the SMTU in conjunction with the government bureaus of labor and justice is in part an attempt to replace enterprise mediation.

There is nothing intrinsically superior to arbitration or litigation versus the more informal modes of negotiation and mediation. Informal modes can be less costly and much faster than the alternatives, and may benefit workers who do not have the resources to withstand lengthy court battles. If recent trends are any indication, however, workers themselves prefer either not to mediate or to mediate only after pressing their claims through to the courts, where they believe they will have a better chance of a fair resolution. Workers often express suspicions of the government's encouragement of early mediation, believing that it has more to do with preserving the "face" of the enterprise and its leaders, as well as Shanghai's reputation as a haven for foreign investment, than with solving their problems. Doubts about mediation are reinforced by the reputation of the trade union as generally ineffective in protecting workers' rights and interests.

During nearly fourteen months of interviews and participant observation at a university legal aid center in Shanghai, I did not encounter a single worker who had received aid from the enterprise trade union in resolving a dispute. Some workers expressed disgust at the behavior of the trade union when, during a dispute, the union becomes the go-between for management, attempting to persuade workers to give up their claims and go quietly into unemployment. One woman who was let go when the joint venture enterprise that employed her was dissolved exclaimed: "Help? The trade union gave me dogshit help. Don't even bring it up" (25). Another who was let go by the largest employer in Shanghai, which had a well-developed enterprise union, also dismissed union legal aid: "Hah! They were only going to make me mediate. What's the point? Mediation has no power. Better just go right to arbitration; quicker and you might get some good results!" (26). Another recipient gleefully described how the trade union representative showed up at court to represent the enterprise, only to be thrown out by the judge (19). The experience of using legal aid and actually having received help from a legal aid organization sharpened the anger that recipients felt toward the trade union by demonstrating what kind of work trade unions could do if they were "real." Or, as one recipient, shaking his head at the naïveté of my questions about legal assistance from the trade union, asserted: "No, no, you don't understand. We don't have real trade unions" (27).

Many workers who turned up at the university legal aid center had first gone to the SMTU main legal aid center, which either recommended the university legal aid center, often referring sensitive or difficult cases to the university center, or were told by other workers, also lodging complaints at the trade union, that the university offered more effective assistance. The low level of trust in the trade union negatively affects the efficacy of out-of-court mediation and negotiation. Since 1995, with the opening up of new legal channels for dispute resolution, workers have become less inclined to agree to mediation, particularly when it is an informal process controlled by government officials and trade union cadres.[22] Mediation rates go up at the litigation stage, however, because there is more trust in the courts, as well as the threat of complete defeat with limited ability to appeal.

A second restraint on trade union legal aid is an unwillingness to accept cases that are politically sensitive or that implicate important companies, especially local state-owned companies with close ties to government offices.[23] Trade union legal aid centers prefer to accept cases that are winnable and simple because these will boost their success rate (which they report to be over 90 percent), and they continue to satisfy legal aid requirements without incurring the ire of the government or the party. These political constraints continue to restrain the scope and impact of trade union legal work. At best, trade union legal aid will serve as an alternative to government legal aid that is often not specialized enough to offer adequate advice on labor issues. The trade union picks up this slack and offers advice and consultation to thousands of workers every year in Shanghai alone. The director estimated that in 2003 the central office received 12,000 requests for consultation, while in 2002 the entire SMTU legal aid system received 21,300 requests for consultation.[24] Trade union legal aid will continue to represent workers in a much smaller number of cases. Its role in mediation, particularly of large collective disputes, will also continue as SOEs restructure and privatize. In some Shanghai districts there is a new requirement that migrant workers with disputes first go through mediation before filing an arbitration claim. These are areas where the trade union will continue to play its traditional role as middleman between the enterprise and the workers. In the balance between workers' protection and social stability, trade union legal aid emphasizes preserving stability.

The trade union also faces other problems endemic to legal aid everywhere but that are becoming particularly severe in China. The trade union legal aid center has difficulty attracting and retaining talented legal staff, especially trained lawyers with knowledge of labor and employment law. Retention is difficult because it offers lower salaries than law firms, and a union legal career is mostly a dead end. Although the legal staff at the SMTU main center is young and well trained, it faces high turnover, with four of the six full-time legal staff leaving between 2002 and 2004. One lawyer who left the SMTU legal aid center after six years explained his decision: "There is no future at the trade union. I can't really defend workers, so why stay? Better just to enter into private practice, where I can choose my clients on my own" (interview, July 24, 2004). Although he continues to represent a small number of workers, many of whom are redirected from the trade union to his law firm, he increasingly represents companies in order to build his client development record and to make more money. The legal aid staff at the district level is much less knowledgeable about labor law, usually receiving only a few hours of training before taking positions as legal consultants.

In addition, the trade union does not offer an incentive structure to encourage the legal staff to take on cases of workers who cannot afford a lawyer. Compensation is not tied to the number of cases accepted, nor is there a minimum number of cases required. This partly explains the low proportion of arbitrated and litigated cases that receive help from the trade union. The former trade union lawyer just quoted estimated that each legal staff member at the SMTU main center took on about ten cases per year, which means a total annual caseload of forty to sixty cases for the center overall. At the university labor legal aid center, a single legal staff member takes on sixty cases per year.

University Legal Aid for Workers

University legal aid centers vary considerably in organization, personnel, goals, and targeted social groups. Even among the limited number of legal aid organizations specializing in labor issues, a wide range of structure, organization, and development strategies exists. At this stage in China's legal aid programs, diversity is welcome as legal aid activists try to reach neglected groups, particularly in the countryside.[25] One Shanghai legal aid center, the Labor Law Service Center for Workers at East China University of Politics and Law (ECUPL), was in 2001 the only university legal aid center to offer legal aid on labor and employment law. It has since grown to be the largest nongovernmental legal aid center in China to offer labor legal aid (in terms of number of cases and consultations received). It continues to have a wide-reaching effect in the Shanghai metropolitan area and is well known in other parts of the country through television and newspaper coverage.

Structure and Personnel

The Labor Law Service Center started as a legal aid center for migrant workers in 2001 as a joint program between a professor at ECUPL and the SMTU. It was greatly supported by the director of the legal department at the SMTU, who had become disillusioned with the trade union's limited ability to offer legal aid. (This was three years after the SMTU set up its own legal aid program.) Although this project received funding from overseas, it was in operation for less than one year. At the end of 2001 the ACFTU central offices formally criticized the center, and the SMTU was implicated in this criticism, which focused on the potential political intentions of the center and its staff. The criticism forced the center to disband temporarily, and the SMTU staff members returned to full-time work at the trade union. Those staff who stayed at the center after its reorganization believe that it occurred because the ACFTU was embarrassed that other organizations were doing "their" work more effectively and with greater societal response, and because at the time the central leadership was not paying much attention to the plight of migrant workers, thus making their work harder to justify politically. After Prime Minister Wen Jiabao's decision to make migrant problems, in particular wage arrears, a major social issue, one legal aid activist commented, "We were just a year too early." This clash with the ACFTU, however, is indicative of a relationship that continues to be both collaborative and competitive.

The center reappeared in 2002 with new overseas funding from NGOs and foreign governments and a new, more general mission to protect workers' rights. There was no longer any formal institutional link to the SMTU. From 2002 the center developed rapidly and expanded its influence through innovative institutional collaborations, use of the Internet, and good working relationships with Shanghai media, including newspapers, television stations, and radio programs. In 2003 the center received on average thirty to forty visits or phone calls daily from workers looking for advice on cases or consultations on employment issues. These figures do not include letters and write-ins to their Web site's BBS service. Two full-time staff members, Teacher Lu and a second retired woman cadre, Teacher Fang, from a large Shanghai SOE, handled the flow of workers. In addition to her consultation work, Teacher Lu served as the legal representative of workers in arbitration or in court, while Teacher Fang worked full-time at the center handling consultations and letters. From 2002 to the end of 2003 the center received over ten thousand visits for consultation and handled over eighty disputes at arbitration or litigation. The number of cases accepted for representation is capped at forty to fifty per year by the overseas funding source, which budgets a certain amount for case representation.

Cases are accepted on the basis of their ability to fulfill three requirements: (1) the case should be representative of an important or common problem for workers; (2) the case should be complicated and difficult to win without professional legal assistance; and (3) the case should be a "hardship" case in which the plaintiff has limited economic resources to sue on his or her own. There is a significant amount of flexibility in deciding whether or not to accept a case. With these requirements the legal aid activists hope to exert an influence beyond each individual case by taking on cases that may attract wide publicity and spur revision of legislation or certain administrative practices. The two full-time legal staff members are assisted by a large group of student volunteers. These students take part in a labor law clinic, also funded by an overseas organization, and are required to spend a portion of their semester consulting or assisting the staff members in their caseload. Enrollment in the clinic doubled between 2003 and 2004 from thirty to sixty students. The director of the center is a university professor who specializes in and practices labor law. Each year a small number of his graduate students also take part in activities at the center, usually by assuming some kind of managerial role while also researching cases and other issues for their own master's theses. This structure is dynamic though unstable because of the high degree of turnover as students leave the clinic program and go on to paid internships, jobs, or apprenticeships at law firms.

In 2003 the center established a "labor legal aid network" which was originally intended to include collaboration with sixteen district-level trade union branches across Shanghai. This network, also funded by an overseas organization, supplies each local office with a computer with Internet access and capability to search the center's database for relevant legislation and regulations as well as past cases. Staffed by center volunteers, these "service stations" offer legal consultation and advice to walk-in visitors. Locations in different parts of Shanghai are also more convenient, especially for migrant workers in Shanghai's industrial suburbs. After a long period of negotiation, however, the planned collaboration with the district trade unions fell through. As with the earlier conflict over the migrant worker center, this was partly due to political sensitivity and fear on the part of the trade union that higher levels disapproved of this kind of collaboration. Nevertheless, two district trade unions continued with the intended plan, and four other locations were established at the neighborhood committee level. Although some of the service stations have been more successful than others, this program increased the center's visibility in the suburbs and nearby development zones.

Media

From its inception the center enjoyed supportive relationships with different types of media in Shanghai. These relationships included a weekly column in *Xinmin Evening News,* one of the most popular papers in the city. This Sunday column featured information and commentary on a current case (without divulging the names of the individuals or employers involved). Graduate student volunteers wrote the columns with the assistance of the main litigator and the undergraduate student volunteers on the case. The column ended with the center's name, address, telephone number, and reception hours.

Other newspapers, including *Labor Daily* (the SMTU paper) and *Xinmin Morning News* (a paper with a younger readership than that of *Xinmin Evening News*), ran similar columns but on a less regular basis. *Labor Daily* has a weekly labor dispute analysis section that features commentary from two opposing legal views. The center often participates in the writing of these columns.

Radio and television also play an important role in the dissemination of and wide social dialogue on legal issues. Television programs on legal issues are numerous, running around the clock. These programs tend to be a mixture of reality TV, with dramatic reenactments of the dispute or crime, followed by the legal proceedings, and ending with academic commentary. They reiterate state propaganda about the rule of law and access to justice, including frequent reiteration of certain principles, including "everyone is equal before the law." Labor disputes feature prominently in these programs, and both the university center and the SMTU legal aid center have been regular participants on these legal programs. With their mixture of melodrama and legal facts, they attract a wide audience and provoke topics for social debate. One well-known Shanghai case in 2004 was that of a domestic worker who fell down a flight of garret stairs while mopping the floor. The case fed into a current policy debate about whether domestic workers should be included in worker compensation plans. This particular case was mentioned several times by legal aid recipients and other people when discussing labor disputes. By the summer of 2004 it had led the municipal government to begin a program for occupational injury insurance for domestic workers.

The media's role in disseminating information about cases and increasing pressure on companies and the government to resolve disputes fairly should not be underestimated. The media are used strategically by legal aid centers to mobilize the public's attention. The media also provide free publicity for the center itself. In interviews with disputants, the vast majority of legal aid recipients reported going to the center after reading the weekly column in *Xinmin Evening News*. They also reported that they went on reading the column long after their own disputes had been settled and continued to monitor and evaluate the current state of labor relations and labor conflict in Shanghai. Disputants who have had their cases published in these media columns reported an overwhelming response to them, to the extent that some of them considered changing their phone numbers. In most cases these disputants were sought out by people who had similar problems with their employers, including contract termination, layoffs, and worker compensation disputes.

A savvy media strategy was combined with a well-developed Internet site that further increased the center's nationwide visibility and influence. By 2004 there were at least five or six similar Web sites that provided information about labor and employment issues, legal consultation, downloadable databases of relevant regulations, laws, and other government documents, and a variety of discussions on current cases or hot legal topics. Some of these sites are run by law firms, some by former labor bureau officials turned human resource (HR) consultants, and some by legal aid centers. According to interviews with legal aid recipients, these resources are used primarily by younger or skilled workers who have access to computers and facility in searching for information. The Web sites are also an important resource for the volunteers who serve at the district service station level, giving them immediate access to relevant information to pass on to the recipients. The commentary and discussion sections of these Web sites provide public space for debates on cases and issues, similar to the debate forums in major newspapers.

Money and the Politics of Protection

Financial resources and funding continue to be critical issues for all types of legal aid. Government legal aid is severely underfunded, with some localities offering no budgetary outlays for legal aid but merely placing a new sign at their offices advertising a service that is mostly nonexistent.[26] In these cases, legal aid has become another unfunded mandate of the central government. Dependence on local financing also creates massive differences in access to justice across regions, with the wealthy coastal and large cities doing generally far better than inland areas and the countryside. Trade union legal aid has the greatest access to resources, as it can make use of monies sent by enterprise-level unions, with 40 percent of the enterprise trade union's total budget (equal to 2 percent of the total wage bill) sent to higher levels. The director of trade union legal aid in Shanghai reported that money is not a problem; the trade union can independently allocate part of its annual budget for legal aid, which currently equals about 100,000 RMB per year. University legal aid centers are funded almost entirely by overseas NGOs, foreign governments, and international institutions.

The dependence on foreign financing creates several problems for university legal aid, however, because it increases the political sensitivity of the legal aid project and leads to regular surveillance by state security bureaus and some degree of self-censorship. Although registration as a student-run organization allows legal aid centers a zone of freedom and autonomy under the university's protection, there is no question that the state continues to monitor these organizations and to look out for any signs of political intent, organizational linkups with other groups or individuals, and contacts with overseas activists or dissidents. Leading figures in legal aid are regularly debriefed by state security personnel and are required to report contacts with foreign organizations and individuals. This system may also rely on internal monitors placed within centers to report on activities. It creates an internal atmosphere that is far more cautious and aware of possible political repression than is the case in post-Mao Chinese society in general, where people personally feel freer to criticize government leaders and policies without fear of reprisal.

The constant fear that the legal aid center was too independent and not well protected politically led to a new institutional collaboration during the spring of 2004. After a year of negotiations, the reception offices of the center moved from their off-campus location (actually the former apartment of the director) to the district's trade union offices (in one of the districts that had participated in the labor service station project). At the trade union office, the center occupies two rooms—a waiting room where recipients fill out their consultation form and a room where recipients can meet with the two full-time staff members. In exchange for providing rent-free space, the district trade union is allowed to use all of the statistics from the legal aid center to send to higher levels as evidence of its legal aid work. In practice, there is not much collaboration between the trade union legal staff and the center staff, which handles most of the trade union's legal aid work. According to the center director, this arrangement makes both economic and political sense. Since the space is free, it saves money. At the same time, he can use the apartment as the administrative office for his burgeoning legal practice, which, not unexpectedly, handles for-fee cases, usually representing employers. Politically, this arrangement gives the center an official affiliation with the trade union, reducing its political vulnerability.

Overwhelming dependence on foreign organizations for funding also runs the risk that legal aid centers may become the victims of donor fatigue or boredom.[27] Although this has yet to occur, with seemingly long-term commitments on the part of some organizations, such as the Ford Foundation, to fund legal aid in China for an extended period of time, legal aid activists are aware of the problem but unsure how to fix it. Charitable donations and philanthropy at the start of the twenty-first century were just beginning to develop and to encourage large corporations and wealthy individuals to donate large sums of money to fund social activism and welfare activities. There is a sense among activists that domestic financial support is important for the sustainable development of legal aid and social organizations; but without changes to the Social Organization Law and the tax code, localization is still a long way off. This lack of private donations also affects the Ministry of Justice legal aid project. In 2002 the overwhelming bulk of its legal aid funding came from the government, with donations and contributions from society making up only 2 percent of the total budget.[28]

Career Paths and Sustainable Development

Just as with trade union legal aid, university legal aid suffers from an inability to professionalize and stabilize its staff and to offer young, good lawyers or other legal staff a chance for career development. The university center is staffed mainly by student volunteers, who then graduate and enter law firms or government organizations. Those who remain interested in practicing labor law will most likely become almost full-time representatives of employers. Because the center is a foreign-funded project that runs on three-year grant cycles and is the creation of one charismatic but extremely overworked professor, there is a sense of extreme fragility and institutional shallowness. Although some of this is attributable to the fact that legal aid has developed only recently in China, there is also reason to believe that university legal aid will face difficulties in growing deeper institutional roots over time. In the case of the labor legal aid staff, the alternative is obvious and grows more lucrative over time: to enter private practice and represent companies, a path that not only offers a good salary but also avoids the political sensitivities and pressure of representing workers. One legal aid practitioner explained to the government that his work on behalf of impoverished workers should not be viewed with suspicion because he also spends some time in his law practice representing companies. He smiled when asked if he thought it ironic that representing capitalists puts him in better stead with the Communist Party.

The university center in Shanghai began with close ties to the SMTU, but these ties were broken due to the continuing political sensitivity of organizations that offer legal aid to workers. Three years later, however, the ties were partially restored through collaboration with a district-level union and the sharing of space and statistics. For political reasons, a collaborative rather than a competitive relationship with the trade union is best for the sustainable development of this university legal aid center. For the trade union, collaboration with the university center brings it added respect from workers and also allows more sensitive and difficult cases to be handled, but not directly by the trade union. Given that many trade union activists are themselves dissatisfied with the ability of the union to protect workers' rights, this arrangement is an improvement, but one within limits imposed from above.

Whereas the politics of protection have been solved at least temporarily by this arrangement, the economics of survival continue to be problematic. Reliance on foreign funding has meant a shoestring budget, which is often complicated by numerous approvals, reapplications, and delays. When the center's two-year funding cycle ended in late 2003, the reapplication process began once again, this time for a three-year cycle. Funding for 2004 was not approved until late that year, held up first by the Ministry of Commerce, which must approve the transfer of foreign capital to the university, and then by the foreign organization itself, which, after a leadership shuffle, decided to review all of its ongoing projects before authorizing new outlays. At the same time, the center's good relations with the media became more complicated due to the media's increased attention to profitability. The average number of workers visiting or calling in daily fell in 2004, as regular newspaper columns ended after an editorial shakeup at *Xinmin Evening News*. The new editor subsequently refused to allow free columns and did not permit publication of the center's name and contact information, which he regarded as free advertising. In negotiations with other newspapers to replace the *Xinmin* column, the problem of payment arose again and again, as the increasingly commercialized press refused to provide publicity without compensation.

The center's director continues to combine legal aid work with his own law practice, through which he can earn a good living and offer employment opportunities to some of his students upon graduation. Few university law professors would be interested in pursuing only legal aid because it would condemn them to the meager salary offered by the university, without any chance of using their legal skills and increasing their reputation in the commercial legal market. The combination of labor legal aid and for-fee legal practice is under fire in China, however, as the largest and most prestigious law offices adopt exclusive guidelines, offering representation only to companies, a practice also common in the United States. Exclusive representation prevents conflicts of interest and increases client trust. In China, however, the adoption of this practice will result in a dramatic decrease in the number of lawyers willing to represent employees.[29] In 2004 one of the largest law firms in China offered the center's director an opportunity to set up a "boutique" branch office in Shanghai, specializing in labor and employment law. The one condition was to give up legal aid and representation of employees completely. Although the offer was rejected because of these conditions, given the political sensitivities of offering legal aid to workers and the economic difficulties of making a living, it is unlikely that many lawyers or law professors will tread such an altruistic path.[30]

Despite these pressing problems of politics and economic sustainability, the center is one of many points in a large and growing social network concerned with labor and employment law, human resource management, legal aid, social responsibility, international labor standards, and related issues. This social network is supported through the media, the Internet, and conferences and training workshops that are funded by universities, international NGOs, and multinational corporations. The network itself is fluid and dispersed but vibrant. The associations involved—the legal aid centers, the lawyers' associations, the media groups, the trade unions, the human resource consulting companies—may themselves be fragile, weak, dependent on the government, or mostly interested in making money. But the strength and resiliency of the network is more than the sum of its individual parts. It is the diversity of interests within the network that allows it to survive and thrive in a political atmosphere in which social organizations are considered suspect and potentially subversive.

Legal Aid and Informed Disenchantment: Toward a Better Understanding of Legal Consciousness

The examination of legal aid institutions, including both their institutional collaborations and continuing problems of politics and funding, shows that labor legal aid is innovative but also extremely fragile. The chance for sustainable development of legal aid for workers is hampered both by political suspicion on the part of the party-state and the economics of representation, which increasingly favors employers. These problems have led to a sense of frustration and disenchantment on the part of legal aid activists, and they also have diverted young legal professionals and even for-fee representation of employees from legal aid. This disenchantment exists, however, not in isolation but within a growing social network of legal aid activists, trade union cadres, print journalists and news reporters, law school professors and students, and lawyers who specialize in labor and employment law.

For the recipients of legal aid, informed disenchantment is produced through the experience of using legal aid to file a suit against one's employer. In most cases this is the recipients' first interaction with the legal system, and therefore they often come to the process with little concrete knowledge of the law but with a sense that their rights have been violated and that the legal system will offer them a chance to protect their rights and interests.[31] As mentioned earlier, this informed disenchantment combines a strong sense of one's legal rights and extensive knowledge of labor law with a critical view of the legal system and one's chances in it.

The educative and interactive aspects of legal aid combine with the systemic problems of China's legal system to produce this disenchantment. The major problems that affect recipients' evaluation of dispute resolution include the length and nature of the process, the inability of the courts to implement their decisions, corruption or suspicion of corruption, and the threat of retribution on the part of the employer. Some of these problems are specific to the labor dispute resolution process itself, whereas others are problems within the legal system more generally.[32] The labor dispute resolution process leads to dissatisfaction because it is lengthy and bureaucratic. Aggrieved workers first go through a nonbinding arbitration hearing before they can file a lawsuit in court. The entire process may take one to two years. This arbitration process is run by labor arbitration committees, which are under the direction of the local labor bureau. This two-step process from arbitration to the courts increases the time and money needed to sue. In Shanghai the fee for labor arbitration is 300 RMB, paid by the person who files the suit (in most cases the worker), whereas the court fee is only 50 RMB. Legal aid recipients overwhelmingly hold negative views of the arbitration process, believing it to be biased in favor of companies and investors, staffed by incompetent members of the labor bureau, and mainly existing as a moneymaking source for the local labor bureau. This negative appraisal is supported by the number of appeals to the court system, which in major Chinese cities now exceeds 60 percent of all arbitrated decisions.

The problems of implementation and corruption exist at both the arbitration and litigation levels and are probably together the most important reasons for the low evaluation of the legal system in general and the labor dispute resolution system in particular. For legal aid recipients, many of whom have endured one to two years of court battles, the failure of implementation is a huge blow to their evaluation of the system because it negates the formal victory and highlights the flaws in the system, especially the ability of large companies, mainly well-connected SOEs, to ignore the law with impunity. After losing a suit or winning a hollow victory, plaintiffs are often subject to ridicule by their former employer and even their former colleagues, who have watched the case carefully with their own grievances in mind, thus adding insult to injury. A young plaintiff, Wei, from a foreign-invested supermarket, unsuccessfully sued his employer for overtime pay. He tried to persuade five co-workers with similar grievances to join him in a collective dispute, but they were too afraid, preferring to wait and see what happened in his case. After the court ruled against him for lack of evidence, the company posted the decision in the employees' break room for all to see (14).[33]

The threat of retribution is often most severe in cases in which the plaintiff's suit has been publicized in the media. It can be exacerbated by an unsuccessful case, in which the media exposure comes to naught and leads to problems in finding a new job. Even staying in one's apartment if the apartment is former *danwei* housing becomes difficult (9). Chai, a kindergarten teacher who was fired when pregnant, used the media to attract public attention to her case; but after her former employer closed the school and left for Canada not only did she receive no compensation, but also she found it difficult to get a new job in education, given the wide media coverage of her case. She became wary of the legal system. "How could it be that this weapon that I am supposed to use to protect myself now comes back to injure me?" she asked (27). Retribution can also be indirect, as employers will threaten to (or actually) inform new employers of an employee's lawsuit during the transfer of his or her personal dossier *(dang'an)* or will share information with other enterprises in the locality about problem workers (23). In some cases, SOEs will use connections with the local government and other SOEs to threaten relatives of the plaintiffs with job dismissal (4).

These aspects of informed disenchantment, when combined with many of the positive and innovate aspects of legal aid, can produce plaintiffs who are more knowledgeable, more strategically minded, and less isolated than before their lawsuits. Similar to what Michael McCann's analysis of the pay equity movement in the United States found, labor legal aid may be more effective outside the court than inside as the movement yields social change through its effects on activists, recipients, and those who come into contact with them either directly (friends, relatives, co-workers) or indirectly through media coverage.[34] Three major effects of legal aid are a sense of increased legal knowledge and ability to articulate one's opinions; an understanding of legal strategy, including how to work the process to one's advantage; and inclusion in a network or community of activists, recipients, and volunteers, which reduces feelings of embarrassment and social isolation.

The legal aid process is much more interactive and educative than the other options a worker might use when suing an employer, such as hiring a lawyer for a fee or going through the process without representation. The effects of legal aid therefore are a by-product of the process itself, which relies heavily on cooperation and division of labor between the litigator, the volunteers, and the recipients. At the university center in Shanghai, the main litigator handles about sixty cases per year, as well as engaging in consultation and advisory work for walk-ins. Therefore, plaintiffs often do much of the preparation work themselves, with oversight from the litigator and a student volunteer. This preparation work often includes the collection of relevant evidence, the writing of the complaint, and sometimes the plaintiff attending arbitration on his or her own.

Knowledge and Articulation

Legal aid recipients therefore feel that legal aid gives them the tools necessary to file a suit against their employers. These tools include knowledge and the ability to express themselves in legal language and a representative who can translate their words into the language of the courts. Hu, a taxi driver, sued his company twice, first for termination of his contract and then for workers' compensation. During the second suit, he noted: "This time I had more confidence, I knew more about my rights. I went several more times to the [legal aid] center for consultation, then I went off to arbitration by myself. I was much better at collecting evidence and understanding the process than before. I would have had no chance without Teacher Lu and the student. The student helped me write my complaint; I didn't know how to write it" (15). A former crane operator on the Shanghai docks expressed similar sentiments after she contested her termination: "What if I didn't have legal aid! I cried at every place, I had never thought of filing a lawsuit, but I would have starved to death if I had stayed at home on 100 RMB a month! I wouldn't have been able to speak were it not for Teacher Lu there to help me speak" (19). A woman working in a local hotel sued with her husband's help after being terminated, but they did not feel that they could master the law alone. Their feeling was that "the law isn't bad; it's the people who are supposed to implement it. . . . We bought a book about labor law at a bookstore and read every line. We wanted to make sure we hadn't done anything wrong. But it wasn't until we went to the legal aid center that we really began to have confidence. Legal aid really should be expanded so that every worker can get it. Right now the law doesn't help us weak groups. . . . We went to the first arbitration alone with our relatives. We didn't know how to speak; we had things to say but couldn't say them" (4).

Like this couple, many legal aid recipients are angry and frustrated with the end result of the legal process but grateful for the knowledge gained. Zhu, a debt collector for a failing SOE, still had hope that he would win at the next appeal: "I've learned enough about the law that I can use it, but I haven't yet found my Judge Bao.[35] I've learned the strategy of how to present evidence and how to win at the next appeal" (8). Yao, an accountant who was fired after reporting irregularities at his company to the government, suspected that his case had not been settled fairly due to the overwhelming political influence of his former state employer. "I protected the country's interest; who protects my interests?" he asked. "We're fools to do this, we get nothing, we get unemployed, we get punished, we're the ones who become unstable. . . . I'll go to Beijing, I'll go the United Nations to get this case settled justly. To have laws that are not followed, it's more rotten than not having laws at all. . . . Legal aid helped me express my views even when I was very frustrated. It's a place where we can speak the truth" (11).

In addition to learning about key laws and regulations and legal procedures, those who become informed about the law also gain other kinds of necessary knowledge, including the ability to know when they are being fairly treated, when they are being coerced or deliberately intimidated, and when the process is being thwarted by corruption and close connections between officials and employers. One former engineer, Li, whose arm had been severed by a machine, reported that when he told the court recorder the amount of economic compensation he was seeking, the recorder mocked him, telling him he was crazy and would never get so much money for his injury. Li knew that it was inappropriate for the court recorder to comment on his case. He also suspected that the recorder was intentionally trying to get him to reduce his demands and to be more willing to mediate and accept less. Li said: "If I hadn't already gone this far and learned so much, I would have been frightened out of my mind. But I wasn't" (18).

Strategy

As with knowledge and articulation, using legal aid can radically affect a plaintiff's approach to the legal process. Plaintiffs learn from experience the differences between the arbitration process and the courts, the most effective way to use the "letters and visits" system in concert with a suit, and how to get the media's attention so that it helps the case in court.[36] The other area where legal aid changes the plaintiffs' behavior is in the collection of evidence, which is often one of the thorniest problems for an employee, since the employer frequently controls access to nearly all the relevant evidence. Yao, a machine operator from an old sewing machine factory, with a "letters and visits" folder six inches thick, reported that he would not sue again. After two years, it had taken too much time and energy, without a successful outcome. Nevertheless, he also said that he now regularly gives advice to his friends and fellow colleagues: "I put a lot of emphasis on making sure that they know how to get the necessary proof and evidence" (3). Like many disenchanted plaintiffs he also continues to hope that something will influence his suit, which went to the Shanghai High Court for a final appeal, for instance, the 2004 addition of a human rights protection clause in the Chinese constitution. A young manager in a large multinational supermarket in Shanghai who sued unsuccessfully for overtime also reported that he would not sue again; it took too much time and was not worth it. But then he paused and said: "But if I had enough evidence, I might try again. I'm more careful about that sort of stuff now. I'm always looking for things that I might need, just in case [of another lawsuit]" (14). Li, the engineer who had lost his arm, was also preparing for another suit because he knew that his company would soon be privatized or closed: "I'm collecting evidence now on the illegal sale of assets, and as soon as they announce the restructuring, I am going to be ready to sue" (18).

Learning new strategies can be particularly important when the grievances are widely shared by workers, thus creating an opportunity for a collective suit, which attracts more public attention and is more worrisome to employers. Legal aid recipients often become the underground organizers of collective disputes as they search out workers with similar complaints and persuade them to join in a suit. This can be difficult to achieve, however, if the workers are still in their positions and prefer to see first what happens to their colleague (14).[37] In one collective dispute represented by the legal aid center, a former worker served as the main strategic organizer of multiple consecutive suits and worked with the center to maintain the workers' shared commitment to victory (20).

Inclusion

Workers who sue are concerned about their social status and their public reputation, often hiding the fact of their lawsuit from their neighbors, friends, and even close relatives. This reticence speaks to the continuing belief, as reported by Du, an old worker who was left with nothing when his SOE was privatized, that "only bad people file suits." Others are embarrassed that they had been fired or laid off, fearing that others will think they had done something wrong. The frequency with which these sentiments are expressed indicates the level of social and psychological barriers to legal mobilization.[38] Most people decide to sue because they have no choice, having exhausted the other options of negotiation, or because their employer rejected any chance for negotiation or reconsideration.[39]

Participation in legal aid can mitigate, at least partially, plaintiffs' feelings of isolation or embarrassment. When workers first go to consult, they enter a space filled with other people like them, and legal aid activists and volunteers listen empathetically to their problems. In the waiting room, recipients share information about their cases and other matters. Some recipients first encountered information about the center from the media or from several open-air consulting forums set up in public locations during the year. Yao, from the sewing machine factory, first heard of the center from a television program and then went to an open-air forum, where he waited in line for five hours. "On TV [the director of the center] always spoke with reason, so I thought that I might have a chance. His line was the longest at the forum, but I waited" (3). During these periods of consultation and waiting, recipients learn that their cases are not unusual, nor are they necessarily a reflection on them. A young worker who also went to a forum was struck by how serious the problems were of the older people crowded around him. "I thought if [the director of the center] can help these people, then surely he should be able to win my case," he reasoned (23). Another woman who burst into tears while looking for help at the trade union offices was told about the center by the other people there (24).

Inclusion in a space or network such as legal aid can be an empowering experience for people who are otherwise discouraged, angry, isolated, and often deeply depressed. Li, the injured engineer, felt that he "went from being someone with a future to something that wasn't even human" (18). For people who have been laid off, summarily dismissed, or otherwise pushed out of their workplace, legal aid becomes the "turning point" from an experience in passive humiliation to an aggressive battle for rights and economic security. Ying, a young Jiangxi woman who sued her employer twice, reported that "as an outsider, who didn't know anyone in Shanghai, the law was my only choice. I never thought about 'letters and visits.' Of course no one would have paid the slightest attention to me. . . . This strengthened my personality; nobody can just take away what is mine. I used to just give up. I sued the second time because I had the time and the experience" (13).

This new sense of empowerment (even while remaining deeply angry with the results of the process) leads many plaintiffs into new roles as "little experts." Their newfound expertise in labor law leads many to give advice, copy materials, introduce friends to legal aid, and even serve as witnesses in the cases of other aggrieved workers. The forklift operator who reported "crying all the time during my lawsuit" is now assisting a relative with his own case: "My husband's brother-in-law now has a workers' compensation case. I helped him with the case at first and then introduced him to the center. . . . Now everyone comes to consult me. I've become a little expert" (19). Yang, the former taxi driver, reported: "Now I give a lot of advice to my friends and other drivers. We drivers, we're exhausted; we have no time to read newspapers or books. I've read and reread the *Two*

Hundred Questions for Older Workers [a book given out by the center] and photocopied it to give to other drivers with problems. We want to restore our rights, but we need to know what procedures, who to look for" (15). Zhang and her husband, who gave up her suit after local officials threatened him with dismissal, are extremely angry, even linking the failed suit to the theory of the "three represents."[40] Zhang said: "Many friends and former colleagues call us and ask us. We've become the experts now. Through the experience I've really learned a lot—how to fight against the government and the higher levels" (4). Her husband exclaimed angrily at the end: "Why do they think so many people are going to Beijing to appeal? Because the law is useless. Those 'three represents' are wrong. What about the interests of the workers?" Old Du, whose case remained up in the air without final implementation, summed up his experience in a way that captures the common path of a legal aid recipient from passivity, to knowledge, to strategy, to anger:

> I didn't know a single thing about labor law [before this experience]. During Mao's time, everything was handled for us, like children. I used to think that only bad people file suit. Now I know everything . . . arbitration, first appeal, second appeal. I'm famous. People ask me for interviews. [After the TV program] my phone started ringing off the hook, didn't stop ringing for a week, all these old workers wanting to know about my case and to resolve their own problems. An old worker from Bayer waited outside my door to talk to me. I gave him some advice and then later served as his witness in court on the question of job transfers in SOEs. I am so angry and frustrated. I wasn't like this before. My poor parents are at home. They are over eighty years old! I'll do anything to help these kinds of cases (9).

"Informed disenchantment" is a direct consequence of people's participation in the state-led project of rule of law. Those who use legal aid have taken the state seriously and responded to changes in the political and judicial arenas. The act of suing one's employers is still firmly within the realm of "legal political behavior," and it remains for the most part an individual act motivated by individual grievances.[41] Suing with the help of legal aid, however, can be an empowering experience that educates and introduces isolated individuals to a community which offers support and strategy.

Labor legal aid organizations play immensely important roles, but within an unwelcoming environment. These organizations remain fragile and subject not only to the pressures of politics but also to the economics of a legal profession that does not reward altruism. As part of a larger network of organizations and individuals that criss-crosses state-society boundaries, however, labor legal aid organizations might become deeply rooted in China. It is significant, after all, that the trade union uses legal aid to do what it cannot, even to the point of appropriating the university legal aid center's records and achievements as its own. In tandem with the media, these legal aid organizations have banded together more than once to attract public attention and shore up needed support. In the case of Chai, the pregnant kindergarten teacher, the judge gave her the name of a reporter, who gave her the name of a legal aid center, which in concert with the media publicized her case. The judge did this in order to make his own ruling easier by balancing the connections of the employer with the pull of public opinion (27). In the case of Old Du, when his former employer continued to refuse to implement the decision, the SMTU, the university legal aid center, and a cooperating law firm all joined together to write letters of support to the higher court. These linkages and relationships cannot be located firmly in time or space because they have no fixed position, but they are indicative of growing public space and community.

It was Samuel Huntington who first argued that institutionalization is critical for the long-term survival of authoritarian regimes.[42] Andrew Nathan revives these ideas with his analysis of China's "authoritarian resilience."[43] In the comparative literature generally, there is persuasive evidence that well-institutionalized single-party regimes are far more likely to endure than are other kinds of authoritarianism.[44] In addition to the more orderly machinations at the top of China's political structure, Nathan credits "the establishment of institutions for political participation and appeal that strengthen the CCP's legitimacy among the public at large" for the party's recovery post-1989.[45] In practice, however, participatory institutions are affected by the milieu in which they exist; their authoritarian antecedents cannot be forgotten. The ability of these institutions to impart legitimacy should be assumed not because of the state's advertisement of their creation, but rather because of the way in which they are experienced by their intended recipients. Workers come away from legal aid and the legal process with a better sense of their own dissatisfaction and with the knowledge that they are part of a large and growing network. It may be that these institutions are not the durable foundations of authoritarianism but rather the bridges that connect actors within the state and society who are looking for change.

10 | Is Labor a Political Force in China?

Since the mid-1990s, labor unrest in China has been described as a source of political and social instability. Surveys undertaken by the Chinese Communist Party have noted the "collective," "antagonistic," "emotional," and increasingly "well-organized" nature of worker petitions and protests.[1] Prominent Chinese academics have focused attention on the plight of the working class—long-term unemployment, poverty, and stark inequity in social distribution—and the potential for dissatisfied workers to become the catalyst for social movements and upheavals.[2] Several China scholars have echoed such concerns. Dorothy Solinger, for instance, has invoked E. P. Thompson's renowned image of the "crowd" in eighteenth-century England to describe the "legitimacy-challenging crowd" formed by the multitude of pauperized, unemployed urban workers.[3] Against such assessments, there are dissenting views on the degree of political challenge posed by Chinese workers. Marc Blecher has found that a majority of workers accept the hegemony of the market economy.[4] Martin Whyte, meanwhile, has written about countervailing tendencies that thus far have prevented worker protests from becoming a serious threat to state authority. These tendencies include the gradualist approach to layoffs, the exit option offered by the buoyant market economy, and the state's usually swift concessions to workers' economic demands.[5]

Despite the differences, these analyses depict workers poised between stability and instability, consent and opposition. Such dichotomous frameworks do not lend themselves to more nuanced questions such as: What actual social and political changes does worker activism champion? And if workers challenge regime legitimacy, what level of the political system is at stake?

Deng Xiaoping's "southern journey" in 1992 to highlight the special economic zones and to reinvigorate the economic reforms sparked widespread privatization and bankruptcy of state-owned enterprises (SOEs), pension and welfare reforms, an influx of global capital, and intensified economic polarization and inequalities. These policies were accompanied by more profound changes in workers' livelihood and politics than in the previous reform decade. In the 1990s labor contention became a localized and cellular force of political challenge and social change, based predominantly on local and cellular mobilization and institution-building. These salient features of labor activism are shaped by the structural tendencies of the reform political economy, especially political decentralization and economic differentiation across and within localities. Moreover, labor protests, at their most effective, but not in all cases, have resulted in not only the repayment of pensions and wages to aggrieved workers, but also more fundamental pension reform, policy changes in local governments' handling of unemployment and bankruptcy procedures, and the punishment of abusive local cadres. Therefore, any workers' "legitimacy challenge" is primarily local. Because political authority has been decentralized and the reach of the state is constrained by market forces, the central government has responded with more laws and more emergency funds.

Protest Politics and Institution-Building

Several influential accounts of Chinese popular struggles, including labor struggles, have concurred on the greater significance of the "heroic," or "movement," mode of politics over institution-building. They point out that this mode of politics is a result of the Chinese state's long tradition of excluding the institutionalized participation of organized political opposition.[6] Indeed, since the June 4, 1989, crackdown on the Tiananmen demonstrations, the political will to exclude organized dissent has persisted with the increase in protests, petitions, and strikes.

Yet at the same time, economic liberalization and increased exchanges with the global community have inadvertently created new opportunities for reforming or creating labor institutions. With limited success, union cadres have sought to increase the organizational leverage of basic-level unions. Among those excluded by the official unions—the unemployed, retirees, migrant workers, and dissidents—some have risked organizing underground unions. In addition, there have been lively but quiet grassroots efforts to build new labor institutions under the rubrics of "service" and "education" rather than unionism or advocacy. A number of these nascent organizations have been established by individuals with "civil courage," which is defined as "daring to act because of one's convictions, even at the risk of a high price for this conviction."[7] Funded by overseas foundations and the transnational social movement community, and professing to enhance workers' capacity and self-protection, a significant number of migrant education centers, service stations, clinics, and legal aid hotlines have sprung up in major cities. Such nascent labor NGOs are poised to engender a new generation of rights-conscious and legally savvy workers. The existence and development of these organizations demonstrate that the self-organizing capacity of Chinese society is growing. Therefore, while workers' political efficacy is debatable, workers constitute a potential force for grassroots social change.

Cellular Activism and Local Effects

Even where they exist, Chinese statistics on popular protests are sketchy and unsystematic. Still, available data consistently depict a general picture of proliferating labor activism since the mid-1990s. The number of "letters and visits" *(xinfang)* and collective petitions *(jiti shangfang)* soared remarkably at the start of the twenty-first century. According to the State Letters and Visits Bureau, in 2000 a total of 10.2 million petition cases were submitted to provincial, county, and municipal offices nationwide, an increase of 115 percent over 1995. Over 76 percent of the petitioners were included in "collective petitions," defined as those involving five people or more. In 2000 the total number of collective cases increased 280 percent and collective petitioners 260 percent over those in 1995. Among the collective petitions in cities, more than 60 percent are lodged by SOE employees.[8]

Furthermore, the volume of labor dispute arbitration increased steadily since the mid-1990s, from 19,098 cases in 1994 to 154,621 cases in 2001. In 1997, out of a total of 70,792 arbitrated disputes, 854 protests (or 1.2 percent of all disputes) were triggered by the arbitration process itself.[9] This rare official statistic, not seen in any other official statistical yearbooks thereafter, provides a glimpse of the tenuous boundary between institutionalized and non-institutionalized conflict resolution.

Finally, despite scattered figures on the numbers of protests and demonstrations from various sources, all concur on a rising trend of popular protests by workers. According to the Ministry of Public Security, collective protests and riots, including labor protests, rose consistently from 8,700 in 1993 to 32,000 in 1999.[10] In 2003 the number of mass incidents reached 58,000, involving 3 million people, and increased to 87,000 incidents in 2005.[11] The labor bureau in Shenzhen, China's most developed export industrial base, with more than 7 million migrant workers, officially registered about six hundred "unexpected" incidents each year from the late 1990s on.[12]

Organization and Mobilization

Despite the occasional neighborhood-based actions, bankruptcy and nonpayment protests are the most common and most politically sensitive. Drawing on field data collected in Guangdong and Liaoning, I describe the dynamics of what can be called "cellular activism." Other scholars have documented cases of worker struggles in other parts of China that follow a similar dynamic.[13] The focus here is on the Liaoyang protests in spring 2002 as an example of the exception that proves the rule. In-depth interviews with key organizers reveal the prevailing logic of cellular activism. Behind the façade of cross-factory participation were protest organizers from one factory who insisted on excluding workers at other factories from participating in planning meetings and the leadership hierarchy. The massive cross-factory turnout was a chance incident that portended the specter of unintended radicalization rather than the result of the workers' strategy or capacity for lateral mobilization.

Generally, young migrant workers and elderly pensioners and laid-off workers pursue both bureaucratic and direct action when a labor dispute arises. Lodging complaints with the government is a well-established channel of political participation under Chinese Communist rule. Dating back to the Communist base areas in the 1930s, petitioning to the letters and visits bureau is an institutionalized and legitimate means of making demands and expressing popular discontent with the government. Even young migrant workers in Shenzhen know about *shangfang*, or petitioning the government, citing examples of rural kin or fellow villagers' petitions to the letters and visits bureaus at home. Officials handling these petitions usually direct workers to labor arbitration committees or pressure state enterprises to redress the workers' grievances. When repeated visits to the bureaus fail to deliver owed pensions, or when migrant workers are frustrated by the pro-employer decisions of labor arbitrators or judges, petitioners may take their demands from the courtrooms to the streets. Many incidents of workers blocking traffic, demonstrating outside government buildings, or marching through downtown streets have their origins in mass outrage against official failure to redress legal and legitimate grievances.

Traffic blockages illustrate how activism can spill over from city government to downtown streets. On the morning of May 22, 2002, more than sixty construction workers went to the petition office of the Shenzhen city government to complain about wage arrears. The office directed them to the labor bureau, which then declared that because the workers had no written contract with the contractor, and could not prove the registration of the construction company for which they worked, the labor bureau was unable to investigate this case of wage arrears. The workers, already frustrated and emotional, again returned to the city government to seek help. When the official there insisted that he could not do anything, the workers yelled at him and angrily marched down the main road. When they arrived at the intersection in front of the huge portrait of Deng Xiaoping in downtown Shenzhen, several of the workers decided to sit down in the road. Others quickly followed, forming a human chain that held up traffic for about fifteen minutes. Some twenty policemen soon arrived, grabbed the workers, and pulled them to the sidewalk but did not arrest them.

One of the three worker representatives, who talked about the workers' anger and their predicament, explained:

All of us are from Sichuan. We have worked for three months for this contractor, and have completed five to six floors every month, working twelve hours each day. But we have never been paid a penny. The boss [the contractor] only loans us money, several hundred RMB a person, from time to time. He said the big boss [the construction company] has a cash problem. We went on strike twice and each time they promised to pay within a week. The last time we went on strike, on May 17, the boss threatened us, announcing in public, "I'll kill anyone who dares to lead a strike again." We realized that we could not trust him anymore, and we began to worry about our personal safety.

Another said:

We workers worked legally and tried legitimate means but got no response. They [the government] are forcing us to shed blood, to take the criminal route. As we left the city government and walked down the street, some of us suggested bombing the company. Others cursed that it's better to be run over by cars than to work without getting paid.

The third one said:

We did not plan this action; it was so natural for everyone to follow once several workers decided to sit down in the road. When the police came to remove us, some workers told them that being arrested was good. At least we wouldn't have to worry about food and lodging.[14]

Savvy and shrewd workers such as these seek to focus public attention on their plight, publicize their grievances ("creating public opinion," as some put it), and undermine the image of the city as stable and therefore capital-friendly. For instance, a popular strategy among migrant workers in Shenzhen is to use the local media to publicize their grievances and to stage public actions to generate social pressures on the government. At the height of the SARS epidemic in 2003, when many restaurants went out of business, leaving their employees without jobs and with unpaid wages, the local government, eager to keep migrant workers in the city and minimize the spread of the epidemic to the countryside, recognized the urgency of paying the migrant workers their back wages, without which they would have been forced to return to their home villages. A group of restaurant workers demanding back wages called up all the major newspapers in Shenzhen and, carrying banners demanding "Return Us Our Blood and Sweat Money" and "You the Public Should Decide for the Working People," organized a march down major city streets. "We wanted to appear on the television news, to alert the local community. We need to make disturbances to create social influence. But only reporters from a few newspapers came," one worker complained.[15]

Similar use of public pressure on local government to address their grievances can be found among retirees and laid-off workers in the northeast. Elderly workers expressly stated that their goal in blocking traffic was to use hierarchical relations as leverage on the local government bureaucracy; they caused disruptions so as to attract the attention of higher-level officials, who could then bring pressure on the subordinate officials directly responsible for their case or on their firm to pay them their wages and pensions.

Two veteran petitioners, who were owed pensions in Shenyang, explained this logic:

> We only want to make one statement by blocking the road: superior officials must come to take a look! We only want our pensions paid. Premier Zhu Rongji himself promised no arrears when he visited Shenyang in 2001. The central government has announced 49 RMB extra subsidies for us retirees. Work unit leaders made us sign a paper saying that they would pay us later, but so far nothing has happened. Providing pensions is Chairman Mao's national policy! Like squeezing toothpaste from a tube. . . . People here say, "Big disturbance, big solution; small disturbance, small solution; no disturbance, no solution."[16]

They continued:

Every time the central government announced publicly that pensions must be paid in full, we became very upset. All of us have television at home and we always watch it. Who would not know about these announcements? Every day, old people gathered in the elderly activity room in our neighborhood, smoking and playing chess, poker, or mahjong. Someone would comment on our unpaid pensions and suggest blocking the road. When we got angry, we would just go instantly, or say, "Tomorrow morning at 8 or 9." Once we arrived at the destination, we did not say a word—no banner, no slogan, just stood there. We just wanted to create public opinion, pressuring leaders of the machinery and electrical works bureau to talk to the enterprise director. Usually included were several hundred retirees, not that many if you consider that we have 1,500 retirees for the entire work unit. Traffic police would arrive several minutes after we began our blockade. They did not intervene, just politely asked which enterprise we were from. They said they were just doing their job, and urged us to try to move toward the sidewalk. Police would come too, and even urge the traffic police not to push us too hard. They were afraid that the elderly people would get hurt. Passers-by who were on bikes were very sympathetic and were curious to know which enterprise we were from. But people in buses or automobiles would swear at us, saying "Those who should die, live." . . . Very soon, local government officials would come, and we would tell them we were owed our pensions and had no money to see the doctor. They usually were very patient. Once they promised to investigate or to get us paid the following week, we would just disband and go home. The more workers present, the higher level of officials would come down."[17]

Leveraging the bureaucratic hierarchy has led workers to petition Beijing. Some worker representatives in my study from Tieling or Fushun in Liaoning formed petition teams of four or five people and took their grievance to the capital. They arduously compiled background materials, studied the relevant laws and regulations, wrote petition letters, consulted with lawyers, and collected trip donations from their co-workers. The workers were disappointed when months later they found out that their petition letters had ended up on the desks of local officials again. When talking with them about their faith in the central government, I found them ambivalent, admitting that the center is responsible for the appointment of the corrupt and irresponsible local cadres. But still they insisted that the center is *more* just and righteous because it issues more regulations favorable to workers' interests. The main problem remains one of local implementation.

A confluence of factors produces this kind of cellular activism. First, the prevailing view among aggrieved workers is that their interests are workplace-specific, and therefore the most effective unit of mobilization is the factory. A gap exists between workers' awareness of common predicaments and the absence of cross-enterprise action, as seen in Tiexi, where residents claimed that retirees in the majority of enterprises blocked the streets. Asked why they did not apply their slogan "Big disturbance, big resolution" to joint action with other factories, a uniform response would be: "It is no use coordinating with retirees from other factories, because some firms are more generous or stronger financially, and their workers get more subsidies. Some leaders take our interests to heart, while others don't care whether we feel cold or warm." And indeed, factories had different subsidy packages for their retired employees, a practice encouraged by the government to increase the benefits of elderly workers whenever the firms could afford it. The problem of pension arrears existed in different degrees across firms, depending on their profitability and the corruption of their cadres. Retirees often bitterly complained of injustices because of unequal retirement benefits across firms. Interviewees in Shenyang complained that the casting factory paid its retirees an average of 600 RMB per month in 2003, while their counterparts in the oil and chemicals or electricity companies were paid more than 1,000 RMB.

At the same time, within firms there are differences in benefits that may appear insignificant to outsiders but are serious to workers. Retirees' pension packages differed according to the starting and termination dates of their employment, with periodic raises given by the central government to pre-Liberation workers (i.e., those who started working before December 1948, when the CCP liberated the northeast) or pre-PRC workers (i.e., before the establishment of the PRC in October 1949). Retirees were further divided by policies that gave special preferential treatment to former workers in positions that involved working in high or low temperatures, or in industries that involved occupational hazards and diseases. Lower-paid retirees were suspicious of the higher-paid retirees because they were able to maintain more comfortable lifestyles, even if they were only partially paid.

Therefore, cellular activism describes not only the locality- or work unit–based unrest but also the intra-firm divisions among workers who have formed themselves into different "interest groups," to use their own terminology. Refined categorizations among laid-off workers (due to illness, enterprise financial difficulties, or bankruptcy) and among pensioners (marked by a specific cut-off date for the beginning of employment and retirement) all involve different entitlements and priorities in receiving payments. These state policy differences reflect what workers call "different interest groups" within work units. Sometimes such a division of interests percolates through workers' families and creates domestic tensions. Family members working for the same enterprise may find their interests at odds with others' due to government policies. In a prolonged protest involving a textile mill in Tieling, Liaoning, management duly paid the pensioners but refused to satisfy the laid-off workers' demand for a severance payment. Such differentiation can cause an elderly parent and a middle-aged son to stop talking to each other.

Workers attribute their plight to local political and economic forces. Since the mid-1980s, SOE reform has emphasized enterprise and managerial autonomy, inter-firm competition, and a performance-based remuneration system, resulting in vast differences in enterprise profitability and wage levels, housing, and medical and retirement benefits. Moreover, fiscal decentralization entails decentralization of budgetary responsibility for welfare. The problem, as Mark Frazier aptly puts it, is that pension and welfare reform is an " unfunded mandate" thrust upon the localities by the center.[18] Consequently, decentralization and market competition have created a kaleidoscope of fine-grained social and economic differentiations across factories in the same locality. And despite the overhaul of the work unit welfare system, Chinese workers' entitlements at work and after retirement continue to be closely tied to their work organizations. The availability of pensions, unemployment benefits, and industrial injury compensation still depends on the employing units' ability and willingness to contribute to insurance funds, pooled at the city or county levels. Migrant workers realize that legal wage levels are set by the local city governments, and the factory as a legal entity bears the responsibility to pay into the social security and injury insurance accounts. Therefore, the localized and workplace-oriented organization of workers' interests results in local and cellular activism.

Both state-owned enterprises and non-state factories share similar ecological and social features that can be conducive to workers' collective action. Dormitories for migrant workers in export factories and residential quarters for state workers are geographically close to the factories, forming self-contained, all-encompassing communities where production and social activities take place. They facilitate communications and the aggregation of interests, especially at the moment of mass layoffs or dismissals.[19]

In brief, workers' cellular activism arises from the local and work unit–based organization of interests and the readily available organizational resources provided by encompassing communities centered on the workplace. Workers' targets are usually local power-holders, because they are the only remaining access points in what is popularly perceived as an agentless and self-regulating market economy. Workers generally seek to exert mass pressure and to leverage the existing bureaucratic hierarchy rather than to pursue the risky path of lateral organization. Cellular resistance and hierarchical political orientation arise from the concrete ways in which interests are constituted. They do not represent a less developed or myopic form of politics, nor do they indicate a traditional culture or conservative mentality.

The Liaoyang Incident: Specter of Class Rebellion?

The specter of a working-class uprising, challenging the prevailing system, appeared during the mass protests in Liaoyang, Liaoning, in the spring of 2002. The international media reported that workers from some twenty factories were involved, demanding the removal of local leaders. These two features distinguished the Liaoyang incident from ordinary worker protests. Interviews with core organizers of the protests, however, actually show that Liaoyang is just another case of prolonged cellular mobilization that evolved, through a "qualitative leap" (the workers' expression) into an unintended radical episode. It began with workers from one factory, the Liaoyang Ferro-Alloy Factory, who had engaged in a four-year struggle with local officials. Liaotie, as the firm was locally known, was once a pillar enterprise employing seven thousand workers in its heyday, the fourth-largest plant in Liaoyang, an industrial city of 1.7 million known for its huge chemical plant, numerous military factories, and steel and industrial equipment and machinery plants. With the appointment of Fan Yicheng as director and party secretary in 1993, the firm's fortunes slipped, and since 1996 production had been periodically suspended. Beginning in 1998 workers made many attempts to petition local and Beijing officials with complaints about managerial corruption, illicit transfers, privatization of state assets, and unpaid wages, pensions, and medical reimbursements. Despite their efforts, the local government did not act to alleviate the workers' plight.

In May 2000, two years before the mass protests, more than one thousand Liaotie workers blocked the main highway from Liaoyang to Shenyang, demanding payment of wages and pensions. Armed police arrived and arrested three of the organizers. The next day, workers regrouped and launched a siege of the city government building, holding a banner reading "Guilty of Arrears." They demanded a solution from the mayor, release of their leaders, and payment of wages. One police source confirmed that at that time, some two thousand workers were still employed at the factory but had not been paid for sixteen months, since 1998, while two thousand laid-off workers and one thousand retired workers had not received their benefits for three to six months.[20] Though the leaders were later released, the workers still did not receive their pay. The only gratification they obtained was that their actions were reported by the overseas media, especially by the Voice of America, which was popular in Liaoyang.

The turning point toward radicalization came in late 2001, when the local government and the court declared Liaotie bankrupt. In an open letter titled "Government Eats Its Words, Workers Demand

Results," workers invoked the Bankruptcy Law and a speech by Chinese president Jiang Zemin in which he urged that "all levels of government officials and bureau cadres must care deeply for the masses, be responsible for them, and promote their interests" to charge local leaders with malfeasance. Liaoyang's leaders, both before and after the bankruptcy of the Liaoyang Ferro-Alloy Factory, never complied, the letter said, with this instruction. The letter continued:

> The Enterprise Law and the Bankruptcy Law both formally require an open and thorough accounting investigation before an enterprise can be declared bankrupt. But our city officials joined hands with enterprise management to blatantly ignore the People's Republic Constitution, the Trade Union Law, and other laws, to ignore the strong opposition of all employees, and to use the threat of force by local public security and armed police, and made four attempts to arrest and harass protesting workers and coerce some worker representatives in the workers' congress to vote for bankruptcy. Why did they do that? Do they dare to explain to the masses? On November 5, 2001, three days before declaring us bankrupt, all the machinery, raw materials, doors, and windows were taken away. Whose fault is this?[21]

The letter went on to list some twenty additional economic demands, such as payment of all back wages, livelihood allowances (182 RMB a month), retirees' enterprise welfare allowances, medical and housing subsidies, certified property rights for housing, and severance payments for laid-off workers.[22]

When I visited this factory at the height of the rebellion in March 2002, open letters and posters depicting the workers' grievances and demands were posted on the walls in the main building. Neatly typed and printed on large 11.5 by 15 inch white paper, these posters were intended as calls to action, addressing their readers as compatriots (tongbao) or the masses (qunzhong) of Liaoyang. One informant likened them to the "black newspapers" (heibao) that he saw in public places in Liaoyang prior to the protest. Smaller flyers were posted in Liaotie's residential quarters, announcing the time and date of the protests. One Liaotie protester related the ease and success of their mobilizing effort while denying that they were "mobilizing" (dongyuan) others, a term that had the connotation of manipulation with subversive intent. The protester explained that "workers in this factory have relatives and spouses in other factories, spreading the news and solidarity across firms. . . . We did not mobilize other factories, but we used 'Open Letters' as a way of encouraging more Liaoyang people to join us. We only posted flyers announcing the time and date of gathering and petitioning in our own residential neighborhoods. But anyone who wanted to find out could come and see these flyers."[23] He went on to explain how initial contacts among factories were made, ironically, at the city government offices. Prolonged official inaction toward the factory-based petitions inadvertently facilitated worker representatives' sustained contact as they repeatedly visited the city government. He pointed out:

All factories had their worker representatives because of so many years of petitioning the government. The government required that workers choose five representatives to present their petitions in order to avoid the gathering of crowds in public places. . . . These representatives from other factories set the specific dates and times of action and spread the news to their own factories so that people who wanted to come would know when to show up. All workers in Liaoyang had their grievances, and most are angry and dare to speak up. They look to the Ferro-Alloy Factory as a leader, because in 2000 our petition aroused the attention of the foreign media, and people knew that our actions were effective in creating pressure. They had hopes of joining us, perhaps because they thought that it would get society's attention.[24]

The people's long-standing rage flared up when Gong Shengwu, the chair of the Liaoyang People's Congress, notorious for his close association with Liaotie's corrupt director, proclaimed on television in Beijing in early March 2002 that there were no unemployed workers in Liaoyang.[25] The actual timing and location of the protest was communicated from Liaotie to other factories through workers' petitions, representatives at each factory, and word of mouth. While work units were prepared with banners, their coordination was loose, if it existed at all. Fearful of infiltration by the police, Liaotie workers had refused to incorporate representatives from other factories into their core leadership group.[26] They held meetings in the Elderly Activities Center in the neighborhood and elected four echelons of representatives, a total of forty people. If the first echelon of leaders was arrested, the second level would take over. Yet worker representatives insisted that they had only disseminated the date and time of their protest and were surprised by the large number of people who showed up. A former party secretary at a local textile mill, one of the twenty or so factories participating in the protest, insisted that workers poured onto the streets only after a significant number of people had started gathering. He explained the variety of disgruntled workers who regarded the local government as the common culprit:

> First, there were laid-off workers who did not get their 180 RMB monthly allowance. Then there were retired workers complaining about not getting the special allowance promised by the central government. The government had stipulated two years earlier that for each year of job tenure, workers should be paid an additional 1.8 RMB in their monthly retirement wage. Retired cadres whose careers dated back to the pre-revolutionary era complained about unequal treatment of retirement. There was a policy for military personnel who were members of the CCP before 1949 to receive 1,800 RMB a month as pension, but those personnel who surrendered to the CCP at the end of the war against Japan were given only half of that amount. The latter group was of course furious.[27]

In addition to the large number of factories involved, the most distinctive aspect of the Liaoyang incident was that workers made political as well as economic demands. Protest banners demanded the removal of enterprise officials, whom workers referred to as "thirteen worms led by Fan Yicheng," the former director of Liaotie and a prime target of the workers' anticorruption demands, and Gong Shengwu, their alleged patron in the government. For these reasons, the government may have cracked down more harshly than in other cases of worker unrest. Yet the sentences of the two imprisoned leaders, Yao Fuxin and Xiao Yuanliang, who were given seven- and four-year prison terms, respectively, apparently had to do with their political background. The seven-page-long indictment emphasized their participation in the outlawed 1998 China Democracy Party, the first opposition party since the founding of the PRC, and their supposed association with hostile foreign elements such as the Voice of America and labor rights groups. Their "incitement and organization of the masses" was the last item listed in the litany of charges. To quell the rebellion, the Liaoyang government promised to investigate and punish the corrupt officials. At the same time, it expediently repaid ordinary workers some of their back salary, health insurance contributions, and severance pay. In November 2002 the government arrested and indicted Fan Yicheng and six other former Liaotie officials. Fan was sentenced to thirteen years on smuggling charges, while the other former officials were given four- to six-year prison terms for engaging in illegal business practices. The city's police chief was fired, and a top Communist Party official was demoted.[28] These punishments were hailed in official publications as an example of the party's serious commitment to fight graft and official corruption.[29]

Thus the Liaoyang case highlights both the potential and the limits of cellular activism. Organizers consciously excluded outside workers from joining the leadership circle. Workers' demands, whether economic or political, were local and enterprise-based. In many of their open letters, the workers pledged support for socialism and the central leadership. While these acts can be interpreted as tactics of self-protection, the fact remains that they did not publicly challenge the regime's legitimacy; at most they challenged the legitimacy of the local government. Initially, the government's inaction fanned the flames of networking across work units. But once workers were arrested, support from other factories quickly collapsed. Moreover, when the government responded to some of Liaotie's demands and cracked down on the leaders, the momentum for work unit–based action slowed and petered out.

Effectiveness and Limits of Labor Activism

Have workers' actions changed policies? Evidence suggests that the regime takes labor unrest seriously and has made maintaining social stability one of its top priorities. In 2002, when the central government earmarked 86 billion RMB (a 28 percent increase over the previous year) for a social security program to make up for the shortfall in pension contributions, the minister of finance explicitly declared that the goal was to ensure social stability.[30] French scholar Jean-

Louis Rocca has interviewed officials in Liaoning and reports that "in many cities social stability is 'bought' by localities through money given to protesters. In doing so, local cadres and workers introduce a kind of 'ritual social bargaining.'" When protests occur, funds from local, provincial and central budgets are provided to prevent them from spreading."[31] Liaoning officials also sought to establish and finance new jobs for laid-off workers. "Job buying," or *goumai gangwei*, gives petty jobs to the unemployed and supplies services to local residents and the community (cleaning, protecting the environment, and help for the disabled and elderly). Protest movements, Rocca points out, have gradually changed the way officials perceive their duties and their relations with the population: "According to officials themselves, social stability has become a very important criterion in the evaluation process of their careers. . . . Most local cadres feel they are trapped between the demands coming from above in terms of stability, the lack of funds and the increasing demands coming from the grassroots."[32]

Workers who have been involved in collective action report getting at least some response from the enterprises or the government, usually in the form of stopgap payment of back wages and pensions. In Shenzhen, workers resorted to protests rather than labor arbitration and lawsuits to obtain back wages. In response to the rampant problem of nonpayment and the increasing number of petitions and mass incidents by migrant workers, the city government since 1997 has set up a "back pay fund," earmarked for making emergency payouts to aggrieved workers. In Shenyang, after a special central government allocation earmarked a social security fund for Liaoning province in 2001, retirees received most of their back pensions, and incidents of road blockages virtually stopped. In addition, the central government hastened the pace of reforming the pension contribution system. Insurance funds are to be pooled at the provincial rather than the city level, thereby expanding the fund-pooling base for workers concentrated in old and failing industrial areas. Since 2001 most of the disputes have been about severance payments to workers who have not reached the official retirement age when their work units are declared bankrupt. Usually these cases also involve back wages and back medical reimbursements. The Liaoning provincial government also took the bankruptcy protests very seriously, especially after the Liaoyang incident. Bankruptcy procedures were revised, with added requirements that before an enterprise can be declared bankrupt, it has to obtain an explicit agreement from the local government that the latter will provide financial support to the workforce for severance payments.[33]

Consequently, workers' protests have thus far failed to produce any fundamental change or challenge to the political system. Despite official concessions to their economic demands, in the vast majority of incidents of worker unrest, enterprise and government officials are seldom reprimanded for financial irregularities and illicit privatization of state assets. The workers' seething discontent over the lack of rule of law, cadre accountability, and party discipline is palpable but remains an unaggregated impulse. Indeed, most workers, especially those who have participated in the protests, appear resigned to the realistic view that they are powerless to bring about fundamental political changes to the prevailing system. Therefore, if workers pose any threat to regime legitimacy at all, it is at the local level, as seen in Liaoyang, where local officials can relatively easily assuage tensions.

(Re)forming Labor Institutions

Official Unions

Despite its expanding network of grassroots unions, the official All-China Federation of Trade Unions (ACFTU) remains a top-down institution subordinate to the government and to the Chinese Communist Party. The 1992 and 2001 revisions of the 1950 Trade Union Law strengthened the legal basis for the union's existence, especially in giving union cadres more legal protection from retaliation by management. The union's subordination to the leadership of the party and government has been reemphasized with the regulation that union chairs at all levels have to be approved by the party at the same administrative level. By law and by the ACFTU's self-proclamation, unions play a "mediator" role between workers and management in situations of work stoppages and strikes, and unions consult with and assist enterprises in restoring production and workplace order.[34] Financially, enterprise unions still depend on the firms in which they function, drawing on 2 percent of the total wage bill of their enterprises.

At the grassroots level, however, there are signs of both new bottom-up initiatives and persistent top-down controls. Some workers and individual cadres have attempted, if only gingerly and not always effectively, to leverage the workplace unions and the workers' congresses to defend workers' interests. Feng Chen has found that in the decade ending in 1999, local unions intervened in an impressive 300,000 labor disputes, in which they also represented individual workers in litigation. Yet he also found that unions are prone to represent workers selectively in cases where labor violations have been exposed by the media and where the management's legal culpability is unmistakable. In some cases, committed union cadres wage "personal crusades against injustice" and might end up losing their jobs. When collective disputes arise, however, the unions' priority is generally to defuse potential protests, communicate workers' demands to the government, and prevent any escalation of tension, for example, by persuading workers to apply for demonstration permits.[35]

There have been recent experiments with direct elections of enterprise union chairs in some economically developed localities as a way to strengthen workers' voices in the official unions. Mirroring the direct elections of village heads, these experiments with union elections reportedly have been carried out in Hangzhou's industrial district, Shenzhen's Shekou Development Zone, Baoan district, Lishu county, of Jilin province, and Huludao city of Liaoning province.[36]

At the same time, the workers' ACFTU remains adamant about monopolizing organizational space. Even when workers' initiatives to form workers' associations were supported by local officials, the ACFTU and the Ministry of Civil Affairs, responsible for overseeing social organizations, have taken swift action to ban them. One such incident occurred in Tangxia, Zhejiang.[37] A migrant worker association was set up by a veteran migrant worker from Guizhou with the support of local village officials who were eager to maintain social stability. Seeing the inability of the "boss unions" set up by the ACFTU to resolve labor disputes, they wanted to preempt the formation of "hometown societies" with a violent bent. The success of the new association drew the attention of the domestic media and evoked the opposition of the ACFTU. The Ministry of Civil Affairs and top party and government officials in Zhejiang province quickly ruled against the association.

Finally, the influx of global capital and the entry of the international anti-sweatshop movement also spawned new grassroots unions in supplier factories producing for multinational corporations. Pressured to comply with the overseas buyers' corporate codes of conduct, some Chinese factories established enterprise unions, with the local ACFTU sending cadres as union chairs, and established labor complaint mechanisms. While limited research has been done on these unions, available preliminary data suggest that they are mostly dominated by managerial and supervisory staff and are motivated primarily by the employers' desire to attract more overseas orders rather than by concerns for labor rights. Ordinary workers are reluctant to join and benefit little from their nominal membership. And local officials have little incentive to participate in enforcing labor standards within these foreign-sponsored firms.[38]

Underground Unionism

Beyond the limits of the official unions, underground union activism waxed and waned throughout the 1990s and early 2000s. Clearly, official unions have largely failed to protect the most vulnerable segments of the working class during the economic reforms. It is estimated that there are 60 million unemployed and laid-off workers in bankrupt SOEs where unions have collapsed, 32 million retirees who have severed relations with their work units, and some 100 million migrant workers, many of whom work in the private and foreign-owned sectors without any union. Haunted by the specter of the Polish Solidarity movement and the networks of autonomous workers' unions that erupted during the 1989 Tiananmen rebellion, the Chinese government has effectively nipped such grassroots-organized dissent in the bud.

Yet despite the relentless repression of the Chinese state, efforts at independent labor organizing have persisted. In the aftermath of the Tiananmen uprising, student-intellectual activists formed the backbone of several independent unions. The Free Trade Union of China (*Zhongguo ziyou gonghui*) was formed in late 1991 by two workers, a teacher, and a small trader, who were also members of the Liberal Democratic Party of China or the Chinese Progressive League, two underground political groups. Its members were soon imprisoned, for terms ranging from two to twenty years. In March 1994 Yuan Hongbing, a university lecturer, Zhou Guoqiang, a lawyer, and others formed the League for the Protection of Laborers' Rights (*Laodongzhe quanyi baozhang tongmeng*), but they were soon arrested or sent away for labor reform. Also in 1993–94 several new college graduates formed the Wage Workers' Federation (*Dagongzhe lianhehui*) in Shenzhen, focusing on migrant labor rights, and published two short-lived newsletters (*Dagong tongxun* and *Dagong guangchang*). Shortly thereafter, three members were arrested and sentenced to two to three years of labor reform.[39]

Given the clandestine nature of these organizations, it is not surprising that not much has been documented about their organizers and their modus operandi. The following first-person report by an activist involved in the Wage Workers' Federation may not be typical of other similar underground labor organizations, but it provides a rare glimpse into the precarious nature of such an undertaking. Li Minqi was a student activist in the 1989 movement. One of a circle of student leaders, he reflected on the political lessons the student activists had learned from their involvement in the Tiananmen protests. He wrote:

> The failure of the 1989 democratic movement, on the one hand, exposed the serious contradictions between the different social classes and groups in the movement, especially that between the middle-class intellectuals and the urban working class, and . . . it exposed the fundamental limits of a democratic movement led by liberal intellectuals under the guidance of Western bourgeois ideology. . . . I began to look to Marxism and later became a Marxist.[40]

Arrested in 1990 for making an anti-government speech and imprisoned for two years, Li Minqi went to Shenzhen in 1993 to meet two of his college-educated Hunan friends, who told him that "they somehow realized that the 1989 democratic movement failed because it failed to mobilize workers effectively. Therefore, to achieve democracy . . . the democratic movement must 'make use of' workers (that's literally how they talked about it) just as the Polish bourgeois intellectuals made use of the Solidarity Union to accomplish the capitalist restoration. This is how they began to be interested in the 'workers' movement.'"[41]

Li's friends started a night school, consciously imitating the methods of the Chinese Communist Party, but so few workers showed up that the school practically failed even to get under way. Using his own money, Li typed up and printed a small ten-page magazine called *Dagong tongxun* and circulated it to some twenty or thirty workers. But after a shortage of money forced him to stop publication, he left Shenzhen. Another Peking University student went to Shenzhen and circulated three issues of another newsletter, *Dagong guangchang*. Li himself left for the United States in 1994 and became a graduate student in economics at the University of Massachusetts, Amherst. His associates were arrested and imprisoned.[42]

In the late 1990s there were other underground efforts to form unions for laid-off and retired workers. In 1998, for instance, Zhang Shanguang was arrested and sentenced to ten years in prison after applying to the local government to register the Shu Pu Association for the Protection of the Rights of Laid-Off Workers in Hunan. In Gansu, Yue Tianxiang and Guo Xinmin established the China Workers' Monitor in 1999, exposing corruption among officials and mismanagement of the company that had laid them off. Yue was given a ten-year prison term and Guo two years. In Taiyuan, Shanxi, sixty-year-old retired worker and labor activist Di Tiangui submitted an application for the establishment of a nationwide National Factories Retiree Association. He was arrested in July 2002.[43]

In Zhengzhou a network of underground labor activists assisted workers, at times successfully, in resisting factory closures. Some of these activists, based in Beijing, Henan, and Chongqing, offered advice to SOE workers fighting illicit mergers, privatization, and land sales of factory premises, sometimes engaging in the risky tactic of physically occupying their plants. In the few reports available on their activities, they are described as fervent remnants of the rebel factions during the Cultural Revolution, some of whom had been imprisoned after the death of Mao Zedong and the fall of the Gang of Four. Others are younger, university-educated New Left Marxists, critical of both the excesses of Mao and the reforms of Deng.[44] In an unusual public demonstration of their organizational skills, four hundred workers from local factories in Zhengzhou reportedly bowed before a statue of Mao to mark the twenty-fifth anniversary of his death. They laid baskets of flowers covered with sheets of paper on which were written elegiac couplets, such as "The great proletarian leader Chairman Mao lives in our hearts forever!" "Defend Mao Zedong's thoughts till death," and "Defend the ruling status of the workers' class till death!" Chinese police later detained four of the workers involved.[45]

Labor NGOs

In response to the repression of organized political dissent, and taking advantage of the opening up of public space, politically concerned intellectuals and professionals have attempted another kind of institution-building. In the 1990s nongovernmental organizations (NGOs) proliferated, strategically shunning the rhetoric and organizational mode of the trade unions. Echoing the official emphasis on providing "education" and "services" to migrant workers, these new organizations exploited the institutional space opened up by the Ministry of Civil Affairs and relied on funding from international foundations, overseas churches, academic institutions, international human rights organizations, and even foreign governments. As in the case of the underground unions, many of the participants are not workers but professionals, academics, and students. In the Pearl River delta region, several of these organizations established and expanded their activities at the turn of the century.

One such organization is the Institute of Contemporary Observation (ICO). Founded in 2001 by a former journalist at the *Shenzhen Legal Daily*, Liu Kaiming, and a handful of academics and lawyers interested in labor issues, the ICO officially registered as a commercial entity. Its list of financial supporters reveals contributions from the forces of globalization (multinational corporations and international agencies, and transnational civil society organizations and foundations) as well as from Chinese institutions. With money from Oxfam (Hong Kong), the Ford Foundation, the Asia Foundation, the University of Oslo, the International Labour Organization, the World Bank, Tsinghua University, Business for Social Responsibility, the International Fair Labor Association, Nike, Adidas, and

Reebok, among others, ICO runs a labor hotline offering legal counseling to workers involved in labor disputes; it conducts and publishes research on industrial injuries, overtime, wage arrears, and dormitory conditions; and it publishes a bimonthly magazine called *Forum: China Labor Research and Support Network*. In 2004 the ICO opened China's first nongovernmental workers' college in one of Shenzhen's factory districts. The Migrant Workers Community College is funded by the Human Rights Committee of the U.S. Congress and co-organized by the Institute for Labor and Employment of the University of California at Berkeley. Evening classes for workers include English, computer skills, auto repair, typing, and small business management. The school claims to "improve migrant workers' education levels, skills, and capacities for further development," "introduce migrant workers to the concepts of citizenship, basic rights, and rule of law," and "improve workers' ability to defend their own interests." It plans to set up mobile education stations in other industrial zones in Shenzhen, Dongguan, and Zhongshan.[46]

Another well-established NGO is the Chinese Working Women Network (CWWN) in Shenzhen. Formed by a group of academics, social workers, and college students in Hong Kong in the mid-1990s, and relying on funding from international labor organizations and foundations, the CWWN runs a mobile clinic that provides services to dormitories in factory districts. Its activity center in Shenzhen offers legal and psychological counseling and educational and recreational activities. While its avowed goal is to enhance worker capacity for self-protection and occupational health education, in actual operation the CWWN staff advises workers involved in labor disputes on how to use the legal system or how to engage in collective bargaining inside the factory.

Other prominent examples of grassroots institutions include a one-man shop called the Workers' Service Center in Panyu, run by a self-trained lawyer who is a former worker. This center caters particularly to the needs of injured workers, and offers support and counseling on legal and medical matters. Another legal clinic active in the Pearl River delta area is the law clinic run by the law school of Zhongshan University in Guangzhou. These organizations operate independently but also maintain collaborative relations, especially in cases of referrals. Similar organizations have been established in

Beijing. A Home for Migrant Women in Beijing has functioned under the auspices of the Women's Federation magazine, offering recreational and training activities for the city's young female migrants. Sociologists from Tsinghua University, with funding from the Ford Foundation and the Asia Foundation, have set up a mobile clinic providing migrant workers in rural industries in Hubei with medical and legal knowledge. Many other legal aid centers are actively involved in helping workers use the legal system. But, due to a paucity of organizational resources and state repression, labor NGOs in China are usually formed through individual conviction, political socialization, and inspiration. At the same time, these grassroots labor organizations contribute to legal reform and raise social demands for legal justice.

This study of local practices of labor struggles and institution-building reveals that whatever "legitimacy challenge" workers manage to mount largely targets local authorities. At times, localized and cellular activism has been effective in bringing about economic and livelihood relief and some social policy reform, while achieving little in dealing with larger political problems such as corruption, lack of accountability, and rule of law. Yet despite the lack of lateral organizational capacity, workers have been able to mobilize resources in what remains of the *danwei* residential communities within the confines of dormitories and factories and seize opportunities provided by the legal system, the labor administration, and the mass media. Likewise, nascent labor institution-building by individuals with civil courage and conviction has embraced a local, pragmatic approach while using resources provided by the global civil society. These institutions seek to empower workers through education and services and to shun political rhetoric and the organization of independent unionism. Consequently, at the start of the twenty-first century, given the persistence of the party-state, Chinese labor has been more effective as a force for social change than as a force for political change.

11 | Between Defiance and Obedience:

Protest Opportunism in China

Ordinary people are often faced with a dilemma in their contentious interactions with an authoritarian state. To enhance their bargaining power, they need to employ some sort of "troublemaking" tactics such as engaging in disruptive activities or forming autonomous organizations. If they go too far, however, radical tactics may not only alienate their constituency but also incur state repression.[1] The choice between efficacy and safety appears to be a tradeoff, and it is very difficult to attain both at the same time. Yet ordinary people sometimes manage to engage in resistance while somehow remaining submissive. Their most common strategy is what James Scott calls "everyday forms of resistance": people carry out covert and individualized resistance while feigning obedience. Can ordinary people also mount public and collective resistance while remaining submissive? Rarely. Yet there are some cases where this happens, as it has in China since the 1990s.

Popular collective actions in China have increased substantially in both frequency and disruptiveness. Considering how little political liberalization there has been in China's high-capacity authoritarian regime, this trend is certainly impressive. Compared to rebellious periods in history, both in China and elsewhere, however, the contention we see today is not particularly striking in frequency, scale, or disruptiveness.[2] More remarkable is the fact that most of these collective actions, even when they involve confrontational tactics, are still generally perceived as essentially submissive rather than rebellious.[3] How have Chinese petitioners achieved the difficult task of maintaining a balance between defiance and obedience?

This chapter seeks to interpret and explain this paradoxical aspect of protest tactics in today's China, which I refer to as "protest opportunism."[4] It is called "opportunism" in that protesters do not take a principled or consistent position toward being either obedient or defiant but are ready to employ any tactics they think useful. As this chapter will show, Chinese protesters have a strong tendency to operate close to authorized channels and to take dramatic actions to demonstrate their obedience. Yet at the same time, when they find them useful, they are ready to engage in activities that implicitly challenge government officials: staging large-scale, public, and disruptive protests, establishing cross-sector ties, or forming semiautonomous or autonomous organizations. They can pursue both strategies at the same time or shift from one to another freely.

James Scott has rightly noted that an analysis of the contradictions of ordinary people's behavior can teach us a great deal about power, hegemony, resistance, and subordination.[5] Without an understanding of protest opportunism, it is impossible to make sense of political contention in today's China. The Chinese case can also contribute to general theories of contentious politics. Like everyday forms of resistance, social movements, rebellions, and revolutions, opportunistic resistance is one of the major forms of popular struggle. By locating this type of resistance within a specific time and space and within specific political and social structures, we can gain a better understanding of the mechanisms and processes of political contention, as well as of the relationship between political institutions and popular contention.

The empirical evidence for this study comes mainly from my fieldwork in Hunan province in 2002. In addition to government archives and interviews with government officials, I relied on in-depth interviews with activists. The analysis of troublemaking tactics is also based on an event catalogue which includes 902 events in City Y, Hunan province, from 1992 to 2002 that I compiled from a series of government reports.

Due to the extensive changes in state-society structures and in state strategies for coping with popular collective action in the reform era, I hypothesize that Chinese petitioners have been tempted to exert pressure on local governments by using "troublemaking tactics," while at the same time integrating them with obedient tactics in an opportunistic way. To test this hypothesis and illustrate how opportunistic troublemaking works, I present four case studies and examine whether or not the four selected petitioning groups have employed both defiant and obedient tactics, and if so, how they have maintained a balance between defiance and obedience. Finally, I look at the impact of protest opportunism on grassroots politics in China.

Hypothesis

Scholars have noted that popular collective action in reform-era China has a tendency to operate near the boundary of authorized channels. Kevin O'Brien and Lianjiang Li's concept of "rightful resistance" offers important insights into this point. They highlight three key elements of "rightful resistance": (1) it operates near the boundary of an authorized channel; (2) it employs the rhetoric and commitments of the powerful to curb political or economic power; and (3) it hinges on locating and exploiting divisions among the powerful.[6]

This concept is confined to moderate forms of collective action. As O'Brien and Li note, "rightful resisters stop short of violence," and "in its basic form, rightful resistance is a rather tame form of contention that makes use of existing (if clogged) channels of participation and relies heavily on the patronage of elite backers."[7] China, however, has witnessed a rise of confrontational collective action since the mid-1990s.[8] Does this mean that Chinese petitioners have begun to give up "rightful resistance"? I argue that when Chinese resisters adopt confrontational tactics, they do not have to become less obedient. Rather, they act as "opportunistic troublemakers."

Generally in China there are three types of troublemaking tactics: disruption, third-party strategies, and symbolic tactics. Disruption is the major form of troublemaking, and it is widely regarded as an important source of protest efficacy.[9] Third-party strategies can also be very powerful.[10] Petitioners in China usually appeal to two types of third parties: elite advocates and the general public. They sometimes also exert pressure on government officials via symbolic actions, which can convey meaning to and provoke emotions from both the targets and the bystanders. Common symbolic tactics include kneeling down, self-mutilation, self-immolation, displaying symbols of grief, singing revolutionary songs, and displaying honorary symbols such as military medals.

In addition to these troublemaking tactics as forms of action, some forms of organization also demonstrate defiance and exert pressure on the government. The Chinese state has always been highly alert to cross-sector coalitions and autonomous organizations.

My central hypothesis is that due to the extensive changes in state-society structures and in state strategies in the reform era, Chinese petitioners have been tempted to employ "opportunistic trouble-making" tactics in bargaining with the government.

The first factor that contributes to the rise of protest opportunism is the transformation of state-society structures. The economic reform has led to an extensive transformation in state-society linkages. In particular, the old authority relationship, which featured "organized dependency," has declined substantially.[11] Faced with a new balance of resources and a new incentive structure, both the state and ordinary Chinese have begun to change their behavior toward each other.

Consequently, in recent years the Chinese state has undertaken dramatic changes in its four major strategies for coping with popular collective action: repression, concession, persuasion, and procrastination. The state's repressiveness has decreased vis-à-vis social protests, and it has largely shifted from punitive to preventive means. Meanwhile, the state has become more inclined to make expedient concessions to troublemaking activities. With the socialist ideology substantially weakened, the state has begun to rely on practical persuasion. Finally, procrastination has begun to play a central role; preventive repression, expedient concessions, and practical persuasion all facilitate procrastination.

These changes in state strategies have had a significant impact on protest behavior, contributing to the rise of public, collective, and disruptive popular resistance. The relative decline in repression has emboldened protesters; expedient concessions have encouraged troublemaking; and procrastination has driven people toward disruptive troublemaking to counter government foot-dragging.

Nevertheless, although state-society structures and state strategies have created considerable space for troublemaking activities, the threat of state repression still hangs like the sword of Damocles over the heads of protesters. Even though the Chinese state began extensive legal reforms more than two decades ago, it still relies mainly on selective and exemplary punishments, which are inherently arbitrary, to deter disruptive collective action. Consequently, while Chinese petitioners find it necessary to maintain obedience, they also understand that a large number of illegal activities are tolerated de facto. Therefore, such arbitrary punishment has led not to passivity but to an opportunistic approach to the law.

Four Cases

To test my hypothesis, and to illustrate how Chinese petitioners maintain a balance between obedience and defiance, I examine the protest strategies of four petitioning groups that engaged in extensive contentious interactions with the government in City Y. For the sake of convenience and confidentiality, I refer to these four groups as A, B, C, and D. Group A is a group of disabled people residing in the urban area. Group B consists of more than a dozen cadres of a branch company of the City Y Supply and Marketing Cooperative. The members of Group C are retired workers from a state-owned factory that employs about a thousand workers. Group D is composed of dozens of demobilized army officers, including staff and workers in state-owned or collective enterprises, and some peasants.

The strategic choices of these four groups are readily observable because they all engaged in contentious actions for at least one year. Two of them, Groups B and C, struggled for seven or eight years; Group A protested for two years, and Group D for about one year.

Although these case studies are mainly based on interviews with the groups' organizers, I have attempted to cross-check their statements with government reports, as well as with interviews with government officials. In the interviews with the protest organizers, I pay the most attention to their troublemaking activities and their obedient actions, as well as their understanding of their relationship with government officials.

Group A: Disabled Urban Residents

In 2000 most cities in China began to ban motorized tricycles for passenger transport because of traffic, environmental, and urban image problems. This policy created serious difficulties for many disabled people who made a living by transporting passengers in their special vehicles. Because of the high unemployment rates, they had virtually no hope of finding alternative sources of income. Not surprisingly, they fiercely resisted this policy.

Troublemaking

The City Y government officially banned motorized tricycles for passenger transport in November 2000. As soon as they heard this news, Group A, together with other motorized tricycle owners who were not disabled, went to the district government to protest. On November 7, 150 tricycle owners joined the protest, and on November 8, 275 joined. Soon after, however, the disabled people decided to act on their own. On December 18, forty-four disabled people paid a collective visit to the city government. Dissatisfied with the official reply from the government, they occupied the reception rooms of the bureau of letters and visits for one night.

Three months later they blocked the gate of the provincial government compound. Although they admitted that this was an "excessively radical action" *(guoji xingwei)*, they downplayed the disruptiveness of the event:

> There are three entrances to the main gate, and we only blocked one on the side, not at the main entrance. Actually, we did not block the entrance. We only sat in by the entrance. We distributed handbills, but we did not display banners. Each of us held a piece of paper on which was written "Disabled" and "City Y." We just wanted to tell people passing by that some disabled people from City Y had come here. We also prepared a placard for a hunger strike, but we did not actually go on a hunger strike.[12]

Later the city government made a significant concession, agreeing to compensate each disabled person 200 RMB a month for one year. Although the petitioners were not fully satisfied, since their ultimate goal was to continue to use the motorcycles for passenger transport, they were considerably pacified by this measure. They did not resume petitioning until the government was about to end the compensation one year later.

On March 15, 2002, which was a national holiday—Help Disabled People Day—they manipulated an officially authorized parade. They slipped in a slogan among those that had been prepared or approved by the official Chinese Alliance of Disabled People which read "Support and Thank the Government for Permitting Disabled People to Use Motorized Tricycles for Passenger Transport." Although this seemed to be a false statement, since the government had never said it would lift the ban, the disabled people claimed that this slogan was in accord with an internal speech given by a vice governor of Hunan province. Whether this was true or not, the slogan annoyed the city government since it publicly challenged its policy and implied that the provincial government did not agree with the city government's policy. Consequently the instigators were summoned to the public security bureau on three occasions to undergo criticism and education. The government also published a disciplinary warning in the local newspapers.

Before the parade, the ban had not been strictly implemented, and disabled people could still use their vehicles for passenger transport without being penalized as long as they were cautious. After the parade, however, the government began to implement the ban strictly. In May the government confiscated five vehicles being used for passenger transport. This triggered another round of conflict.

When they could not recover their three-wheelers, twenty-six disabled people, demonstrating indomitable spirit and solidarity, went all the way to Beijing to submit a petition. In response, the city and district governments dispatched four officials to Beijing to bring the protesters back to the city. The local officials partially accepted Group A's bargaining conditions, agreeing to release the confiscated vehicles on the condition that the owners sign a written statement that they would not use their vehicles for passenger transport again. The interviewees seemed satisfied with their partial success and expressed a willingness to repeat their strategy if need be. If future demands were not met satisfactorily, the interviewees said, "We will first give them [the local government] a warning and then go to Beijing again."

Moderation

The first example of moderate behavior can be found in an official report by the bureau of letters and visits:

> On November 14, 9:30 am, forty-seven disabled people from both ZY and H districts who were owners of motorcycles lined up to enter the government compound and attempted to apply for administrative reconsideration of the policy to ban passenger transport with motorized tricycles. . . .[13] They expressed their support for the policy generally, and their willingness to give up their vehicles spontaneously. Yet they claimed that the policy would deprive them of their source of income. . . . The deputy director explained to them the rationale behind the policy and told them that the procedure of administrative reconsideration could not legally be applied in this case. The deputy director praised the disabled tricycle owners for their civilized behavior on this visit. . . . In response, the disabled owners warmly applauded. At 10:30, they lined up again and exited the government compound.[14]

During this event the protesters' behavior was so obedient that it appeared that they were convinced. They applauded a speech that rejected their demand and lined up in an orderly fashion when entering and exiting the government compound.

The complainants also refrained from forming alliances with disabled people from other cities, even though such collaboration might have been more forceful. They regarded such action as inappropriate:

> We City Y people should go [to upper-level government] by ourselves, they [people in other cities] should go by themselves. On this issue we should not go together. Going together would violate the party's policies. Establishing ties [*chuanlian*] would give our action a political nature, and our petition would become a political

event. Since we disabled people live close to the limits of the law, we should be careful so as not to violate the law.

While they refrained from petitioning jointly with disabled people in other cities, however, they maintained relationships with them in order to share information. From disabled petitioners in other cities they acquired some internal documents, including a supportive speech by Deng Pufang, chairman of the Chinese Alliance of Disabled People, which proved to be very useful for their petition.

They also showed restraint with respect to the provincial games held in City Y in the summer of 2002. An interviewee reported:

> Yesterday an officer from the city police came to my work unit to see me. He warned me that we should not launch a petition during the period of the provincial games. I said we would not petition on two occasions: the first was during times of fighting floods and sending disaster relief, and the second was during important events. I said that I know that you [the government] have your own business to attend to, and we will not disturb you then. Only when you do not have important things to handle will we pay you a visit.

Relationship with the Government

The interviewees believed that their relationship with the government was quite positive. They said, "The Alliance of Disabled People in the city and the district have praised us highly." This may have been true, to judge from some favorable descriptions of this group in government reports. They also mentioned that officials who met them were usually quite nice. In return, they showed their understanding of the government and its policies, at least superficially. Such apparent mutual understanding could not disguise the tension within their relationship, however. The interviewees claimed that "overall, the city government has not paid enough attention to the cause of helping disabled people. When we visited the Alliance of Disabled People in the city, they didn't care about us. They treated us like terrorists, like bin Laden." Obviously they were aware that the government was concerned about their troublemaking activities. As one of the interviewees said, they lived close to the limits of the law. But as another interviewee claimed, "The most important point is that we are not against the party or against the society." Not surprisingly, their description of their relationship with the government was not wholly consistent. Nor were their actions, which fluctuated between confrontational and obedient strategies.

Group B: Retired Cadres from a Small State-Owned Company

Group B consisted of about twenty cadres in a small state-owned enterprise. Like many others in City Y, this company had difficulty paying pensions and health insurance to its retirees. Probably because of its small size, the group of petitioners had a strong incentive to form a coalition with other similar groups. Although Group B is small, its core leader, Mr. L1, is well known among retiree pensioners in City Y. I first ran across his name when reading a government report on which the mayor had written an instruction specifically requiring relevant government agencies to control him and educate him against establishing illegal ties with other groups. He seemed to be the mastermind of a coalition of retirees of forty-seven different enterprises that was established around 2002.

Pensioners in these forty-seven enterprises had experienced similar contention with the government. Their goals had also changed over time. Most had started their struggle around 1995, when their enterprises were undergoing structural reform. At first, their major goal was to get the government to pay their basic salary on time. When this goal was achieved, they demanded that the local government add to their salaries a subsidy of 51 RMB, as stipulated by the central government. When some of them successfully forced the government to comply with this initial request, they followed up with demands for health insurance and back pay. In 2002 they then made a remarkably bold demand: as retirees from enterprises, they demanded a status equal to that of retirees from administrative and nonprofit work units.

Troublemaking

Mr. L1 would not talk about specific protest events, but he was willing to speak generally about the tactics he and his group had employed in their petitioning. Their two favorite tactics were writing joint letters to provincial and central government officials, and collectively and repeatedly visiting the city government. They did not write individual letters or pay collective visits to upper-level government officials because these two tactics were either useless or unnecessary:

> I have almost never written anything in my own name. Letters from famous people may be able to attract attention, but letters from ordinary individuals seldom get any response. We have written many joint letters [to upper-level government officials]. Whenever we found some policies that had not been implemented thoroughly, we would write letters. I have never visited the upper-level government, not even the provincial government. I have no objection to those who want to do so, but I think the effect would be the same [as writing letters to upper-level government officials]. But we have frequently visited the city government. It is our "staple diet" [jiachang bianfan].[15]

Generally, he was satisfied with the effect of these two trouble-making tactics. "They are useful," he said:

> At first the government was extremely intransigent [tieban yikuai]. For example, as to the subsidy of 51 RMB, the officials in the social security bureau told me in 2000 that it was impossible for them to pay it since the local government did not have any money. I said, "I don't believe it. The subsidy is stipulated in official policy, and I don't believe you can cover the sky with only one hand." So we organized many collective visits. . . . Now this problem has been solved for those enterprises owned directly by the city government.

He believed that collective action was not only useful but also legitimate and legal:

> Sometimes they [government officials] criticized us for having too many people join the petitions. We believe we have not violated the law. In a TV opera, Black Face [heilian], there is an old comrade who spent two or three years collecting ten thousand signatures for a joint letter to accuse the party secretary. It was the party secretary, not the old comrade, who was finally punished. If our action were not legal, such an opera would not have been shown on TV. Fur-

thermore, we also rebuked the officials, saying that if our action was illegal, you [the government] violated the law before we did, since you did not fulfill your obligation as stipulated by law.

As an old party cadre, he was well aware that although the coalition of retirees from the forty-seven enterprises was a very powerful weapon for the petitioners, it was very troubling from the viewpoint of the government. So he downplayed the mobilizing efforts in establishing the coalition:

They [the government] especially oppose ties across industrial sectors. I told them that we did not establish such ties deliberately. We old comrades often got together to chat about things. On occasion we found that the local government had not implemented national policies and laws, and we felt it necessary to report such problems to the upper-level government. We thus all wanted to write letters jointly. Our action has always been voluntary.

According to him, the coalition was formed naturally rather than from explicit organizational efforts. Asked about the future of the coalition, he was optimistic: "Previously we had only fourteen work units, and now we have forty-seven. The number will increase in the future. Other enterprises can join us if they are willing. But they'd better join spontaneously."

Moderation

Group B has never engaged in severely disruptive action. Asked about his opinion of the disruptive tactics taken by Group C and many other groups, Mr. F replied:

It is not right to block the gate [of the government compound]. We have never done such things as blocking gates. Old people may sometimes hurl curses, and easily become emotional. Yet never will we engage in acts of smashing and seizing, or blocking roads or bridges. We do not support radical behavior that violates principles. Such actions are not right and also provide them [the government] with a chance to "pull our queue." We need to act within the boundary of the law.

He did not regard minor disruptive activities that took place in the course of collective action as a problem. From his perspective this is normal, and justifiable given the cause. According to him, old comrades would not do such things even as a last resort. He noted: "We old people cherish quiet. We cannot stand noise even when we watch TV. Why would we want to make noise in the government?" While minor disruption is normal, they would avoid deliberately organizing seriously disruptive activities.

Mr. F was careful to distinguish the coalition from a formal organization. Though enthusiastic about a large coalition for collective action, he refrained from organizing cross-sector or cross–work unit associations. In his understanding, the regime permits associations within a work unit, but organizing across work units could cause trouble. In each enterprise that made up the coalition there existed an association of senior people. According to him the best form of organization is the party team of retirees, since it is "perfectly legal." He had actually organized such a party team within his own work unit. He said, however, that he would not establish any formal organization across work units: "If you want to form such an organization, you need to get approval from the government, which is almost impossible. If you form it without approval, they [the government] can say you violated the law. So why ask for trouble?"

Relationship with the Government

Despite their often intense struggles with the government, Mr. F believed that he and the other comrades were behaving as party cadres. "We will absolutely never do anything antiparty or antisocialist," he said. "Most of us are Communist Party members whose mission is to defend the laws of the nation and the socialist system."

He was also aware of the possibility of repression but not especially concerned about it. He sought security from the law. "We have never demanded anything without a legal basis," he claimed. "Whenever we do something, including writing letters, I consult things like the Law on Marches and Demonstrations and the Regulations on Public Security Management." He did not take threats by the government seriously. Once an official threatened him, saying that the police had been looking for him for several months. He commented with scorn:

"The police could not be so stupid. I have been home all the time. This is only a bluff."

In his view, coercive measures taken by the local government were not a deterrent. He talked about his experience after the mayor instructed that he be controlled. In response, he wrote another letter to upper-level governments, accusing the mayor of vindictively attacking the petitioners. He also sent a copy of that letter to the mayor: "The mayor was fine about it, and did not do anything to me, although he must have felt pretty uncomfortable reading my letter."

He also believed that many officials were reluctant to carry out coercive measures. The city government required that the party secretary and the manager of their company monitor and control the pensioners, but the company leaders were reluctant to comply: "They would not do anything without pressure from the government even though they need to protect their official posts." He was confident that their cause was just and that the government officials actually acknowledged it.

Group C: Retired Workers from a Large State-Owned Enterprise

Group C consisted of several hundred retirees from a large SOE. It was part of the coalition of the aforementioned forty-seven enterprises. Yet joining this coalition to write joint letters was but a minor part of its long struggle. The earliest protest recorded in the government report was a collective visit by two hundred people to the city government in 1994. Group C changed its demands over time in a process similar to that of many other enterprises, as described earlier.

Troublemaking

In its long struggle with the government, Group C experimented with almost every major variety of troublemaking activity: large, disruptive, public, and symbolic actions, as well as skip-the-level visits. Government reports record a series of large-scale collective petitioning by Group C: in June 1994, more than 200 participants (with pensioners from another factory); in December 1995, 150 participants; in February 1996, more than 300 participants; in May 1996, 85 participants; in October 1996, 350 participants; in September 1999, 40 participants; in September 2000, 240 participants; in June 2001, 400 participants (with pensioners from three other enterprises); in September 2001, more than 200 participants.

Mrs. W1 described their experience as a logical reaction to the government's bureaucratic behavior:

> At first we sent written requests to the government through four or five representatives. According to the Regulations for Letters and Visits, there should be no more than five people. We knew the policy. But they [the government] won't receive you or pay attention to your request if you don't have many people making a commotion. On December 24, 2000, before the Spring Festival, I went with another retired representative to submit our petition. We waited about one month, but there was no response. When we went to the bureau of letters and visits again to ask a bespectacled official whether our petition had been submitted to the mayor, it turned out that it was still in the drawer. They had not even read it. We thus were forced to return en masse.[16]

Strictly speaking, her narrative is misleading, since it implies that Group C did not begin a large-scale collective action until it experienced bureaucratic obstruction in December 2000. As stated earlier, however, the group actually started its collective action much earlier.

Members of Group C believed that collective visits were fairly effective. Mrs. G talked about how the government increased their pension payments: "At first, they [the government] just gave us 80 RMB [per month], and then they added several RMB when we made a real commotion. Later on, our pensions were increased to 130 RMB, and after we struggled for another several years, we got 200 RMB. They treated us like kids, and wouldn't give us [our pensions] unless we made a fuss."

To "make a real commotion" (chaode lihai), they repeatedly used disruptive and public tactics. Mrs. G's narrative presents such troublemaking as nothing but a natural and necessary extension of normal visits. For example, she talked about the protesters' occupation of a government office for one night:

> We went there to ask for rice [pensions]. We clamored until half past twelve o'clock [am]. We could not go home so late. There was no boat, and it was very cold. We are all elderly people, and most of

us aren't in good health. Since the office was warm, we decided to
stay overnight. The director of the office despised us and called the
police. The police came with batons and handcuffs. But they said,
"It is right for you to ask for rice," and then they left.

She also talked casually about their experience of blocking the gate
of the city government compound: "At that time, only several old
comrades blocked the entrance, while hundreds of other comrades
sat down inside the government compound."

Like Mr. L1, Mrs. W1 justified her troublemaking activities as a
rightful cause. She often said, "We are old comrades educated by
Mao Zedong Thought. We do not like to make trouble. We have
been forced to beg for rice. Collective visits are always exhausting, especially for us old comrades. If the government had paid the pensions as it should have, we wouldn't have made collective visits even
if you had begged us."

Moderation

According to Mrs. W1, the protesters always sent warnings before
they actually started disruptive or public actions. Their threats were
seldom empty, but they also hoped to resolve the problem without
recourse to troublemaking.

When forced to engage in disruption, they nevertheless managed
to maintain discipline: "Before we went to petition, we told workers
not to shout abuses or damage goods. We always emphasize discipline. As a result, we have never damaged a cup, a window, or a chair.
Sometimes we even cleaned the office before we left. We have paid
visits in a civilized way."

Like Group A, they also refrained from disrupting the provincial
games held in City Y:

The manager of our factory passed on warnings [from the govern-
ment] to our several representatives. He said anybody who plotted
or organized activities to disturb the provincial games would be de-
prived of their salaries or even arrested. He said the government
had convened an emergency meeting to make this decision. We replied that we were not afraid of this kind of warning. But we knew
enough not to pay collective visits during the provincial games. We
are City Y people ourselves, and holding these provincial games is

an honor for all of us. Therefore, we did not disturb them. We are old enough to understand this.

Relationship with the Government

Mrs. W1 often referred to the attitude of the government as "they treated us like kids." From the protesters' perspective, the government preferred to buy them off with small favors whenever they engaged in troublemaking activities. The protesters did not believe that the government really wanted to resort to heavy-handed repression. Like Mr. L1, Mrs. W1 regarded the government's threats of force as a bluff. She expressed defiance:

> Once an official said we had violated the Regulations for Public Security Management. We replied that it was not the time for them to label us with such a hat [*daimaozi*]. When the police threatened to arrest five representatives if we went on with the march the next day, I replied: "If you want to arrest me, I can help you do that. I have nothing to fear. My mom died when I was only eight, and I became a child bride at twelve. I have never been involved in adultery, burglary, or embezzlement of public property. We are just asking for rice, and asking for rice does not violate the law. If you arrest one person, we will send several hundred people to ask for him or her back. Where there is repression, there is resistance. You'd better talk rather than threaten us."

As mentioned earlier, Mrs. W1 referred to the petitioners as "old comrades," and she liked to say: "We are all old comrades who have been educated by Mao Zedong Thought. We will not make trouble."

Group D: Demobilized Army Officers

Group D was a group of demobilized army officers who participated in the Sino-Vietnam War of 1979. Demobilized military officers have been a continuing concern for the regime as a possible threat to political stability for three reasons. First, they have a strong mobilizing capacity. There exist throughout the country de facto associations of demobilized soldiers. Second, they are better educated than the average population and have an excellent understanding of public policies and laws. Third, despite the fact that they have made sacrifices for the nation, many of them are living in poverty. Consequently, many veterans harbor deep grievances against the state.

Group D did not start its contentious activity until the restructuring of SOEs and collective enterprises began in the mid-1990s. Although this group included some peasants, its core leaders worked in collective or state-owned enterprises. These demobilized army officers faced unemployment as a result of the industrial reforms. With an average age of forty, they found it very difficult to get other jobs. They consulted brochures of central policies and laws and discovered that "many favorable policies and laws affecting demobilized army officers had not been implemented by the local government." Yet their demands were not limited to the implementation of central policies. They also made proactive claims, demanding new policies beneficial to demobilized soldiers.

Troublemaking

Like Group C, Group D combined the major varieties of troublemaking: collective, public, symbolic, and disruptive. But its exercise of these various tactics was relatively tame compared to that of Group C.

Group D justified its actions in terms similar to those of the other groups: "We have to petition collectively. Individual petitions never work and attract no attention." According to a government report, Group D's largest collective petition movement occurred in January 2002, when twenty-six demobilized army officers paid a highly charged visit to the district government. That July they planned a large event, a march on Army Day, but they failed to carry it out due to forceful measures taken by the government. They also paid several visits to the government, each time with five representatives. During every petition drive, they claimed to represent about three hundred Sino-Vietnam War veterans in their district.

According to members of Group D, the planned march was a response to the government's having broken its promise: "Previously, every time we visited the government it promised to issue a document that would solve our problems. Then in June it said it would not issue the document, and therefore we would get nothing. We comrades-in-arms became indignant since we had been deceived. This is why we submitted an application for the march."

The veterans adopted symbolic tactics that emphasized their military background. In the Points of Attention drafted for their planned march on Army Day, it was required that everyone wear old-style military uniforms and carry medals and certificates of military service or disability. The organizers stipulated that the participants should sing revolutionary songs during the march, such as "The Internationale" and the "Three Disciplines and Eight Points of Attention."[17]

Although members of Group D had not yet undertaken skip-the-level visits when I interviewed them, they clearly had such an intention. They acknowledged that ultimately they might need to go to the capital. One of the interviewees said, "We will not give up until we have visited Beijing."

Although their petitioning tactics did not seem especially confrontational, their organizational activities caused deep suspicion on the part of the party-state. The government archives include a speech by a major local leader requesting that the district government declare the association of comrades-in-arms illegal, and that the police collect information and evidence about their activities for future use in the case of a possible crackdown.

Group D's mobilizing rhetoric is highly militant. The following are excerpts from a proposal the group circulated to all Sino-Vietnam War veterans in their district:

> Comrades-in-arms: we will not form an illegal organization or do anything illegal. But if we cannot attain our goal, we will have to submit petitions level by level. We must use our power of unity to change the leaders' opinion of us and struggle to obtain the concern of the upper-level leaders. . . . In order to defend our dignity, we shall always be on call, ready to sacrifice everything we have. Comrades-in-arms: Let's act![18]

Since this group was characterized by an autonomous organization, illegal assemblies, and militant language, it is understandable why the government was so suspicious of it, even though its activities were not as disruptive as those of other groups, such as Group C.

Moderation

Group D refrained from large-scale actions. This was a self-conscious strategy: "We shall try to limit the number of participants. When there are too many participants, we shall divide into groups and petition separately." As mentioned earlier, usually only five representatives delivered their petitions. Apparently they did this to avoid possible repression by the government. They usually refrained from publicizing their actions, as noted in their program of action: "To reduce the social impact [of our petition], we had better not wear army uniforms while petitioning." They also emphasized discipline and eschewed disruption, as also indicated in their program of action: "We should maintain strict discipline while petitioning; petitioners should strictly comply with party discipline, national laws, and the Three Main Disciplines and the Eight Points of Attention. We shall petition in a civilized way, without hurling curses, wrangling bitterly, coming to blows, or damaging public property."

Relationship with the Government

Although, among the four, Group D had the most strained relationship with the government, it did not challenge the legitimacy of the regime. In fact, several times the four leaders emphasized, "We have all been Communist Party members for more than twenty years; none of us will act recklessly." In their program of action, one of their principles was "to strengthen our confidence, and trust the party." They said:

> Since the establishment of the PRC, the party and the country have taken the greatest care of us. After the War to Resist U.S. Aggression and Aid Korea, the War of Resistance to U.S. Aggression and Aid to Vietnam, and the Sino-Vietnam War, the party Central Committee and the State Council issued timely policy documents that gave us priority in job assignments, provided us with economic security, and confirmed our values. We are deeply confident that the party and the country are greatly concerned about us.[19]

Analysis

In this section I provide a systematic comparison of the four groups to illustrate further the key features of their protest strategies and to analyze whether or not these findings support the hypothesis regarding protest opportunism.

The struggles of these four groups share remarkable similarities. First, all of the participants portrayed themselves as loyal members of the regime and explicitly rejected any activities directed against the party-state. Even Group A, the disabled urban residents, who belonged to one of most marginalized segments of the population, appeared to understand the government's position on issues such as fighting floods and sending in disaster relief, as well as holding the provincial games. The members identified themselves as citizens of City Y who shared interests with their government. Organizers of Group B, who were retired cadres, and Group D, who were demobilized army officers, emphasized that they were Communist Party members. Similarly, members of Group C, the retired workers from an SOE, described themselves as "a generation educated by Mao Zedong Thought."

Consistent with these self-identifications, all of the groups demonstrated a strong tendency to operate close to the boundary of authorized channels. For example, Group A challenged public policy by slipping a subversive slogan into an authorized parade. Both Groups A and C occupied government offices as an extension of a legal form of petitioning. Unsurprisingly, they always tried to portray their actions as a natural outgrowth of legal claim-making, downplaying any disruption and mobilization effort. Furthermore, they showed a certain sympathy toward government officials. For example, they refrained from making trouble when the government was most vulnerable.

At the same time, all of the groups demonstrated some tendency to overstep prescribed bounds: staging large-scale, public, and disruptive protests; forming cross-sector coalitions; and establishing autonomous or semiautonomous organizations. They all insisted that troublemaking tactics were essential. For most of them, troublemaking constituted a necessary but not sufficient condition for success. Without any troublemaking activities, their demands were almost certain to be ignored. As the popular saying goes, "Big troublemaking leads to big solutions, small troublemaking to small solutions, and no troublemaking to no solution." It is worth noting that troublemaking is not confined to these groups that have actually carried it out. Many other groups have not engaged in sustained troublemaking activities, but only because they lack the necessary resources and capacity.

In the course of their resistance, the groups all demonstrated an impressive degree of defiance. They often treated officials' threats as bluffs. This is not to suggest that they were unafraid. Actually, as Dorothy Solinger indicates, the mindset of protesters in contemporary China is a mixture of daring and fear.[20] They are aware of a sizable space for resistance within which repression is considered unlikely. Still, they can never exclude the possibility of punishment. What fuels their defiance is a combination of legal consciousness, understanding of the strategies of government officials, and belief in the righteousness of their cause.

Equally defiant and obedient, the petitioners exhibit a host of contradictions: (1) between words and deeds, for example, while they all verbally denounced disruption, they all engaged in various forms of disruptive activities; (2) among words, for example, Group A portrayed its relationship as both positive and tense; (3) among deeds, for example, although members of Group C engaged in many disruptive actions, they sometimes cleaned the offices they had occupied before they departed; and (4) among the actions of the various groups. The petitioners, however, did not seem concerned about such contradictions. Instead, what they were most worried about was protest efficacy and personal safety.

Despite these remarkable similarities, the four groups also demonstrated quite different behavioral patterns. For example, while Group A refrained from acting together with disabled petitioners from other areas, Group B did not hesitate to form cross-sector coalitions, although it did refrain from establishing a formal organization beyond the work unit. In contrast, Group D was not afraid of forming a lateral organization.

As rational actors, the members of these groups tended to choose strategies that they perceived as legitimate and effective. The case studies indicate, however, that these groups sometimes had different understandings of the effectiveness and legitimacy of the various strategies. While Group A found collective visits to Beijing very effective, for instance, leaders of Group B believed that such skip-the-level collective visits incurred higher costs and would not make much difference.

The groups also differed in terms of their perceptions of the boundary line separating permissible from impermissible actions. Close observation reveals that their perceptions were largely consistent with the strengths and needs of each group. In other words, the various groups tended to regard what they could do and needed to do as appropriate behavior, and what they could not or did not need to do as inappropriate. For example, the leaders of Group B, which had a small constituency but could find many other similar groups, had a strong incentive to form a large coalition for collective action, and therefore regarded such action as legitimate. In contrast, Group A had no intention of forming such a coalition, and therefore believed that establishing such a coalition amounted to political provocation. In another situation, while Group B regarded it as inappropriate to establish a formal organization, Group D thought it was legitimate, largely because its organizational capacity was its most powerful weapon.

The groups demonstrated a certain tradeoff in balancing their collective action strategies. For example, while Group D favored a strong organization, it tended to refrain from large-scale activities and widespread publicity. Conversely, Group C enjoyed a large number of participants but was not enthusiastic about developing a strong organizational presence.

The similarities and differences among these groups' protest strategies underline their opportunistic approaches. They are ready to employ any useful tactic available, no matter whether it is defiant or obedient. Moreover, for the sake of effective and sustained struggle, they all find it necessary to employ both defiant and obedient tactics.

These features are not confined to the four groups studied here. Among petitioning groups, a tendency to employ troublemaking tactics is prevalent, as indicated by the remarkable rise of confrontational protests throughout the country since the late 1990s. As I have noted, even those groups that have not carried out considerable troublemaking activities have demonstrated such a motivation. What they usually lack, however, are the resources and capacity for mobilization. In the meantime, among petitioners, and especially among those who have engaged in effective troublemaking activities, the tendency to indicate obedience is also widespread. One of the most striking slogans in China is "We don't want democracy, we want food" *(buyao minzhu yao chifan),* which appeared during a demonstration by the unemployed in Shenyang city, Liaoning province.[21] What is important here is not whether those petitioners really rejected democracy, but that they had a strong incentive to show their obedience. A similar case is a statement by some Hunan peasants who were trying to organize an autonomous peasant association: "Be loyal to the Communist Party forever."[22] In the post-Mao era, when ordinary people no longer need to demonstrate their loyalty in such an ostentatious way, such postures usually can be found only among those who have engaged in defiant activities. Paradoxically, the Chinese people are obligated to show their obedience only when they have been defiant.

These findings about the prevalent tendency to integrate defiant and obedient activities among contemporary Chinese petitioners confirm the hypothesis regarding protest opportunism.

Effects on Grassroots Politics

To some extent protest opportunism has changed the political landscape in grassroots China. Through protest opportunism, the silent masses have begun to have a voice on some policy issues and have started to restrain the behavior of local cadres in a more effective way than previously.

Citizen complaints and protests in China generally restrain local cadres in two ways. First, they report the misdeeds and crimes of local cadres to concerned agencies or to higher authorities. Second, they create pressure on local government to meet their demands. The first form of restraint can ensure the accountability of local cadres for their behavior, and the second can ensure their responsiveness to citizens' preferences.[23] The first form of restraint has worked throughout the PRC regime, where policy feedback and cadre monitoring have been the main functions of the citizen input system. Indeed, the Chinese state has traditionally allowed or often even encouraged ordinary citizens to report problems with local bureaucrats, although such encouragement has not always been consistent across different levels of bureaucracy and across time. In contrast, the second form of restraint is relatively new. Only in the 1990s did ordinary people begin frequently to use official channels of petitioning to assert their claims through collective action. These two types of restraint also demonstrate different citizen-government relations. For the first kind, as Jean Oi points out, "the upward flow of information of the mass line is turned on or off like a faucet by the state from above," not by the strivings of ordinary people from below.[24] In contrast, ordinary people play a more aggressive role in the second kind of restraint, and the state has less control over the process. Of course, these two types of restraint are not mutually exclusive. Many petitioners make their claims to specific interests and rights by framing their grievances as the result of the shortcomings of local cadres.[25]

For either type of restraint to work, petitioners must first obtain an effective government response. How much impact does protest opportunism have in such situations? Here I draw on other evidence to supplement these four case studies to make two preliminary arguments: (1) opportunistic troublemaking tactics generally increase the likelihood of government concessions; and (2) while obedient tactics do not directly create pressure on local governments, they help sustain collective struggles and therefore are indirectly conducive to government concessions.

A quantitative analysis suggests that troublemaking tactics are significantly correlated with the possibility of prompt government response.[26] Here I present a qualitative study, which can better capture the nuances of government responses.

Of course, protest tactics are not the only factor that affects the possibility of government concessions. There are at least two other important factors: (1) the validity of the claims, namely, whether or not the petitions are based on solid evidence and consistent with relevant laws and policies; and (2) the nature of the issues expressed in the protests, in particular, whether or not the government is concerned about the issues involved and whether or not the government has the capacity to respond to them promptly. Yet despite these two other factors, troublemaking tactics usually still have a significant impact on protest outcomes.

As to the validity of the claims, undoubtedly the more valid the claims, the more likely they are to obtain a favorable government response. Determining the validity of the claims, however, usually requires a substantive investigation, and a majority of cases never get the chance to be seriously investigated. In order to trigger serious investigations, troublemaking tactics are often needed. Also, in many cases there is no fixed answer as to whether or not the petitioners' demands are legitimate; only by sustained efforts can they force the state to recognize their claims. Furthermore, a majority of claims recognized as largely valid are nevertheless ignored. As Zhou Zhanshun, the chief of the State Bureau of Letters and Visits, noted, about 80 percent of all letters and visits to state agencies in China are valid or partly valid.[27] Since only a very small number of petitions obtain a response, in most cases it is other factors such as troublemaking tactics that make a difference.

Another relevant factor is whether or not the government is particularly concerned about the issues expressed in the complaints or protests. The Chinese state has often distinguished "burning issues" *(redian wenti)* from ordinary issues. The broadly defined burning issues offer few clues as to whether the government will respond, since they are so broad as to include a majority of issues connected with the protests. But for a few genuinely burning issues in a narrow sense, petitions are substantially more likely to receive a prompt response. Such burning issues have shifted over time. For example, in about 1997 the overcharging of tuition fees and other study costs by middle and primary schools was a burning issue. Protests on this issue were therefore responded to in a relatively prompt way. On March 5, 1997, seven representatives of students' parents in District ZY, City Y, delivered to the municipal government a petition signed by over one thousand parents complaining about inappropriate school fees. This event was immediately reported to the city leaders and to the provincial government, and both the provincial and city party secretaries wrote instructions on this issue. Consequently, the city party committee swiftly investigated the issue and reduced the fees.

For such issues, troublemaking tactics are not always necessary. Sometimes a letter is enough to trigger a substantive response. In some cases the state is actively looking for the information expressed in the petitions rather than passively responding to them. This is also true for most petitions about misdeeds and crimes of cadres. Nevertheless, protesters still often find troublemaking tactics very useful in such cases for three reasons. First, the flow of information usually exceeds bureaucratic capacity, and therefore by using troublemaking tactics, petitioners can distinguish their claims from those of others. Second, petitioners often need to overcome bureaucratic inertia or the tendency of bureaucrats to cover up their subordinates' errors. Finally, whether or not an issue will become a burning issue depends to a large extent on how many people have been involved in the protests and how disruptive they have been.

Not surprisingly, the state is particularly concerned with only a small portion of protest issues. In most cases, state agencies are at best moderately concerned. At the same time, they have a strong incentive not to make concessions to collective resistance, mainly for two reasons. First, concessions often require the difficult task of diverting resources, changing official agendas, and amending or even aborting policies. Local officials often find that their time is insufficient, their energy limited, and their budgets very tight. They also have a strong interest in maintaining the policies that they or their superiors made.

The second major concern of local officials involves the negative consequences of concessions. Giving in to resistance may undermine a local government's authority. By demonstrating the weakness and vulnerability of the government, concessions may inadvertently encourage copycats to resist. Furthermore, concessions by one government agency will often create pressure on other agencies to make similar concessions. Therefore, the party-state often reminds its agents not to make concessions too readily. When local officials have strong incentives not to make concessions, troublemaking tactics are essential for successful protests, since moderate petitions are usually met with procrastination and persuasion. Thus in the case of Group A, in response to its first collective visit, the mayor wrote the following instruction: "As to the ban, it is understandable that some people would hold different opinions. We should do solid work in persuading them to accept the policy."[28] Although he also instructed the concerned agencies to relieve the specific difficulties of those people affected by the ban, such measures were largely a formality. A compensation of 400,000 RMB to Group A would have been inconceivable without their sustained troublemaking activities. With respect to this concession, a cadre in charge revealed the general reluctance: "We were exchanging stability with money."[29]

Sometimes local governments failed to meet the petitioners' demands not because they were unwilling to do so but because it was beyond their capacity. Some issues require systematic adjustment of institutions or policies, sometimes even at the national or provincial levels. For instance, Group D's demand for a substantial improvement in the welfare of demobilized army officers could not be met by the city government. Therefore, the city government was determined to adopt a highhanded posture on this issue. Activists in Group D were obviously aware of this difficulty and therefore claimed that they were prepared to struggle for five years or more. Of course, even when a thorough solution is impossible in the short term, troublemaking activities have often forced local governments to make expedient concessions. As the experiences of Groups B and C reveal, expedient concessions, though often quite limited, are better than nothing for people living in bleak poverty.

As to obedient tactics, they usually cannot directly create pressure on local governments. Without troublemaking tactics, obedient tactics in fact generally amount to nothing. Nevertheless, this is not to suggest they are meaningless. Rather, they have two important effects. First, through obedient tactics, petitioners can demonstrate that they are reasonable claim makers. Second, and more important, obedient tactics can help sustain collective struggles. In short, obedient tactics help protesters define their behavior as reasonable, legitimate, and legal, even though they may have broken some laws.

Due to protest opportunism, collective, public, and disruptive popular resistance in China to some extent has functioned, ironically, in the routinized way of political participation. In a political system where most institutionalized forms of political participation are only a formality, protest opportunism has provided ordinary people with a voice, and has forced some restraints on local officials. Of course, we should not idealize protest opportunism. Unlike institutionalized participation, it has often created disorder, disrupting normal social activities and delaying or obstructing some important public policies. Moreover, in order to realize their interests and defend their rights, ordinary people may need to pay high costs, and sometimes may even incur state repression. After all, such government-citizen interaction patterns, however routinized they may be, are not ultimately protected in China by entrenched political and legal institutions. Finally, protest opportunism can give ordinary people a voice and can restrain government officials only on a limited range of issues and at certain levels of government. Protest opportunism works effectively mainly for issues for which ordinary people have both strong incentives and a relatively high capacity for resistance. Such protests, however, very rarely have a direct impact on the actions of provincial or higher-level government.

12 | In Search of the Grassroots:
Hydroelectric Politics in Northwest Yunnan

In their introduction to *Chinese Society: Change, Conflict, and Resistance*, Elizabeth Perry and Mark Selden point out that China's impressive record of economic growth in recent years has been the envy of the world, largely because the growth suggests the making of a remarkably flexible and inventive state capitalist system.[1] Yet they remind us that this flexibility has not gone uncontested. Rather, it has provoked a dizzying array of confrontations with the state: tax riots, labor strikes, inter-ethnic conflicts, prodemocracy demonstrations, anticorruption and antipoverty campaigns, and even mass suicides. At the same time, since the late 1990s, the Chinese state has directed its rural populations to govern themselves by becoming more active participants in a state-orchestrated "mass democracy" movement by electing their village heads and village committees. Village elections, petitions, and strikes are clearly unprecedented developments in the People's Republic. Nevertheless, while China's citizens are now demanding that local officials be held accountable to the new logic of state-orchestrated participation, and many are demanding that the state address myriad forms of corruption, the mounting health care crisis, the growing problem of social and economic inequalities, and the forces of environmental destruction, it remains unclear just how effective rural residents are in mobilizing against large-scale development projects.

These contradictions between "mass democracy" and

citizen demands for state accountability have become especially evident in the early years of the twenty-first century in the multi-ethnic border region of northwest Yunnan. In this largely mountainous region, where three of Asia's great rivers—the Salween (Nu), the Yangtze (Jinsha), and the Mekong (Lancang)—drop off the Tibetan plateau and produce some of the most stunning gorge country in the world,. the Chinese state has established new institutional structures for grassroots participation in governance and, at the same time, embarked on the building of large-scale hydroelectric projects. This chapter argues that instead of producing a silent or immobilized populace, grassroots participation in government has incited new forms of political action, organizing, and protest.[2] Building on Perry and Selden's vision of an inventive state capitalist system and its unruly others, I show how mostly urban-based activists have attempted to build links with mountain residents and creatively use the media—newspapers, weekly journals, television, videography, public photography exhibits, teach-ins, and the distribution of petitions on the Internet—to contest the building of a multi-tiered dam project on the Nu, or Angry River, in northwest Yunnan.

These activists have drawn national, regional, and international attention to the Yunnan provincial government's obsession with dams, an obsession driven by China's rapidly increasing energy needs and by the economic logic that provinces and sub-provincial units can make large profits from selling energy to other parts of China, or to other countries such as Thailand, Vietnam, and Laos.[3] They have also built on a decade of organizing and protest in northwest Yunnan. Confrontations with the Chinese state in that area throughout the 1990s often emerged around the exploitation of the region's natural resources. Some of this activism came in the form of candid reappraisals of the effects of three decades of socialist development on the environment, a situation not unlike that which Judith Shapiro describes in moving detail in her study, *Mao's War against Nature*.[4] Most environmental and anti-dam activists concerned about the fate of northwest Yunnan, however, are concerned less about the history of socialism than they are about the social and economic inequalities that have emerged under the economic reforms: corrupt land-leasing schemes, unequal access to non-timber products (mushrooms, medicinal herbs, etc.), the changing state definitions of what constitutes collective and state forests, and even the selling of mountaineering permits on "sacred" mountains.[5]

In organizing to protect the Nu River from hydroelectric development, nongovernmental organizations in Kunming and Beijing have built on this recent history of regional environmental activism by linking up with transnational river activists concerned with the effects of Yunnan's dam projects on downstream communities in Thailand, Myanmar (Burma), Laos, Vietnam, and Cambodia. International Rivers Network (IRN), Probe International, Rivers Watch East and Southeast Asia, Oxfam America, Greenpeace International, and a host of other international environmental organizations have put immense pressure on the Chinese government by funding environmental NGOs in China, coordinating international petitions, and pressuring the press outside China to cover the issue. Indeed, much of the international coverage of the protests against the Nu dam project has celebrated the transnational dimensions of the movement. This transregional and transnational activism seems to support recent writings that have argued that the nation-state is now irrelevant in the age of globalization. Unquestionably, certain forms and practices of globalization have brought into China an unprecedented mobility of capital, goods, people, and ideas, as well as activist connections, which have created new spaces in which to challenge the Chinese government. Yet the mobility, traffic, and networking across national borders have not "hollowed out" national sovereignty, nor have they denied citizens new forums for collective action.[6] Rather, they have enabled newly emergent forms of local, regional, and transnational collective action to challenge the state on multiple levels and scales in northwest Yunnan and indeed throughout much of China. It is to these challenges, and some of their contradictions, that we now turn.

Setting the Stage

In the mid-1990s, the Yunnan Construction Bureau began to prepare an application to be submitted to UNESCO to create a "natural" world heritage site in northwest Yunnan, known as the *sanjiang bingliu,* or the Three Parallel Rivers. After many years of work, these efforts finally paid off when UNESCO officially approved the application in July 2003. The Three Parallel Rivers Natural World Heritage Site consists of eight geographical clusters of protected areas spread across a 1.7 million hectare expanse of land, and includes the upper reaches of the Nu, Lancang, and Jinsha rivers (the last becoming the Yangtze farther downstream), which are all part of the larger expanse of the Hengduan Mountains, linking northwest Yunnan and western Sichuan to the Himalayan range. These mighty rivers originate on the Tibetan plateau in the Tibetan Autonomous Region (TAR). When they enter Yunnan, they abruptly turn south and, at one place, flow within seventy-five kilometers of one another, forming extreme altitudinal gradients and a diverse array of ecosystems, from the desert-like dryness on the valley floors to the frigid alpine zones on the mountain peaks and passes.

Official approval of the heritage site—the largest in all of China—was championed in the Chinese media as a great success. Yunnan government officials claimed publicly in press briefings and at official celebrations that the *sanjiang bingliu* would preserve some of China's most diverse ecosystems and, by virtue of the sheer abundance of natural scenic spots, bring tourists to the region. Since the imposition of the Natural Forest Protection Plan, which banned logging on much of the Tibetan plateau in 1998 and forced many county governments to look for alternative means to generate cash, tourism has emerged as the preferred means of development.[7] For the government, the approval was a victory against skeptics, such as the staff at the Nature Conservancy (TNC) and many Chinese environmental activists in Yunnan, who had consistently argued that mass tourism would never benefit local villagers and that it would ultimately lead to large-scale infrastructure development projects, such as the building of new roads and airports.[8] The government argues that development projects, such as the *sanjiang bingliu*, are the only way to bring modernization to the mostly ethnic minority populations who live in the mountains of northwest Yunnan.

Residents of these areas, however, are rarely, if at all, involved in the planning for development initiatives. At most, they are used as informant-consultants to provide local knowledge and information about plant use, herding practices, firewood collection, and other forms of resource use. Local villagers and ethnic minorities are not antidevelopment. Most of the mountain residents with whom I worked, for example, welcome the building of roads. They support such initiatives because they see them as easing the burden of transporting goods to distant villages, providing faster access to middle schools, and giving villagers with severe illnesses easier access to hospitals in county seats. Most mountain residents are tired of isolation, eager for development, and ready for change.

The construction of dams, however, seems to be an altogether different issue. Less than one year after UNESCO's acceptance of the *sanjiang bingliu* application, various environmental activist groups began to organize to oppose the government's plan to dam the Nu River. Their protests quickly attracted the attention of the Chinese and international media. One of the issues of concern was how a massive dam project had found its way into the heritage site. Despite all the public support for Yunnan's quest to win the world heritage designation, few had bothered to notice that the protected sites technically begin above three thousand meters.[9] Harnessing the river's hydroelectric power had been part of the provincial government's agenda from the very beginning of the application process. Although the world heritage site refers to three of Asia's great rivers, the rivers themselves ironically are not part of the heritage site. Some of the activists who organized public opposition to the dam saw the exclusion of the rivers as a perversion of the very spirit of a "natural" world heritage site; others, especially those who worked to prepare the application to UNESCO but were never privy to the final document, saw it as a betrayal.

Media Activism

The debate over the Nu River dam project began on June 14, 2003, when Yunnan television reported that a new hydropower development corporation had been created to explore hydropower development on the upper reaches of the Nu River in Yunnan. Subsequently, numerous reports on the dam appeared in the print media. Rumored in the press to be the brainchild of one of Li Peng's sons, this new corporation was created when the China Huadian Corporation, the Yunnan Development Investment Company, the Yunnan Electricity Group's Hydropower Construction Company, and the Yunnan Nu River Electricity Group signed an agreement to pool resources and funds, with an initial 200 million RMB to dam the river.[10] At the signing ceremony held in Kunming in June 2003, the newly constituted development corporation revealed an ambitious plan to build a thirteen-step dam system over the next twenty years, with the first one, the 180,000-kilowatt Liuku station, slated to begin in September 2003.

The Nu River is one of the last un-dammed major rivers in China. It originates on the southern slope of the Tanggula Mountain range in Qinghai, flows through the imposing Gaoligong Snow Mountain range in Tibet and Yunnan, and twists and turns through deep canyons and seemingly impassable gorges for some 2,018 kilometers before it finally enters Myanmar and becomes the Salween. The proposed dam project is situated in the heart of the Hengduan Mountain range, part of the eastern wing of the Himalayas, now part of the Three Parallel Rivers World Heritage Site. Ironically, UNESCO approved the Chinese government's bid for the Three Parallel Rivers World Heritage Site just weeks after the Nu River Hydropower Development Company was created. This world heritage site is the largest one in all of China. Environmental activists, conservation botanists, and many government officials involved in forestry and nature reserve management insist that this area contains some of the best-preserved varieties of plant and animal life in all of China, if not the world. World Wildlife Fund (WWF), Conservation International, TNC, and other organizations, including several Kunming-based environmental groups, recognize this area as one of the world's greatest biodiversity hotspots.[11]

Organized activism against the Nu River dam project did not necessarily originate in China. It began in other countries, such as Thailand, Vietnam, Cambodia, and Laos, which were affected by Yunnan's dam projects. For example, in late 1995, the 1,250-megawatt Manwan dam was completed on the Mekong, which is now connected to a grid serving Kunming's growing power demands. Soon thereafter construction began on a dam in Jinghong in southern Yunnan, followed shortly thereafter by the Xiaowan dam, the largest in Yunnan, which supplies electricity to Yunnan and Guangdong. Yunnan government officials have made it abundantly clear that these dams are part of a provincial development strategy to make money by targeting the regional electricity market, which, they argue, will in turn alleviate poverty on the upper reaches of the Nu. By the late 1990s, as Yunnan continued to position itself as the key supplier of electricity to other provinces in southern China, as well as to countries throughout mainland Southeast Asia, Yunnan was cooperating with the Japanese government and with several American commercial interests to develop additional hydro projects on the Mekong.

In 1996, government officials in Cambodia began to protest to China that dam projects on the Mekong River in Yunnan were decreasing the flow of water into the Tonle Sap. Later that year, the Vietnamese government complained that these dam projects threatened to reduce water flow to the southern Mekong delta, on which Vietnam relies for 60 percent of its agricultural output. By the start of the new millennium, NGOs and other water and fishery rights organizations in Southeast Asia began to pressure the Chinese government. Several months after the creation of the Yunnan Huadian Nu River Hydropower Development Company in June 2003, the Southeast Asia Rivers Network, for example, with an office in Bangkok, publicly criticized the project and called on the Chinese government to consult with countries downstream before building the dam. On December 16, 2003, the Thai director of the Southeast Asia Rivers Network submitted a protest letter to the Chinese ambassador at the PRC embassy in Thailand, demanding that the Chinese government suspend the project immediately. The protest letter was endorsed by over eighty different environmental, community development, and human rights organizations based in Thailand and Myanmar. The letter argued that the Nu River was shared by three countries, with a wide range of peoples of different ethnicities who depended on the river for their livelihood, both for fisheries and for fertilization of the land. Moreover, the river flowed through some of the most spectacular scenery in all of west China, including the Three Parallel Rivers World Heritage Site. In January 2004, the California-based IRN sent a letter to the director of UNESCO's World Heritage Center, in which it was noted that nine of the thirteen proposed dams were located within the Three Parallel Rivers World Heritage Site. In March 2004, the IRN then organized a petition, signed by seventy-six organizations based in over thirty different countries, which was sent directly to China's president, Hu Jintao, calling for a detailed study of the environmental and social impacts of the dams.

At the same time, behind the scenes in Beijing's Zhongnanhai government compound, certain authorities in the central government complained in September 2003 to Premier Wen Jiabao that the Yunnan government should not have permitted the creation of a new hydroelectric corporation without the authorization of Beijing. In fact, however, in August 2003, the National Development and Innovation Committee had already reviewed and approved the hydropower plans for the Nu River. In late September, China's National Environmental Protection Bureau held a closed-door meeting in Beijing, where thirty experts in zoology, forestry, farming, and geology opposed the Nu River dam proposal. They argued that it had been poorly thought out, was driven excessively by the profit motive, adversely affected the biodiversity of the region, and further strained relations between the government and the region's multi-ethnic minority populations. Some of these experts had worked as consultants to the committee that prepared the application for the Three Parallel Rivers World Heritage Site application. A major rift had thus occurred between conservation-minded experts, many with strong ties to the Chinese Communist Party and the Chinese government, and those within the government pushing for the exploitation of Yunnan's rivers.

As news of this meeting began to leak out in Beijing in late 2003, the Southeast Asia Rivers Network contacted certain environmental groups in Beijing, most notably Liang Congjie's Friends of Nature *(ziran zhiyou)* and Wang Yongchen's Green Volunteers *(lüjia yuan)*, as well as Yu Xiaogang's Yunnan Green Watershed *(Yunnan luse liucheng)*, based in Kunming. It asked them to join the campaign, first started in Thailand, to halt the Nu River dam project. Consequently, these and other activists in Beijing adopted a media strategy used successfully by the wildlife photographer and environmental activist Xi Zhinong. Working as a photographer for the Yunnan forestry bureau in the early 1990s, Xi Zhinong found out that the government of Deqin county (the county that forms the border of Yunnan and the TAR) was engaged in illegal logging in the Baima Nature Reserve. He initially pointed out to Deqin county officials, and then to the provincial government, that the logging scheme would destroy some of the last remaining habitats of the endangered snub-nosed monkey. Shunned by the Yunnan provincial government, Xi and his wife, Shi Lihong, then a journalist for the English edition of *China Daily* and with strong family connections at CCTV, managed to air a documentary on national television exposing the plight of the endangered monkey. Soon thereafter, a number of "Green Camps" were formed on college campuses in Beijing, which, after several months of planning, embarked on a long overland trek to the Baima Nature Reserve to meet with government officials, nature reserve personnel, and village residents. Their investigative tour was widely publicized in China. Eventually, after the intervention of a high-ranking official in the State Council, the central government ordered an end to the illegal logging. The county official who had brokered the deal was replaced.[12]

Many of the activists and experts involved in the spring campaign to oppose the Nu River dam project knew all about Xi Zhinong's media-savvy campaign to stop the illegal logging scheme in the Baima Nature Reserve, and some had been connected to the 1995 investigative tour to the reserve. This successful campaign provided a strategy for the current campaign. In February 2004, twenty journalists, environmental protection volunteers, and conservation scholars in Beijing joined up with activists in Yunnan and embarked on their own investigative tour. For nine days, from February 19 to 24, they traveled along the Nu River, held meetings with local officials, collected stories from village residents about their fears and anxieties concerning the dam construction (which mostly involved issues of relocation), and took photographs and recorded videos. Returning to Beijing in early March, they began preparations for a major educational exhibition of their findings, which they had hoped to hold on March 14, the International Day of Action against Dams. Under pressure from the government, however, they canceled this action. Instead, they proceeded to create a Web site, which could be accessed in both Chinese and English.[13] It seemed that even with some government opposition, little could be done to stop the dam construction on the Nu River, scheduled to begin in September 2004.

But then the situation took an unexpected turn. With the Nu River Web site up and running, plans were under way to attempt another photographic exhibition at the Xidan Bookstore in central Beijing. Around the same time, in early April, the Hong Kong *Mingbao Daily* reported that on April 1 Premier Wen Jiabao had ordered suspension of the dam project. Though Premier Wen stated he was concerned that the dam project had become too controversial, he made no direct mention of activist groups in Southeast Asia or of the protest letter submitted to the PRC embassy in Bangkok. Rather, he called for a more extensive study of the dam project proposal and for more involvement of the scientific and environmental communities. Within days, environmental groups in Yunnan and Beijing claimed a great victory. People involved in the campaign to stop the dam were surprised, but also exuberant; as one activist said, it was like waking up from a dream and realizing that the dream was in fact reality. Word of the premier's decision spread across Chinese- and English-language Web sites and chat rooms. Even the *New York Times* took note, running a front-page article on April 9 titled, "Premier Orders Halt to a Dam Project Threatening a Lost Eden."

While those involved celebrated the campaign as a success, competition emerged behind the scenes over who should get credit for organizing the opposition to the dam. Among activists in Beijing and Kunming, there is arguably not enough recognition of the role that the Bangkok-based Southeast Asia Rivers Network played in the early phases of the movement. Divisions have also emerged among the journalistic, scholarly, and NGO communities. Some journalists have claimed in post-movement meetings among several of the Beijing organizers that they were the crucial force, arguing that without the media attention on the February investigative tour, nothing would have happened. Academic and environmental activists claim that the campaign was successful because they worked behind the scenes to persuade key government officials to put pressure on Wen Jiabao and then worked publicly through creative use of the press and through public teach-ins to educate the people about the potential devastation the dam project would bring to the biodiversity of the Nu River region. Wen Jiabao, they assert, did not just fear the controversy within and among different government organizations and the new hydro project corporation, but, more important, he also feared the growing opposition to the dam. As one activist put it to me, "He feared the will of the masses."[14] In fact, no one really knows exactly what propelled Wen Jiabao to halt the building of the thirteen dams on the Nu River.

In Search of the Grassroots

Therefore, it would appear that the activism against the Nu River hydroelectric scheme was largely the result of the energies and concerns of various Kunming- and Beijing-based environmental organizations, most notably Yu Xiaogang's Yunnan Green Watershed and Wang Yongchen's Beijing Green Volunteers, which had responded to the Bangkok-based Southeast Asia Rivers Network's initial protests. In almost all of the Web-based accounts of the event, as well as in much of the Chinese- and English-language news coverage, there is strikingly little mention of (1) whether or not local cadres in the various villages and townships slated for dam sites supported or opposed the dam, and (2) what role village residents played in the public opposition to the dam. It also needs to be mentioned that much of the protest against the dam was based on a preservation ethic that focused on the natural attributes of the region, especially its biodiversity and water resources (in part due to the fact that the Nu River was believed to lie within the Three Parallel Rivers World Heritage Site), and not based sufficiently on the economic and social effects of relocating eighty thousand residents. Moreover, journalists in China have accused international environmental organizations such as the Nature Conservancy of supporting the dam project on the basis of the positive benefits (clean energy, tourism opportunities, etc.) credited to the American hydropower experience.[15]

Although the protests are a grassroots movement, we must recognize that the space for this grassroots movement has been riddled by numerous contradictions, as a wide range of actors, some based in China, many based outside of China, have brought sometimes radically different understandings, relations, and agendas to the question of why the Nu River project should be opposed, and on what grounds. Additionally, if we define the grassroots as always reflecting the concerns of local residents, then it would appear that resistance to the dam was not a grassroots movement. To see the opposition as a grassroots movement, the term would need to be expanded to incorporate the activities, mobilization strategies, and media skills of various international and metropolitan-based environmental groups, and the ways in which these groups worked across national, regional, and local administrative boundaries to bring pressure to bear on the Chinese government. Even if we take a more transnational approach to the analysis of the grassroots, we would have to acknowledge that intense debates still rage as to just how much this activism across borders is giving voice to the people living in the Nu River valley. At the very least, we would have to recognize that there is, in fact, no single voice that characterizes the people of the Nu River valley.

I became aware of this when one informant described the role of the residents of the Nu River region in opposing the dam. She had been involved in the mid-1990s Baima Nature Reserve campaign, which had exposed the secret deal the then Deqin county governor made to clear a section of the reserve illegally. After the Green Camp investigative tour to Deqin county, and the subsequent media attention to the plight of the snub-nosed monkey, the county governor, as pointed out earlier, was removed from office.[16] Village residents living in the vicinity of the reserve were clearly not the driving force behind the campaign. In fact, most villagers living in the vicinity of the Baima Nature Reserve were largely indifferent to the fate of the snub-nosed monkey.[17] Before the logging ban was instituted in 1998, many villagers earned extra income working for county and prefecture logging companies. Some admitted that they had illegally hunted the monkey (as well as other animals such as the snow leopard), because the skins and various internal organs of these animals could be sold on the black market. In short, the exposure of the illegal logging scheme was a metropolitan-based environmental triumph. Environmental activists learned a lesson, not about the power of the people at the village and township levels to speak out against an environmental injustice, but rather about the power of using the media to turn a then little-known monkey into a national cause.

My informant and several of her friends had participated in the investigative tour of the proposed dam sites, but she was cautious in her assessment of the future of the sites. She emphasized that the Nu River dam project had only been suspended, not defeated. In her estimation, it was one thing to take on a county official over the fate of the snub-nosed monkey; it was quite another to take on the powerful

energy interests pushing to dam the Nu. Moreover, despite its success, the Baima movement in the mid-1990s did not represent the
concerns of many local residents. This time around, the environmental organizations that led the opposition to the dam spent much
more time talking to local residents and local cadres, inquiring
whether they were for the dam or opposed to it. In addition, she
pointed out that Wen Jiabao had called for a more intensive study
and environmental assessment before the plans for the dam could
proceed. This meant that the scientists and environmental experts
whom Wen Jiabao recruited to study the dam project further would
not include the activist groups that had organized the opposition.[18]
And most important, it would not include input from the people
most affected by the dam, those living in the Nu River region.

Other informed observers and participants in Beijing and
Kunming also expressed cautious assessments on the fate of the
dam. A Kunming informant, who has worked extensively in the
Liuku region of the Nu River valley, the site proposed for the construction of the first dam, related that there had been considerable
debate in village meetings about just what the dam would mean for
local people and their livelihoods. Although many upland village
residents were sympathetic to the argument of the government and
the hydroelectric corporation that the dam would bring jobs to the
region and provide much-needed electricity to upland villages, local
schools, and hospitals, village residents who live in the valleys and
along the river's edge were concerned that they would be relocated
to upland regions less suitable for cultivating rice and other staple
foods. Moreover, local cadres who openly opposed the dam were
hesitant to join forces with the environmental organizations in village meetings because they feared that they would lose their jobs or
be criticized by higher-ranking party authorities. To team up with
metropolitan-based environmental groups was risky because such
groups are viewed as operating largely outside the party-state system.
They are also sometimes viewed, whether correctly or not, as lacking
the political connections to ensure that local participation in the
movement will not backfire.

Local cadres and leaders of village committees are restrained by
the fact that they not only have to deal with the specter of future hydroelectric schemes, but also have to address a host of other issues:

access to poverty alleviation programs, government support for dealing with animal husbandry problems (such as livestock illnesses,
etc.), and outside companies that want to turn villages into ethnic
tourist destinations.[19] Their ability to negotiate these issues, which
for many invariably is a question of how to enhance the livelihood of
their communities, depends on their connections, however tenuous,
to prefecture- and provincial-level bureaus and offices. Finally, because the Nu River valley and the mountains surrounding the river
are heavily populated by ethnic minority nationalities, such as the
Lisu, Yi, and Tibetans, many mountain residents are hesitant to join
protest campaigns organized by outsiders. They fear that their participation will be viewed as an ethnic-based movement, which runs
the risk of undermining national unity, a crime against the state.

Grassroots Activism in the Age of Globalization

I began this chapter by pointing out a contradiction: although the
Chinese state has encouraged increased village participation in local
forms of governance, it has also invited new forms of investment in
large-scale development projects. In places such as the Nu River region of northwest Yunnan, market and state forces are pushing for
the development of roads, mass tourism, and hydroelectric dams.
The planning for these projects, however, rarely includes the active
participation and input of the people most affected by them. Moreover, village committees and other institutional structures set up
to encourage local participation in governance issues have not been
the locus of grassroots organizing or popular protest. As seen in
the campaign to oppose the Nu River dam, much of the organizing came from metropolitan-based or international environmental
organizations, which adroitly, and indeed quite impressively, used
the media, the Web, and journalistic connections to push their
cause.

The suspension of the dam project no doubt had much to do with
their efforts. The organizers also drew attention to what they believed were the deleterious effects of such a large-scale development
project on the biodiversity of the region, and, in some instances,
they attempted to give voice to the concerns of the people living
along the Nu River. Residents of the Nu River region participated in

some of the oppositional activities, such as attending meetings organized by Kunming-based environmental groups and signing petitions. In one instance, about two dozen local leaders and residents from the Nu and Mekong river regions traveled to Kunming to attend three days of activist training sessions and to participate in a one-day public forum. This widely attended forum focused not only on the question of how best to organize against the powerful interests of state capitalism in China, but also on the dangers of using the movement as a rights-based form of resistance. As I have pointed out, the opposition to this particular large-scale development project is not an example of the grassroots standing up to energy interests, unless we are willing to expand the usual definition of the grassroots as emanating from local peoples, local concerns, and local demands. In this particular instance, we need to look at the grassroots from the perspective of translocal and transnational forms of organizing and mobilization. At the same time, we need to recognize that this transnational space, where activists work across national, cultural, economic, and social borders and boundaries, is characterized as much by its contradictions as it is by its opening up a new utopian space of transnational civil society.

As we rethink the meanings and associations of the metaphor of the grassroots, we might also ask how recent theories of globalization are relevant to our understandings of collective action and protest in contemporary China. Many theorists have suggested that the "global" signals a revolutionary break with the past, that a new form of governmentality is now appearing, based in the flow and movement of global institutions, and that organizing against any and all forms of capital exploitation must, if it is to be effective, cut across local and national borders.[20] Clearly, in previous and ongoing dam projects in Yunnan, there is some validity to the argument that effective collective actions, if they are to be successful, cannot be centered only on local or national concerns. As seen in the campaign against the damming of the Nu River, downstream communities and activist groups based in Thailand, Cambodia, Vietnam, and Myanmar, with the help of international groups, such as the Southeast Asia Rivers Network, attempted to put pressure on the Chinese government by calling attention to the effects of dams on the livelihood of the people living in other downstream countries. It is not surprising that rivers which, like the Nu and the Mekong, originate in China and then flow into the territories of other nation-states present a case of regionally based contested sovereignties. Yet, as we have seen in this particular instance, transnational concerns, and the activities and strategies of groups outside China that challenge China's claims to build dams based on its sovereign right to do so, largely dropped out of the picture. The movement increasingly turned away from the more complicated transnational regional context of Southeast Asia and inward to the human and biological future of the Nu River region in Yunnan.

This occurred not simply because various Beijing- and Kunming-based activist groups refused to think about what the dams would mean for people in downstream countries, or simply because these activists could think only in nationalist terms. Indeed, many of the activists I know are cosmopolitan nomads, often living abroad, constantly attending meetings, workshops, and even protests (such as the World Social Forum) outside China; they are also pervasively suspicious of how the Chinese Communist Party mobilizes support for itself through appeals to national protection or national sentiment. The turning away from the transnational dimensions of the movement occurred mostly because of the perceived dangers of raising the issue of national sovereignty that the Nu River hydroelectric scheme immediately suggests. Although many activists are unsure about the relationship between hydroelectric corporations and the state (and how and why decisions are made at central and provincial levels which allow these interests to incorporate and seek investment funds), they know that challenging the authority of prefectural and provincial leaders can be politically risky. The relationship between the state and the processes of marketization in the energy sector is also unclear. Thus many activists struggle with the vexing question of just how to define the enemy. Is it the central government? Is it global capitalism? Is it corrupt provincial leaders who have been promised kickbacks if a dam wins approval? Or is it local cadres who have been seduced by the promises of development and modernization that these dams claim to represent? Part of the effectiveness of large-scale hydroelectric schemes in Yunnan is that the enemy seems at once, as Perry and Sheldon state, to be the very "inventiveness and flexibility of the state," as well as the myriad and often hidden ties that this "creative" state system has with non-state, regional, and global capital interests.

The anthropologist Michel-Rolph Trouillot has observed that the globalized world of the new millennium remains characterized by complex encounters between individuals, collectivities, and governmental bureaucracies.[21] His observation suggests not the retreat of the state in the new age of global capital, but an increased governmental presence in the lives of citizens everywhere. And yet this "shadow of the state," as Ralph Miliband termed it several decades ago, has hardly gone unchallenged.[22] Almost everywhere in the world—the anti-WTO protests that started in Seattle in 1999, the Chiapas movement in Mexico, the labor strikes and other forms of protest that have erupted in China in the early years of the twenty-first century, and so forth—we see challenges to the power, claims, and projects of governments. Trouillot argues that these varied confrontations, which are often simultaneously confrontations with capital, have led analysts of globalization to observe that not only is the nation a bygone remnant of the modernist era of the twentieth century, but also so too has the state become irrelevant, economically, socially, and culturally. Michael Hardt and Antonio Negri argue, for example, that in place of the state there are now new organizational configurations of "imperial sovereignty"—what they call Empire—that adroitly sidestep national state power.[23] In the new millennium, they predict, real power will be lodged in trans-state organizations: nongovernmental organizations, global corporations, the World Bank, the International Monetary Fund, and even corporations such as Halliburton, with its multiple, offshore subsidiaries. These trans-state organizations are seemingly everywhere at once, and yet are accountable to no one.

This chapter has attempted to tell a slightly different story. As seen in the account of the Nu River dam, the power of the nation-state at the beginning of the twenty-first century appears more visible and encroaching, but also less effective and relevant. In China, collective action at the grassroots depends increasingly on this dual, almost schizophrenic nature of the state. In northwest Yunnan, the Chinese state is promoting grassroots participation and mass democracy through village elections and other means at the same time that it pushes forward with economic liberalization, rampant growth and modernization, and large-scale development projects. The mobilization of grassroots collective action to fight social injustices, corruption, malfeasances, and neglect, and to empower those who are marginalized, silenced, or ignored in the process of state-orchestrated economic liberalization, is an unprecedented development in China's recent history, one that suggests real social change may be possible. At the same time, the increased demand for energy in China's metropolitan areas and the specter of profits for provincial leaders and would-be capitalists in Yunnan and elsewhere, who are aware of the hydroelectric potential of the great Nu and Mekong rivers as they fall off the Tibetan plateau, suggest a completely different battle, one perhaps with less room for optimism. This, then, may be the legacy of the ongoing protests against hydroelectric schemes in northwest Yunnan: the mixing of hopes and despair, triumphs and struggle.

YUEZHI ZHAO
SUN WUSAN

13 | Public Opinion Supervision:
Possibilities and Limits of the Media
in Constraining Local Officials

Public opinion supervision *(yulun jiandu)* emerged as a buzzword in Chinese media and politics in the 1990s. Like many other words in the Chinese political lexicon, the term is ambiguous. Nevertheless, a prevailing definition connotes the use of critical media reports to supervise government officials. Popular opinion and anecdotal evidence reveal a positive role of critical media reporting in constraining local officials. For example, it is said that local officials "do not fear citizen appeals but are afraid of press exposure" *(bupa shanggao, jiupa shangbao)*. A township official interviewed in Zhejiang observed that when villagers saw journalists, some would say, "Those who dismiss officials are coming." And *Focus Interviews (Jiaodian fangtan)*, CCTV's most celebrated public opinion supervision program, is said to be so powerful that Liang Jianzeng, the director of the CCTV News Commentary Department, which is responsible for the program's production, reported that a county propaganda official had said: "Since *Focus Interviews* reporters arrived in the village and produced one program after another to expose and attack grassroots officials when in conflict with party secretaries and village leaders, farmers now have the nerve to threaten: 'Watch out, or I will take you to *Focus Interviews*.' . . . *Focus Interviews* has spoiled the farmers."[1]

Such claims should not be taken at face value. Nevertheless, the rise of public opinion supervision signifies both the emergence of more assertive media outlets and the central leadership's more conscious use of the media to curb the systematic bureaucratic corruption and mounting crisis in local governance. Although the supposed power of the media to carry out political and moral persuasion and the government's power to dismiss officials are two different matters, media outlets are sometimes effective in disciplining local officials because they are part of the party-state structure. Yet it is precisely the same structure that undermines the media system's consistency in exercising such a supervisory role and limits its potential as an independent social force. Moreover, we argue that the use of public opinion supervision in legitimating monopolistic party power through the public display of the central leadership's paternalistic commitment to the people is more significant than the actual ability of the media to restrain local officials in their everyday exercise of power.

Continuity and Change in the Media's Role in Mediating Relations

Although the specific definition of public opinion supervision as news media supervision of government officials is often taken to be part of a new discourse on political liberalization in reform-era China, the term "critical reporting" (piping baodao) and the writing of critical reports on local officials are not new in Chinese journalism. There are institutional continuities between public opinion supervision and critical reports as instruments of governance in the PRC. Although the party has always insisted that the role of the media is to be its mouthpiece, the Chinese Communist Party Central Committee issued its Decision to Carry out Criticism and Self-Criticism on Newspapers and Periodicals as early as April 1950, with the purpose of "strengthening the linkages between the party and the masses, to ensure the democratization of the party and the state, and to accelerate social progress."[2] In addition to writing positive propaganda for public consumption, China's journalists had the responsibility to provide "internal reference material" for restricted circulation within the party leadership.[3] Through internal reporting, which is almost by definition investigative, critical, and problem-oriented, journalists were to identify flaws in the party's policies and miscarriages of these policies at the local levels, report on social problems, and suggest specific reforms and disciplinary actions against delinquent local officials.

The party journalists' role in mediating the relationship between upper-level party leadership and grassroots officials derives from the party's view of the media as an integral part of the party-state's governmental apparatuses and its model of political communication, that is, "from the masses, to the masses." As a form of internal communication within the party hierarchy, internal reference material does not play any role in the public mediation of the relationship between the central leadership and the general public. It underscores the party's paternalistic nature and its predisposition to deal internally with problems of power abuses and policy failures. Moreover, recurring ideological struggles, plus the media's lack of a self-interested institutional imperative in the pre-reform period, made it very difficult for journalists to pursue critical internal reporting in any consistent manner.

The reform era ushered in the party's conscious incorporation of critical reporting in the public media as part of its ideological, disciplinary, and administrative apparatuses. A 1980 party Central Committee document explicitly states that "the party's press should carry out criticism and self-criticism," defining the targets of criticisms to include both social phenomena and specific individuals.[4] A 1981 party document further defines the dual ideological and administrative role of critical media reporting. It not only acknowledges the role of the critical press in strengthening the linkage between the party and the masses, and in enhancing "the reputation of the party and the press," but also encourages various levels of the party to use critical media reporting to facilitate administrative work.[5] While journalists continued to write internal reference reports, more critical reports appeared in the media, as the party tried to demonstrate publicly its benevolent intention to respond to popular concerns, and as media outlets struggled to rebuild their own credibility after the Cultural Revolution.

By the mid-1980s the reformist discourse of public opinion supervision had replaced the Maoist language of "criticism and self-criticism." Compared with the old terminology, this new discourse expressed liberal aspirations for a more autonomous media system as an external check on the party-state's absolute power. In 1987, in a breakthrough in official discourse, and as a sign of the party's growing appreciation of the role of critical media reporting in governance, party general secretary Zhao Ziyang explicitly promoted public opinion supervision in the party's Thirteenth National Congress report.[6] Despite the general tightening up of media control in the post-1989 period, Jiang Zemin echoed the same endorsement of public opinion supervision in his report to the party's Fifteenth National Congress in 1997.[7] A reiteration of the party's commitment to public opinion supervision can be found in the February 2004 Regulations on Inner-Party Supervision of the Communist Party of China. The document states that the news media should play the role of public opinion supervision through internal or open reports "under the leadership of the party" and "according to relevant rules and procedures." In addition, party organizations and party officials at various levels "should emphasize and support public opinion supervision, listening to opinions, and promoting and improving work."[8]

The apparent continuity between the pre-1989 and post-1989 official endorsements of public opinion supervision, however, conceals significant differences. The pre-1989 discourse was articulated in the context of relaxed media censorship and a wider call for greater press freedom. It expressed a liberal democratic aspiration for increased public participation in the state's decision-making processes and a more autonomous role of the media in supervising not only government officials but also the party-state on major policy issues. It was articulated in the promise in the report of the party's Thirteenth National Congress to inform members of the public about important events and to involve them in discussions of major issues. In contrast, the post-1989 discourse was promoted in the context of tightened media control, a narrower, though more urgent, anticorruption agenda, and the party-state's pressing need to achieve both ideological legitimacy and administrative effectiveness over local authorities as it confronts the contradictions of China's capitalist revolution unleashed by Deng's 1992 call for accelerated market reforms. In particular, it was articulated at a time when the party leadership was beginning to face intensified tensions between the promises of a nominally socialist state and a developmental process that had led to a corrupt bureaucracy, a brutally exploitative economy, and a highly stratified, fractured, and conflictual society.[9]

Thus as China embraces the market economy and integration with the global market system, the question of how to accommodate the varied and often conflicting interests of different social groups while maintaining stability has become the most profound governmental challenge. In meeting this challenge, on the one hand, the party leadership prohibits open media discussion of the political implications of the reforms by subscribing to Deng's "no debate" decree.[10] It also imposes a sustained news blackout on so-called "mass events" *(qunti shijian),* particularly organized protests by workers, farmers, and urban residents who have endured the multifaceted negative consequences of "accumulation by dispossession" in the process of China's capitalistic developments.[11] On the other hand, the party leadership has mobilized the news media to provide "correct guidance to public opinion" and to defuse growing social tensions. Within this context, a highly publicized response by party leaders on national television to exposed cases of power abuse, bureaucratic delinquency, and inhumane economic exploitation plays an important ideological role. It projects a caring image and symbolically affirms the leadership's commitment to the people, enhancing its legitimacy and demonstrating its sincerity in dealing with China's problems.[12]

From an administrative point of view, drastic changes in central-local power relations and the central leadership's decreasing authority over local officials have forced the leadership to search for new methods of governance.[13] Since the 1980s the changes in central-local financial relationships have resulted in profound changes in central-local political-economic relationships. On the one hand, as George Gilboy points out, "understanding that local economic growth promotes social and political order, the CCP tolerates, and even rewards, officials who use any means to produce local investment and employment."[14] On the other hand, the central government, especially since the 1990s, has raised the central share of national budgetary revenues while transferring expenditure responsibility downward to lower-level governments.[15] As a result, local governments at the county level and below not only have become relatively autonomous political-economic agents but also are trapped in a profound imbalance between resource extraction and obligations of service delivery.[16] This policy has turned many local officials, particularly township-level officials in the grain-growing regions of central China, into single-minded "tax officials" who depend on direct and sometimes coercive extractions from farmers for delivering basic services such as education and family planning, and even their own salaries.[17]

At the same time, this change has transformed local governments in regions with village and township industries into de facto entrepreneurs with a focus on economic growth at the expense of maintaining social justice and securing workers' welfare.[18] Moreover, the state's efforts to strengthen the machinery of political power in rural society by establishing an excessively large but inadequately funded corps of township officials have intensified plundering of farmers by local officials, creating further tensions between officials and villagers. In central China the agrarian crisis has brought about "the reemergence of lineage, religious, cult and even criminal organizations."[19] Signs of this crisis in local governance, according to Yu Jianrong, are a widespread fiscal crisis at the township level (analyzed by Jean Oi and Zhao Shukai in their chapter in this book), the growth of organized resistance by villagers, and the invasion of "black and evil forces" *(hei'e shili)* in local governance.[20] Instead of implementing central policies, these "black" social forces have privatized public power and openly defied central authority. For example, they have denounced central documents that ban illegal fees on farmers as "black documents" and "dog farts."[21] Consequently, as Jonathan Unger observes, farmers want more assertion of central power in order to enforce central edicts and to provide greater protection from predatory local officials. Unger writes that "Beijing, for its part, is increasingly willing today to promote the viewpoint among disgruntled peasants that errant local cadres are to blame for their plight, painting itself as a good, caring government."[22]

The news media have emerged as the central party leadership's major tool for achieving this objective. Because the news media are relatively autonomous from other functionary parts of the state bureaucracy, they play a unique surveillance role for the central leadership, serving as its eyes and ears on local situations. Although media outlets are integral parts of the party-state, they are not part of the government's administrative structure. The party gives them institutional authority to investigate and to report, but the unique status of the media allows them to bypass the government's bureaucratic hierarchy. A CCTV crew, for example, can go directly to a village to investigate without going through the provincial, county, and township bureaucracies. Moreover, public media exposure not only helps to undermine bureaucratic protection but also increases the political and moral pressures on the bureaucracy to deal with the problem. The whole nation, particularly the central leadership, is watching. Though government officials may not be accountable to the public, they are ultimately accountable to the central leadership, whose awareness of inaction could spell the end of one's political career. In short, the media's public nature and their unique role as an integrated but relatively autonomous part of the party-state make them a powerful ideological tool for creating a closer identity between the party and the public at a time of increased political alienation. They also act as a cost-effective administrative instrument for the central leadership to reassert control over an unruly and dysfunctional bureaucracy that threatens the very existence of the party-state itself. The widespread post-1992 corruption and crisis in local governance gave the media an unprecedented role in this process.

At the same time, just as the reform process has turned local governments into relatively autonomous political-economic agents, it has turned news organizations into relatively autonomous political-economic entities, with an institutional imperative to win popular support through public opinion supervision. The development of a market economy in the post-Mao era has led to the commercialization of media operations, the proliferation of media outlets, and the growth of television as the most popular medium.[23] By the start of the twenty-first century, almost all media institutions were dependent on commercialized financing and were forced to survive in increasingly competitive media markets. To establish credibility and ensure their own political survival, many commercially oriented media outlets have taken pains to curb corrupt practices, such as accepting bribes in exchange for favorable news reporting.[24] In addition, a flexible personnel system has allowed these news organizations to recruit and nurture a new generation of enterprising young journalists with a reformist ethos and a strong sense of social responsibility. Although they are fully aware of the American muck-raking tradition and the liberal notion of watchdog journalism, they also are acutely aware of the permissible political boundaries. They improvise a unique form of professionalism in both practical and normative terms.[25] For example, they pick their targets carefully and work within the constraints of an evolving regime of propaganda discipline that clearly defines certain topics and individuals as off-limits to critical reporting.[26] These enterprising journalists constitute the backbone of public opinion supervision.

The Making and Power of Public Opinion Supervision

The rise of public opinion supervision, then, is the result of the complicated interaction between the central leadership's ideological and administrative imperatives and the self-interests of the media within the broader context of China's ongoing political, economic, and social transformation. Specifically, the most significant step toward the rise of public opinion supervision in the post-1992 period was initiated at the top of the party's propaganda hierarchy. At the end of 1992, Xu Xinhua, journalism bureau head of the party's Propaganda Department, relayed to Yang Weiguang, then president of CCTV, the central party leadership's new directive to the media: to provide "correct guidance to public opinion" through the discussion of current social issues on national television. Startled by the extraordinary nature of this instruction, Yang asked for a written directive. The party delivered the directive in its 1993 propaganda guidelines.[27] With this, Yang set in motion a series of reforms that led to the creation of CCTV's first current affairs magazine program, *Oriental Horizon (Dongfang shikong)*, in May 1993, and the establishment of CCTV's News Commentary Department at the end of that year, which has produced the country's most celebrated public opinion supervision programs, *Focus Interviews* and *News Probe (Xinwen diaocha)*. Since its inception in 1994, *Focus Interviews* has garnered a national audience of 273 million, or approximately one quarter of the total national audience of 1.094 billion.[28] Its overwhelming success led to the popularization of its form of public opinion supervision in the country's media system. Also, the growing importance of the Internet as a new medium for initiating and circulating critical stories, along with encouragement from the top leadership, propaganda officials, and journalism scholars, turned public opinion supervision into a prominent discourse in Chinese media and politics.

The first critical report on *Focus Interviews* aired on April 3, 1994, the third day after the program's debut. It established the archetypal public opinion supervision story. The story, titled "Beijing Outskirts: A Cemetery Is Being Built on Farmland," exposed how a village in Shunyi county, for short-term economic gain, violated state policy and illegally sold farmland to build a cemetery. The news tip came from an anonymous caller. Three journalists were dispatched to investigate the case. Without first approaching the local officials, they went directly to film the cemetery and interviewed its custodian and villagers. The journalists then approached the village party secretary, who abruptly terminated the interview when he realized the critical nature of their investigation. Finally, the journalists visited the land administration bureau of Shunyi county and interviewed other officials. When the program was broadcast, relevant central government departments expressed concern, sent an investigative team to the village, and asked the journalists to accompany the team to report on the resolution of the problem.[29]

These events epitomize the process and purpose of public opinion supervision. First, there is the information from the public, by far the most important source for this type of content. Although the news media and professional journalists carry out critical reporting, the public plays a crucial role in this process. On an average day in the early 2000s, *Focus Interviews* received approximately 300 letters, 20 in-person visits, 130 telephone calls, 300 e-mails, and 400 paged messages.[30] Many of these suggest program topics, raise local issues of concern, and express individual and collective complaints against local officials. In fact, 90 percent of the program's critical topics are derived from audience letters and calls.[31] Thus while the central leadership consciously incorporates the news media as an instrument of power, ordinary Chinese, often as a last resort in their struggles against bureaucratic oppression and economic exploitation, have also tried to assert their claims by urging the media to investigate their complaints and trying to put the issue of social justice on the media's agenda.[32]

Second, as seen in the cemetery exposé, the journalists' investigations focused on a target related to an issue that has broad policy relevance. Contrary to the routine news-gathering procedure in which local propaganda officials often accompany journalists, in this case journalists from a central-level media organization bypassed several levels of bureaucracy, reached the village directly, and confronted the party secretary without advance notice. The camera exposed the "true face" of a local official responsible for the violation of state policy. The on-the-spot performances by local officials in front of the camera—explaining, defending, contradicting, denying, and acknowledging their own wrongdoing—make for audience-grabbing critical reports. Furthermore, although the story is specific, it is also typical. It is a symptom of the Chinese version of "enclosure," that is, the reckless misappropriation of farmland for commercial gains in the wave of the market-oriented development unleashed by Deng's 1992 pronouncements during his Southern Tour. In fact, the problem had already prompted the central leadership to issue edicts to curb such misappropriations.

Therefore, such a target accentuates the policy agenda of the central leadership and provides an example for strengthening the implementation of central policy. Not only has *Focus Interviews* developed an entire set of criteria to identify and nurture a story with broad policy relevance, but also it has cultivated effective methods of investigation, including covert investigations in which journalists hide their identities and their cameras. It has also developed effective strategies of presentation to maximize the dramatic effects of an exposé, such as weaving engaging narratives out of factual evidence and personalizing stories.[33] Moreover, just as the incorporation of vox populi interviews with ordinary people—the symbolic incarnation of the "public" in public opinion supervision—is an essential ingredient, so is the inclusion of comments by experts and by government officials with policy authority. Yet as standard practice, the journalists limit the targets of exposure to the local levels without implicating higher-level officials in the policy violation. No township-level officials, for example, were interviewed in the report on the cemetery.

The third element is that the selection and treatment of the topic should not stir up social unrest and undermine political stability at the same time that it generates positive official reaction and effective mobilization of party-state bureaucracies for problem solving. The sequence of events has become routine: first, the program exposes an instance of power abuse, policy violation, consumer fraud, industrial accident, or social injustice. The party leadership sees the program, becomes concerned, and telephones subordinates, telling them to investigate. State Council and ministerial-level investigation teams are dispatched to the location, emergency meetings are convened at various levels of the party-state bureaucracy, and the targeted problem is quickly dealt with. For example, in 2001 Politburo members issued as many as thirty directives *(pishi)* in response to more than twenty *Focus Interviews* reports and demanded bureaucratic action. In 2002 the State Council General Office further institutionalized this process by issuing a document demanding that concerned departments provide feedback reports on the implementation of party leaders' directives with regard to specific problems exposed by *Focus Interviews*.[34]

Therefore, the power of public opinion supervision is not only real as far as its specific targets are concerned but also at times all-encompassing. First, because of its incorporation into the governmental process, its power is punitive rather than simply persuasive. Media exposure often leads to harsh legal and administrative punishments of the government officials and businesses involved. Not surprisingly, public opinion supervision has a high degree of "killing power."[35] Second, this power is governmental, not only because it typically induces the state to take disciplinary actions, but also because its execution is directly linked to the level of the party-state administration to which the media outlet belongs. Finally, this power can be productive because it not only creates an environment conducive to the implementation of new policies and regulations but also on occasion can lead to policy changes.

The case of industrial poisoning in Baigou township, Hebei province, for example, encompasses all three dimensions of the power mentioned here.[36] Shortly after the 2002 Spring Festival, *Dahe bao* (Dahe Daily), a market-oriented newspaper in Zhengzhou city, Henan province, reported cases of young women migrant workers from the local Xuchang area suffering from benzene poisoning, resulting in several deaths.[37] These women had all worked in luggage factories in Baigou township in neighboring Hebei province. On the basis of information provided by the victims and medical experts, the report claimed that the factory owners in Baigou were responsible, as the glue used for making the luggage contained benzene, which is toxic when used under improper working conditions. Unlike in many other cases of industrial incidents and labor abuse in China, the hometown media of the affected workers were not constrained by local protectionism. Thus not only were they able to report on the problem, but also their verdict on the guilt of the factory owners was unquestioningly accepted by the Xuchang city authorities, who called an emergency meeting in which they sought to "rescue" the workers and negotiate with the Baigou township government to improve working conditions.[38] The involvement of the Xuchang municipal government quickly helped define the nature of the case not only as one of business negligence but also as the failure of local officials to protect workers.

Following the report in *Dahe bao*, newspapers in Beijing reported on the issue. These reports caught the attention of relevant central government ministries and prompted central government intervention. An investigative team consisting of members of six government departments went to Baigou with a broad mandate to investigate overall labor conditions in the area. Subsequently, factories that failed to follow regulations were closed down, workers were sent to undergo health examinations, and factory owners were subjected to legal education. The government made the problem of unsafe working conditions in factories a matter for central government supervision of local officials.

When *Focus Interviews* picked up the story on March 27, 2002, the case reached the pinnacle of power and led to an all-out mobilization of the governmental structure. Premier Zhu Rongji watched the program and issued a whole set of instructions the following day. First, he linked this incident to a related occurrence in Beijing, defining it as a national problem and calling for severe punishment of those involved in illegal industrial production, tax evasion, use of child labor, and violation of labor protection regulations. Second, he called for the protection of the workers' welfare and compensation for impaired workers. Third, he called for the development of new, detailed regulations with regard to labor protection in enterprises involved in the use of dangerous materials. Finally, he called for a national alert, demanding nationwide examination of the problem and correction of the situation.[39] A reorganized and more powerful State Council investigation team, consisting of members of eight government ministries and departments, was dispatched to Baigou immediately.

The impact on Baigou was instantaneous: eight business operators were legally prosecuted; the top two party and government leaders of the township, the party secretary and the township leader, were dismissed; and 1,100 substandard family workshops, accounting for about one third of all factories in the township, were shut down. Repercussions also extended to the national level: shortly before May Day, 2002, a State Council document reported to the national bureaucracy about the Baigou incident and asked other localities to draw a lesson from it. On May 19 the State Council enacted a new set of labor protection regulations titled Regulations on Labor Protection in Workplaces Using Dangerous Material. Although these regulations were already in the making before the Baigou case, the event provided an opportunity for the state to maximize publicity and dramatize its relevance. This case epitomized "rule by television": through television, the central leadership affirmed its administrative power and its ability to mobilize the entire party and state bureaucracy, and, most important, demonstrated its penetration of local-level politics and economics. The timing was also crucial because the central leadership needed such a story right before May Day, as it reaffirmed the state's commitment to the working class.[40]

Media reporting on the circumstances surrounding the death of Sun Zhigang, a young university graduate from Wuhan, further increased the power of public opinion supervision. On March 20, 2003, Sun, who had just moved to Guangzhou to start a new job, was beaten to death while in the custody of the Guangzhou police because he had failed to carry an identification card. A local newspaper, the *Nanfang dushi bao* (Southern Metropolis News), disclosed the case. Although CCTV initially remained silent, the story was picked up by other media outlets and received wide circulation and commentary on the Internet, generating pressure on Guangzhou authorities to intervene. An investigation was ordered, and those responsible for Sun's death were identified. More than twenty local officials, police functionaries, and their hired thugs were subjected to party and administrative discipline, with more than ten of them receiving legal punishment and one sentenced to death. More significantly, the media coverage went beyond Sun's death to challenge the state policy that empowered the police to detain him in the first place.[41] The media reported and amplified legal opinion arguing against the unconstitutional and discriminatory nature of the detention policy. The case galvanized existing elite and popular criticism of the state's discriminatory policy toward the rural population, especially migrant workers. In August 2003 the state abolished the custody system and prohibited local police from detaining rural migrants or imposing fines on them.[42]

Whereas the Baigou case addressed state regulation of businesses and the state's role in protecting workers' welfare, the Sun Zhigang case involved a fundamental civil right and the justice of a major state policy. Moreover, whereas there was little mobilization of public opinion beyond the initial media reports in the Baigou case, in the Sun Zhigang case there was sustained mobilization of public opinion in the media until the state undertook a major policy change. Most significant, whereas central-level media outlets such as *Focus Interviews* choose targets far down the bureaucratic ladder (county level and below), and provincial media outlets, including the well-known *Nanfang zhoumo* (Southern Weekend), muckrake only in other provinces in a practice known as "[public opinion] supervision in a different jurisdiction" *(yidi jiandu),* the Sun Zhigang case was unprecedented in that a local newspaper exercised public opinion supervision in its own city. Furthermore, instead of targeting local government departments with less political clout, the newspaper targeted the powerful law-and-order apparatuses of Guangzhou city. Yet the aftermath of this exposure, in which the Guangzhou city authorities carried out a retaliatory investigation into the finances of the paper and arrested three of its journalists, illustrates the power of bureaucratic resistance.[43]

Local Bureaucratic Resistance and Backlash against Public Opinion Supervision

Although public opinion supervision is significant because it affects not only individual local officials but also government policies in some cases, its role in improving local governance is limited. First, given that the problem of local governance is most acute in the rural areas, the amount of critical news reporting in national media outlets focusing on governance in the rural areas is quite limited. For example, of the 396 *Focus Interviews* critical reporting topics between 1994 and 1998, 190, or 40.8 percent, focused on urban settings. Only 119 cases, or 30.1 percent, were concerned with issues in villages and townships.[44] While such a ratio is highly disproportionate to the actual ratio of urban to rural residents in the population, not to mention the gravity of the rural governance problem, it is consistent with the overall systemic urban bias of the Chinese news media.[45] More significantly, *Focus Interviews'* more articulate urban audiences have already complained about its "disproportionate" concentration on rural issues. Consequently, in its future evolution the program faces the challenge of how to accommodate the viewing preferences of this core audience.[46] Economic interests in the media industry favor urban audiences, who are the most desired targets of domestic and foreign advertisers. Given that competition for advertising and the core affluent urban audience have intensified in the post-WTO Chinese media market, it is unlikely that the media will increase coverage of rural issues.

Second, in contrast to national media outlets, especially CCTV, which is known to be closely followed by the central leadership, the capacity of local media, inclusive of provincial, municipal, and county-level media outlets, to bring pressure to bear on local officials is more limited. Thus although CCTV's Liang Jianzeng reported a 100 percent resolution rate for problems exposed by *Focus Interviews,* a national survey of 661 media workers revealed a very different picture.[47] Only 7 percent reported that all the problems they had reported were addressed, 32.7 percent reported that a majority of the problems were addressed, and more than 32 percent reported that a small portion was addressed. Significantly, 13 percent reported no solution at all to their reported problems.[48] In fact, local officials who are described as "only afraid of central-level media, not local media," seem to be quite common.[49] County-level media outlets, which are geographically close to villagers and are theoretically equipped to criticize village and township-level officials, are virtually useless in this regard. As one interviewee in Zhejiang observed, if central-level media can hardly criticize county-level officials, county-level media can hardly touch village-level officials. County-level media outlets operate strictly as party mouthpieces and as instruments of local boosterism. They have a high level of integration with the local power structure and a low level of professionalism. The director of a county-level television station, for example, is typically the director of the county's broadcasting bureau. With such a local power structure, as one interviewee noted, to criticize local affairs means criticizing the work of colleagues and even superiors. Moreover, smaller geographic settings mean more closely knit interpersonal and social networks among journalists, power holders, and other potential targets of criticism.[50] One interviewee in Zhejiang noted that when the county television station broadcast a critical report about the maintenance of street sanitation, it provoked animosity between officials in two related government departments. Instead of blaming the two departments, the county leadership blamed the television station for creating the bureaucratic tension. Consequently, the television station abandoned critical reporting.

Third, although the central leadership has come to appreciate the ideological and administrative role of public opinion supervision, there is still the constant fear that the media may become too critical and thus pose a threat to political stability. Any change in the macropolitical climate, particularly power struggles at the top and increased instances of social unrest from below, could undermine the central leadership's commitment to critical reporting in actual practice, if not in principle. Even if the central party leadership is in a more self-confident and unified mood and thus willing to tolerate more critical reports, rank-and-file bureaucratic resistance is formidable. For example, it is well known that there are two lines of traffic flowing from all over the country to CCTV headquarters. One consists of the powerless grassroots people, typically poor individuals with personal or collective grievances and petitions. Their only resources are tears and personal resolve. The other consists of the targets of these complaints and possible news investigations. These are government and business officials armed with local influence, ample cash, and connections to higher-level party and government leaders. If the purpose of the first group is to get journalists to investigate and report on their cases, the purpose of the second is to kill a story, a task in which they leave no official or personal relations and bureaucratic resources unexploited.

In some cases, village leaders are able to mobilize township, county, and even provincial officials to go to Beijing as a group in order to find all sorts of excuses to kill a damaging story. According to insiders, at least 70 percent of *Focus Interviews* programs are the targets of such bureaucratic interference.[51] The level of interference at local media outlets is even higher. The director of Shanghai Television's News Center, for example, reported that between 80 and 90 percent of critical reports were the subject of such intervention.[52] This intrabureaucratic pressure acts as a strong countervailing force to the power of media exposure. A widely circulated article in 2003 describes how *Focus Interviews* had become victimized by bureaucratic resistance, resulting in a drop in critical reports from a high of 47 percent of total stories in 1998 to 17 percent in 2002.[53] Although a concerted effort, backed up by the central leadership, boosted the program's critical content in 2004 to the unprecedented level of more than 50 percent, the targets of critical reports have shifted from local officials to social problems that do not have easily identifiable official targets.[54]

Most significantly, ad hoc and unorganized local bureaucratic resistance against critical media reporting has recently evolved into highly organized resistance, leading in 2005 to a major setback in the central leadership's use of the media as a means of constraining local officials. According to a widely circulated report by Ji Shuoming of *Yazhou zhoukan* (Asia Weekly), propaganda officials from seventeen provinces and metropolitan areas, including those from Guangdong, Hebei, Henan, and Shanxi provinces, sent a joint petition to the party Central Committee demanding that the central leadership step up control over central-level media outlets and stop the media's practice of "[public opinion] supervision in a different jurisdiction."[55] In the petition, local officials claimed that although they have been able to control media outlets within their own jurisdictions, critical reporting by central-level media outlets on local problems had stirred up popular discontent and escalated social conflicts, thus becoming the main source of social instability.

In response, the General Office of the CCP Central Committee issued a directive calling for a halt to "[public opinion] supervision in a different jurisdiction," with a new rule requiring reporters from central-level media outlets to inform local authorities when writing critical reports about them. Furthermore, according to Ji Shuoming, the party Central Propaganda Department, in its detailed guidelines on the implementation of this new directive, proposed two "whenevers": whenever issuing a critical story about a different jurisdiction, permission must be sought from that jurisdiction's party propaganda department, and whenever issuing a critical media report involves a leading official, permission must be sought from that official's superior.[56] Because the term "[public opinion] supervision in a different jurisdiction" in this discourse applies not only to the practice of media outlets from one province reporting critically on another province, but also to the practice of central media outlets reporting critically on problems in the provinces, this has effectively undermined the relative autonomy and authority of the central-level media vis-à-vis local governments, compelling journalists to turn their critical focus away from local officials. Whereas the triumph of local officials over the central leadership in this instance is a sign of their increased power vis-à-vis the central leadership, local officials, in their resistance against the current form of top-down public opinion supervision, have also unwittingly exposed its ultimate limits. After all, the central leadership does not allow central-level media outlets to expose corruption inside Zhongnanhai and to report critically on problems of power abuse at the central levels.

Apart from this recent institutionalization of local resistance and the central leadership's capitulation to local power, there are other forms of local resistance to and retaliation against critical media reporting. It is not unusual for journalists to be subjected to blackmail and death threats. Violent attacks against journalists have increased, and local police have not always been protective of endangered journalists. Although the official journalists' association, the All-China Federation of Journalists, established the Committee to Protect the Rights and Welfare of Journalists in August 1998, the organization has little power and autonomy and is not likely to have much impact in protecting investigative journalists. There have also been an increasing number of cases in which local law-and-order agencies detained journalists or punished them for reporting critical stories. The Guangzhou city authorities' embezzlement charges against three *Nanfang dushi bao* journalists for the paper's exposure of Sun Zhigang's death as well as the SARS epidemic is a well-known case of bureaucratic retaliation against the news media through legal means. It reveals the increasing sophistication of bureaucratic power in muffling the media. Although intense domestic and international media pressure, together with the reported intervention of central-level officials, secured the release from prison of the paper's editor in chief, Cheng Yizhong, by the end of 2005 central authorities had fired top editors at the *Xinjing bao* (Beijing News) for its critical reporting on various occasions, including its exposure of the June 11, 2005, bloody crackdown on farmers protesting against land seizures in Dingzhou city, Hebei province.[57] In late January 2006 the central authorities ordered the closure of *Bing dian* (Freezing Point), a weekly supplement to the *Zhongguo qingnian bao* (China Youth Daily) and arguably the only central-level print media outlet known for its in-depth investigative stories and its persistent role in public opinion supervision.[58]

In the same month, another journalist, Li Chanqing of the *Fuzhou ribao* (Fujian Daily) in Fujian province, became the latest casualty of local official retaliation against public opinion supervision. Li was on trial in a Fuzhou court for "fabricating and spreading false terroristic information" by reporting on a dengue fever outbreak. The real reason, according to Western news reports, however, was Li's publication of articles in support of Huang Jingao, the former party secretary of Lianjiang county in Fujian, who was at the center of a ferocious power struggle involving anticorruption politics. Huang had created a national sensation in a high-profile case of public opinion supervision by posting an extraordinary letter on the *People's Daily* Web site in August 2004 saying that his efforts to root out bribery had been stymied by a corruption fraternity in which officials protect one another from scrutiny and stating that he had worn a bulletproof vest for six years for fear of retaliation by the targets of his anticorruption investigations. But in a vicious counterattack by Fuzhou and Fujian officials, Huang's letter was quickly removed from the Web site, and further media comments were banned. Moreover, Huang was not only quickly denounced by the Fujian authorities and fired as Lianjiang party chief but also charged with fifty counts of corruption and sentenced to life in prison in November 2005.[59] Then, on February 2, 2006, Wu Xianghu, deputy editor in chief of *Taizhou wanbao* (Taizhou Evening News), died in a Hangzhou hospital after failing to recover from an October 2005 assault by traffic police officers who stormed the newspaper's editorial office to protest a critical report the paper had published. This assault happened despite the fact that the newspaper conducted the investigation at the invitation and in the company of relevant Taizhou city authorities, and that the Taizhou City Party Discipline Committee had previewed and approved the report.[60]

Although a wave of unprecedented protests by individuals both inside and outside *Zhongguo qingnian bao* led the central authorities to allow *Bing dian* to resume publication on March 1, 2006 (but only with the purge of the chief editor), events like these not only send chilling messages throughout the media system and demonstrate the limits of the central leadership's commitment to public opinion supervision, but also highlight the complicated power struggles over the party's anticorruption campaign in general and over media-based public opinion supervision in particular. The absence of opposition political parties and independent citizens' groups, together with the lack of an independent judicial system and the lack of transparency in the Chinese political process, deprive the media of important allies to carry out thorough investigations into official wrongdoing and to defend their right to conduct critical reporting. As a matter of fact, although the Chinese constitution formally endorses press freedom, journalists have no legally defined and enforceable rights to report. Although they are called upon to defend citizens' rights under the law, in practice their own constitutional rights are still denied. At the same time, they have been subjected to an increasing number of libel cases brought by officials and businesses.[61] The resulting chill is especially dangerous in a society that is not used to having its problems scrutinized and publicized by the media.[62] When the central leadership itself censors the news and fires or even jails journalists at will to keep itself in power, it is not surprising that lower-level bureaucrats and unlawful elements are doing the same to protect their own interests.

Although the high-profile national television treatment of a local case of injustice demonstrates the power of the central leadership and its ability to penetrate into the micro-politics of power at the local levels, this is the exception rather than the rule. As far as the everyday practice of local governance is concerned, the impact of critical media reporting is limited, even before the curbing of "[public opinion] supervision in a different jurisdiction." Although the consensus of local officials interviewed in Zhejiang is that it is better to have some critical media reports than none at all, the media do not register as a significant factor in constraining local officials. The chances of a CCTV television crew showing up in a village are very small. Thus few local officials would consider the overwhelming "killing power" of *Focus Interviews* in their everyday practice of power. As one township official remarked in an interview, it is not a question of whether or not one is afraid of being exposed by the media; it is a question of dealing with the everyday imperatives of the job. For some, it is a case of rational risk calculation. For those who are already corrupt, it is a case of "dead pigs not being afraid of boiling water," as one interviewee put it.

Yet the problem in local governance, especially governance in rural China, is not simply a problem of the behavior of local officials. As noted earlier and discussed in other chapters in this book, it is systemic. Although media exposure and other forms of disciplinary action may lead to the removal of specific officials, they do not change the local power structure. The role of the media, in the context of an overwhelming structural power that shapes the actions of local officials, is limited. As one interviewee commented, an official can be dismissed, but the replacement will likely turn out to be the same. The current crisis in rural governance is rooted in China's political economy, particularly the persistent extractive policy of the central government toward the countryside during the processes of industrialization and modernization.[63] Thus if the lack of economic opportunities in the rural areas and the temptations of power have drawn many into the ranks of local officialdom, as Qunjian Tian notes, the discrepancy between extractive demands and service obligations in the Chinese political economy has also put local officials in an unenviable position.[64] By targeting individual rural officials and personalizing the rural problem, *Focus Interviews* types of media exposure systematically conceal structural problems in the broad Chinese political economy of development.

Not surprisingly, critics of *Focus Interviews* and similar kinds of programs have noted their role in sustaining the party's hegemony.[65] By individualizing, localizing, and moralizing the problem, this type of "morality discourse in the marketplace" avoids "a critical interrogation of overall social structure."[66] Moreover, the phenomenon of urban-based media outlets exposing rural officials on behalf of disenfranchised farmers contains a profound irony and hypocrisy: these media outlets and journalists are themselves the beneficiaries of China's uneven path of development that produces the crisis in rural governance in the first place. Although the elimination of agricultural taxes may have provided some relief for farmers, Chinese farmers are facing even more devastating consequences from China's move to a market economy, including land seizures and environmental degradation. Increasing incidents of violent confrontations between government and business interests on the one side and farmers on the other as exemplified in 2005 by the environmentally related April 10 incident in Huashui village, Dongyang city, Zhejiang province, and the land enclosure–related June 11 incident in Shengyou village, Dingzhou city, Hebei province, underscore the escalation of social conflicts and the deepening of the crisis in governance in the Chinese countryside. These internationally reported stories from rural China, together with the recurring mining disasters and the state's inability to improve industrial safety in this sector, dwarf the scope and severity of the problems exposed in the Chinese media's successful public opinion supervision stories of the mid-1990s and early 2000s, such as the archetypical Shunyi and Baigou stories discussed in this chapter.

The Internet as a New Venue for and Site of Struggle over Public Opinion Supervision

Since the late 1990s the Internet has opened up a new venue for public opinion supervision. Compared with the conventional media, the Internet provides a freer space for the discussion and critique of state policies—be it China's WTO entry, Chinese foreign policy, or the wisdom of spending a fortune to stage the 2008 Olympics. In this sense the Internet, especially in the form of BBS, has significantly expanded the definition of public opinion supervision to public supervision of the fundamental direction of the country. This notion is closer to the one espoused by liberal political forces in the pre-1989 discourse on the subject.

The Internet has also played a significant role in strengthening and expanding the kind of public opinion supervision practiced by the media. As Xu Jilin observes, the Internet has been instrumental in increasing exposure of official corruption by local journalists whose reports in the conventional media are suppressed by local authorities, and also by individuals who feel that they are the direct victims of corruption and who do not have access to regular media.[67] In these cases the Internet has provided potential initial sources for further investigation and reporting by conventional media. It has created a concerted public opinion supervision environment in certain instances, leading to the kind of government intervention discussed in this chapter.

In a more recent development, Web sites dedicated exclusively to the cause of public opinion supervision have emerged to amalgamate the role of the conventional media in this regard. One such example is the China Petition Network (www.chinacomplaint.com), whose debut in 2004 attracted domestic and foreign media attention.[68] Self-described as a "public sentiment early-warning mechanism" based on the requirements of the top leadership to be kept informed of public opinion, the network heralds its own establishment as a "milestone in the course of democratic supervision," and it claims that it will "endeavor to supervise officials at all levels throughout the country and their governance."[69] More interestingly, although the network presents itself as a non-state *(minjian)* force, it seems to have an elaborate infrastructure, prominently featuring the icons of major central party-state institutions—from the party's Central Discipline Inspection Commission to the National People's Congress. Furthermore, the network asserts that it is considering "collaboration" with official media and party-state agencies.[70] Although it is difficult to determine the Web site's exact institutional background, it is possible that high-level state authorities, or at least some elements within the top leadership, played a role in appropriating, if not establishing, this network as an extension of the state's governmental power in cyberspace.

An apparently less well resourced but potentially more independent Web site is the China Public Opinion Supervision Network (www.yuluncn.com), created by freelance investigative writer Li

Dexi. Li's network became a national sensation in 2003, when he posted a story exposing Li Xinde, a deputy mayor of Jining city in Shandong province, for corruption. Li's initial story led to reports in the mainstream media and the quick downfall of Li Xinde. This was highly significant because a deputy mayor is an important official in China. Even the official media have not initiated an exposé of any officeholder of Li's rank. Arguing that the mainstream media are inadequate, Li Dexi sought to establish his Web site as a "brand" in public opinion supervision.[71] In May 2005, perhaps as a sign of the growing strength of Internet-based public opinion supervision forces, a number of self-proclaimed "independent anticorruption" and rights-protection Web sites, including Li's Web site, announced the formation of an alliance in an attempt to become more effective in their anticorruption crusade and in their resistance against government censorship.[72] Thus just as local officials have organized themselves in resistance against public opinion supervision by the official media, independent Chinese voices on the Internet are organizing among themselves in the effort to serve as a check on government officials.

Jean Oi notes that while village committee elections are a pressure valve that allows peasants to vent their dissatisfaction, they do so in a way that directs "the responsibility for continued poverty and poor leadership in villages away from central authorities."[73] Public opinion supervision in the *Focus Interviews* formula has the same impact of sustaining the party-state's monopoly on power and the current power structure in Chinese society. Through their exposés, the media are smoothing the rough edges of the current Chinese political economic transformation and policing the political, economic, and social boundaries of an emerging authoritarian market society that is predicated on "accumulation by dispossession." Instead of counting on the media to expose the local officials who have failed them, members of China's disenfranchised social groups would be better off if they were allowed to organize and struggle collectively for a better deal in China's current social transformation.

This does not mean that the media have no positive role to play in local governance. Rather, in China the local is national, and the behavior of local officials is shaped by national policies, as the news stories discussed in this chapter illustrate. Therefore, the media's role in constraining local officials must be understood within the broader context of Chinese social development and wider discussions of the role of the media in constraining all levels of political and economic power in China. For this to be effective, the media must be able to target higher-level officials and to do so in conjunction with independent political groups and civil society organizations.

Though the current form of public opinion supervision as an integral part of the party-state's disciplinary power is overwhelming in specific cases, it is highly reactive and therefore limited in function. Effective media power should be able to express independent popular views and deliberate on major political issues. Moreover, the subject of public opinion *(yulun)* includes more than media organizations. Different social interests, especially disenfranchised social groups, should have access to media organizations beyond their currently limited roles as victims of power abuse and petitioners against arbitrary official power. Similarly, supervision *(jiandu)* does not necessarily have to mean negative exposure. Its broader definition, as implied in the pre-1989 discourse on political democratization, includes the public's oversight of society's fundamental direction of development. Finally, there is the question of the media's own governance and the need for society's supervision of the media's power, which has also been abused by media officials and practitioners, sometimes even in the name of public opinion supervision.[74]

The Internet has demonstrated some potential to expand both the depth and scope of public opinion supervision by including criticisms of the state's major domestic and foreign policies, undermining local media censorship, exposing higher-level officials, and offering a venue for direct participation by individuals such as Li Dexi. Ironically, however, the Internet is able to demonstrate this potential partly because of its more limited nature as a mass medium in comparison to the reach of television. Moreover, the state has the power to shut down Web sites and censor the Internet. As the influence of the Internet grows, central and local officials are stepping up efforts to constrain it on the one hand and to harness it for their own propaganda objectives on the other. Meanwhile, the political economy of the Internet will probably display an even stronger elite and urban bias than conventional print and broadcast media. All of these factors make it difficult to be optimistic about the role of the Internet in constraining local officials.

Notes

Contributors

Notes

1. Introduction

The authors thank Paul Cohen and Ben Read for helpful comments on an earlier version of this chapter.

1. Margaret Levi, *Of Rule and Revenue* (Berkeley: University of California Press, 1988); Joel S. Migdal, *Strong Societies and Weak States* (Princeton: Princeton University Press, 1988).

2. Explorations of this question for earlier periods of Chinese history include Brian E. McKnight, *Village and Bureaucracy in Southern Sung China* (Chicago: University of Chicago Press, 1971); John R. Watt, *The District Magistrate in Late Imperial China* (New York: Columbia University Press, 1972); T'ung-tsu Ch'ü, *Local Government in China under the Ch'ing* (Cambridge, Mass.: Harvard University Press, 1962); and Kan-Yu Wang, *The Local Government of China* (Chungking: China Institute of Pacific Relations, 1945).

3. For a general overview of these successive reform efforts, focusing on the issue of centralization versus decentralization, see Paul A. Cohen, "The Post-Mao Reforms in Historical Perspective," *Journal of Asian Studies*, 47, no. 3 (August 1988): 518–540.

4. Azizur Rahman Khan and Carl Riskin, "Income and Inequality in China: Composition, Distribution and Growth of Household Income, 1988 to 1995," *China Quarterly*, no. 154 (June 1998): 221–253; Andrew G. Walder, "Markets and Income Inequality in Rural China: Political Advantage in an Expanding Economy," *American Sociological Review*, 67, no. 2 (April 2002): 231–253.

5. Ding Xuguang, *Jindai Zhongguo difang zizhi yanjiu* (A Study of Local Self-Government in Modern China) (Guangzhou: Guangzhou chubanshe, 1993), pp. 15ff.

6. Philip A. Kuhn, "Late Ch'ing Views of the Polity," in Tang Tsou, ed., *Select

Papers from the Center for Far Eastern Studies: Political Leadership and Social Change at the Local Level in China, from 1850 to the Present, no. 4 (Chicago: University of Chicago, 1981), pp. 1–18.

7. John H. Fincher, *Chinese Democracy: The Self-Government Movement in Local, Provincial and National Politics, 1905–1914* (Canberra: Australian National University Press, 1981), pp. 16–22.

8. Mark Elvin, "The Gentry Democracy in Chinese Shanghai, 1905–14," in Jack Gray, ed., *Modern China's Search for a Political Form* (Oxford: Oxford University Press, 1969), pp. 41–43.

9. Ibid., pp. 52–54; Mark Elvin, "The Administration of Shanghai, 1905–1914," in Mark Elvin and G. William Skinner, eds., *The Chinese City between Two Worlds* (Stanford: Stanford University Press, 1974), pp. 239–262.

10. Fincher, *Chinese Democracy*, pp. 41–43. The expanded electorate chose an "electoral college" that elected the council directors.

11. Ibid., pp. 45–46.

12. Yang Zhong, *Local Government and Politics in China: Challenges from Below* (Armonk, N.Y.: M. E. Sharpe, 2003), p. 31.

13. Roger R. Thompson, *China's Local Councils in the Age of Constitutional Reform, 1898–1911* (Cambridge, Mass.: Council on East Asian Studies, Harvard University, 1995), p. 125.

14. Cited in Kung-ch'üan Hsiao, *Rural China: Imperial Control in the Nineteenth Century* (Seattle: University of Washington Press, 1960), p. 647, n. 10.

15. Harold E. Gorst, *China* (New York: E. P. Dutton, 1899), pp. 82–85.

16. Arthur H. Smith, *Village Life in China* (Boston: Little, Brown, 1970), pp. 170–171.

17. Ibid.

18. Hsiao, *Rural China*, p. 274.

19. Fincher, *Chinese Democracy*, pp. 136–138.

20. Thompson, *China's Local Councils*, pp. 131–136.

21. On rural resistance under the New Policies, see Roxann Prazniak, *Of Camel Kings and Other Things: Rural Rebels against Modernity in Late Imperial China* (Lanham, Md.: Rowman and Littlefield, 1999). On the relationship between popular protest and revolution, see Joseph W. Esherick, *Reform and Revolution in China: The 1911 Revolution in Hunan and Hubei* (Berkeley: University of California Press, 1976).

22. Fincher, *Chinese Democracy*, p. 218.

23. Ibid., p. 222.

24. Thompson, *China's Local Councils*, pp. 3–4.

25. Philip A. Kuhn, "Local Taxation and Finance in Republican China," in Susan Mann Jones, ed., *Proceedings of the NEH Modern China Project, 1977–78: Political Leadership and Social Change at the Local Level in China from 1850 to the Present*, no. 3 (Chicago: University of Chicago, 1979), pp. 121–122.

26. Susan Mann Jones, "The Organization of Trade at the County Level: Brokerage and Tax Farming in the Republican Period," in Jones, *Proceedings of the NEH Modern China Project*, p. 86.

27. Prasenjit Duara, *Culture, Power, and the State: Rural North China, 1900–1942* (Stanford: Stanford University Press, 1988).

28. Philip A. Kuhn, "Local Self-Government under the Republic: Problems of Control, Autonomy, and Mobilization," in Frederic Wakeman Jr. and Carolyn Grant, eds., *Conflict and Control in Late Imperial China* (Berkeley: University of California Press, 1975), pp. 283–285.

29. David Tsai, "Party-Government Relations in Kiangsu Province, 1927–1932," in *Select Papers from the Center for Far Eastern Studies*, no. 1 (Chicago: University of Chicago, 1976), pp. 85–118.

30. For an example of village elites thumbing their noses at state efforts to impose democratic elections, see Sidney D. Gamble, *North China Villages: Social, Political, and Economic Activities before 1933* (Berkeley: University of California Press, 1963), pp. 151–152. In some villages, however, reasonably fair elections apparently did take place. See ibid., pp. 167–169; and Martin C. Yang, *A Chinese Village: Taitou, Shantung Province* (New York: Columbia University Press, 1945), pp. 175ff.

31. Kuhn, "Local Self-Government under the Republic," pp. 286–287.

32. Ding Xuguang, *Jindai Zhongguo difang zizhi yanjiu*, pp. 203–205.

33. Zhong, *Local Government and Politics in China*, pp. 35–37. See also Li Defang, *Minguo xiangcun zizhi wenti yanjiu* (A Study of Rural Self-Government in Republican China) (Beijing: Renmin chubanshe, 2001).

34. John Fitzgerald, "The Politics of the Civil War: Party Rule, Territorial Administration and Constitutional Government," in Werner Draguhn and David S. G. Goodman, eds., *China's Communist Revolutions: Fifty Years of the People's Republic of China* (New York: RoutledgeCurzon, 2002), pp. 61–62.

35. Guy S. Alitto, "Rural Reconstruction during the Nanking Decade: Confucian Collectivism in Shantung," *China Quarterly*, no. 66 (June 1976): 213.

36. Charles W. Hayford, *To the People: James Yen and Village China* (New York: Columbia University Press, 1990).

37. Shirley S. Garrett, *Social Reformers in Urban China* (Cambridge, Mass.: Harvard University Press, 1970); Robin Porter, *Industrial Reformers in Republican China* (Armonk, N.Y.: M. E. Sharpe, 1994); Jun Xing, *Baptized in the Fire of Revolution: The American Social Gospel and the YMCA in China, 1919–1937* (Cranbury, N.J.: Lehigh University Press, 1996).

38. The "representative congress" was proposed as the appropriate type of municipal government to rule Shanghai after the Three Workers' Armed Uprisings in 1926–27, but by the time of the Canton Uprising in December 1927, the CCP announced the formation of what turned out to be a very short-lived "soviet" government.

39. Mark Selden, *The Yenan Way in Revolutionary China* (Cambridge, Mass.: Harvard University Press, 1971), p. 128.

40. Ibid., p. 132.

41. Ibid., p. 134.

42. James R. Townsend, *Political Participation in Communist China* (Berkeley: University of California Press, 1967), pp. 104–105. In the election law of 1979, direct elections were extended to county-level people's congresses; in 1980 these were held throughout China. See Andrew J. Nathan, *Chinese Democracy* (New York: Knopf, 1985), chap. 10.

43. Townsend, *Political Participation,* pp. 105–106.

44. John P. Burns, *Political Participation in Rural China* (Berkeley: University of California Press, 1988), p. 87.

45. John P. Burns, "The Election of Production Team Cadres in Rural China: 1958–74," *China Quarterly,* no. 74 (June 1978): 273–296. In some places, however, team head elections were considered radical and reckless right up until the Third Plenum of December 1978. See the discussion in Huang Shu-min, *The Spiral Road: Change in a Chinese Village through the Eyes of a Communist Party Leader* (Boulder, Colo.: Westview Press, 1989), pp. 136–138.

46. Burns, *Political Participation in Rural China,* p. 108.

47. Ibid., p. 119.

48. A. Doak Barnett, *Communist China: The Early Years, 1949–55* (New York: Praeger, 1964); Ezra Vogel, *Canton under Communism: Programs and Politics in a Provincial Capital, 1949–1968* (Cambridge, Mass.: Harvard University Press, 1969).

49. Michel Oksenberg estimated that as many as 70 to 80 percent of sub-village leaders may have been purged in some provinces. Michel Oksenberg, "Local Leaders in Rural China, 1962–65," in A. Doak Barnett, ed., *Chinese Communist Politics in Action* (Seattle: University of Washington Press, 1969), p. 184. Adopting a far more conservative purge estimate of between 5 and 10 percent of grassroots cadres, Richard Baum nevertheless came up with a figure of 1.25 to 2.5 million. Richard Baum, *Prelude to Revolution: Mao, the Party, and the Peasant Question, 1962–66* (New York: Columbia University Press, 1975), p. 104.

50. Ibid., p. 8.

51. Ibid., p. 9.

52. For a discussion of these practices in Cultural Revolution Shanghai, see Elizabeth J. Perry and Li Xun, *Proletarian Power: Shanghai in the Cultural Revolution* (Boulder, Colo.: Westview Press, 1997).

53. Tang Tsou, "Back from the Brink of Revolutionary-Feudal Totalitarianism," in Victor Nee and David Mozingo, eds., *State and Society in Contemporary China* (Ithaca: Cornell University Press, 1983), pp. 53–88; Frederick C.

Teiwes, "The Chinese State during the Maoist Era," in David Shambaugh, ed., *The Modern Chinese State* (New York: Cambridge University Press, 2000), pp. 105–160.

54. Merle Goldman, *Sowing the Seeds of Democracy in China: Political Reform in the Deng Xiaoping Era* (Cambridge, Mass.: Harvard University Press, 1994); and Merle Goldman, *From Comrade to Citizen: The Struggle for Political Rights in China* (Cambridge, Mass.: Harvard University Press, 2005).

55. Minxin Pei, *From Reform to Revolution: The Demise of Communism in China and the Soviet Union* (Cambridge, Mass.: Harvard University Press, 1994).

56. Like many grassroots reforms in China, the village committee elections originated from spontaneous experiments (in this case in two counties in Guangxi province) and then were endorsed and encouraged by the central authorities. See Zhong, *Local Government and Politics in China*, p. 163.

57. See, among many others, He Baogang and Lang Youxing, "Cunmin xuanju dui xiangcun quanli de yingxiang" (The Impact of Village Elections on Village Power), *Xianggang shehui kexue xuebao* (Hong Kong Journal of Social Sciences), no. 16 (Spring 2000): 99–124; Li Lianjiang and Kevin J. O'Brien, "The Struggle over Village Elections," in Merle Goldman and Roderick MacFarquhar, eds., *The Paradox of China's Post-Mao Reforms* (Cambridge, Mass.: Harvard University Press, 1999), pp. 129–144; Li Lianjiang, "The Empowering Effect of Village Elections in China," *Asian Survey*, 43, no. 4 (July–August 2003): 648–662; Kevin J. O'Brien and Li Lianjiang, "Accommodating 'Democracy' in a One-Party State: Introducing Village Elections in China," *China Quarterly*, no. 162 (June 2000): 465–489; Robert Pastor and Qingshan Tan, "The Meaning of China's Village Elections," *China Quarterly*, no. 162 (June 2000): 490–512; Daniel Kelliher, "The Chinese Debate over Village Self-Government," *China Journal*, no. 37 (January 1997): 63–90; Yang Zhong and Jie Chen, "To Vote or Not to Vote: An Analysis of Peasants' Participation in Chinese Village Elections [Jiangsu]," *Comparative Political Studies*, 35, no. 6 (August 2002): 686–712; Jean C. Oi and Scott Rozelle, "Elections and Power: The Locus of Decision-Making in Chinese Villages," *China Quarterly*, no. 162 (June 2000): 513–539; Anne F. Thurston, *Muddling toward Democracy: Political Change in Grassroots China* (Washington, D.C.: U.S. Institute of Peace, 1998); Melanie Manion, "The Electoral Connection in the Chinese Countryside," *American Political Science Review*, 90, no. 4 (December 1996): 736–748; Tianjian Shi, "Voting and Nonvoting in China," *Journal of Politics*, 61, no. 4 (November 1999): 1115–39; Tianjian Shi, "Economic Development and Village Elections in Rural China," in Zhao Suisheng, ed., *China and Democracy: The Prospect for a Democratic China* (New York: Routledge, 2000), pp. 233–252; Tianjian Shi, "Village Committee Elections in China," *World Politics*, 51, no. 3 (April 1999): 385–412; Sylvia Chan, "Research Notes on Villagers' Com-

mittee Election: Chinese-Style Democracy," *Journal of Contemporary China*, no. 19 (November 1998): 507–521.

58. Thomas P. Bernstein and Xiaobo Lü, *Taxation without Representation in Contemporary Rural China* (New York: Cambridge University Press, 2003).

59. On the abortive attempts to separate party and government, see Shiping Zheng, *Party vs. State in Post-1949 China: The Institutional Dilemma* (New York: Cambridge University Press, 1997), chap. 8.

60. Stanley B. Lubman, *Bird in a Cage: Legal Reform in China after Mao* (Stanford: Stanford University Press, 1999).

61. Minxin Pei, "Citizens v. Mandarins: Administrative Litigation in China," *China Quarterly*, no. 152 (December 1997): 832–862.

62. Kevin J. O'Brien, "Rightful Resistance," *World Politics*, 49, no. 1 (October 1996): 31–55.

63. On the relationship between civil society and political reform in contemporary China, see also Muthiah Alagappa, ed., *Civil Society and Political Change in Asia: Expanding and Contracting Democratic Space* (Stanford: Stanford University Press, 2004); Timothy Brook and B. Michael Frolic, eds., *Civil Society in China* (Armonk, N.Y.: M. E. Sharpe, 1997); Baogang He, *The Democratic Implications of Civil Society in China* (New York: St. Martin's Press, 1997); Gordon White, Jude Howell, and Shang Xiaoyuan, *In Search of Civil Society: Market Reform and Social Change in Contemporary China* (New York: Oxford University Press, 1996).

64. Recent research on nation size suggests that the fear of democratization leading to dismemberment is not unfounded: "Democratization should lead to the creation of many new countries, which is precisely what we observed after the collapse of the Soviet Union." Alberto Alesina and Enrico Spolaore, *The Size of Nations* (Cambridge, Mass.: MIT Press, 2003), p. 12.

65. Samuel P. Huntington, *Political Order in Changing Societies* (New Haven: Yale University Press, 1968), p. 363.

66. Marshall I. Goldman, *What Went Wrong with Perestroika* (New York: Norton, 1992).

67. This situation is not only a product of the post-Mao reforms, however. During the Maoist era as well, scholars have remarked upon local defiance of central authority. See, for example, Vivienne Shue, *The Reach of the State: Sketches of the Chinese Body Politic* (Stanford: Stanford University Press, 1988), chap. 2.

68. Cheng Li, *China's Leaders: The New Generation* (Lanham, Md.: Rowman and Littlefield, 2001), p. 198.

69. Shelley Rigger, *Politics in Taiwan: Voting for Democracy* (New York: Routledge, 1999).

70. Huntington, *Political Order in Changing Societies*, pp. 344–345.

71. Melanie Manion, *Corruption by Design: Building Clean Government in Main-*

land China and Hong Kong (Cambridge, Mass.: Harvard University Press, 2004); Yan Sun, *Corruption and Market in Contemporary China* (Ithaca: Cornell University Press, 2004).

72. Dali L. Yang, *Remaking the Chinese Leviathan: Market Transition and the Politics of Governance in China* (Stanford: Stanford University Press, 2004).

2. Village Elections, Transparency, and Anticorruption

I am grateful to Harvard University and Salem State College for support for this research. I also thank Professor Gao Xinjun of the China Center for Comparative Politics and Economics in Beijing for his invaluable assistance in Henan and Professors Gao and Zhao Yuezhi for their comments and suggestions. Sections of this paper draw on Richard Levy, "The Village Self-Government Movement: Elections, Democracy, the Party, and Anticorruption: Developments in Guangdong," *China Information*, 17, no. 1 (2003): 28–65.

1. See, for example, Gunter Schubert, "Village Elections in the PRC: A Trojan Horse of Democracy?" at www.uni-duisburg.de/Institute/OAWISS/download/doc/discuss19.pdf (accessed August 13, 2004), which provides an excellent summary of Western and Chinese scholars' approaches to many of these issues; the works of Yu Keping, He Zengke, and their colleagues at the China Center for Comparative Politics and Economics in Beijing and the associated Innovations and Excellence in Local Chinese Government Project at www.chinainnovations.org (accessed February 24, 2006); analysis from the EU-China Training Programme on Village Governance at www.chinarural.org/euchinaprog (accessed February 24, 2006); the writings of Guo Zhenglin, Wu Chongqing, Liu Xintang, Liu Ya, Li Fan, Wang Yugan, Xiao Tangbiao, and Wang Jinhong; the Web sites of the Ministry of Civil Affairs, www.mca.gov.cn and www.chinarural.org, as well as www.chinaelections.com and www.univillage.org (all accessed February 24, 2006).

2. The level of regional economic development and degree of development of the private sector, the strength of various state and party organizations and orientation of township leadership, the strength and locus of control of village enterprises, and so forth, are significant factors in analyzing variations in village elections and village-level corruption. See, for example, Jean C. Oi and Scott Rozelle, "Elections and Power: The Locus of Decision-Making in Chinese Villages," *China Quarterly*, no. 162 (June 2000): 513–539; Anne F. Thurston, "Muddling toward Democracy," United States Institute of Peace, at www.usip.org/pubs/peaceworks/pwks23.html (accessed February 24, 2006); and Yan Sun, *Corruption and Market in Contemporary China* (Ithaca: Cornell University Press, 2004), chap. 4. Though not

focusing on village-level corruption, Sun outlines different forms of corruption that develop in regions with different combinations of state, entrepreneurial, and social strength. Nonetheless, because provincial regulations vary widely and play an important role in establishing the ground rules for elections, they remain a useful node for analysis.

3. I contrast a "new, more economically based elite," composed of entrepreneurs, enterprise owners, factory managers, and so forth, with an "older, more politically based elite," composed of village leaders and party members who came to their positions through more traditional party recruitment and appointment practices. Those who did not enter these structures because they were entrepreneurs and those who became entrepreneurs once they had entered these structures are not two distinct elites. Rather they are two overlapping but not identical groups with both shared and contrasting interests and modes of operation. Lang Youxing, in "From Economic Elite to Political Administrator: The Recruitment of Village Power-Holder and Village Elections in Rural Zhejiang," an unpublished paper, suggests that "village elections provide an institutional opportunity for village economic elites to enter into village power centers and then change the recruitment pattern of village power-holders." He summarizes the works of Ole Odgaard, Jonathan Unger, Bruce Dickson, J. Dearlove, and Jude Howell. He Zengke, "Nongcun zhili zhuanxing yu zhidu chuangxin" (Governance Transition and Institutional Innovation in Rural Areas), *Jingji shehui tizhi bijiao* (Comparative Economic and Social Systems), no. 6 (November 2003): 74–82, analyzes the *haixuan* method of direct nomination and direct election of village committees as a form of attack on party-dominated village leadership.

4. Professor Gao Xinjun of the China Center for Comparative Politics and Economics in Beijing facilitated my interviews with village leaders in Xinmi city. The Center's long-term research in Xinmi city has resulted in the publication of Rong Jingben et al., *Cong yalixing tizhi xiang minzhu hezuo tizhi de zhuanbian* (Transformation from a Pressurized System to a Democratic System of Cooperation) (Beijing: Zhongyang bianyi chubanshe, 1998), and *Zailun cong yalixing tizhi xiang minzhu hezuo tizhi de zhuanbian* (Further Discussion on the Transformation from a Pressurized System to a Democratic System of Cooperation) (Beijing: Zhongyang bianyi chubanshe, 2001), and numerous publications by Professor Gao. Because Professor Gao has conducted research in these villages for over ten years, he has developed a degree of trust and openness with the leaders, which was extended to me. This became particularly clear in a discussion of whether a village official competing for office in the municipal government had used private or collective funds to hand out "gifts" of 3,000 RMB per person before the vote.

5. Elections in Guangdong in 2002 were organized under the so-called one law and two methods [of implementation], *yifa liangbanfa*, that is, the Provisional Organic Law on Village Committees (1987) and, subsequently, the Organic Law (November 4, 1998), and "Guangdongsheng shishi 'Zhonghua renmin gongheguo cunmin weiyuanhui zuzhifa' banfa" (Guangdong Province's Methods for Implementing the PRC Organic Law on Village Committees) (hereafter "Methods for Implementing") (November 27, 1998), supplemented by Lin Jianwen's "Guangdongsheng shishi 'Zhonghua renmin gongheguo cunmin weiyuanhui zuzhifa' banfa shiyi" (Explanation of Guangdong Province's Methods for Implementing the "PRC's Organic Law on Village Committees") (December 12, 1998); as well as "Guangdongsheng cunmin weiyuanhui xuanju banfa" (Guangdong Province Methods for Village Committee Elections) (July 27, 2001). These were subsequently supplemented by "'Guangdongsheng cunmin weiyuanhui xuanju banfa' shishi xize (shixing)" ([Provisional] Detailed Regulations for Implementing "Guangdong Province's Methods for Village Committee Elections") (January 11, 2002); and Guangdong Civil Affairs Department, "Cunmin weiyuanhui xuanju guicheng" (Election Rules for Village Committees), in Guangdongsheng minzhengting, Guangzhoushi minzhengju, *Nongcun weiyuanhui jianshe falü, fagui, wenjian* (Laws, Regulations, and Documents on the Construction of Village Committees) (December 2001); and Minzhengbu jiceng zhengquan he shequ jianshesi, ed., *Zhonghua renmin gongheguo cunmin weiyuanhui xuanju guicheng* (PRC Rules for Implementing Village Committee Elections) (Beijing, 2001). (Only 50,000 copies of this book were printed for China's some 800,000 villages.) In Henan, the 2001–2002 elections were conducted under "Henansheng shishi 'Zhonghua renmin gongheguo cunmin weiyuanhui zuzhifa' de banfa" (Henan's Methods for Implementing the "PRC's Organic Law on Village Committees") (hereafter "Henan's Methods") (November 2001). Henan is one of a few provinces that has only this regulation, whereas most provinces have both "Methods for Implementing the Organic Law" and "Methods for Implementing Village Elections." Also in November 2001, the provincial government promulgated "Wosheng disijie cunmin weiyuanhui huanjie xuanju gongzuo qingkuang huibao" (Report on the Work Situation in Our Province's Fourth Round of Village Elections), unpublished paper. Yu Weiliang provides an analysis of the similarities and differences among the various laws and regulations promulgated by China's thirty-one provinces, autonomous regions, and municipalities directly under central control in "31 geshengji cunweihui xuanju difangxing fagui zhi bijiao" (Comparison of Local Village Election Rules in 31 Provinces), in *Quanguo cunweihui xuanju qingkuang fenxi hui lunwenji* (Collected Works of the Discussion Meeting on Analyzing the National Situation in

Village Committee Elections) (hereafter *Xuanju qingkuang*) (Ningbo: Minzheng jiceng zhengquan he shequ jianshesi, November 2001), pp. 277–295. Unless otherwise noted, contrasts among such regulations are drawn from this article. An English version of Yu Weiliang's article "A Comparative Study of Village Committee Election Procedures in Thirty-one Provinces" can be found at www.chinarural.org/euchinaprog/ WebSite/eu/UpFile/File770.pdf (accessed April 1, 2006).

6. Guangdong's rapid economic development has also resulted in an unusual degree of urbanization, with previously rural villages encircling urban and/or manufacturing centers, rapidly urbanizing, and becoming very wealthy while maintaining their legal status as villages. Whereas inland villages still rely largely on agriculture, and the key issues facing village cadres remain agricultural taxes and family planning, agricultural production is virtually nonexistent in many urban villages. The main source of income is either land rental (as factory or commercial sites) and/or collective enterprises, that is, factories run independently or as joint ventures on these land parcels. Since taxes are usually deducted from collective income and paid by the village government, the key issue for cadres in these villages is ownership and management of the land which, if the villages are to be absorbed into the adjacent cities, would revert to the urban government.

7. Levy, "Village Self-Government," p. 41.

8. In the fourth round of elections, the Henan Civil Affairs Department received some 900,000 RMB from the provincial Department of Finance for 48,000 villages, whereas the villages where I interviewed each spent between 500 and 2,000 RMB. In contrast, the 2001–2002 elections in Guangzhou alone cost some 53 million RMB, of which villages spent 31 million RMB, with one village spending some 400,000 RMB.

9. Because of the focus on Guangdong and Henan, I have also included comparative data from the prior round of elections in these two provinces.

10. Interviews in Xinmi city in 2004 anecdotally revealed turnout rates significantly lower than the reported provincial rate.

11. Li Jiangtao et al., *Minzhu de genji: Guangdong nongcun jiceng minzhu jianshe shixian* (The Basis of Democracy: The Practice of Building Grassroots-Level Rural Democracy in Guangdong) (Guangzhou: Guangdong renmin chubanshe, 2002), p. 46. If party vice secretaries who are village leaders are also counted, the degree of party control is noticeably higher.

12. See Schubert, "Trojan Horse."

13. See "1999 nian Henansheng cunmin weiyuanhui huanjie xuanju qingkuang zongjibiao" (Statistical Totals of 1999 Henan Village Election Situation) on the Ministry of Civil Affairs Web site, www.chinarural.org/ readnews.asp?newsid={E0C84495-E0B1–11D6-A7FF-009027DDFA1E} and

www.chinarural.org/readnews.asp?newsid={E0C84497-E0B1–11D6-A7FF-009027DDFA1E}(accessed May 2002).

14. "Wosheng disijie cunmin weiyuanhui huanjie xuanju gongzuo qingkuang huibao." This represents a reduction of 14,931 VC members, though it is unclear whether this is a result of reducing the size of the VCs or of unsuccessful elections.

15. Although many entrepreneurs seek local political office, others avoid it because of how it will affect their business prospects. Here the new VL estimated that he would lose 20,000–30,000 RMB per year by serving. Another entrepreneur on Village 5's VC was hesitant about joining the party despite pressure to do so because he felt that if he was evaluated poorly, it would hurt his reputation as a businessman.

16. Several villagers reported that the winner provided what he had promised. Anthony Kuhn, "China's Newly Rich Are Getting Political," *Wall Street Journal,* August 17, 2004, p. A14, cites two similar examples in Yiwu city, Zhejiang, along with tolerance of this practice by the Yiwu authorities. See also Lang Youxin, "From Economic Elite," on the "Yiwu phenomenon."

17. According to one source, Henan's provincial regulation originally followed the Organic Law, that is, "an appropriate number of women," but was revised after suggestions by the Women's Federation. Nevertheless, this stipulation was not stressed when the elections were implemented because election officials were satisfied that some 20 percent of VC members were women and few complaints were received. This 20 percent, however, is higher than the reported figure of 16.1 percent. Interviews in Xinmi revealed that in 2004, four out of five villages had a female member. Regulations vary widely across provinces. At one end, Hunan, which also requires one woman per VC, states that if no woman is included among the candidates for the VC, the VEC can declare this illegal and can organize another nomination process to avoid the problems and costs associated with invalidating the final election. According to Huang Peisheng, "Hunansheng diwujie cunweihui huanjie xuanju qingkuang" (The Situation in the Fifth Round of Village Elections in Hunan Province), in *Xuanju qingkuang,* pp. 192–193, this practice resulted in 98.5 percent of the VCs having at least one woman. At the other end of the spectrum, Tibet seemed to have the lowest percentage of female VC members; see Cha Si, "Xizangzizhiqu disijie cunweihui huanjie xuanju qingkuang" (The Situation in the Fourth Round of Village Elections in the Tibetan Autonomous Region), in *Xuanju qingkuang,* pp. 240–242.

18. Yang Chengyong, "Guanyu 'Guangdongsheng cunmin weiyuanhui xuanju banfa' de jige wenti" (A Few Problems about "Methods [for Implementing] Village Committee Elections in Guangdong"), in *Guangzhoushi cunweihui xuanju gongzuo yantaohui ziliao huibian* (Collected Materials from

the Research and Discussion Conference on Guangzhou Village Committee Elections), March 27–28, 2002, unpublished conference proceedings.

19. Hebei reported that only 48 percent of newly elected VCs had female members, thus lowering the national average; see Wang Mankui, "Guanyu jinyibu zuohao cunweihui xuanju gongzuo de jianyi" (Suggestions for Improving Village Election Work), in *Xuanju qingkuang*, pp. 23–26.

20. See Yang Cuiping, "Cunweihui xuanjuzhong de funü canyu" (Women's Participation in Village Elections), in *Xuanju qingkuang*, pp. 313–320; and Yu Weiliang, "A Comparative Study of Village Committee Election Procedures," p. 3.

21. Yang Cuiping, "Cunweihui xuanjuzhong de funü canyu," provides a good analysis of many of the factors cited in this discussion.

22. In Village 5 we were invited to the party secretary's home for lunch. Since his wife was in town for the day, he called the female member of the VC to his house to cook the meal, but she was not invited to take part in the interview. In Village 2 the female vice leader was not reelected because, according to the party secretary, she did not have adequate status. No further election was held to fill the position, however. Instead, a person was hired to fulfill these duties without being a member of the VC.

23. The Ministry of Civil Affairs held a conference on methods to increase women's participation in village self-government in Beijing, August 13–14, 2004.

24. Numerous Chinese terms, including *qiyejia* (entrepreneur/enterprise owner), *nengren* (an undefined term generally translated as "an able person"), *xianfuren* (the newly rich), *changzhang* (factory director/owner), *kuangzhang* (mine director/owner), *jingying* (elite), and so forth are often conflated in official documents and in the discourse of both local officials and villagers despite the positive overtones of *nengren* and the more mixed overtones of *xianfuren*. Although vast numbers of *nengren* and newly rich are private entrepreneurs, others are officials and/or managers in collective enterprises, and the newly rich have frequently become private entrepreneurs through a variety of means. Here I use "entrepreneur" as an inclusive term unless another specific term was used by the interviewees or in the documents.

25. Zhejiang, which also encouraged the notion of the "two strengths" *(shuangqiang)* as a prerequisite for good VC candidates, claimed that 30 percent of VC members province-wide were newly rich, whereas in Yiwu municipality, 60 percent of VLs, and VC members in general, were said to be newly rich; Jiang Shouxun, "Xianfu qunti jingxuan 'cunguan' xianxiang de fenxi he sikao" (Thoughts and Analysis of the Phenomenon of Newly Rich Groups Standing in Elections for Village Officials), in *Xuanju qingkuang*, pp. 101–105; Zhou Bingquan, "'Xianfu qunti' jingxuan

'cunguan' xianxiang de diaocha yu sikao" (Research and Thoughts on the Phenomenon of "Newly Rich Groups" Competing in Elections for "Village Officials"), unpublished paper; also Lang Youxin, "From Economic Elite."

26. "Guangdongsheng lixun gongzuo qingkuang zongjibiao" (Summary Chart on the Situation in the Changeover Work [From Management Districts to Village Committees] in Guangdong Province), in Minzhengbu jiceng zhengquan he shequ jianshesi nongcunchu, *1999 niandu nongcun jiceng minzhu zhengzhi jianshe ziliao huibian* (Collected Materials on Democratic Construction of Basic-Level Rural Democracy in 1999) (Beijing, 2000), pp. 606–607; Li Jiangtao et al., *Minzhu de genji*, pp. 46, 130, cites inconsistent data on this factor.

27. See, for example, Wang Jinhong, "Cunmin zizhi yu Guangdong nongcun cunji zhili de fazhan" (Rural Self-Government and the Development of Village-Level Governance in Guangdong) (Guangdong, 2002), unpublished paper, available at http://211.91.135.86/ccrs01/big/cmzzygdncc.htm (accessed April 1, 2006); Li Jiangtao et al., *Minzhu de genji;* Jiang Shouxun, "Xianfu qunti"; and Zhou Bingquan, "'Xianfu qunti' jingxuan 'cunguan.'"

28. See also Zhao Shukai, "Xiangcun zhili: Zuzhi he chongtu" (Governance in Villages: Organization and Conflict), *Zhanlüe yu guanli* (Strategy and Management), no. 6 (November 2003): 1–8; and Jonathan Unger, *The Transformation of Rural China* (Armonk, N.Y.: M. E. Sharpe, 2002). Many townships and, where possible, villages have enacted various provisions to attract investment and give preferential treatment to investors; see, for example, Guankouzhen weiyuanhui renmin zhengfu, "Qianjinzhong de Guankouzhen" (Guankou Township in Progress), March 2002. Zhao Shukai suggests that government should be reduced in size and play only a minimal role in a market economy. Gao Xinjun, "Chuyu tizhi chongtu yu maodun jiaodianzhong de xiangzhen dangzheng" (Recent Reforms at the Township Level: Political Interests and Institutional Conflict), *Makesizhuyi yu xianshi* (Marxism and Reality), no. 2 (April 2004): 51–57, notes that Guankou township had requested that every party and government cadre set up or introduce an enterprise in the township by 2003 (although 50 percent did not do so).

29. Mao Dan, Ren Qiang, and Yu Ruyan, "Guanyu cunmin zizhi de sange nanti de zhengzhixue fenxi" (A Political Analysis of Three Difficult Issues in Village Autonomy), *Kaifang shidai* (Open Times), no. 1 (November 2003): 113–122.

30. Ironically, Wenzhou's local regulation stating that a candidate who causes significant losses to the village collective economy must reimburse the villagers for any related losses may well further discourage non-entrepre-

neurs from vying for VC positions. See "Woguo shouge cunguan dangxuan xieyi qianding cunguan zuocuo shiqing yao peichang" (First in Nation Contract Signed by VC Candidates Guaranteeing That They Will Compensate for Any Losses From Their Mistakes), in *Xuanju qingkuang*, p. 329.

31. See, for example, He Zengke, "Nongcun zhili zhuanxing"; Lang Youxin, "From Economic Elite"; Jiang Shouxun, "Xianfu qunti"; Zhou Bingquan, "'Xianfu qunti' jingxuan 'cunguan.'"

32. Because I had limited opportunities to interview villagers in Henan, this inference about the villagers' perception of entrepreneurs/*nengren* is drawn from the village leaders' explanations of how entrepreneurs came to be elected, from the numbers of entrepreneurs on the VCs, and from numerous articles to that effect. Kuhn, "China's Newly Rich," reinforces this notion, citing one farmer as saying, "Entrepreneurs who become village chiefs are already wealthy enough, so at least they don't have to embezzle public funds," and claiming that other villagers point out that entrepreneurs often serve without pay or use their personal funds to pay for the wining and dining of official patrons and clients. See also Bao Shenghua, "Furen dangxuan cunguan: 'Jingji nengren' jiaoban 'daode quanwei'" (When Rich People Get Elected as Village Leaders: "Entrepreneurs" Challenge "Moral Authority"), at http://news.xinhuanet.com/newscenter/2003–09/15/content_1081369.htm (accessed January 2006).

33. "Rules Required to Guide Rural Elections," *China Daily*, April 12, 2004, at www.chinadaily.com.cn/english/doc/2004–04/12/content_322427.htm (accessed February 24, 2006).

34. He Zengke, *Fanfu xinlu: Zhuanxingqi Zhongguo fubai wenti yanjiu* (New Path to Combat Corruption: Research on the Issue of Corruption in Transitional China) (Beijing: Zhongyang bianyi chubanshe, 2002), pp. 29ff., also argues that the newly wealthy are increasingly willing to spend a considerable amount of money to help their children get into local legislative and administrative organs.

35. On a scale in which 10 is seen as highly clean and 0 as highly corrupt, China received a score of 3.2 (down from 3.4 in 2003), tying it with Morocco, Senegal, Sri Lanka, and Surinam at 78 among 159 countries in Transparency International's 2005 "Corruption Perception Index," at http://ww1.transparency.org/cpi/2005/cpi2005.sources.en.html#cpi (accessed January 2006). In her introduction, Yan Sun, *Corruption and Market*, argues, however, that new frameworks, including an interactive model of the development of reforms and the development of corruption, are needed to understand corruption in China. In contrast to widely held theories, a high degree of corruption has been combined with a high rate of economic growth, and government withdrawal from the economy has led to an increase rather than a decrease in the size and scope of corruption. See also Jean C. Oi, "Market Reforms and Corruption in Rural

China," *Studies in Comparative Communism*, 32, nos. 2–3 (Summer 1989): 221–234.

36. Huang's letter making such allegations, at http://www.zonaeuropa.com/20040815_2.htm (accessed April 1, 2006), was published in *Renmin ribao* (People's Daily), August 11, 2004, and removed from the *Renmin ribao* Web site the following week. Huang was initially condemned for breaking party rules and was required to conduct a self-examination and subsequently charged with corruption and sentenced to life in prison.

37. On the varied definitions of corruption in China, see Richard Levy, "Corruption, Economic Crime and Social Transformation since the Reforms: The Debate in China," *Australian Journal of Chinese Affairs*, no. 33 (1995): 1–25; Levy, *"Fubai:* Differing Chinese Views of Corruption since Tiananmen: Does a Road Paved with Corruption Lead to Socialism?" *International Journal of Public Administration*, 23, no. 11 (2000): 1863–98; Levy, "Corruption in Popular Culture," in Perry Link, Richard Madsen, and Paul Pickowicz, eds., *Popular China: Unofficial Culture in a Globalizing Society* (Lanham, Md.: Rowman and Littlefield, 2002), pp. 39–56; and Kin-man Chan, "Corruption in China: A Principal-Agent Perspective," in Hoi-kwok Wong and Hon S. Chan, eds., *Handbook of Comparative Public Administration in the Asia-Pacific Basin* (New York: Marcel Dekker, 1999), p. 299. Although bribery is also a crime, these economic crimes are not generally targeted in anticorruption campaigns. Unger, *Transformation*, pp. 55–58, argues that in some areas in Guangdong "officials are not considered corrupt unless they grossly overstep the amounts that other local officials take for themselves," and that in Xiqiao district in Guangdong, factory owners pay village cadres a fee for each loom that remains off the tax roll but regard these payments as gratuities rather than instances of corruption. For an up-to-date Chinese theoretical discussion of corruption, including aspects related to village elections, see He Zengke, *Fanfu xinlu.*

38. "Rules Required to Guide Rural Elections," *China Daily*, April 12, 2004, places the amount at 2.3 million RMB.

39. "Minzhengbu tongzhi: Zuohao 2004 nian cunmin weiyuanhui huanjie xuanju gongzuo" (Ministry of Civil Affairs Circular: Do 2004 Village Election Work Well) (March 1, 2004), at www.mca.gov.cn/search/detail.asp?title=%C3%F1%D5%FE%B2%BF%CD%A8%D6%AA%A3%BA%D7%F6%BA%C32004%C4%EA%B4%E5%C3%F1%CE%AF%D4%B1%BB%E1%BB%BB%BD%EC%D1%A1%BE%D9%B9%A4%D7%F7&Ftype=Acontent&keyword=%B4%E5%CE%AF%BB%E1%D1%A1%BE%D9 (accessed January 2006).

40. He Zengke, *Fanfu xinlu*, p. 43, and interviews.

41. Zhou Bingquan, "'Xianfu qunti.'"

42. That is, only the Public Security Bureau, which for legal and political reasons rarely becomes involved in such issues, can use subpoenas to coerce

testimony. Other investigatory agencies must rely on research; see Gong Hui and Shen Jianliang, "Liangge huixuan anli yinchu de wenti" (Issues Arising from Two Cases of Vote-Buying), in *Xuanju qingkuang*, pp. 321–323.

43. See Levy, "Village Self-Government," pp. 51–52.

44. See Wu Feng, "Zhili cunweihui xuanju 'huixuan' de shixian yu sikao" (Thoughts and Practice on Managing "Vote-Buying" in Village Elections), and "Huixuan cunguan weihe nanyi chuli?" (Why Is It So Difficult to Control Vote-Buying in Electing Village Officials?), both in *Xuanju qingkuang*, pp. 184–187, 330–332.

45. "Rules Required to Guide Rural Elections," *China Daily*, April 12, 2004.

46. Rong Jingben et al., *Zailun cong yalixing tizhi*, p. 410.

47. See Yu Weiliang et al., *Cunwu gongkai shouce* (Transparency in Village Affairs: A Reference Manual) (Beijing: EU-China Training Programme on Village Governance, 2003), at http://www.chinarural.org/euchinaprog/euweb/NewsInfo.asp?NewsId=686 (accessed January 2006).

48. "Henan's Methods," art. 36.

49. See "Guangdongsheng cunwu gongkai tiaoli" (Guangdong Province Rules on Making Village Affairs Open to the Public), passed May 31, 2001 at the 26th meeting of the 9th session of the Standing Committee of the Guangdong People's Congress; "Methods for Implementing," art. 14; and a 1999 provincial notice on transparency in Minzhengbu jiceng zhengquan he shequ jianshesi nongcunchu, *1999 niandu nongcun jiceng minzhu zhengzhi jianshe ziliao huibian*, pp. 3–6.

50. Nevertheless, Nanhai's transparency apparently was not adequate to prevent 7.4 billion RMB in bad loans at the Nanhai Bank of Industry and Commerce, resulting in a loss of more than 1 billion RMB and numerous Nanhai leaders stepping down from their posts; see http://news.sohu.com/20040923/n222198472.shtml (accessed January 2006).

51. A significant amount of team-level fiscal information was missing when the system was reviewed in October 2001 and January–February 2002. One cadre did mention that, for proprietary reasons, certain village fiscal data are not posted, although private records are kept. Xiqiao's Web site also included a wide range of materials, at www.xiqiao.gov.cn (accessed May 2004).

52. See Yu Weiliang, "A Comparative Study of Village Committee Election Procedures," p. 3; "Henan's Methods," art. 8; and Suo Nan and Liu Zhide, "Qinghaisheng diwuci cun(mu)weihui huanjie xuanju qingkuang" (The Situation in the Fifth Round of Village Elections in Qinghai), in *Xuanju qingkuang*, pp. 255–258.

53. See Wang Xiansheng and Luo Xiaoming, "Guangdongsheng dierjie cunweihui huanjie xuanju qingkuang" (The Situation of Guangdong's Second Round of Village Elections), in *Xuanju qingkuang*, pp. 201–204.

Numerous reports—for example, speeches at the March 2002 Guangzhou Conference (collected in *Guangzhoushi cunweihui xuanju gongzuo yantaohui ziliao huibian*)—suggest problems in pre-election audits in the first round of elections, particularly in poor villages. Wang Jinhong, *Cunmin zizhi*, p. 11, reports that in 2002 all the villages he observed had completed their audits of the prior VC in a timely way, though according to Li Jiangtao et al., *Minzhu de genji* (of which Wang is a co-author), in numerous villages audits and accounts were not publicized. In some cases this led to postponement of the elections.

54. Art. 24 of "Guangdongsheng cunwu guanli banfa (shixing)" (Guangdong Methods for Administering Villages [Provisional]) (December 12, 2001) calls for audits of village party secretaries, village leaders, leaders of collective economic organizations, accountants, and cashiers by higher-level governments or outside auditors.

55. Tianhe district's December 2000 "Guanyu nongcun caiwu guanli de zanxing guiding (shixing)" (Temporary Guidelines on Fiscal Management in Rural Villages [Provisional]), in *Tianhequ nongcun guizhang zhidu wenjian huibian* (Collection of Documents on Tianhe District's System of Regulation for Rural Villages) (April 2001).

56. Zhonggong Humenshi jiwei Dongguanshi jianchaju, eds., *Fanfu changlian de shixian yu lilun tan* (A Practical and Theoretical Exploration of Fighting Corruption and Promotion of Honest Government) (Guangzhou: Guangdong renmin chubanshe, 2001), pp. 327–335. Yu Weiliang et al., *Cunwu gongkai shouce*, p. 70, suggests that village accountants not be members of the VC but be hired by either the VA or the VRA.

57. Minzhengbu jiceng zhengquan he shehui jianshesi, ed., *Cunmin zizhi anli xuanping* (A Selective Review of Village Self-Government Cases) (Beijing: Zhongguo shehui chubanshe, 2001).

58. See Unger, *Transformation*, pp. 55–58.

59. See *Xuanju qingkuang*, pp. 44–46, 72–77, 83–85, 123–126, 131–136.

60. A similar analysis is also suggested by Kuhn, "China's Newly Rich."

61. See Levy, "Village Self-Government," pp. 54–55, on other problems with China's current anticorruption policies.

3. The Implementation of Village Elections and Tax-for-Fee Reform

I thank the Fulbright Program (2000–2001), University of California, Pacific Rim Fellowship (2000–2001), University of Kansas Research Center and New Faculty General Research Fund (2004), and University of Kansas Policy Research Institute (2004). In addition, I am grateful to Elizabeth Perry, Merle Goldman, Kevin O'Brien, Maria Edin, Li Lianjiang, Thomas Bernstein, Jean Oi, and Nancy Myers for their suggestions and comments, and my good friends and colleagues at Northwest University, Xi'an.

1. Justin Yifu Lin et al., "Urban and Rural Household Taxation in China: Measurement and Stylized Facts," Working Paper, China Center for Economic Research, Peking University (2002).

2. See Joel S. Migdal, *Strong Societies and Weak States* (Princeton: Princeton University Press, 1988), pp. 2–8; Gabriel A. Almond and G. Bingham Powell Jr., *Comparative Politics: A Developmental Approach* (Boston: Little, Brown, 1966); Peter J. Katzenstein, ed., *Between Power and Plenty* (Madison: University of Wisconsin Press, 1978).

3. Robert W. Jackman, *Power without Force: The Political Capacity of Nation-States* (Ann Arbor: University of Michigan Press, 1993), p. 156.

4. Ibid.

5. Edgar Kiser and Xiaoxi Tong, "Determinants of the Amount and Type of Corruption in State Fiscal Bureaucracies: An Analysis of Late Imperial China," *Comparative Political Studies,* 25, no. 3 (October 1992): 300–331.

6. Thomas Bernstein and Xiaobo Lü, "Taxation without Representation: Peasants, the Central and the Local States in Reform China," *China Quarterly,* no. 163 (September 2000): 742–763; Lü Xiaobo, "The Politics of Peasant Burden in Reform China," *Journal of Peasant Studies,* 25, no. 1 (October 1997): 134.

7. Kevin O'Brien and Lianjiang Li, "Selective Policy Implementation in Rural China," *Comparative Politics,* 31, no. 2 (January 1999): 172; Maria Edin, "State Capacity and Local Agent Control in China: CCP Cadre Management from a Township Perspective," *China Quarterly,* no. 173 (March 2003): 35–52.

8. Bernstein and Lü, "Taxation without Representation," p. 742.

9. Ibid., p. 743.

10. Lü Xiaobo, "The Politics of Peasant Burden in Reform China," p. 136.

11. Bernstein and Lü, "Taxation without Representation," p. 762.

12. O'Brien and Li, "Selective Policy Implementation in Rural China," p. 172.

13. Melanie Manion, "The Cadre Management System, Post-Mao: The Appointment, Promotion, Transfer, and Removal of Party and State Leaders," *China Quarterly,* no. 102 (June 1985): 227.

14. In the 1990s the administrative hierarchy below the province consisted of the municipal *(shi)* or district *(qu),* county *(xian),* town *(zhen),* and township *(xiang)* levels. The village is below the township level, but the township is the lowest administrative level. In our sample we have towns and townships. A town contains a number of households with an urban registration and typically has a small "urban" center, whereas none of the residents in a township has an urban registration. In the sample, several townships became towns, but for consistency the term "township" is used for both.

15. O'Brien and Li, "Selective Policy Implementation in Rural China," p. 172.

16. David S. G. Goodman, "The Politics of Regionalism: Economic Development, Conflict and Negotiation," in David S. G. Goodman and Gerald Segal, eds., *China Deconstructs: Politics, Trade, and Regionalism* (New York: Routledge, 1994), pp. 1–20; Yan Huai, "Organization Hierarchy and the Cadre Management System," in Carol Lee Hamrin and Zhao Suisheng, eds., *Decision-Making in Deng's China: Perspectives from Insiders* (Armonk, N.Y.: M. E. Sharpe, 1995), pp. 39–50.

17. O'Brien, and Li, "Selective Policy Implementation in Rural China," p. 172.

18. Ibid.

19. Bernstein, and Lü, "Taxation without Representation," p. 742.

20. Edin, "State Capacity and Local Agent Control in China," p. 36.

21. O'Brien and Li, "Selective Policy Implementation in Rural China," p. 172; Edin, "State Capacity and Local Agent Control in China," p. 36.

22. Edin is mostly concerned with the promotion of economic growth policies rather than burden reductions or the Organic Law. Even though economic growth might be considered a popular policy, in her research she does not set out to test this hypothesis. I thank Maria Edin for bringing this to my attention.

23. Wang Xiong, "Sheng shijie renda changweihui diliuci huiyi bimu" (The Sixth Plenum of the Standing Committee of the Tenth Provincial People's Congress Comes to a Close), *Shaanxi ribao* (Shaanxi Daily), September 29, 2003, p. 1; Feng Jing, "Tax Reform Helps Ease Burden on Farmers," *Beijing Review*, 44, no. 17 (May 3, 2001): 21.

24. Wang Xiong, "Sheng shijie renda changweihui diliuci huiyi bimu."

25. Ibid.

26. The 2000 data used in this analysis come from a survey of thirty-four villages conducted in Shaanxi province between October and November 2000. The survey was a random multi-stage sample of thirty-four villages in six counties. Within each village, nine households were randomly selected from the household registration list *(huji)* supplied by the village accountant. In addition to the nine villager respondents, the village leader, party secretary, and accountant were also interviewed.

27. O'Brien and Li, "Selective Policy Implementation in Rural China," p. 172.

28. I thank Kevin O'Brien for helping to clarify this point.

29. O'Brien and Li, "Selective Policy Implementation in Rural China," p. 172; Bernstein and Lü, "Taxation without Representation," p. 742.

30. Lin et al., "Urban and Rural Household Taxation in China."

31. See Linda Jakobson, "Local Governance: Village and Township Elections," in Jude Howell, ed., *Governance in China* (Lanham, Md.: Rowman and Littlefield, 2004), pp. 97–120; Bai Gang and Zhao Shouxing, *Xuanju yu zhili* (Elections and Governance) (Beijing: Zhongguo shehui kexue chubanshe, 2001), pp. 300–322; Fan Yu, "Xiangzhen zhengfu shifou

youquan rending cunmin xuanjude jieguo" (Whether or Not the Township Government Should Be Entitled to Villager Election Outcomes) (January 2003), at www.chinaelections.org/ (accessed August 27, 2004).

32. Ibid.

33. John James Kennedy, "The Face of 'Grassroots Democracy' in Rural China: Real versus Cosmetic Elections," *Asian Survey*, 42, no. 3 (May–June 2002): 456–482.

34. Township involvement in village elections is different from township interference. The township officials help register eligible voters, set up voting booths, monitor vote counts, and even mediate debates and campaign speeches. Therefore, the presence of township government officials can also ensure a "free and fair" election.

35. The village nomination categories were determined through quantitative and qualitative means. In the questionnaire, villagers were asked about the election and nomination processes. Specifically, they were asked how the candidates in the most recent election were nominated: by the villagers, the village representative assembly, the party branch, the township, or other. Unfortunately, for whatever reason, when we asked this question of the nine households in a village, my Chinese colleagues and I often received inconsistent answers within the same village. In order to reconcile the cases in which the opinions of villagers in a single village are inconsistent, we developed a single village measure. To do so, we aggregated the nomination data across households to the village level using a "majority rule" procedure. See Tianjian Shi, "Economic Development and Village Elections in Rural China," *Journal of Contemporary China*, no. 22 (November 1999): 425–442. In addition, the majority of villagers must also be consistent with at least two of the village cadre responses. All three cadres were asked the same set of questions as the villagers regarding the village election process. Enumerators also conducted lengthy sit-down interviews with the leader, party secretary, and village accountant in each village. Finally, in the 2004 sample we conducted additional interviews with the principal of the elementary school and the cadre in charge of family planning. The school principals in particular were well-informed, educated, and typically quite candid about village elections and relations among cadres and villagers.

36. For an excellent discussion of the regressive tax system and the negative effect on the poorest rural households, see Lin et al., "Urban and Rural Household Taxation in China"; and Tao Ran and Mingxing Liu, "Government Regulations and Rural Taxation in China," *Perspectives* (Overseas Young Chinese Forum), 5, no. 2, at http://www.oycf.org/Perspectives/ 25_063004/6.pdf (accessed April 1, 2006).

37. One important implication of the tax reform is that township revenues have dried up. In one township the cadres whom we interviewed said that

they had not been paid in over twenty months. In 2000, when we visited Township 51, there were over sixty cadres on the payroll, and the government offices were teeming with activity. In 2004 the same office complex was deserted, and the only cadres in the complex were the party secretary and the government head. For further discussion of the fiscal crisis affecting township government, see the chapter in this volume by Jean C. Oi and Zhao Shukai.

38. Xu Wang, *Mutual Empowerment of State and Peasantry: Village Self-Government in Rural China* (New York: Nova Science, 2003), pp. 60–62.

39. Bai Gang and Zhao Shouxing, *Xuanju yu zhili*, p. 310; Bernstein and Lü, "Taxation without Representation," p. 742; Wang, *Mutual Empowerment of State and Peasantry*, p. 61.

40. These data are from personal interviews with County 5 township party secretaries and government heads in November 2000, March 2001, and June 2004.

41. In the 2000 and 2004 surveys I asked villagers and cadres the question: "Some villagers believe the last election was fair, while others believe it was unfair. Thinking of the last village election, where do you place it on a scale of 1 to 5, where 1 means that the last election was conducted fairly and 5 means that the last election was conducted unfairly?"

42. Interview with Township 51 party secretary, June 5, 2004.

43. Ibid.

44. Robert A. Dahl, *Polyarchy: Participation and Opposition* (New Haven: Yale University Press, 1971); Adam Przeworski, *Democracy and the Market: Political and Economic Reforms in Eastern Europe and Latin America* (New York: Cambridge University Press, 1991).

45. The use of handbills and big-character posters has a long history in China, most recently during the Cultural Revolution. In fact, one of the democratic elements of the Cultural Revolution was the opportunity for average citizens to criticize local cadres openly using pamphlets and posters. See Maurice Meisner, *Mao's China and After: A History of the People's Republic*, 3rd ed. (New York: Free Press, 1999), p. 327.

46. The median family income in 2004 was 7,500 RMB for C5, 8,500 RMB for C3, and 3,500 RMB for C6. In 2004 the exchange rate was 8.24 RMB to the U.S. dollar.

47. According to *Zhongguo nongcun zhuhu diaocha nianjian 2003* (China Rural Household Survey Yearbook 2003) (Beijing: Zhongguo tongji chubanshe, 2003), in 2002 the middle (annual net income) per capita rural income was 2,164 RMB. Thus, the household income is estimated at 8,656 RMB ($4 \times 2{,}164$).

48. Shi, "Economic Development and Village Elections in Rural China," pp. 425–442.

49. O'Brien and Li, "Selective Policy Implementation in Rural China," p. 172.

50. In the 2004 survey we had official questionnaires for the township party secretaries and specific questions regarding the rotation of county and township leading cadres.

51. Even though the party secretary in C6 had not been transferred in over twelve years, and at his age had no possibility of further promotion, he still had an incentive (i.e., fiscal punishments for noncompliance) to implement provincial and central policies because of the need for local development funds and tax remittances from the provincial and central governments.

52. Daniel Kelliher, "The Chinese Debate over Village Self-Government," *China Journal*, no. 37 (January 1997): 63–90; Jean C. Oi, "Economic Development, Stability, and Democratic Village Self-Governance," in Maurice Brosseau, Suzanne Pepper, and Shu-ki Tsang, eds., *China Review, 1996* (Hong Kong: Chinese University Press, 1996), pp. 125–144.

53. According to an interview with the township party secretary in C5 (Township 51), the current county party secretary had been in office since 2001, and the previous county party secretary had served from 1997 to 2001 (interview, June 2004).

54. Edin, "State Capacity and Local Agent Control in China."

55. This is similar to the policy retrenchment that occurred during the cyclical political campaigns of the Maoist era. G. W. Skinner and Edwin Winckler demonstrate that although the party had the political capacity to influence rural communities (i.e., to close down local markets), it did not have the capacity to maintain these political campaigns for an extended period of time. Therefore, local rural markets would open and close with the high tide and retrenchment of the political campaigns. See G. W. Skinner and Edwin A. Winckler, "Compliance Succession in Rural Communist China: A Cyclical Theory," in Amitai Etzioni, comp., *A Sociological Reader on Complex Organization* (New York: Holt, Rinehart and Winston, 1969), pp. 410–438.

4. Fiscal Crisis in China's Townships

We thank Kay Shimizu for research assistance and Yuen Yuen Ang for useful comments on an earlier draft of this chapter.

1. Vladimir Gimpelson and Daniel Treisman, "Fiscal Games and Public Employment: A Theory with Evidence from Russia," *World Politics*, 54, no. 2 (January 2002): 145–183.

2. The ten provinces are Hebei, Shanxi, Shandong, Zhejiang, Anhui, Hunan, Sichuan, Gansu, Ningxia, and Shaanxi. Research in these provinces, counties, and townships was carried out between January and December 2003. In addition, we also conducted research in a county in Hebei in the sum-

mer of 2004. These sites were intentionally selected. We knew in advance the likely fiscal situation of each county and township. We selected a few relatively well off areas but focused on those areas likely to have fiscal difficulties so that we could delve into these problems more deeply. We thank the Ford Foundation for its generous support, with special thanks to Sarah Cook for her encouragement in overseeing the project.

3. See Jean C. Oi, *Rural China Takes Off: Institutional Foundations of Economic Reform* (Berkeley: University of California Press, 1999), for a more detailed explanation of this system.

4. The one exception to this system was found in a relatively underdeveloped township where a "county unified planning" *(xianji tongchou)* system was adopted. In this system the county pays directly for a portion of the township expenditures, namely, the salaries of the public employees of the township, while the township remains responsible for all of its other expenses. In this township in our sample, the county took 25 percent of the central taxes, which is the amount that all counties are allowed to keep, and 60 percent of the local taxes that in other counties are retained entirely within the township. In return, the county paid the salaries of those in the township with an official bureaucratic position *(bianzhi)* and all public employees, including teachers. All other township expenditures, however, had to be taken care of by the township in accord with the "eating in separate kitchens" principle. Fieldwork by Zhao Shukai in 2004 in another county suggests that this new *xianji tongchou* system is spreading, especially in the more backward regions, to ensure that the wages of government personnel are guaranteed.

5. Since the 1994 fiscal reforms, the extra-budgetary funds are more formally called the second budget *(dier yusuan)*, but still commonly referred to as *yusuanwai*.

6. These are the agricultural tax, the agricultural and forestry special products tax, the slaughter tax, and the land-use tax.

7. This was implemented in twenty provinces beginning in 2002. The policy is also often referred to in the literature as *feigaishui*.

8. For those areas that have special agricultural products, there is a special agricultural products tax and a surcharge on that tax. Peasant households pay either the agricultural or the special agricultural products tax and its associated surcharge, but not both.

9. As of December 2005 there were only three provinces that had not yet totally abolished their agricultural tax and associated surcharge.

10. See Thomas Bernstein and Xiaobo Lü, *Taxation without Representation in Contemporary Rural China* (New York: Cambridge University Press, 2003); Oi, *Rural China Takes Off*.

11. Survey data came from over one hundred villages. See Jean C. Oi and Kaoru Shimizu, "Costs and Benefits of Rural Industrialization: A Reassess-

ment," paper presented at the International Conference on Grassroots Democracy and Local Governance in China during the Reform Era," National Chengchi University, Taipei, November 2–3, 2004.

12. Occasionally a few are still sent even though the system ended in 2002. See "Jiaoyubu, gong'an bu, renshi bu, laodong baozhangbu 'Guanyu jinyibu shenhua pudong gaodeng xuexiao biyesheng jiuye zhidu gongzuo gaige youguan wenti de yijian'" ("Suggestions for Further Deepening Reforms of the System for Employing Graduates" Jointly Proposed by the Ministry of Education, Ministry of Public Security, Ministry of Personnel, and Ministry of Labor and Social Security), in *Zhongguo jiaoyu nianjian 2003* (China Education Yearbook 2003) (Beijing: Renmin jiaoyu chubanshe, 2003), pp. 792–793.

13. Authors' China interviews (hereafter CI) 62204.

14. For a discussion of previous attempts to reduce peasant burdens, see Jean C. Oi, "Old Problems for New Leaders: Institutional Disjunctions in Rural China," in Yun-Han Chu, Chih-cheng Lo, and Ramon H. Myers, eds., *The New Chinese Leadership: Challenges and Opportunities after the 16th Party Congress* (New York: Cambridge University Press, 2004), pp. 141–155.

15. Also see Ray Yep, "Can 'Tax-for-Fee' Reform Reduce Rural Tension in China? The Process, Progress and Limitations," *China Quarterly*, no. 177 (March 2004): 42–47.

16. CI 101202.

17. CI 101302.

18. Cited in Justin Yifu Lin et al., "Rural Direct Taxation and Government Regulations in China: Economic Analysis and Policy Implications," unpublished ms., August 2002.

19. Xiao Junyan, "Rural Economic Situation in the First Half of 2002 and Outlook for the Whole Year," *China Development Review*, 4, no. 4 (October 2002): 47–60.

20. Guojia tongjiju, "Shangbannian nongmin xianjin shouru renjun 1345 yuan, tongbi zengzhang 16.1%" (Farmers' Per Capita Cash Income Reaches 1345 RMB in the First Half of the Year, Which Is a 16.1% Increase Over Last Year), July 27, 2004, quoted in "Nongyebu buzhang Du Qinglin: Zai hongguan tiaokongzhong jiaqiang nongye" (Minister of Agriculture Du Qinglin On Promoting Agriculture Using Macro Adjustment), *Renmin ribao* (People's Daily), August 10, 2004.

21. Salaries consist of various items *(xiang);* local officials often talk about being about to pay four or six out of eight *xiang*.

22. See Oi, "Old Problems."

23. Wen Jiabao, "Jiejue 'sannong wenti' shi quanbu gongzuo de zhongzhong zhizhong" (Solving the Problems of "Agriculture, Rural Areas, and Farmers" Is a Top Priority of All Work), *Renmin ribao* (People's Daily), March 6, 2004, p. 2.

24. See Oi, *Rural China Takes Off*, chap. 2.
25. It has been reported by Owen Brown in the *Wall Street Journal* that the 2004 budget earmarked 39.6 billion RMB in transfer payments to make up for the cuts in the agricultural tax and other surcharges. This represents a 9.1 billion RMB increase compared with the 2003 budget. Owen Brown, "Local Governments to Rack Up Debt, Worrying Beijing," *Wall Street Journal*, April 12, 2004, p. A18.
26. CI 101002.
27. One township among our twenty never received any transfers even though it was in need.
28. See Jean Oi and Kay Shimizu, "The Uncertain Road of Industrialization," unpublished ms., 2006; also CI 112805.
29. The impact of this category varied within different townships. In the five that identified it as a source of debt, the amounts ranged from 5 percent to 86 percent of a township's debt.
30. In the five townships where this category was a source of debt, the debt constituted different proportions of the total, ranging from 20 percent to 70 percent.
31. CI 112805.
32. Wen Jiabao, "Jiejue 'sannong wenti.'"
33. On *dingzihu*, see Lianjiang Li and Kevin J. O'Brien, "Villagers and Popular Resistance in Contemporary China," *Modern China*, 22, no. 1 (January 1996): 28–61.
34. For detailed discussion of the cadre evaluation system, see Susan H. Whiting, *Power and Wealth in Rural China: The Political Economy of Institutional Change* (New York: Cambridge University Press, 2001); and Maria Edin, "State Capacity and Local Agent Control in China: CCP Cadre Management from a Township Perspective," *China Quarterly*, no. 173 (March 2003): 35–52. Also see Kai-Yuen Tsui and Youqiang Wang, "Between Separate Stoves and a Single Menu: Fiscal Decentralization in China," *China Quarterly*, no. 177 (March 2004): 71–90.
35. On the façade of compliance during the Mao period, see Jean C. Oi, *State and Peasant in Contemporary China: The Political Economy of Village Government* (Berkeley: University of California Press, 1989); also Vivienne Shue, *The Reach of the State: Sketches of the Chinese Body Politic* (Stanford: Stanford University Press, 1988).
36. This is under the double alternative management *(shuang daiguan)* system. See Oi, "Old Problems."
37. See Jean Oi, "Patterns of Corporate Restructuring in China: Political Constraints on Privatization," *China Journal*, no. 55 (January 2005): 115–136.
38. WY township.
39. We do know of a case in which an official who took out a loan was trans-

ferred. He then found it very difficult to receive repayment from the township.

40. BZ township.

41. See, for example, Yongshun Cai, "Collective Ownership or Cadres' Ownership? The Non-agricultural Use of Farmland in China," *China Quarterly,* no. 175 (September 2003): 662–680.

42. Xiaolin Guo, "Land Expropriation and Rural Conflicts in China," *China Quarterly,* no. 166 (June 2001): 422–439.

43. See, for example, "Chinese Protester Dies over Land Dispute: Local Residents Sue Government over Evictions," *Radio Free Asia,* October 29, 2003; also see Zhao Ling, "Nongmin weiquan zhongxin chuxian zhongda bianhua" (Significant Shift in Focus of Peasants' Rights Activism), *Nanfang zhoumo,* September 2, 2004, p. 4. Also see Sally Sargenson, "Subduing 'the Rural House-Building Craze': Attitudes toward Housing Construction and Land Use Controls in Four Zhejiang Villages," *China Quarterly,* no. 172 (December 2002): 927–955; and also work by Peter Ho.

44. The 2005 figure represents a 6.6% increase over 2004. The date of the Ministry of Public Security news release was January 19, 2006. "Editor's Note," *Jamestown Journal,* 6, no. 2 (January 20, 2006); and Li Fan, "Unrest in China's Countryside," *Jamestown Journal,* 6, no. 2 (January 20, 2006), both at www.jamestown.org/publications_details.php?volume_id=415&issue_id=3592&article_id=2370693 (accessed February 25, 2006).

45. Joseph Kahn, "Chinese Premier Says Seizing Peasants' Land Provokes Unrest," *New York Times,* January 21, 2006, p. A3. The article also reports government figures which state that in 2004, new factories, housing, offices, and shopping malls had consumed about 5 percent of the total arable land in the previous seven years.

46. Geoffrey York, "Peasants Fighting Back in Rural China," *Globe and Mail* (Toronto), June 18, 2005, p. A13.

47. Didi Kirsten Tatlow, "In Riot Village, the Government Is on the Run," *South China Morning Post,* April 13, 2005, p. 6.

48. Michel Oksenberg, "Getting Ahead and Along in Communist China: The Ladder of Success on the Eve of the Cultural Revolution," in John Lewis, ed., *Party Leadership and Revolutionary Power in China* (New York: Cambridge University Press, 1970), pp. 304–347.

49. A similar attitude pervaded interviews in county agencies where officials similarly had not been paid for several months, and in some cases for over a year.

5. Direct Township Elections

For generous financial support, I thank the Asia Foundation, the Harry Frank Guggenheim Foundation, the Research Grants Council of Hong Kong, and Hong Kong Baptist

University. I also acknowledge a grant from the Research and Writing Initiative of the Program on Global Security and Sustainability of the John D. and Catherine T. MacArthur Foundation. For helpful comments on earlier drafts, I thank Merle Goldman, Baogang He, John Kennedy, Young-Choul Kim, Elizabeth Perry, Victor Shih, Lily Tsai, Rob Weller, an anonymous reviewer, and especially Kevin O'Brien.

1. See, among others, Robert A. Dahl, *A Preface to Democratic Theory* (Chicago: University of Chicago Press, 1956); Giovanni Sartori, *Theory of Democracy Revisited* (Chatham, N.J.: Chatham House, 1987); Ian Shapiro, *The State of Democratic Theory* (Princeton: Princeton University Press, 2003).

2. On Peng Zhen's view that villagers' self-government is preparation for direct democracy at the township and county levels, see Lianjiang Li and Kevin J. O'Brien, "The Struggle over Village Elections," in Merle Goldman and Roderick MacFarquhar, eds., *The Paradox of China's Post-Mao Reforms* (Cambridge, Mass.: Harvard University Press, 1999), p. 131. For a Western report on the Buyun election, see Michael Laris and John Pomfret, "Ssshhh! This Is a Secret Election; Chinese Quietly Test Democratic Waters," *Washington Post*, January 27, 1999, p. A15.

3. "Zhonggong zhongyang guanyu zhuanfa 'Zhonggong quanguo renda changweihui dangzu guanyu quanguo xiangji renmin daibiao dahui huanjie xuanju gongzuo youguan wenti de yijian' de tongzhi" (The Party Central Committee's Notice on Transmitting "Suggestions of the Party Group of the Standing Committee of the National People's Congress in Regard to a Number of Questions Concerning the Reelection of Township-Level People's Congresses"), issued in July 2001.

4. Interviews with officials at the Guangdong Provincial People's Congress, Guangzhou, September 2001; interviews with two senior scholars at the Chinese Academy of Social Sciences, August 2001. Also see Shi Weimin, *Gongxuan yu zhixuan* (Open Selection and Direct Election) (Beijing: Zhongguo shehui kexue chubanshe, 2000), p. 412.

5. On "open selection," see Melanie F. Manion, "Chinese Democratization in Perspective: Electorates and Selectorates at the Township Level," *China Quarterly*, no. 163 (September 2000): 764–782; Tony Saich and Xuedong Yang, "Innovation in China's Local Governance: 'Open Recommendation and Selection,'" *Pacific Affairs*, 76, no. 2 (Summer 2003): 185–208. For a report on the "open selection" of county government heads in Jiangsu, see Li Nan, "Yige xianzhang de dansheng" (The Birth of a County Government Head), *Zhongguo xinwen zhoukan* (China Newsweek), no. 46 (December 15, 2003): 20–23.

6. For Zhu Rongji's response, see Xinhua she, "Zhu Rongji zongli huijian zhongwai jizhe huida jizhe ti wen" (Zhu Rongji Meets with Foreign and Domestic Journalists and Answers Their Questions), *Renmin ribao* (People's Daily), March 16, 2000, pp. 1, 4.

7. See John Pomfret, "Taking on the Party in Rural China: Reformer Risks Livelihood for Direct Elections," *Washington Post,* September 27, 2003, p. A14.

8. Useful Chinese sources on the Buyun election include Tang Jianguang, "Zhixuan xiangzhang" (The Direct Election of a Township Head), *Nanfang zhoumo* (Southern Weekend), January 15, 1999, p. 2; Shi Weimin, *Gongxuan yu zhixuan,* pp. 428–453; Li Fan et al., *Chuangxin yu fazhan* (Innovations and Development) (Beijing: Dongfang chubanshe, 2000), pp. 96–102. On the Nancheng township election, see Li Fan, "Zhongguo xiangzhen xuanju gaige de dadan changshi: Nancheng xiang de xiangzhang zhixuan" (A Courageous Experiment with Township Electoral Reforms: Direct Election of the Township Head in Nancheng Township), *Beijing yu fenxi* (Background and Analysis), no. 30 (Beijing: World and China Institute, April 29, 2001).

9. Baogang He and Youxing Lang, "China's First Direct Election of the Township Head: A Case Study of Buyun," *Japanese Journal of Political Science,* 2, no. 1 (May 2001): 21.

10. Joseph Y. S. Cheng, "Direct Elections of Town and Township Heads in China: The Dapeng and Buyun Experiments," *China Information,* 15, no. 1 (2001): 135.

11. Lianjiang Li, "The Politics of Introducing Direct Township Elections in China," *China Quarterly,* no. 171 (September 2002): 707–708.

12. Saich and Yang, "Innovation in China's Local Governance," p. 205.

13. Cai Dingjian, ed., *Zhongguo xuanju zhuangkuang de baogao* (Reports on the Current Situation of Elections in China) (Beijing: Falü chubanshe, 2002), pp. 235–241.

14. Lianjiang Li, "Direct Election of Township Heads: Perspectives of Chinese Peasants," in John Wong and Yongnian Zheng, eds., *China's Post-Jiang Leadership Succession* (River Edge, N.J.: World Scientific, 2002), pp. 231–260.

15. See Shi Weiqin, "Pingba zhen 'shuanggui' gaigezhe diaocha" (An Investigation of the "Double Restriction" of a Reformer in Pingba Town), *Zhongguo shehui daokan* (Guide to Chinese Society), no. 10 (October 2003): 21–25; Li Fan, "Chengkou xian Pingba zhen zonghe zhengzhi tizhi gaige jishi" (A True Record of a Comprehensive Political Reform in Pingba Town of Chengkou County), *Gaige neican* (Inside Information on Reform), no. 29 (October 20, 2003): 16–20; Pomfret, "Taking on the Party"; Matthew Forney, "Taking a Stand," posted on March 1, 2004, at www.time.com/time/asia/2004/china_reform/story.html (accessed January 10, 2006).

16. Li, "The Politics of Introducing Direct Township Elections," p. 713.

17. Gao Xinjun, "Woguo xian xiang liangji zhengzhi tizhi gaige de shuguang:

Henansheng Xinmi shi cunji minzhu zhengzhi zhidu jianshe diaocha" (The Twilight of the Reform of Political Systems at County and Township Levels: An Investigation on the Construction of Village Democracy in Xinmi County, Henan Province), *Jingji shehui tizhi bijiao* (Comparative Economic and Social Systems), no. 6 (December 1998): 15.

18. Xin Qiushui, "57 ming xiangzhen ganbu zai zuotanhuishang tichu cunmin zizhi yihou cunzai zhe 14 ge zenmoban" (57 Township Officials Raise 14 Questions about What Should Be Done after the Establishment of Villagers' Self-Government), unpublished paper, 2001, p. 6.

19. Interviews, township party secretary and township government head, Fujian, July 1997; township party secretary, Hebei, 1995; deputy township party secretary, Hebei, 1999; township party secretary, Jiangxi, July 2001; township party secretary and deputy party secretary, Hebei, August 2004.

20. On the reconstruction of township government, see Vivienne Shue, "The Fate of the Commune," *Modern China*, 10, no. 3 (July 1984): 259–283.

21. National Statistics Bureau, *Zhongguo tongji nianjian 2004* (China Statistical Yearbook 2004) (Beijing: Zhongguo tongji chubanshe, 2004), p. 21.

22. Here I mean "administrative villages" *(xingzheng cun)*, which are usually equivalent to the brigades of the commune era. Most administrative villages are natural villages, though a large natural village is sometimes divided into two or more administrative villages, and several small natural villages can be combined into one administrative village. Each administrative village has its own village committee.

23. On revisions of the Organic Law, see Shi Weimin, *Gongxuan yu zhixuan*, pp. 283–297. The constitution as amended in 2004 extends the terms of office of the township people's congress and the township government from three to five years (art. 98).

24. See Manion, "Chinese Democratization in Perspective," pp. 764–782.

25. See Ma Rong, Liu Shiding, and Qiu Zeqi, eds., *Zhongguo xiangzhen zuzhi diaocha* (Investigations of the Organization of Towns and Townships in China) (Beijing: Huaxia chubanshe, 2000).

26. For an analysis of the impact of the 1994 tax reform on township governments, see Thomas P. Bernstein and Xiaobo Lü, *Taxation without Representation in Contemporary Rural China* (New York: Cambridge University Press, 2003), pp. 107, 248–249. For more analyses of the reform, see Le-Yin Zhang, "Chinese Central-Provincial Fiscal Relationships, Budgetary Decline, and the Impact of the 1994 Fiscal Reform: An Evaluation," *China Quarterly*, no. 157 (March 1999): 115–141; Pak K. Lee, "Into the Trap of Strengthening State Capacity: China's Tax-Assignment Reform," *China Quarterly*, no. 164 (December 2000): 1007–24.

27. For analyses of conflicts between villagers and township officials, see Bernstein and Lü, *Taxation without Representation;* Lianjiang Li and Kevin J.

O'Brien, "Villagers and Popular Resistance in Contemporary China," *Modern China*, 22, no. 1 (January 1996): 28–61.

28. In March 1998, for instance, Premier Zhu Rongji said in a nationally televised news conference that many government agencies collected fees in spite of state regulations, imposing onerous burdens on the people and causing seething popular discontent. See Xinhua she, "Jiujie quanguo renda yici huiyi juxing jizhe zhaodaihui Zhu Rongji zongli deng da jizhe wen" (Premier Zhu Rongji and Others Answer Questions at the Press Conference Held by the First Meeting of the Ninth National People's Congress), *Renmin ribao* (People's Daily), March 20, 1998, pp. 1, 3. From January 1, 1995, to December 31, 2004, 313 articles containing the words "arbitrarily collect fees" *(luan shoufei)* and "township government" *(xiangzhen zhengfu)* appeared in *Renmin ribao*.

29. See Li Xueju, Wang Zhenyao, and Tang Jinsu, eds., *Zhongguo xiangzhen zhengquan de xianzhuang yu gaige* (The Current Situation of Township Government and Its Reforms) (Beijing: Zhongguo shehui chubanshe, 1994).

30. See Li and O'Brien, "The Struggle over Village Elections," pp. 131–132.

31. Interviews with officials at the Ministry of Civil Affairs, Beijing, July 1994.

32. Jiang Zemin, "Hold High the Great Banner of Deng Xiaoping Theory for an All-Round Advancement of the Cause of Building Socialism with Chinese Characteristics into the 21st Century," September 12, 1997, *Beijing Review* 40, no. 40 (October 6–12, 1997), p. 24.

33. See Lai Hairong, "Jingzheng xing xuanju zai Sichuansheng xiangzhen yiji de fazhan" (The Development of Competitive Elections at the Township Level in Sichuan Province), *Zhanlüe yu guanli* (Strategy and Management), no. 2 (April 2003): 57–70; Bao Yonghui and Shi Yonghong, "Suqian 'gongtui jingxuan' xiangzhen yi ba shou" (Open Recommendations and Competitive Elections of No. 1 Township Leaders in Suqian), *Liaowang xinwen zhoukan* (Outlook Newsweekly), no. 37 (September 15, 2003): 46–48; Yao Lifa, "Hubei Jingshan xian Yangji zhen de xuanju gaige" (Electoral Reforms in Yangji Town, Jingshan County, Hubei), in Li Fan, ed., *Zhongguo jiceng minzhu fazhan baogao 2002* (2002 Report on the Development of Grassroots Democracy in China) (Xi'an: Xibei daxue chubanshe, 2003), pp. 358–373; Huang Weiping and Zou Shubin, eds., *Xiangzhen zhang xuanju fangshi gaige: Anli yanjiu* (Case Studies of Reforms of Township Head Elections) (Beijing: Shehui kexue wenxian chubanshe, 2003), pp. 240–247, 262–268, 306–314.

34. Zou Shubin, "Dapeng: 'San lun liang piao zhi' gaige qiaoran zhongzhi" (The Quiet Termination of the "Three-Round-Two-Ballot System" in Dapeng), *Zhongguo gaige* (China Reform), no. 7 (July 2003): 18–19.

35. Shi Weimin, *Gongxuan yu zhixuan*, pp. 411–427; Li Fan et al., *Chuangxin yu fazhan*, pp. 71–79; Shi Weiqin, "Muji Linyi de xiangjian minyi diaocha"

(Witnessing a Rural Public Opinion Survey in Linyi), *Zhongguo shehui daokan* (Guide to Chinese Society), no. 5 (May 1999): 13–16.

36. Jiang Zuoping and Li Yin, "Jiceng minzhu jianshe xin kandian" (New Highlights of Grassroots Democratic Construction), *Liaowang xinwen zhoukan* (Outlook Newsweekly), no. 49 (December 8, 2003): 26–29; Tang Jianguang, "Zhixuan dangdaibiao" (Direct Election of Party Congress Deputies), *Zhongguo xinwen zhoukan* (China Newsweek), no. 3 (January 17, 2003): 16–18.

37. On extending direct elections to the county level, see Du Runsheng, "Women qian nongmin tai duo" (We Owe the Peasants Too Much), in his introduction to Li Changping, *Wo xiang zongli shuo shihua* (I Told the Premier the Truth) (Beijing: Guangming ribao chubanshe, 2002), pp. 2–3.

38. Tian Shubin, Li Ziliang, and Wang Yan, "Yunnan Honghe zhou 'dadan' gaige 'zhitui zhixuan xiangzhen zhang'" (A "Bold" Reform in Honghe Prefecture of Yunnan: "Popular Nomination and Direct Election of Township Heads"), *Banyuetan* (Fortnightly Chats), no. 21 (November 10, 2004): 16–20.

39. On the use of local samples, see Melanie F. Manion, "Survey Research in the Study of Contemporary China: Learning from Local Samples," *China Quarterly*, no. 139 (September 1994): 741–765.

40. "Xialie geji zhengfu lingdao shifou yinggai you xuanmin yi ren yi piao zhijie xuanju chansheng?"

41. I.e., (1) "xiang zhen zhang," (2) "xianzhang," (3) "shizhang," 4) "shengzhang," (5) "guojia zhuxi."

42. I.e., (1) "bu yinggai," (2) "yinggai dan muqian bu kexing," (3) "yinggai erqie muqian jiu keyi shixing."

43. For a discussion of a high level of education as a necessary condition of democracy, see Seymour Martin Lipset, "Some Social Requisites of Democracy: Economic Development and Political Legitimacy," *American Political Science Review*, 53, no. 1 (March 1959): 78–81.

44. See Li Fan et al., *Chuangxin yu fazhan*, p. 141; Tang Jianguang, "Zhixuan xiangzhang," p. 2.

45. Shi Weimin, *Gongxuan yu zhixuan*, pp. 440–444. Interview with the head of a city organization department, Sichuan, February 2004.

46. For a discussion of odds and the odds ratio, see Tamás Rudas, *Odds Ratios in the Analysis of Contingency Tables* (Thousand Oaks, Calif.: Sage, 1998).

47. Interview with a rural researcher, Beijing, December 2003; interview with the director of a city organization department, Sichuan, February 2004.

48. For discussions about the power struggles between elected village directors and appointed party secretaries, see Li and O'Brien, "The Struggle over Village Elections," pp. 141–142; Guo Zhenglin and Thomas P. Bernstein, "The Impact of Elections on the Village Structure of Power:

The Relations between the Village Committees and the Party Branches," *Journal of Contemporary China*, 13, no. 39 (May 2004): 257–275.

49. Interview with the director of a city organization department, Sichuan, February 2004.

50. "Xiangzhen ganbu shi xian lingdao de nuli."

51. On the institutional constraints of township officials, see Kevin J. O'Brien and Lianjiang Li, "Selective Policy Implementation in Rural China," *Comparative Politics*, 31, no. 2 (January 1999): 167–186; Lu Xueyi and Li Chunguang, "Wei nongcun xiangzhen ganbu shuo jiju hua" (Say a Few Words on Behalf of Rural Township Cadres), *Lingdao canyue* (Leadership References), no. 23 (August 15, 2001): 1–9.

52. Interviews with township party secretary, Hebei, 1993; township party secretary, Hebei, 1994; deputy township party secretary, Hebei, 1995; township party secretary, Hebei, 2002; deputy township government head, Hunan, 2003; director of a city organization department, Sichuan, 2004.

53. Interview with township party secretary, Hebei, August 2004.

54. See Leng Xiao, "Xiangguan nandang" (It Is Hard to Be a Township Leader), *Nanfeng chuang* (Winds on a Southern Window), no. 7 (July 2001): 30–32; Liu Jian et al., "Nongcun wending: Yige ningzhong de huati" (Rural Stability: A Grave Topic), *Banyuetan (neibuban)* (Fortnightly Chats) (internal edition), no. 4 (April 1999): 12.

55. Zha Qingjiu, "Minzhu buneng chaoyue falü" (Democracy Must Not Overstep the Law), *Fazhi ribao* (Legal Daily), January 19, 1999, p. 1; Zhang Jinming, "Buyun xiangzhang zhixuan de beijing, guocheng yu xiaoguo" (The Background, Process, and Effects of the Direct Election of the Government Head of Buyun Township), typescript.

56. "Zhijie xuanju xiangzhang weifan xianfa."

57. "Zhixuan xiangzhang fuhe yiqie quanli shuyu renmin de xianfa jingshen."

58. Nonresponse rates were unusually high, perhaps because these two issues were deemed controversial.

59. While it is logical for one to agree that direct elections accord with the "constitutional spirit" but not the constitution, it is somewhat illogical to agree that direct elections accord with the constitution but not the "constitutional spirit." Still, 132 respondents held this position.

60. Zha Qingjiu, "Minzhu buneng chaoyue falü."

61. In the Pingba case, "violating the principle that the party manages cadres" was a major charge the county leadership brought against the reform-minded township party secretary; see Shi Weiqin, "Pingba zhen 'shuanggui,'" p. 21.

62. For more discussions of the party's monopoly over cadre recruitment, see Melanie Manion, "The Cadre Management System, Post-Mao: The Appointment, Promotion, Transfer and Removal of Party and State Leaders,"

China Quarterly, no. 101 (March 1985): 203–233; John P. Burns, "China's *Nomenklatura* System," *Problems of Communism*, 36, no. 5 (September–October 1987): 36–51; John P. Burns, ed., *The Chinese Communist Party's Nomenklatura System* (Armonk, N.Y.: M. E. Sharpe, 1989).

63. Interviews with two senior scholars, Beijing, December 2002.

64. Interviews with local officials, Yunnan, 2001, and Sichuan, 2004.

65. Interview with a former head of the city organization department, Guangzhou, November 2003.

66. "Zhijie xuanju weifan dang guan ganbu de yuanze."

67. "Dang guan ganbu de shizhi jiushi dang peiyang ganbu, rang renmin xuanze."

68. "Xianxing de ganbu xuanba zhidu quefa toumingdu he gongzhengxing."

69. "Zhijie xuanju you zhu yu jiejue mai guan mai guan wenti."

70. "Wen: Too Soon for China Democracy," December 10, 2003, at www.cnn.com/2003/WORLD/asiapcf/east/12/10/china.wen.rights.ap/ (accessed January 10, 2006).

71. "Jingji fazhan shuiping bugou gao, zhixuan xiangzhang tiaojian bu chengshou."

72. "Nongmin you nengli zhijie xuanju xiangzhen zhang."

73. "Zhijie xuanju xiangzhang hui cujin jingji fazhan."

74. "Zhijie xuanju xiangzhang you li yu fan fubai."

75. "Zhijie xuanju xiangzhang you li yu jiaqiang dang de lingdao."

76. "Zhijie xuanju xiangzhang you li yu jiaqiang fazhi jianshe."

77. The most popular way of measuring the reliability of a construct scale is to calculate Cronbach's alpha coefficient, between 0 and 1. A commonly accepted threshold for this coefficient is 0.70.

78. Interviews with government officials and policy researchers, Hebei, 1995, 1997, 2004; Fujian, 1997; Jiangxi, 1997; Guangdong, 2003; Shaanxi, 2003; Beijing, 1999, 2003; Sichuan, 2004.

79. For an analysis of instrumentalism in Chinese debates over village elections, see Daniel Kelliher, "The Chinese Debate over Village Self-Government," *China Journal*, no. 37 (January 1997): 63–90.

6. The Struggle for Village Public Goods Provision

1. Although the state officially maintains that the township is the lowest level of government, both government officials and citizens consider village officials part of the state. The party's formal ruling apparatus extends all the way down to the village level and controls the appointment of the half of the village government that consists of the village party branch (the other half being the village committee, which is supposed to be popularly elected). Village governments, which include both the village committee

and the village party branch (often composed of many of the same people anyway), are fully responsible for carrying out the business of the state: collecting state taxes, enforcing state directives such as the birth control policy, and organizing public goods and services. As it does with the township government, the central government gives village governments the right to collect village taxes and rights over residual revenue from taxes and nontax revenues. The only substantive differences between village governments and higher-level governments is that village officials are technically not on the state payroll (although their salaries are officially set by the township government), and village governments, lacking coercive resources of their own, must rely on the township police. From the perspective of China's 800 million villagers, village officials have almost complete authority and discretion over issues within the village community.

2. Township governments rarely offer village officials promotion to higher levels of government as a potential reward for good behavior. See Scott Rozelle, "Decision-Making in China's Rural Economy: The Linkages between Village Leaders and Farm Households," *China Quarterly*, no. 137 (March 1994): 99–124.

3. Pilot counties employ more administrative resources and pressure to implement village democratic reforms. This selection strategy allows us to use pilot county status as an instrument for the implementation of democratic institutions and to use two-stage least squares instrumental variable estimation in order to deal with potential endogeneity. In order to administer the survey, I trained groups of Chinese graduate and undergraduate students and traveled with them to the various counties and townships from which villages were sampled. Results were coded in the field.

4. Dummy variables for the eight counties from which the villages were randomly sampled are also included.

5. The potential social fragmentation as reflected by the number of surname groups is constructed by subtracting the percentage of households in the largest surname group from 1.

6. Regression tables available at https://dspace.mit.edu/handle/1721.1/32528. This analysis uses seemingly unrelated regression (SUR) to estimate the effects. The SUR method allows disturbance terms across outcome measures to be correlated during hypothesis testing. When different public goods provision outcomes are only imperfectly correlated due to idiosyncratic factors, the confidence interval around the estimated impact of an explanatory variable is considerably narrower than the confidence interval for a single outcome. This strategy allows us to be more certain that the estimated impact is accurate. Edward Miguel uses a similar strategy to evaluate public goods provision in Kenya and Tanzania. See Edward Miguel, "Tribe or Nation? Nation Building in Public Goods in Kenya versus Tanzania," *World Politics*, 56, no. 3 (April 2004): 327–362.

7. Using the seemingly unrelated regression method which allows us to perform joint hypothesis tests across outcomes, we cannot reject the null hypothesis that no relationship exists between village head party membership and village public goods provision (p–value = .99). This model included the full set of controls: geographic and demographic factors (distance from county seat, number of natural villages, terrain, village population, surname fragmentation, and county dummies), economic factors (village income per capita, village government assets, per capita village tax revenue), and institutional factors (implementation of village democratic reforms, party membership of village head, percentage of village officials with party membership, the existence of a temple manager, and the existence of a village-wide lineage). Missing data were deleted listwise.

8. Using the seemingly unrelated regression method, again we cannot reject the null hypothesis that no relationship exists between the percentage of village officials who are party members and village public goods provision as measured by the six indicators (p–value = .51). This model included the full set of controls: geographic and demographic factors (distance from county seat, number of natural villages, terrain, village population, surname fragmentation, and county dummies), economic factors (village income per capita, village government assets, per capita village tax revenue), and institutional factors (implementation of village democratic reforms, party membership of village head, percentage of village officials with party membership, the existence of a temple manager, and the existence of a village-wide lineage). Missing data were deleted listwise.

9. Using the SUR method, when all controls are included in the model, a joint hypothesis test suggests that there may be some relationship between performance contracts and public goods provision, although, strictly speaking, we cannot reject at a 90 percent confidence level the null hypothesis that there is no relationship ($p = 0.11$).

10. Tables of these and other fitted values in the chapter can be viewed at https://dspace.mit.edu/handle/1721.1/32528. These fitted values are based on the estimates produced by the SUR analysis with a full set of controls. The 95 percent confidence interval for the probability of paved roads was (38, 55) with a contract and (50, 66) without a contract. For the mean per capita investment, the 95 percent confidence interval was (49, 127) with a contract and (22, 92) without a contract. For the mean percentage of usable classrooms, the 95 percent confidence interval was (89, 99) with a contract and (83, 92) without a contract.

11. For five of the outcomes (roads, paths, classrooms, newness of school building, and the availability of running water), democratic institutions had only a small and statistically insignificant impact. For two of these outcomes (school building and water), the estimated effect was negative, and for three of these outcomes, the estimated effect was positive. For only one

outcome, per capita investment, did the implementation of democratic institutions have a notable though modest effect; but using the seemingly unrelated regression method and including all control variables, we cannot reject the null hypothesis that no relationship exists between the implementation of democratic institutions and village public goods provision (p-value = .34). This model included the full set of controls: geographic and demographic factors (distance from county seat, number of natural villages, terrain, village population, surname fragmentation, and county dummies), economic factors (village income per capita, village government assets, and per capita village tax revenue), and institutional factors (performance contracts, party membership of village head, percentage of village officials with party membership, the existence of a temple manager, and the existence of a village-wide lineage). Missing data were deleted listwise.

12. Like ordinary least squares regression (OLS), seemingly unrelated regression is an inadequate technique if we are not certain of the causal direction between public goods provision and the implementation of democratic institutions. It seems plausible, for example, that villages that already have good public goods provision may be more likely to implement village democratic reforms because village officials are confident of popular support or because village officials who provide services conscientiously may be more likely to believe in progressive reforms. In order to deal with this problem of potential endogeneity, I also estimated a two-stage least squares model (2SLS) using a county's status as a pilot county for democratic reforms as an instrument for a village's level of implementation. Pilot county status is an appropriate instrument because it is determined by the provincial government without regard for conditions at the village level and is causally prior to the implementation of democratic reforms. In short, the same conclusions result from 2SLS instrumental variables estimation. When two-stage least squares estimation was used to estimate the impact of democratic reforms on public goods provision, the result was indeterminate. The direction and magnitude of the estimated effect on five out of the six outcomes (investment, roads, paths, classrooms, and water) vary widely depending on what control variables are included in or excluded from the estimation. For one outcome, the newness of the village school building, the implementation of democratic reforms had a consistent but modest positive effect. A Hausman test, moreover, comparing the differences between SUR/OLS estimates and 2SLS estimates finds that the differences are not statistically significant. Therefore, we cannot reject the null hypothesis that the implementation of democratic reforms is exogenous, which suggests that the SUR estimates are more efficient than the 2SLS estimates.

13. The standard deviation for this first difference is 17 RMB, and the ninety-fifth confidence interval (−21, 45).

14. Rhys H. Williams and N. J. Demerath III, "Religion and Political Process in an American City," *American Sociological Review,* 56, no. 4 (August 1991): 424.

15. In many places temples were the only village-wide organizations, and it was the temple of a village that defined the village as a distinct, discrete community. See Prasenjit Duara, *Culture, Power, and the State: Rural North China, 1900–1942* (Stanford: Stanford University Press, 1988); and G. William Skinner, "Marketing and Social Structure in Rural China: Part I," *Journal of Asian Studies,* 24, no. 1 (November 1964): 6.

16. Clifford Geertz, *Negara: The Theatre State in Nineteenth-Century Bali* (Princeton: Princeton University Press, 1980).

17. Russell Hardin, "The Street-Level Epistemology of Trust," *Politics and Society,* 21, no. 4 (December 1993): 516–520.

18. When the strength of temple institutions is measured by the percentage of households participating in temple reconstruction projects, the results are similar. See Lily L. Tsai, "The Informal State: Governance, Accountability, and Public Goods Provision in Rural China" (Ph.D. diss., Harvard University, 2005).

19. Using the seemingly unrelated regression method, we can reject the null hypothesis that village temple institutions have no impact on public goods provision at a 99 percent confidence level (p-value = .001). This SUR model included the full set of controls: geographic and demographic factors (distance from county seat, number of natural villages, terrain, village population, surname fragmentation, and county dummies), economic factors (village income per capita, village government assets, and per capita village tax revenue), and institutional factors (implementation of village democratic reforms, performance contracts, party membership of village head, and percentage of village officials with party membership). Missing data were deleted listwise.

20. Again, I also used two-stage least squares to estimate the effect of temple institutions as reflected by the existence of a temple manager in case temple institutional strength is an effect of village public goods provision rather than a cause. In this case, whether or not a village had a legacy of temple institutions from before 1949 was used as an instrument for estimating the current existence of temple institutions. The results from two-stage least squares estimation corroborate the results from seemingly unrelated regression analysis. In fact, the coefficient estimates produced by two-stage least squares are in general larger than the estimates produced by seemingly unrelated regression. Village temple institutionalization as measured by the existence of a temple manager has a positive effect on

five of the public goods provision outcomes (investment, roads, paths, school building, and running water) and is statistically significant for water. For one outcome—the percentage of classrooms usable in rain—the coefficient estimate was negative but statistically insignificant. This result may be by chance or it may have to do with the fact that villages with sufficient resources wait until the school building is in disrepair before building a new one. Similar results were obtained regardless of what controls were included or excluded.

21. These fitted values are based on estimates produced by seemingly unrelated regressions with the full set of controls. These estimates were much smaller than the estimates produced by two-stage least squares and thus reflect a conservative idea of the impact of temple institutions. The 95 percent confidence interval for the mean percentage of classrooms with a temple manager is (94, 100) and (84, 92) without a temple manager. Since there is no overlap in their confidence intervals, we can be quite certain that villages with temple institutions are in fact quite different from villages without temple institutions. The 95 percent confidence interval for the mean probability of running water with a temple manager is (47, 77) and (41, 51) without a temple manager.

22. Using the seemingly unrelated regression method, we can reject the null hypothesis that the coefficient estimate on village-wide lineage institutions is equal to 0 at a 95 percent confidence level (p-value = .05). The estimated relationship between village-wide lineage institutions and village governmental public goods provision was positive for five outcomes (investment, roads, paths, newness of school, and water) and statistically significant or close to significant for three of these outcomes (investment, roads, and paths). For one outcome (classrooms), the coefficient estimate was negative but not statistically significant. This analysis included the full set of controls: geographic and demographic factors (distance from county seat, number of natural villages, terrain, village population, surname fragmentation, and county dummies), economic factors (village income per capita, village government assets, and per capita village tax revenue), and institutional factors (implementation of village democratic reforms, performance contracts, party membership of village head, and percentage of village officials with party membership). Missing data were deleted listwise. Results were similar regardless of which control variables were included or excluded. Estimates yielded by two-stage least squares in which a historical legacy of lineage activity before 1949 is used as an instrument for current lineage institutions corroborate the results from seemingly unrelated regression analysis. In fact, the coefficient estimates produced by two-stage least squares are in general larger than the estimates produced by seemingly unrelated regression. The effect estimated by two-

stage least squares is positive for five outcomes (investment, roads, paths, school building, and water) and statistically significant for investment, school building, and water. The estimated effect is negative and statistically insignificant for classrooms. When all control variables are included, the estimated effect of village-wide lineage institutions is positive for the same five outcomes and statistically significant for investment, roads, paths, and school building. Again, the estimated effect is negative and insignificant for classrooms.

23. As with temple institutionalization, these fitted values are based on estimates produced by seemingly unrelated regression with a full set of controls. These estimates were also much more conservative than the estimates produced by two-stage least squares. The 95 percent confidence interval for investment with village-wide lineage institutions is (52, 256) and (45, 99) without lineage institutions. The level of uncertainty around these estimates is quite low as we can see from the lack of overlap in their 95 percent confidence intervals. The 95 percent confidence interval for the mean probability of paved roads is (63, 100) with lineage institutions and (44, 56) without lineage institutions.

24. After the departure of the observation group, subsequent election irregularities in the 2000 U.S. presidential election were the source of considerable merriment to local officials in charge of supervising village elections in the township. Numerous officials commented on the irony of U.S. observers offering them advice on how to improve their elections when authorities in the United States seemed to be doing a far worse job than they were.

25. On a village in North China where norms of maintaining community-wide relations are stronger than the distinctions between different sub-lineage groupings within the village, see Ellen R. Judd, *Gender and Power in Rural North China* (Stanford: Stanford University Press, 1994), pp. 54–55.

26. Guandi (a Taoist god evolved from the historical figure of a third-century military hero) is popularly worshiped in local village temples throughout rural China as a guardian deity. Since local village temples often honor numerous deities from different religious traditions together with local deities unique to their village and ancestral spirits, it is difficult to classify these groups as strictly temple or lineage groups.

27. Jean Oi, *Rural China Takes Off: Institutional Foundations of Economic Reform* (Berkeley: University of California Press, 1999).

28. When the index measuring the implementation of democratic reforms was interacted with the existence of temple groups and the existence of village-wide lineage groups, there was no statistically significant or substantively interesting interaction effect that was consistently positive or negative. Although there was some evidence that in villages with solidary

groups the implementation of democratic reforms was associated with more investment in public goods, the impact of democratic reforms on other public goods provision outcomes was sometimes negative and sometimes positive. In other words, the implementation of democratic reforms does not seem to have a major effect on village public goods provision either in villages with solidary groups or in villages without solidary groups.

29. Fubing Su and Dali L. Yang, "Elections, Governance, and Accountability in Rural China," paper presented at the International Symposium on Villager Self-Government and the Development of Rural Society in China, Ministry of Civil Affairs of the PRC and the Carter Center, Beijing, September 2001.

30. Jean Oi, "Communism and Clientelism: Rural Politics in China," *World Politics,* 37, no. 2 (January 1985): 252.

31. Lowell Dittmer and Xiaobo Lü, "Personal Politics in the Chinese 'Danwei' under Reform," *Asian Survey,* 36, no. 3 (March 1996): 255.

32. David Wank, "Business-State Clientelism in China: Decline or Evolution?" in Thomas Gold, Doug Guthrie, and David Wank, eds., *Social Connections in China: Institutions, Culture, and the Changing Nature of* Guanxi (New York: Cambridge University Press, 2002), p. 113.

33. Pittman Potter, "*Guanxi* and the PRC Legal System: From Contradiction to Complementarity," ibid., p. 183.

34. See Thomas Bernstein and Xiaobo Lü, *Taxation without Representation in Contemporary Rural China* (New York: Cambridge University Press, 2003). See also Margaret Levi, *Of Rule and Revenue* (Berkeley: University of California Press, 1988).

7. Inadvertent Political Reform via Private Associations

1. This categorization is hardly exhaustive. Another type of reform acts by increasing the transparency of officials' behavior to the public and to the media. Yet another focuses on the inculcation of norms, professional ethics, and corporate identity within the ranks of bureaucrats.

2. This in turn is a subcategory of a broader category of reforms operating through bottom-up pressure. This subcategory includes conscious state efforts to endow citizens with more rights, as well as unwitting processes that give individuals more mobility or exits from the bureaucrats' authority or provide them with more information.

3. The YWH were first authorized for new neighborhoods *(xinjian xiaoqu)*. Since then, all neighborhoods under commercial property management (including older, formerly state-owned housing) have, in principle, become eligible to form homeowners' committees.

4. Samuel P. Huntington, "Will More Countries Become Democratic?" *Political Science Quarterly*, 99, no. 2 (Summer 1984): 203.

5. Larry Diamond, "Toward Democratic Consolidation," in Larry Diamond and Marc F. Plattner, eds., *The Global Resurgence of Democracy*, 2nd ed. (Baltimore: Johns Hopkins University Press, 1966), p. 231. Though agreeing with Diamond's basic point, I would argue against such a clear-cut differentiation of civil society's functions by regime type.

6. Michael Walzer, "The Civil Society Argument," in Ronald Beiner, ed., *Theorizing Citizenship* (Albany: State University of New York Press, 1995), p. 170.

7. See also Mark E. Warren, *Democracy and Association* (Princeton: Princeton University Press, 2001), pp. 85–86; and Jonah D. Levy, *Tocqueville's Revenge: State, Society, and Economy in Contemporary France* (Cambridge, Mass.: Harvard University Press, 1999), pp. 1–16, esp. p. 2.

8. Ariel C. Armony, *The Dubious Link: Civic Engagement and Democratization* (Stanford: Stanford University Press, 2004); Sheri Berman, "Civil Society and the Collapse of the Weimar Republic," *World Politics*, 49, no. 3 (1997): 401–429; Nancy Bermeo and Philip Nord, eds., *Civil Society before Democracy: Lessons from Nineteenth-Century Europe* (Lanham, Md.: Rowman and Littlefield, 2000); Jason Kaufman, *For the Common Good? American Civic Life and the Golden Age of Fraternity* (New York: Oxford University Press, 2002).

9. Examples of work that undertakes this kind of disaggregation, in addition to the items cited later in this chapter, include Joshua Cohen and Joel Rogers, "Secondary Associations and Democratic Governance," *Politics and Society*, 20, no. 4 (1992): 393–472; Nancy L. Rosenblum, *Membership and Morals: The Personal Uses of Pluralism in America* (Princeton: Princeton University Press, 1998); Dietlind Stolle and Thomas R. Rochon, "Are All Associations Alike? Member Diversity, Associational Type, and the Creation of Social Capital," in Bob Edwards, Michael W. Foley, and Mario Diani, eds., *Beyond Tocqueville: Civil Society and the Social Capital Debate in Comparative Perspective* (Hanover, N.H.: University Press of New England, 2001); and Helmut K. Anheier, *Civil Society: Measurement, Evaluation, Policy* (London: Earthscan, 2004).

10. Elizabeth Perry raised this possibility in comments on an earlier draft.

11. Internal democracy and horizontal, as opposed to vertical, orientation are discussed in Jonathan Fox, "How Does Civil Society Thicken? The Political Construction of Social Capital in Rural Mexico," *World Development*, 24, no. 6 (June 1996): 1089–1103; and Robert D. Putnam, *Making Democracy Work: Civic Traditions in Modern Italy* (Princeton: Princeton University Press, 1993), pp. 173–174.

12. Warren, *Democracy and Association*, discusses autonomy on pp. 62–69.

13. On associations generally, examples include Tony Saich, "Negotiating the State: The Development of Social Organizations in China," *China Quar-*

terly, no. 161 (March 2000): 124–141; and Kenneth W. Foster, "Associations in the Embrace of an Authoritarian State: State Domination of Society?" *Studies in Comparative International Development,* 35, no. 4 (Winter 2001): 84–109. Contributions to the debate on civil society include Thomas Gold, "Bases for Civil Society in Reform China," in Kjeld Erik Brödsgaard and David Strand, eds., *Reconstructing Twentieth-Century China: State Control, Civil Society, and National Identity* (Oxford: Clarendon Press, 1998), pp. 163–188; Thomas B. Gold, "The Resurgence of Civil Society in China," *Journal of Democracy,* 1, no. 1 (Winter 1990): 18–31; Elizabeth J. Perry and Ellen V. Fuller, "China's Long March to Democracy," *World Policy Journal,* 8, no. 4 (Fall 1991): 663–685; Yanqi Tong, "State, Society, and Political Change in China and Hungary," *Comparative Politics,* 26, no. 3 (April 1994): 333–353. A current and thorough review is Mary E. Gallagher, "China: The Limits of Civil Society in a Late Leninist State," in Muthiah Alagappa, ed., *Civil Society and Political Change in Asia: Expanding and Contracting Democratic Space* (Stanford: Stanford University Press, 2004), pp. 419–452.

14. E.g., Gordon White, Jude Howell, and Shang Xiaoyuan, *In Search of Civil Society: Market Reform and Social Change in Contemporary China* (Oxford: Clarendon Press, 1996).

15. Notable arguments along these lines include Andrew G. Walder, "The Quiet Revolution from Within: Economic Reform as a Source of Political Decline," in Andrew Walder, ed., *The Waning of the Communist State: Economic Origins of Political Decline in China and Hungary* (Berkeley: University of California Press, 1995), pp. 1–24, esp. p. 16; and David L. Wank, *Commodifying Communism: Business, Trust, and Politics in a Chinese City* (New York: Cambridge University Press, 1999), pp. 178–187, 202.

16. On questioning whether the newly rich will form representative organizations, see Christopher Earle Nevitt, "Private Business Associations in China: Evidence of Civil Society or Local State Power?" *China Journal,* no. 36 (July 1996): 25–43; Margaret M. Pearson, "The Janus Face of Business Associations in China: Socialist Corporatism in Foreign Enterprises," *Australian Journal of Chinese Affairs,* no. 31 (January 1994): 25–46. On mixed evidence, see Jonathan Unger, "'Bridges': Private Business, the Chinese Government, and the Rise of New Associations," *China Quarterly,* no. 147 (September 1996): 795–819; Bruce J. Dickson, "Cooptation and Corporatism in China: The Logic of Party Adaptation," *Political Science Quarterly,* 115, no. 4 (Winter 2000): 517–540. On business interest groups, see Scott Kennedy, *The Business of Lobbying in China* (Cambridge, Mass.: Harvard University Press, 2005).

17. Robert P. Weller expresses the question in these terms in *Alternate Civilities: Democracy and Culture in China and Taiwan* (Boulder, Colo.: Westview Press, 1999), pp. 14–16. Outside the China context, this idea is also put forward

in Chris Hann, "Introduction: Political Society and Civil Anthropology," in Chris Hann and Elizabeth Dunn, eds., *Civil Society: Challenging Western Models* (London: Routledge, 1996), pp. 1–26.

18. Evan McKenzie, *Privatopia: Homeowner Associations and the Rise of Residential Private Government* (New Haven: Yale University Press, 1994). See also Edward J. Blakely and Mary Gail Snyder, *Fortress America: Gated Communities in the United States* (Washington, D.C.: Brookings Institution Press, 1997).

19. Teresa P. R. Caldeira, *City of Walls: Crime, Segregation, and Citizenship in São Paulo* (Berkeley: University of California Press, 2000), esp. chap. 7.

20. On laudable examples, see Donald R. Stabile, *Community Associations: The Emergence and Acceptance of a Quiet Innovation in Housing* (Westport, Conn.: Greenwood Press, 2000). On overstated criticism, see Rosenblum, *Membership and Morals,* chap. 4.

21. Robert Jay Dilger, *Neighborhood Politics: Residential Community Associations in American Governance* (New York: New York University Press, 1992), pp. 104–130. Dilger concludes: "In some ways RCAs [residential community associations] are like sleeping tigers. When left alone, they are of little concern to those around them, but once aroused from their sleep, they are clearly a force to be reckoned with at the local level" (p. 130).

22. Benjamin L. Read, "Democratizing the Neighbourhood? New Private Housing and Home-Owner Self-Organization in Urban China," *China Journal,* no. 49 (January 2003): 31–59. Li Zhang's December 2003 paper "Governing at a Distance: The Politics of Privatizing Home and Community in Neoliberalizing China," discusses power relations among the state, developers, and homeowners in Kunming. Deborah Davis presents a case study of a Shanghai neighborhood in "Urban Chinese Homeowners as Citizen-Consumers," in Sheldon Garon and Patricia Maclachlan, eds., *The Ambivalent Consumer* (Ithaca: Cornell University Press, 2006). Published Chinese-language analyses include Xia Jianzhong, "Zhongguo gongmin shehui de xiansheng: Yi yezhu weiyuanhui wei li" (The First Signs of China's Civil Society: The Case of the Homeowners' Committees), *Wen shi zhe* (Literature, History, and Philosophy), no. 3 (2003): 115–121; Xia Jianzhong, "Beijing chengshi xinxing shequ zizhi zuzhi yanjiu: Jianxi Beijing CY yuan yezhu weiyuanhui" (A Study of Autonomous Organizations in Urban Beijing's New Communities: Learning from the Homeowners' Committee in Beijing's CY Gardens), *Beijing shehui kexue* (Beijing Social Sciences), no. 2 (2003): 88–94; Zhang Jing, "Gonggong kongjian de shehui jichu" (Social Foundations of the Public Sphere), Working Paper 2001.004, Institute of Sociology and Anthropology, Peking University (2001); and Gui Yong, "Lüe lun chengshi jiceng minzhu fazhan de keneng ji qi shixian tujing: Yi Shanghaishi wei li" (On the Development of Grassroots Democracy in Urban Areas: A Case Study of Shanghai City), *Huazhong keji daxue xuebao*

(shehui kexue ban) (Central China Science and Technology University Journal [Social Sciences Edition]), 15, no. 1 (February 2001): 24–27.

23. Studies of Chinese housing policy include Deborah S. Davis and Hanlong Lu, "Property in Transition: Conflicts over Ownership in Post-socialist Shanghai," *European Journal of Sociology*, 44, no. 1 (April 2003): 77–99; Deborah S. Davis, "From Welfare Benefit to Capitalized Asset: The Recommodification of Residential Space in Urban China," in Ray Forrest and James Lee, eds., *Housing and Social Change: East-West Perspectives* (London: Routledge, 2003); Ya Ping Wang and Alan Murie, *Housing Policy and Practice in China* (New York: St. Martin's Press, 1999); Ya Ping Wang and Alan Murie, "Commercial Housing Development in Urban China," *Urban Studies*, 36, no. 9 (August 1999): 1475–94; Yanjie Bian et al., "Work Units and Housing Reform in Two Chinese Cities," in Xiaobo Lü and Elizabeth J. Perry, eds., *Danwei: The Changing Chinese Workplace in Historical and Comparative Perspective* (Armonk, N.Y.: M. E. Sharpe, 1997); and Min Zhou and John R. Logan, "Market Transition and the Commodification of Housing in Urban China," *International Journal of Urban and Regional Research*, 20, no. 3 (September 1996): 400–421.

24. Zhonghua renmin gongheguo jianshebu ling 1994 nian 33 hao, "Chengshi xinjian zhuzhai xiaoqu guanli banfa," reprinted in Beijingshi juzhu xiaoqu guanli bangongshi, *Beijingshi wuye guanli wenjian huibian* (Compilation of Documents on Real Estate Management in the City of Beijing), vol. 1 (February 1998), pp. 1–5. The management methods went into effect on April 1, 1994.

25. The Ministry of Construction Web site records these regulations *(xingzheng fagui)* at www.cin.gov.cn/law/admin/2003062002.htm (accessed February 25, 2006). They went into effect on September 1, 2003.

26. In fact, many new neighborhoods have no Residents' Committee in at least the first few years after they are built.

27. The figure of 77,431 Residents' Committees in 2003 is given in the *Zhongguo minzheng tongji nianjian 2004* (China Civil Affairs Statistical Yearbook) (Beijing: Zhongguo tongji chubanshe, 2004), pp. 82–83. RCs *(jumin weiyuanhui)* are now sometimes referred to as Community Residents' Committees. Their total numbers have declined in recent years as local governments have merged multiple smaller RCs into larger ones. My own work on Residents' Committees includes "Revitalizing the State's Urban 'Nerve Tips,'" *China Quarterly*, no. 163 (September 2000): 806–820; and Benjamin L. Read and Robert Pekkanen, "The State's Evolving Relationship with Urban Society: China's Neighborhood Organizations in Comparative Perspective," unpublished paper. My dissertation, "State, Social Networks, and Citizens in China's Urban Neighborhoods" (Harvard University, May 2003), contains a full literature review. Other recent works include Robert

Benewick, Irene Tong, and Jude Howell, "Self-Governance and Community: A Preliminary Comparison between Villagers' Committees and Urban Community Councils," *China Information,* 18, no. 1 (March 2004): 11–28; and Allen C. Choate, "Local Governance in China, Part II: An Assessment of Urban Residents Committees and Municipal Community Development," Asia Foundation Working Paper no. 10, November 1998. Among recent Chinese-language studies is Lei Jieqiong, chief ed., *Zhuanxing zhongde chengshi jiceng shequ zuzhi* (Grassroots Community Organization in Urban Transition) (Beijing: Beijing daxue chubanshe, 2001).

28. Interview with Shanghai housing official Xin Yiming, June 30, 2004.

29. Beijing had established 566 YWH by the end of 2003, according to an interview with Beijing housing officials Zou Jinsong and Li Lanying, July 23, 2004.

30. Susan L. Shirk, for example, highlights the "particularistic" nature of relationships between local units and their overseeing bodies in *The Political Logic of Economic Reform in China* (Berkeley: University of California Press, 1993).

31. McKenzie, *Privatopia,* p. 145, describes the U.S. Common Interest Developments as "a prefabricated framework for civil society in search of a population."

32. This much is a general feature of homeowners' groups, which often see maintaining home resale values as a primary purpose. Interestingly, many of my homeowner informants seemed to regard property values as only indirectly related to YWH matters, with prices depending more on rapidly changing conditions in the broader market than on circumstances that the homeowners' group could itself hope to control.

33. On the limits of legal recourse, see also the chapters by Yongshun Cai and Mary Gallagher in this volume.

34. Harvey Molotch, "The City as a Growth Machine: Toward a Political Economy of Place," *American Journal of Sociology,* 82, no. 2 (September 1976): 309–332. A relevant application to China is Yan Zhang and Ke Fang, "Is History Repeating Itself? From Urban Renewal in the United States to Inner-City Redevelopment in China," *Journal of Planning Education and Research,* 23 (March 2004): 286–298.

35. The names of the six categories are my own and do not derive from any Chinese-language terms.

36. The assertion that internal democracy and external autonomy go together is a simplification. In some cases, for example, the YWH are created through the self-initiated efforts of homeowners, who then appear to stop holding elections once their most pressing goals are achieved. This claim appears valid as a broad generalization nonetheless.

37. As several of the previously cited studies of homeowners' organizations in

the United States and elsewhere attest, factional bickering among such groups is hardly unique to China.

38. This much is clear from interviews with homeowner activists and government officials in Beijing, Shanghai, and Guangzhou.

39. The Ministry of Construction's January 2004 policy on compensation for demolition and relocation *(chaiqian)* is one such example; for the text of this policy, see www.china.org.cn/chinese/2003/Dec/457254.htm (accessed February 25, 2006). Another is the 2003 law strengthening farmers' claims to contracted land, the *Nongcun tudi chengbao fa*. See www.china.org .cn/chinese/PI-c/196651.htm (accessed February 25, 2006).

40. For example, cases in which no deed has been issued for a purchased property, or in which more than one deed exists for the same property.

41. On "letters and visits," see the chapters by Xi Chen and Ching Kwan Lee in this volume.

42. Kevin J. O'Brien, "Rightful Resistance," *World Politics,* 49, no. 1 (October 1996): 31–55.

43. To be sure, other organizers deny having any political agenda and see their purpose as merely that of protecting homeowners in their transactions with developers and property managers.

44. Interview with a prominent homeowner activist and onetime People's Congress candidate, July 21, 2004.

45. For these details I am indebted to Professor Chen Youhong of People's University.

8. Civil Resistance and Rule of Law in China

1. John Reitz, "Constitutionalism and Rule of Law: Theoretical Perspectives," in Robert D. Grey, ed., *Democratic Theory and Post-Communist Change* (Upper Saddle River, N.J.: Prentice-Hall, 1997), p. 112.

2. Mark Brzezinski, *The Struggle for Constitutionalism in Poland* (New York: St. Martin's, 1998), p. 81.

3. John Reitz, "Progress in Building Institutions for the Rule of Law in Russia and Poland," in Grey, *Democratic Theory and Post-Communist Change,* pp. 147–148.

4. Laifan Lin, "Judicial Independence in Japan: A Re-investigation for China," *Columbia Journal of Asian Law,* 13, no. 2 (1999): 185–202.

5. See, among others, Randall Peerenboom, *China's Long March toward Rule of Law* (New York: Cambridge University Press, 2002); Stanley B. Lubman, *Bird in a Cage: Legal Reform in China after Mao* (Stanford: Stanford University Press, 1999).

6. Richard H. Fallon Jr., "'The Rule of Law' as a Concept in Constitutional Discourse," *Columbia Law Review,* 97, no. 1 (January 1997): 7–9.

7. Yin Xiaohu, *Xin Zhongguo xianzheng zhilu, 1949–1999* (The Constitutional Development of New China, 1949–1999) (Shanghai: Shanghai jiaotong daxue chubanshe, 2000), p. 277.

8. Peerenboom, *China's Long March toward Rule of Law.*

9. Ibid., chap. 10.

10. Yu Jianrong, "Tudi chengwei Zhongguo nongcun shouyao wenti" (Land Use Becomes the Most Conflictual Issue in Rural China), *Liaowang dongfang* (Oriental Outlook), September 9, 2004.

11. Yongshun Cai, "Collective Ownership or Cadres' Ownership? The Non-agricultural Use of Farmland in China," *China Quarterly*, no. 175 (September 2003): 662–680; Xiaolin Guo, "Land Expropriation and Rural Conflicts in China," *China Quarterly*, no. 166 (June 2001): 422–439; David Zweig, "The 'Externalities of Development': Can New Political Institutions Manage Rural Conflict?" in Elizabeth Perry and Mark Selden, eds., *Chinese Society: Change, Conflict, and Resistance* (New York: Routledge, 2000), pp. 120–142.

12. Wang Fang, "Chaiqian: Yu falü tongxing" (Housing Demolition: In Line with the Law), *Fazhi ribao* (Legal News Daily), January 10, 2001.

13. According to a survey of twelve thousand citizens in ten provinces in 2004, construction was reported as the most corrupt sector in China (32.2 percent). See *Lianhe zaobao* (United Morning Post), January 27, 2004; Yongshun Cai, "Irresponsible State: Local Cadres and Image Building in China," *Journal of Communist Studies and Transition Politics*, 20, no. 4 (December 2004): 20–41.

14. Interview, China, 2004.

15. Wang Fang, "Chaiqian: Yu falü tongxing."

16. Ren Bo, "Chaiqian zhisu" (Lawsuits on Housing Demolition), *Caijing* (Finance), no. 13 (2003): 24–28.

17. Wang Jun, "Jingcheng chaiqianhu de 'luocha' shenghuo" (Different Lives of Homeowners), *Liaowang* (Outlook), no. 6 (February 9, 2004): 38–39.

18. Song Zhenyuan, Zhou Guohong, and Cui Lijin, "Chaiqian chengwei qunzhong shangfang jiaodian" (Housing Demolition Becomes the Focus of the Masses' Complaints), *Beijing qingnian bao* (Beijing Youth Newspaper), November 13, 2003, p. 1.

19. Wang Xiaoxia, "Chaiqian heidong" (The Black Box of Housing Demolition), *Zhongguo jingji shibao* (China Economic Times), September 24, 2003, p. 2.

20. Sun Jie, "Nanjing xiugai chaiqian fagui jiejian shichang jiage gusuan fangfa" (Nanjing Revised Regulations on Housing Demolition and Adopted Some Assessment Criteria Based on Market Prices), *Xiandai kuaibao* (Modern Express), October 10, 2003.

21. Song Zhenyuan, Zhou Guohong, and Cui Lijin, "Chaiqian chengwei qunzhong shangfang jiaodian."

22. Quanguo renmin daibiao dahui changwu weiyuanhui fazhi gongzuo weiyuanhui, ed., *Zhonghua renmin gongheguo falü huibian* (Laws of the People's Republic of China) (Beijing: Falü chubanshe, 1996), p. 32.

23. Zhang Fan, "Zhuanjia fansi: Chaiqian beihou you zhong da falü wenti" (Experts' Reflection: Some Important Legal Issues Surrounding Disputes over Housing Demolition), *Zhongguo jingji shibao* (China Economic Times), October 22, 2003.

24. Lei Feng and Chen Jieren, "Chaiqian zhihuo" (The Trouble Caused by Housing Demolition), *Falü yu shenghuo* (Law and Life), October 15, 2003.

25. Interview with a lawyer, China, 2004.

26. Ju Jin, "Tuitujixia de beiju, Nanjing chaiqian zifen shijian diaocha" (Tragedy under the Bulldozer: An Investigation into the Self-Immolation in Nanjing), *Waitan huabao* (Waitan Panorama), September 3, 2003.

27. Yongshun Cai, "Managed Participation in China," *Political Science Quarterly*, 119, no. 3 (Fall 2004): 425–452; Tianjian Shi, *Political Participation in Beijing* (Cambridge, Mass.: Harvard University Press, 1997).

28. See the chapter by Mary Gallagher in this volume.

29. See the chapter by Xi Chen in this volume.

30. Xiao Han, "Rang fa lilian rongru minqing" (Put Law into People's Practice), *Nanfeng chuang* (Window for Southern Wind) (December 15, 2002): 31–33.

31. From 1999 to 2002 the land management agency was listed as the most frequently sued agency. *Zhongguo falü nianjian 2000–2003* (China Law Yearbook 2000–2003) (Beijing: Zhongguo falü nianjian she chuban, 2000–2003); p. 1211 (in 2000 volume, for 1999); p. 1258 (in 2001 volume, for 2000); p. 1240 (in 2002 volume, for 2001); p. 1321 (in 2003 volume, for 2002).

32. Tao Feng and Xie Chunlei, "Zhejiang fayuan 'chaiqian' bianfa" (The Change of Rules Regarding "Housing Demolition Cases" in the Courts of Zhejiang), *Nanfang zhoumo* (Southern Weekend), October 10, 2003, p. 4.

33. Yongshun Cai, *State and Laid-Off Workers in Reform China: The Silence and Collective Action of the Retrenched* (New York: Routledge, 2006), p. 39.

34. Wu An and Liu Liu, "Jianrui de hutong baoweizhe" (A Strong Protector of Lanes), *Sanlian shenghuo zhoukan* (Sanlian Life Weekly), December 30, 2002, pp. 17–21.

35. Ren Bo, "Chaiqian zhisu," pp. 38–39.

36. Liu Zhiming and Sun Zhan, "Youchanzhe de weiquan kunjing" (The Plight of Property Owners Defending Their Rights), *Zhongguo xinwen zhoukan* (News Weekly), no. 36 (September 29, 2003): 30–33.

37. Yongshun Cai and Songcai Yang, "State Power and Unbalanced Legal Development in China," *Journal of Contemporary China*, 14, no. 42 (February 2005): 114–134.

38. Xie Guangfei, "Meiti baoguang Shanghai chaiqian bei fengsha, you ren ceng baodao chaiqian shu xiemi" (Media Reports on Housing Demolition Were Banned in Shanghai to Prevent the Release of So-Called National Secrets), *Zhongguo jingji shibao* (China Economic Times), November 25, 2003, p. 3.

39. Zheng He, "Zhongyang paichu silu diaocha xiaozu tuji jiancha gedi chaiqian jiufen" (The Central Government Sent Four Groups to Investigate Conflicts Arising from Housing Removal), *Ershiyi shiji jingji baodao* (Twenty-first Century Economic Report), September 27, 2003, p. 1.

40. Cai, "Managed Participation in China"; Laura M. Luehrmann, "Facing Citizen Complaints in China, 1951–1996," *Asian Survey*, 43, no. 5 (September–October 2003): 845–866.

41. Zhao Ling, "Chaiqian shinian beixi ju" (The Ten-Year History of Housing Removal), *Nanfang zhoumo* (Southern Weekend), September 4, 2003, pp. 1, 2.

42. Interview, China, 2004.

43. Also see Yongshun Cai, "China's Moderate Middle Class: The Case of Homeowners' Resistance," *Asian Survey*, 45, no. 5 (September–October 2005): 777–799.

44. Reported in *Neibu canyue* (Internal References), no. 9 (1999): 18–19.

45. See http://news.bbc.co.uk/chinese/simp/hi/newsid_1950000/newsid _1953400/1953443.stm (accessed March 10, 2006).

46. See http://news.bbc.co.uk/chinese/simp/hi/newsid_2990000/newsid _2996400/2996481.stm (accessed March 10, 2006).

47. Tu Ming, "Xiang weigai kaidao, taoluo hechu" (Dangerous Houses Should Be Revamped, But How?), *Zhongguo gaige* (China Reform), no. 7 (2003): 43–47.

48. Xie Guangfei and Chen Xiaofeng, "Beijing yeman chaiqian shijian diaocha" (An Investigation into Compulsory Housing Demolition in Beijing), *Zhongguo jingji shibao* (China Economic Times), November 5, 2003, p. 2.

49. Interview with residents, China, 2004.

50. Xie Guangfei and Chen Xiaofeng, "Beijing yeman chaiqian shijian diaocha."

51. Liu Shengliang and Gao Kefen, "Baoli chaiqian jiangzhao jingfang yanda" (Demolition with Force Will Be Punished by the Police), *Beijing qingnian bao* (Beijing Youth Newspaper), October 30, 2003.

52. Interview with residents, China, 2004.

53. Ju Jin, "Tuitujixia de beiju, Nanjing chaiqian zifen shijian diaocha."

54. Hu Jie, "Zhu Zhengliang Beijing zifen yihou" (After Zhu Zhengliang's Self-Immolation in Beijing), *Nanfang dushi bao* (Southern Metropolis News), September 23, 2003.

55. See the Chinese Web site of BBC, at http://news.bbc.co.uk (accessed September 25, 2003).

56. Zhao Ling, "Chaiqian shinian beixi ju."

57. See the Web site of the State Resource and Housing Management Bureau of Beijing municipality, at www.bigtfgi.gov.cn (accessed September 28, 2003).

58. Su Min, "Liangfen chengshi fangwu chaiqian wenjian shixing, chaiqian gujia ying suihang jiushi" (Two Directives Regarding Housing Demolition Will Take Effect, and the Assessment of Prices Will Be Based on the Market), *Zhongguo qingnian bao* (China Youth Daily), January 1, 2004, p. 1.

59. Xie Guangfei and Wang Xiaoxia, "Yanda chaiqian fubai rang xingzheng ganyu tuichu chaiqian lingyu" (Combating Corruption and Stopping Administrative Intervention in Housing Demolition), *Zhongguo jingji shibao* (China Economic Times), October 15, 2003, p. 2.

60. Shi Zhe, "Guangzhou: Huanjie chaiqian maodun de changshi" (Guangzhou: A Trial of Reducing Conflicts in Housing Demolition), *Nanfang zhoumo* (Southern Weekend), September 4, 2003, p. 3.

61. For example, the Shanghai government placed very specific requirements on the procedures for housing demolition. Li Yongle, "Shanghai lifa 'wenming chaiqian'" (Shanghai Made Laws to Regulate Housing Demolition), *Lianhe zaobao* (United Morning Post), November 10, 2003, p. 5.

62. Bai Yanlong, "Beijing 13 jia chaiqian danwei you weifa chaiqian xingwei, shoupi 'chuju'" (Licenses of Thirteen Housing Demolition Companies in Beijing Were Revoked Because of Law Violations), *Zhongguo qingnian bao* (China Youth Daily), October 25, 2003, p. 1.

63. Interview, China, 2004.

64. Sun Jie, "Nanjing xiugai chaiqian fagui jiejian shichang jiage gusuan fangfa."

65. Interview, China, 2004.

66. Tao Feng and Xie Chunlei, "Zhejiang fayuan 'chaiqian' bianfa" (The Change of Rules in Cases Regarding "Housing Demolition" in the Courts of Zhejiang), *Nanfang zhoumo* (Southern Weekend), October 9, 2003, p. 3.

67. Zuo Zhijian, "Nanjingshi chengshi chaiqian guanli banfa zheng xiuding, zhengqiu gaoyuan yijian" (Nanjing Is Revising Its Regulations on Housing Demolition by Seeking the Advice of the Supreme Court), *Ershiyi shiji jingji baodao* (Twenty-first-Century Economic Report), September 27, 2003, p. 3.

68. Duan Hongqing, "Dengdai zuigao fayuan chaiqian sifa jieshi" (Awaiting the Supreme Court's Interpretation of Articles on Housing Demolition), *Caijing* (Finance), June 7, 2004, pp. 41–44.

69. Zuo Zhijian, "Nanjingshi chengshi chaiqian guanli banfa zheng xiuding, zhengqiu gaoyuan yijian."

70. Talks with two city officials, China, 2005.

71. Samuel Huntington, *Political Order in Changing Societies* (New Haven: Yale University Press, 1968), p. 359.

9. "Hope for Protection and Hopeless Choices"

1. For general information including history and relevant regulations and laws on legal aid, see www.legalinfo.gov.cn (accessed February 25, 2006). A useful time line of the development of legal aid is found at www.legalinfo.gov.cn/flyz/2004–08/29/content_129072.htm (accessed September 5, 2004).

2. Li Xun, "Falü yuanzhu shinian: Cong bangzhu qiongren dao weihu zhengyi" (Ten Years of Legal Aid: From Helping the Poor to Defending Justice), *Nanfang zhoumo* (Southern Weekend), September 2, 2004, p. 6.

3. Benjamin Liebman goes into greater detail on variations of legal aid services as offered through the Ministry of Justice's legal aid project and summarizes five different approaches. This chapter discusses the Shanghai approach, which utilizes lawyers from private law firms to staff legal aid centers. Benjamin L. Liebman, "Legal Aid and Public Interest Law in China," *Texas International Law Journal*, 34, no. 2 (Spring 1999): 211–286.

4. Zhou Xianglin, "Yifa weihu zhigong hefa quanyi, nuli tansuo zhigong falü yuanzhu qudao" (Protect Workers' Legal Rights and Interests through the Law, Work Hard to Explore Channels for Workers' Legal Aid), unpublished Shanghai Municipal Trade Union report, 2003; Guan Huai, "Lun dui woguo zhigong de falü yuanzhu" (A Discussion of Our Country's Legal Aid for Workers), at www.labournet.com.cn/lilun/fileview.asp?title=%C2%DB %B6%D4%CE%D2%B9%FA%D6%B0%B9%A4%B5%C4%B7 %A8%C2%C9%D4%AE%D6%FA&number=al017707.txt (accessed April 4, 2006).

5. Randall Peerenboom, *China's Long March toward Rule of Law* (New York: Cambridge University Press, 2002).

6. For a discussion of the democratic nature of legal aid and legal mobilization, see Frances Kahn Zemans, "Legal Mobilization: The Neglected Role of the Law in the Political System," *American Political Science Review*, 77, no. 3 (Sept. 1983): 690–703; Michael W. Giles and Thomas D. Lancaster, "Political Transition, Social Development, and Legal Mobilization in Spain," *American Political Science Review*, 83, no. 3 (Sept. 1989): 817–833.

7. The emphasis here is on how workers' legal (and non-legal) activism can be increased through their participation in the legal process, which contrasts in some ways with emphasis on the legal process as a method of bureaucratization and routinization. See, for example, Ching Kwan Lee, "From the Specter of Mao to the Spirit of the Law: Labor Insurgency in China," *Theory and Society*, 31, no. 2 (2002): 192.

8. Steven Levitsky and Lucan Way, "The Rise of Competitive Authoritarianism," *Journal of Democracy*, 13, no. 2 (April 2002): 51–65; Jason Brownlee, "Durable Authoritarianism in an Age of Democracy" (Ph.D. diss., Princeton University, 2004).

9. Larry Diamond, "Thinking about Hybrid Regimes," *Journal of Democracy*, 13, no. 2 (April 2002): 33.

10. Sally Engle Merry finds similar disappointments in her study of working-class Americans using the lower courts, in *Getting Justice and Getting Even: Legal Consciousness among Working-Class Americans* (Chicago: University of Chicago Press, 1990).

11. Empirical studies of the Chinese legal system, including the provision of legal services, are now becoming more common. See Donald C. Clarke, "Empirical Research into the Chinese Judicial System," in Erik G. Jensen and Thomas C. Heller, eds., *Beyond Common Knowledge: Empirical Approaches to the Rule of Law* (Stanford: Stanford University Press, 2003). One of the advantages of the empirical data used in this project is that they were collected directly from a legal aid center.

12. Legal aid recipient interviews are identified parenthetically with a number, while other interviews are identified parenthetically by a date. All names are pseudonyms.

13. This project uses three different methods to study the effects of legal aid and the patterns of legal mobilization among Chinese workers. Each method is designed to capture a different population. A four-city household survey examined the general population's "knowledge, attitude, and practice" of labor law and labor dispute resolution. Analysis of the database of the legal aid organization's consultation records tells us what kinds of people, with what kinds of problems, actually search out legal aid and legal resolution of their problems. Finally, the in-depth interviews of the legal aid recipients provide much more fine-grained analysis of recipients' changing legal consciousness and patterns of legal mobilization, as well as other types of contentious behavior that are used in concert with the legal process. This chapter deals only with those who have received legal aid, which is a small but growing subset of the population.

14. Luan Jun and Deng Rong, "Gaoxiao falü yuanzhu zuzhi qingkuang de yanjiu" (Research on the Situation of University Legal Aid Organizations), *Fayuan zhi chuang* (Window on the Court), 12, no. 5 (2003).

15. Lin Fengzhang, "Woguo falü yuanzhu de kunjing fenxi" (Analysis of the Difficulties of Our Country's Legal Aid), *Fujian shifan xueyuan xuebao (zhexue shehui kexue ban)* (Journal of Fujian Teachers University [Philosophy and Social Science Edition]), no. 3 (2002).

16. Wang Jun et al., "Dui Shanghaishi xianxing falü yuanzhu zhidu de sikao" (Reflections on the Current Legal Aid System in Shanghai), *Huadong*

zhengfa xueyuan xuebao (Journal of East China University of Politics and Law) no. 2 (2000): 71.

17. The negative experiences that these respondents had with government legal aid reflect the well-known problems of government-run legal aid. They may also be, however, a function of selection bias in the sample. Those workers who had positive experiences with government legal aid would not have needed to search out additional help at the university centers.

18. Wang Jun et al., "Dui Shanghaishi xianxing falü yuanzhu zhidu de sikao."

19. *Laodong baozhang bao* (Labor and Security Newspaper), September 16–22, 2004, p. 1.

20. *Zhongguo sifa xingzheng nianjian* (China Judicial Administration Yearbook) (Beijing: Falü chubanshe, various years).

21. Zhou Xianglin, "Yifa weihu zhigong hefa quanyi, nuli tansuo zhigong falü yuanzhu qudao."

22. Mary E. Gallagher, "'Use the Law as Your Weapon': Institutional Change and Legal Mobilization in China," in Neil J. Diamant, Stanley B. Lubman, and Kevin J. O'Brien, eds., *Engaging the Law in China: State, Society, and Possibilities for Justice* (Stanford: Stanford University Press, 2005), pp. 54–83.

23. Li Xun makes this charge about government legal aid as well. Li Xun, "Falü yuanzhu shinian."

24. *Shanghai nianjian* (Shanghai Yearbook) (Shanghai: Shanghai renmin chubanshe, various years).

25. See prepared remarks by Benjamin L. Liebman, "Roundtable on Access to Justice in China," Congressional Executive Committee on China, July 12, 2004, at www.cecc.gov/pages/roundtables/071204/index .php?PHPSESSID=5ffd24815bf8f2f64d1c65feb213c177 (accessed August 1, 2004).

26. Li Xun, "Falü yuanzhu shinian"; Mou Xiaoai, "Falü yuanzhu fendan feiyong zhidu ruogan wenti yanjiu" (Research on Several Problems on Fee Sharing Structure in Legal Aid), *Huadong zhengfa xueyuan xuebao* (Journal of East China University of Politics and Law), no. 3 (2002): 26–35.

27. Reliance on foreign organizations can create problems that go beyond simple economic dependence. On this point, see Michael William Dowdle, "Preserving Indigenous Paradigms in an Age of Globalization: Pragmatic Strategies for the Development of Clinical Legal Aid in China," *Fordham International Law Journal*, 24 (2000–2001): S56–S82.

28. Xu Hui, "Legislation and Implementation of Legal Aid in China," in *Zhongguo renquan niankan, 2003* (The Chinese Yearbook of Human Rights, 2003) (Beijing: Shehui kexue wenxian chubanshe, 2004), pp. 467–472.

29. Ethan Michelson, "The Practice of Law as an Obstacle to Justice: Chinese Lawyers at Work," *Law and Society Review*, 40, no. 1 (2006): 1–38.

30. There is no room in this chapter, unfortunately, to discuss representation

offered on contingency, made famous in China by Zhou Litai, a Chongqing lawyer who worked on workers' compensation cases in Shenzhen. Zhou reappeared in the press with a vengeance in 2004 when he sued one of his clients for failing to pay his legal fees.

31. This is a statement not about the general population but rather about people who seek out legal aid. The fact that these recipients are self-selected probably means that they have relatively high expectations of the legal system.

32. For a much more detailed discussion of the dispute resolution process, see Virginia Harper Ho, *Labor Dispute Resolution in China: Implications for Labor Rights and Legal Reform* (Berkeley: Institute of East Asian Studies, University of California, 2003).

33. See also Mei Minyou, "Falü panjue zen nengcheng baitiao" (How Can a Legal Ruling Become an IOU?), *Gongren ribao* (Workers' Daily), November 27, 2002, at http://www.yn.xinhuanet.com/ynnews/zt/2003/flbt/wen/x02.htm (accessed April 4, 2006).

34. Michael W. McCann, *Rights at Work: Pay Equity Reform and the Politics of Legal Mobilization* (Chicago: University of Chicago Press, 1994).

35. Judge Bao is a famous character in Chinese history and literature, known for his attention to justice and upholding the law.

36. "Letters and visits" is shorthand for the petitioning process that many Chinese citizens use to alert the government about their grievances and to ask for compensation or redress. Most government agencies have a "letters and visits" office that processes these complaints. See Carl F. Minzner, "Xinfang: An Alternative to the Formal Chinese Legal System," *Stanford Journal of International Law*, 42 (Winter 2006): 103–180.

37. See "Buliaojie xin laodong fagui, gongsi zao lianhuan tousu mianlin guanmen" (Companies Don't Understand New Labor Regulations, Copy-Cat Claims Lead to Closure"), *Gongren ribao* (Workers' Daily), June 3, 2004, available at http://www.longhoo.net/gb/longhoo/news/shijing/node100/userobject1ai202456.html (accessed April 4, 2006).

38. Patricia Ewick and Susan Silbey define legal mobilization as "the ways in which citizens initiate legal action." Patricia Ewick and Susan S. Silbey, *The Common Place of Law: Stories from Everyday Life* (Chicago: University of Chicago Press, 1998), p. 18.

39. In Ewick and Silbey's study of New Jersey, they also find a very bottom-heavy "dispute pyramid," with only a few disputes pushed to the top in the form of legal trials. "It turns out that although almost any social interaction could, in theory, become a matter of contest and dispute, few do." Ibid., p. 19. Labor grievances in particular are often just "lumped" because people prefer to keep their jobs.

40. Many legal aid recipients linked their problems to high politics, including

the "three represents theory," the single-party system, and lack of civil and political freedoms. One young worker who reluctantly accepted a mediation agreement during a collective court case muttered under his breath, "I guess my mind's not at ease yet because I haven't studied the 'three represents.'" The "three represents theory" was coined by former Chinese president and CCP general secretary Jiang Zemin and enshrined in the Chinese constitution in 2004. It stipulates that the Chinese Communist Party represents the advanced productive forces, advanced culture, and fundamental interests of the Chinese people. This is a significant departure from the Marxist emphasis on class and the CCP's historic relationship to workers and peasants.

41. Kevin J. O'Brien, "Neither Transgressive nor Contained: Boundary-Spanning Contention in China," *Mobilization: An International Journal*, 8, no. 1 (2003): 51.

42. Samuel Huntington, *Political Order in Changing Societies* (New Haven: Yale University Press, 1968).

43. Andrew J. Nathan, "Authoritarian Resilience," *Journal of Democracy*, 14, no. 1 (January 2003): 6–17.

44. Barbara Geddes, "What Do We Know about Democratization after Twenty Years?" *Annual Review of Political Science*, 2 (June 1999): 115–144.

45. Nathan, "Authoritarian Resilience," p. 7.

10. Is Labor a Political Force in China?

1. Zhonggong zhongyang zuzhibu ketizu, *Zhongguo diaocha baogao: 2000–2001 xin xingshi xia renmin neibu maodun yanjiu* (China Survey Report: A Study of the Internal Contradictions among the People in the New Situation, 2000–2001) (Beijing: Zhongyang bianyiju chubanshe, 2001); Research Department, Politics and Law Committee, ed., *Weihu shehui wending diaoyan wenji* (Research Papers on Maintaining Social Stability) (Beijing: Falü chubanshe, 2001).

2. Wang Shaoguang, Hu Angang, and Ding Yuanzhu, "Jingji fanrong beihou de shehui bu wending" (Social Instability beneath Economic Prosperity), *Zhanlüe yu guanli* (Strategy and Management), no. 3 (2002): 26–33.

3. Dorothy Solinger, "The New Crowd of the Dispossessed," in Peter Hays Gries and Stanley Rosen, eds., *State and Society in 21st-Century China* (New York: RoutledgeCurzon, 2004), pp. 50–66.

4. Marc Blecher, "Hegemony and Workers' Politics," *China Quarterly*, no. 170 (June 2002): 283–303.

5. Martin King Whyte, "Chinese Social Trends: Stability or Chaos?" in David Shambaugh, ed., *Is China Unstable? Assessing the Factors* (Armonk, N.Y.: M. E. Sharpe, 2000), pp. 143–163.

6. Mark Selden, "Labor Unrest in China, 1831–1990," *Review*, 18, no. 1 (Winter 1995): 69–86; David Strand, "Protest in Beijing: Civil Society and Public Sphere in China," *Problems of Communism*, 39, no. 3 (May–June 1990): 1–19; Elizabeth J. Perry and Ellen V. Fuller, "China's Long March to Democracy," *World Policy Journal*, 8, no. 4 (1991): 663–685.

7. Richard Swedberg, "Civil Courage ('Zivilcourage'): The Case of Knut Wicksell," *Theory and Society*, 28, no. 4 (1999): 501–528. Swedberg maintains that acts of civil courage are particularly important for the development of civil society in places where freedom of expression is not guaranteed or when one is confronting a hostile majority.

8. Zhou Zhanshun, "Guanyu dangqian xinfang gongzuo qingkuang de tongbao" (A General Report on the Current Situation of Petition Work), *Renmin xinfang* (People's Petitions), no. 7 (2001): 13–16.

9. *Zhongguo gonghui tongji nianjian, 1998* (Chinese Labor Union Statistics Yearbook, 1998) (Beijing: Zhongguo tongji chubanshe, 1999), table 2–36.

10. Minxin Pei, "Beijing Drama: China's Governance Crisis and Bush's New Challenge," *Policy Brief* (Carnegie Endowment for International Peace), no. 21 (November 2002).

11. Murray Scot Tanner, "Protests Now Flourish in China," *International Herald Tribune*, June 3, 2004, p. 7; Joseph Kahn, "Pace and Scope of Protest in China Accelerated in '05," *New York Times*, January 20, 2006, p. 10.

12. *Shenzhen laodong nianjian, 1998–99* (Shenzhen Labor Yearbook, 1998–99) (Beijing: Zhongguo laodong chubanshe, 2000), p. 103; and *Shenzhen laodong nianjian, 2000–2001* (Shenzhen Labor Yearbook, 2000–2001) (Beijing: Zhongguo laodong chubanshe, 2002), pp. 109 and 115.

13. William Hurst and Kevin J. O'Brien, "China's Contentious Pensioners," *China Quarterly*, no. 170 (June 2002): 345–360; Feng Chen, "Subsistence Crises, Managerial Corruption, and Labour Protests in China," *China Journal*, no. 44 (July 2000): 41–63; Feng Chen, "Industrial Restructuring and Workers' Resistance in China," *Modern China*, 29, no. 2 (April 2003): 237–262; Stephen Philion, "The Discourse of Workers' Democracy in China as a Terrain of Ideological Struggle" (Ph.D. diss., University of Hawaii, 2004).

14. Interview with three worker representatives in Shenzhen, May 23, 2002.

15. Interview in Shenzhen, May 14, 2003.

16. Interview in Shenyang, December 24, 2002.

17. Interview in Shenyang, July 4, 2003.

18. Mark W. Frazier, "China's Pension Reform and Its Discontents," *China Journal*, no. 51 (January 2004): 97–114. See also Dorothy Solinger, "Path Dependency in the Transition to Unemployment and the Formation of a Safety Net in China," unpublished ms., August 2003. The notion of a cellular social structure in China, of course, is not new. See, for instance, Vivienne Shue, *The Reach of the State* (Stanford: Stanford University Press, 1988).

19. A major difference between the two types of communities is that a state worker's residence survives the termination of his employment, in contrast to a migrant worker's itinerant status and lack of a permanent dwelling in the city. Thus, labor struggles in the northeast have the potential to be sustained for longer periods of time, up to several years in some cases.

20. "Chinese Police Battle Up to 5,000 Workers over Unpaid Wages," Agence France-Presse, May 16, 2000.

21. Open letter dated March 8, 2002. It was posted near the entrance of the factory even after the mass rally on March 18, 2002.

22. In a letter to the Liaoyang People's Government, dated June 25, 2002, signed by more than one hundred Liaotie employees, workers explained in detail their economic demands, for instance, why they did not accept the government's proposal to transfer severance compensation to workers' social security accounts. They wanted both severance compensation and social security accounts.

23. Interview in Liaoyang, August 5, 2003.

24. Interview in Liaoyang, August 5, 2003.

25. John Pomfret, "With Carrots and Sticks, China Quiets Protestors," *Washington Post*, March 22, 2002, p. A24.

26. Interview in Liaoyang, August 5, 2003, and personal communication with Philip Pan, *Washington Post* reporter.

27. Interview in Liaoyang, March 25, 2002.

28. Erik Eckholm, "2 Promoters of Worker Protests in China Get Prison Sentences," *New York Times*, May 10, 2003, p. 4.

29. Jiang Chenggang, "Liaoyang Tiehejin da an chachu jishi" (A Report on the Liaoyang Ferro-Alloy Case Investigation), *Dangfeng yuebao* (Party Discipline Monthly), no. 5 (2003): 18–22.

30. "Xiang Huaicheng at NPC Meeting: Social Security System Needed to Ensure Stability," Xinhua, March 6, 2002, in FBIS-CHI-2002–0306.

31. Jean-Louis Rocca, "The Invention of Social Policies in Marketizing China: The Case of Migrant Workers and Precarious Urban Workers," paper presented at the Conference on Employment and Social Security, Shanghai, September 11–13, 2003, p. 6.

32. Ibid., pp. 8–9.

33. In a study of a military enterprise in Shenyang, enterprise officials reported that they had received instructions regarding a new bankruptcy policy prompted by the unrest in Liaoyang and other places in Liaoning. See Li Erjin, "The Making of the Xiagang Worker List" (M.Phil. thesis, Tsinghua University, Beijing, June 2003).

34. Article 27 of the 2001 Trade Union Law.

35. Feng Chen, "Between the State and Labour: The Conflict of Chinese Trade Unions' Double Identity in Market Reform," *China Quarterly*, no. 176 (December 2003): 1006–28.

36. Christopher Bodeen, "China Trade Union to Allow Direct Election of Local Leaders," Associated Press, September 26, 2003; Bill Taylor, Chang Kai, and Li Qi, *Industrial Relations in China* (Cheltenham, U.K.: Edward Elgar, 2003), p. 113.

37. Philip P. Pan, "When Workers Organize, China's Party-Run Unions Resist," *Washington Post*, October 15, 2002, p. A11.

38. Pun Ngai, "The Moral Economy of Capital: Transnational Corporate Codes of Conduct and Labour Rights in China," unpublished ms., 2004; Anita Chan and Hong-zen Wang, "Raising Labor Standards, Corporate Social Responsibility and Missing Links—Vietnam and China Compared," paper presented at the Conference on Labor Reform in China, University of Michigan, March 21–22, 2003.

39. Raymond W. K. Lau, "China: Labour Reform and the Challenge Facing the Working Class," *Capital and Class*, no. 61 (Spring 1997): 45–81; Trini W. Y. Leung, "Labour Fights for Its Rights," *China Perspectives*, no. 19 (September–October 1998): 6–21.

40. Li Minqi, "Response to Lau's 'China: Labour Reform and the Challenge Facing the Working Class,'" *Capital and Class*, no. 65 (Summer 1998): 22.

41. Ibid.

42. Chan Wai-fong, "'Collusion by Officials' in Abuses of Workers," *South China Morning Post*, June 13, 1994, p. 5, describes some of the contents of the newsletters.

43. "Imprisoned Chinese Labor Activist Di Tiangui's Life in Danger," China Labor Watch press release, August 19, 2002.

44. Jiang Xueqin, "Fighting to Organize," *Far Eastern Economic Review*, 164, no. 35 (September 6, 2001): 72–75; Matthew Forney and Neil Gough, "Working Man Blues," *Time* (Asia edition), April 1, 2002; Philion, "The Discourse of Workers' Democracy."

45. "Chinese Police Detain Four Workers Mourning Mao," Reuters World Report, September 10, 2001.

46. Brochure of the Migrant Workers Community College (2004).

11. Between Defiance and Obedience

1. For a comparison of the advantages of radical and moderate protest strategies, see Ann-Marie Szymanski, *Pathways to Prohibition: Radicals, Moderates, and Social Movement Outcomes* (Durham, N.C.: Duke University Press, 2003).

2. See Elizabeth J. Perry, *Challenging the Mandate of Heaven: Social Protest and State Power in China* (Armonk, N.Y.: M. E. Sharpe, 2001).

3. This can be illustrated by the Chinese term to describe such actions: visits *(shangfang)*. Meaning citizens' "visits" to government, this type of collective action differs from rebellious action. Even very disruptive and large-

scale events are described as "visits," although sometimes the adjective "unusual" is added, and they are referred to as "unusual visits" *(yichang shangfang)*.

4. This is a technical term and does not carry any negative connotation.

5. James C. Scott, *Domination and the Arts of Resistance: Hidden Transcripts* (New Haven: Yale University Press, 1990), p. x.

6. Kevin J. O'Brien, "Rightful Resistance," *World Politics,* 49, no. 1 (October 1996): 33.

7. Ibid., p. 34; Kevin O'Brien and Lianjiang Li, *Rightful Resistance in Rural China* (New York: Cambridge University Press, 2006), p. 68.

8. There is much academic and journalistic evidence. For example, see Murray Scot Tanner, "China Rethinks Unrest," *Washington Quarterly,* 27, no. 3 (Summer 2004): 137–156; Kathy Chen, "Chinese Protests Grow More Frequent, Violent," *Wall Street Journal,* November 5, 2004, p. A10.

9. See, for example, Doug McAdam, "The Framing Function of Movement Tactics: Strategic Dramaturgy in the American Civil Rights Movement," in Doug McAdam, John D. McCarthy, and Mayer N. Zald, eds., *Comparative Perspectives on Social Movements: Political Opportunities, Mobilizing Structures, and Cultural Framings* (New York: Cambridge University Press, 1996); Frances Fox Piven and Richard A. Cloward, *Poor People's Movements: Why They Succeed, How They Fail* (New York: Vintage Books, 1977); Sidney G. Tarrow, *Power in Movement: Social Movements and Contentious Politics,* 2nd ed. (New York: Cambridge University Press, 1998).

10. Michael Lipsky, "Protest as a Political Resource," *American Political Science Review,* 62, no. 4 (December 1968): 1144–58.

11. See Andrew Walder, *Communist Neo-Traditionalism: Work and Authority in Chinese Industry* (Berkeley: University of California Press, 1986).

12. Interview, City Y, September 2002.

13. Administrative reconsideration is an administrative procedure through which citizens request the government to reconsider its decisions.

14. Government documents collected in City Y, July 2002.

15. Interview, City Y, September 2002.

16. Interview, City Y, July 2002.

17. This is the People's Liberation Army code of discipline, which emphasizes that army officers should not disturb civilians.

18. Documents collected in City Y, September 2002.

19. Interview, City Y, September 2002.

20. Dorothy Solinger, "The New Crowd of the Dispossessed: The Shift of the Urban Proletariat from Master to Mendicant," in Peter Hayes Gries and Stanley Rosen, eds., *State and Society in 21st-Century China: Crisis, Contention, and Legitimation* (New York: RoutledgeCurzon, 2004), pp. 50–66.

21. Liu Binyan, "Xueji qian de sisuo" (Thoughts in Front of the Bloodstain), at http://bjzc.org/bjs/bc/50/06 (accessed January 8, 2005).

22. Yu Jianrong, "Dangdai Zhongguo nongmin weiquan zuzhi de fayu yu chengzhang: Jiyu Hengyang nongmin xiehui de shizheng yanjiu" (Growth and Development of Peasants' Organizations of Rights Defense in Contemporary China: An Empirical Study of the Hengyang Peasant Association), *Zhongguo nongcun guancha* (China Rural Survey) no. 2 (2005): 57–64, 71.

23. For a discussion of accountability and responsiveness, see the introduction to Adam Przeworski, Susan C. Stokes, and Bernard Manin, eds., *Democracy, Accountability, and Representation* (New York: Cambridge University Press, 1999).

24. Jean C. Oi, *State and Peasant in Contemporary China: The Political Economy of Village Government* (Berkeley: University of California Press, 1989), p. 228.

25. Ying Xing and Jin Jun refer to this tactic as the "problemization of issues" *(wentihua)*. See Ying Xing and Jin Jun, "Jiti shangfangzhong de 'wentihua' guocheng: Xi'nan yige shuidianzhan de yimin de gushi" (The Process of "Problemization" in Collective Visits: A Story of Migration Caused by Construction of a Hydroelectric Plant in Southwest China), *Qinghua shehuixue pinglun* (Tsinghua Sociological Review), special issue (2000): 80–109.

26. Xi Chen, "The Art of Troublemaking: Protest Tactics and Their Efficacy," paper presented at the annual meeting of the American Political Science Association, Chicago, 2004.

27. Wang Yongqian and Huang Haiyan, "Guojia xinfang juzhang: Diaocha xianshi chaoguo 80% de shangfang you yiding daoli" (Chief of the State Bureau of Letters and Visits: Research Demonstrates That Over 80 Percent of Petitions Are More or Less Reasonable), *Banyuetan,* November 16, 2003, at www.china.org.cn/chinese/2003/Nov/446032.htm (accessed April 1, 2006).

28. Government report collected during my fieldwork, 2002.

29. Interview with a local official, City Y, July 2002.

12. In Search of the Grassroots

This chapter is part of a larger research project exploring issues of globalization, environmental activism, and state development agendas in the upland multi-ethnic border regions of northwest Yunnan. This research began in the summer of 2000 with a grant from Duke University's Vice Provost for Interdisciplinary Studies. A Fulbright Faculty Research grant and a Fulbright-Hays grant provided funding for fieldwork in Kunming and the Diqing Tibetan Autonomous Region in northwest Yunnan for eleven months in 2001–2002. Several subsequent trips to China have been funded by generous grants from the Vice Provost for International Studies at Duke and from the Asia/Pacific Studies Institute. A first draft was presented at the Media and Citizenship in China conference at Oxford

University, August 31–September 2, 2004, organized by Rachel Murphy and Vanessa Fong. I thank the participants in this conference and the Fairbank Center October 2004 conference on Grassroots Political Reform for their many insightful comments and suggestions, with a special thanks to Deborah Davis, Merle Goldman, and Rob Weller.

1. Elizabeth Perry and Mark Selden, "Introduction: Reform and Resistance in Contemporary China," in Elizabeth J. Perry and Mark Selden, eds., *Chinese Society: Change, Conflict, and Resistance* (New York: Routledge, 2000), pp. 1–19.

2. For a discussion of environmental justice movements associated with the much more visible Three Gorges dam, see Jun Jing's excellent essay "Environmental Protests in Rural China," in Perry and Selden, *Chinese Society: Change, Conflict, and Resistance,* pp. 143–160. For one of the best discussions of water resource issues in China, see Ma Jun, *Zhongguo shui weiji* (China's Water Crisis) (Beijing: Zhongguo huanjing kexue chubanshe, 1999), translated by Nancy Yang Liu and Lawrence R. Sullivan as *China's Water Crisis* (Norwalk, Conn.: Eastbridge, 2004).

3. My understanding of the Nu River protests has benefited greatly from the work of Erik Nielsen of the Environmental Policy Group at MIT. See Erik Nielsen, "Dam It! How National and Transnational Civil Society Actors Influence Domestic Environmental Policy-Making in China: A Case Study of Damming the Nu River in Yunnan Province," paper presented at the Harvard East Asia Graduate Student Conference, March 5–6, 2005; and Erik Nielsen, "Beyond Borders: Emerging Forms of Transnational Advocacy for Improved Transboundary Environmental Governance in the Greater Mekong Sub-Region," paper presented at the Mobile Workshop on Land Use History in Montane Mountain Southeast Asia, January 15–27, 2005. For a discussion of energy politics and development issues in Guizhou province, see Tim Oakes, "Building a Southern Dynamo: Guizhou and State Power," *China Quarterly,* no. 178 (June 2004): 467–487.

4. Judith Shapiro, *Mao's War against Nature: Politics and the Environment in Revolutionary China* (New York: Cambridge University Press, 2001).

5. For a discussion of the complex and often contested role of international environmental nongovernmental organizations such as the Nature Conservancy in issues involving development, inequality, and environmental protection, see Ralph Litzinger, "The Mobilization of 'Nature,'" *China Quarterly,* no. 178 (June 2004): 488–504. For a trenchant critique of the effects of economic growth on China's environment, see Elizabeth C. Economy, *The River Runs Black: The Environmental Challenge to China's Future* (Ithaca: Cornell University Press, 2004).

6. Tessa Morris-Suzuki, "For and against NGOs: The Politics of the Lived World," *New Left Review,* no. 2 (March–April 2000): 63–84.

7. Two major events led to the logging ban. First, the Yellow River completely

stopped flowing for 267 days in 1997; second, major flooding occurred on the Yangtze during the summer of 1998. In response, provincial governments in southwest China issued prohibitions on forest logging. This was followed in late 1998 by the implementation of a nationally instituted program called the Natural Forest Protection Program, or NFPP, which called for the reduction of or complete ban on logging in seventeen designated provinces (including Yunnan), established plans for the restoration of degraded lands, and called for a complete overhaul of the forestry industry. In 1999 Zhu Rongji toured six provinces in western China and subsequently put forth the idea of the Sloping Land Conservation Program (SLCP), which was approved by the State Council in 2000. Whereas the NFPP is a government program aimed to help state forest enterprises abandon or revise traditional logging operations, the SLCP is a public payment scheme that subsidizes farmers to convert their farmland back to trees or grassland. For an assessment of the NFPP and the SLCP, see Xu Jintao, Eugenia Katsigris, and Thomas A. White, "Implementing the Natural Forest Protection Program and the Sloping Land Conservation Program: Lessons and Policy Recommendations," China Council for International Cooperation on Environment and Development, October 2002. See also Chris Clarke, "Logging on Top of the World," *Earth Island Journal,* 14, no. 3 (Fall 1999): 32–33; and "Ecosystem Profile: Mountains of Southwest China," on the Web site of the Critical Ecosystem Partnership Fund, at http://cepf.net/xp/cepf/where_we_work/Southwest_China/cull_strategy .htm. (accessed February 25, 2006). For a broader historical perspective, see S. D. Richardson, *Forests and Forestry in China* (Washington, D.C.: Island Press, 1990).

8. Many people are familiar with the astonishing economic transformations that came to Lijiang in the late 1990s. The remaking of Lijiang into a major Chinese national and international destination owes much to the flow of relief money into the county after the 1996 earthquake and to UNESCO's 1997 decision to declare the old town of Dayan, in the heart of Lijiang city, a cultural world heritage site. Similar changes are coming to the "Tibetan" town of Zhongdian, the administrative seat of the Diqing Tibetan Autonomous Region, which lies some two hundred kilometers to the northwest of Lijiang. In May 2002 Zhongdian, with the approval of China's State Council, officially changed its name to Xianggelila, or Shangri-la, to help fuel tourist growth. The best discussion of this process is found in Tang Shijie, *Menghuan gaoyuan* (The Illusory Plateau) (Kunming: Yunnan jiaoyu chubanshe, 2000). See also Yue Gang, "From Shambhala to Shangri-la: A Traveling Sign in the Era of Global Tourism," in Jin Yuanpu and Tao Dongfeng, eds., *Cultural Studies in China* (Singapore: Eastern Universities, 2004), pp. 165–183; and Ben Hillman, "Paradise under Construction," *Asian Ethnicity,* 4, no. 2 (June 2003): 175–188.

9. Two documents describing UNESCO's decision to award the nomination can be found at www.worldheritagesite.org/sites/parallelriversyunnan .html (accessed February 24, 2005). The first is the minutes of the World Heritage Committee's meeting in Paris from June 30 to July 5, 2003, where the decision was made to approve the site. The second is the technical evaluation of the application, submitted to UNESCO by the International Union for the Conservation of Nature.

10. See, for example, Oliver August, "Tiger Dam Drives Thousands from Valley of Shangri-La," *Times* (London), November 9, 2004, at http:// threegorgesprobe.org/tgp/index.cfm?DSP=content&contendID=11831 (accessed February 24, 2006). In this brief survey of the late 2004 controversy over the damming of the Tiger Leaping Gorge on the Jinsha River, the author says that Huaneng, the state power company controlled by Li Xiaopeng, Li Peng's son, which helped to build the Three Gorges dam, has also been actively involved in dam projects in northwest Yunnan. Li Peng's son's involvement in both the Nu and Jinsha dam projects has been widely discussed in Chinese chat rooms and in e-mail exchanges.

11. To date there has been little analysis of the discovery, creation, and mapping of biodiversity hotspots in China in the 1990s. For a preliminary analysis, see Ralph Litzinger, "Contested Sovereignties and the Critical Ecosystem Partnership Fund," *PoLar (The Political and Legal Anthropology Review)*, 29, no. 1 (2006): 1–14. For a discussion of biodiversity assessment in another part of the world, see James E. Gordon, "The Practice and Circulation of Biodiversity Assessment in Tropical Mexico," *Social and Cultural Geography*, 7, no. 1 (February 2006): 35–51.

12. This is, of course, a simplified version of what was in fact a complex process of trans-local mobilization, letter writing, and behind-the-scenes negotiations which included Liang Congjie's NGO, Friends of Nature, the environmental activist Tang Xianyan, and Song Jian, then a member of China's State Council. For a full account, see Shen Xiaohui, *Xueshan xunmeng* (In Search of the Snow Mountain) (Shenyang: Shenyang chubanshe, 1998).

13. This Web site, www.nujiang.ngo.com, could be accessed throughout the later part of 2004 and much of 2005. By the end of 2005, it had disappeared from the Web.

14. From an interview in Beijing, May 2004. The issue of competition over who should get credit for the suspension of the dam is also reported by Kristen McDonald, a fellow at the Human Rights Center at the University of California, Berkeley, who did research among activist organizations in Kunming during the summer of 2004. She writes: "When Premier Wen Jiabao announced the suspension of the Nu River dam project, rather than using the success to bolster the anti-dam campaign, NGO leaders and media activists immediately began to fight over credit for the triumph.

Was it AIRC's [Asian International Rivers Center] leader, who had mar-
shaled the scientific community to point out the flaws in the plan? Was it
the media, who had aired probing stories on TV and run scathing indict-
ments in the press? Was it members of the Chinese Academy of Social Sciences, who had issued a report to Wen Jiabao that apparently had made
him aware of the issue in the first place? Or was it the letter from 76 different civil society groups in 33 different countries sent to China's President
Hu Jintao, voicing criticisms of the dam?" See Kristen McDonald, "'Great
Western Development' for Whom? Dams and Resource Equity in China's
Yunnan Province," report to the Human Rights Center Summer Fellowship Program, University of California, Berkeley, February 4, 2005.

15. See Luo Li's report on TNC's participation in a government-sponsored
conference assessing the social and economic impact of the dam at http://
chinarivers.com/NYT%20Article/Gaoligong.html (accessed February 24,
2006).

16. In an ironic twist of fate, after the county governor retired from government service in 2000, he was hired by the Nature Conservancy to head up
its field office in the town of Zhongdian (Xianggelila). This move, as we
might expect, angered many of the veteran activists from the mid-1990s,
who continued to see the governor as a corrupt official with little care or
concern for the region's biodiversity. When I asked various TNC staff why
they had hired this man, the uniform response was that despite his unsa-
vory past, he still possessed strong connections with county, prefecture,
and provincial leaders, and thus could help push forward various TNC
projects.

17. According to fieldwork in the Baima Nature Reserve region in 2001–2002.

18. There is some credibility to her argument. A rumor reached me in early
October 2005 that Yu Xiaogang was being criticized behind the scenes by
government officials and provincial party cadres in Yunnan, and that there
was some concern that the government might move to close down his
Yunnan Green Watershed, which is housed on the campus of the Yunnan
Academy of Social Sciences. While Yu's activities continue to be closely
watched by the Chinese government, he was permitted to travel to the
United States in April 2006 to receive the Goldman Environmental
Prize. The annual prize awards $125,000 to "environmental heroes" from
each of the world's six inhabited continental regions. See http://www
.goldmanprize.org (accessed August 1, 2006).

19. For a discussion of conflicts between mass tourism and ecotourism initiatives in northwest Yunnan, see Li Bo and Xie Hongyan, "Jisha—Women
you yige meng" (Jisha Village: We Have a Dream), *Wenhua dili* (Cultural
Geography) (February 2003): 1–17.

20. For a sampling of work addressing these issues, see Michael Hardt and An-

tonio Negri, *Empire* (Cambridge, Mass.: Harvard University Press, 2000), and *Multitude: War and Democracy in the Age of Empire* (New York: Penguin, 2004); Margaret E. Keck and Kathryn Sikkink, *Activist beyond Borders: Advocacy Networks in International Politics* (Ithaca, N.Y.: Cornell University Press, 1998); Richard Warren Perry and Bill Maurer, eds., *Globalization under Construction: Governmentality, Law, and Identity* (Minneapolis: University of Minnesota Press, 2003); and Aihwa Ong and Stephen J. Collier, eds., *Global Assemblages: Technology, Politics, and Ethics as Anthropological Problems* (Malden, Mass.: Blackwell Publishing, 2005).

21. Michel-Rolph Trouillot, "The Anthropology of the State in the Age of Globalization: Close Encounters of the Deceptive Kind," *Current Anthropology*, 42, no. 1 (February 2001): 125–138.

22. Ralph Miliband, *The State in Capitalist Society* (New York: Harper Books, 1969), cited,, ibid., p. 125.

23. Hardt and Negri, *Empire* and *Multitude.*

13. Public Opinion Supervision

1. Liang Jianzeng, *Jiaodian fangtan hongpishu* (Red Book of Focus Interviews) (Beijing: Wenhua yishu chubanshe, 2002), p. 69.

2. Sun Xupei, *Dangdai Zhongguo xinwen gaige* (Journalism Reform in Contemporary China) (Beijing: Renmin chubanshe, 2004), p. 142.

3. See Michael Schoenhals, "Elite Information in China," *Problems of Communism*, 34, no. 5 (September–October 1985): 65–71; Jennifer Grant, "Internal Reporting by Investigative Journalists and Its Influence on Government Policy," *Gazette* (Leiden), 41 (1988): 53–65.

4. Zhonggong zhongyang xuanchuanbu, Zhonggong dang'anguan bianyanbu, eds., *Zhongguo gongchandang xuanchuan wenxian huibian (1957–1992)* (A Collection of Documents on Propaganda by the Central Committee of the Communist Party of China, 1957–1992), 4 vols. (Beijing: Xuexi chubanshe, 1996), p. 574.

5. Wang Qianhua and Wei Yongzheng, *Yulun jiandu yu xinwen jiufen* (Public Opinion Supervision and Legal Disputes over News) (Shanghai: Fudan daxue chubanshe, 2000), p. 6.

6. For a detailed discussion of the reformist discourse on the news media and the party's Thirteenth National Congress, see Yuezhi Zhao, *Media, Market, and Democracy in China: Between the Party Line and the Bottom Line* (Urbana: University of Illinois Press, 1998).

7. For a detailed description of the party's mechanisms of media control, see He Qinglian, *Zhongguo zhengfu ruhe kongzhi meiti* (Media Control in China), at www.hrichina.org/fs/downloadables/pdf/downloadable-resources/MediaControlALL.pdf?revision_id=20206 (accessed January 24,

2006); see also Yuezhi Zhao, *Communication in China: Capitalist Reconstruction and Social Contestation* (Lanham, Md.: Rowman and Littlefield, forthcoming).

8. Zhonggong zhongyang, "Zhongguo gongchandang dangnei jiandu tiaoli (shixing)" ([Provisional] Regulations on Inner-Party Supervision of the Central Committee of the Chinese Communist Party), *Xinhua Net*, February 17, 2004, at http://news.xinhuanet.com/newscenter/2004–02/17/content_1318358.htm (accessed August 30, 2004).

9. For relevant literature, see He Qinglian, "China's Listing Social Structure," *New Left Review*, no. 5 (2000): 69–99; Maurice Meisner, *The Deng Xiaoping Era: An Inquiry into the Fate of Chinese Socialism, 1978–1994* (New York: Hill and Wang, 1996); Elizabeth J. Perry and Mark Selden, eds., *Chinese Society: Change, Conflict, and Resistance*, 2nd ed. (New York: RoutledgeCurzon, 2003); Sun Liping, *Duanlie: 20 shiji 90 niandai yilai de Zhongguo shehui* (Cleavage: Chinese Society since the 1990s) (Beijing: Shehui kexue wenxian chubanshe, 2003).

10. That is, to forgo any discussion about whether the reform policies are "socialist" or "capitalist." See Joseph Fewsmith, *China since Tiananmen: The Politics of Transition* (New York: Cambridge University Press, 2001).

11. For "accumulation by dispossession," see David Harvey, *The New Imperialism* (New York: Oxford University Press, 2003).

12. For further discussion, see Yuezhi Zhao, "Watchdogs on Party Leashes? Contexts and Implications of Investigative Journalism in Post-Deng China," *Journalism Studies*, 1, no. 4 (November 2000): 577–597.

13. Sun Wusan, "Piping baodao zhouwei zhili jishu" (Critical Reporting as an Administrative Technique), *Xinwen yu chuanbo pinglun 2002* (Journalism and Communication Review 2002) (Wuchang: Wuhan daxue chubanshe, 2002), pp. 123–138.

14. George J. Gilboy, "The Myth behind China's Miracle," *Foreign Affairs*, 83, no. 4 (July–August 2004): 33–48.

15. Qunjian Tian, "Agrarian Crisis, WTO Entry, and Institutional Change in Rural China," *Issues and Studies*, 40, no. 2 (June 2004): 68.

16. Ibid., p. 70.

17. Yu Jianrong, "Nongcun hei'er shili he jiceng zhengquan tuihua: Xiangnan diaocha" (Rural Dark and Evil Forces and the Regression of Local Governments), *Zhanlüe yu guanli* (Strategy and Management), no. 5 (2003): 5.

18. Sun Liping, *Duanlie*.

19. Tian, "Agrarian Crisis," p. 73.

20. Yu Jianrong, "Nongcun."

21. Ibid., p. 2.

22. Jonathan Unger, "Power, Patronage, and Protest in Rural China," in Tyrene White, ed., *China Briefing, 2000: The Continuing Transformation* (Armonk, N.Y.: M. E. Sharpe, 2000), p. 88.

23. For substantive discussion of the commercialization of the Chinese media, see Zhao, *Media, Market, and Democracy in China;* Daniel C. Lynch, *After the Propaganda State: Media, Politics, and "Thought Work" in Reformed China* (Stanford: Stanford University Press, 1999); Chin-Chuan Lee, ed., *Power, Money, and Media: Communication Patterns and Bureaucratic Control in Cultural China* (Evanston: Northwestern University Press, 2000).

24. Zhao, *Media, Market, and Democracy in China;* Yuezhi Zhao, "Underdogs, Lapdogs, and Watchdogs: Journalists and the Public Sphere Problematic in China," in Gu Xin and Merle Goldman, eds., *Chinese Intellectuals between State and Market* (New York: RoutledgeCurzon, 2004), pp. 43–74.

25. See Zhongdang Pan, "Improvising Reform Activities: The Changing Reality of Journalistic Practice in China," in Lee, *Power, Money, and Media,* pp. 68–111; Zhongdang Pan and Ye Lu, "Localizing Professionalism: Discursive Practices in China's Media Reforms," in Chin-chuan Lee, ed., *Chinese Media, Global Contexts* (New York: RoutledgeCurzon, 2003), pp. 215–236; Zhao, "Watchdogs on Party Leashes?"; Zhao, "Underdogs, Lapdogs, and Watchdogs."

26. Hai Ming, "Xinwen shencha guocheng zhong de quanli shijian xingtai yanjiu" (A Study of the Practice of Power in the Process of News Production), at http://academic.mediachina.net/academic_xsjd_view.jsp?id= 1180 (accessed March 24, 2006); Guo Zhenzhi, *Cong "Jiaodian fangtan" lei zhuanti baodao kan yulun jiandu zuoyong* (An Examination of the Role of Public Opinion Supervision through a Study of Focus Interviews and Similar Feature Programs), unpublished manuscript, 2001; Sun Wusan, "Piping baodao zhouwei zhili jishu." For an insider's point of view, see Liang Jianzeng, *Jiaodian fangtan hongpishu.*

27. Sun Jie, "Jiaodian de baogao" (A Report on Focus), in Yuan Zhengming and Liang Jianzeng, eds., *Yong shishi shuohua: Zhongguo dianshi jiaodian jiemu toushi* (Speaking with Facts: An Examination of Focus Programs on Chinese Television) (Shanghai: Shanghai renmin chubanshe, 2000), pp. 3–4; Liang Jianzeng, *Jiaodian fangtan hongpishu,* pp. 4–13.

28. Guo Zhenzhi, *Cong "Jiaodian fangtan,"* p. 7.

29. Liang Jianzeng, *Jiaodian fangtan hongpishu,* pp. 14–15.

30. Ibid., pp. 82–83.

31. Sun Jie, "Jiaodian fangtan de shijian yu yulun jiandu de celüe" (The Praxis of Focus Interviews and Strategies in Public Opinion Supervision), *Xinwen jizhe* (The Journalist), no. 1 (1999): 40–41. The other two sources for critical reports are central government departments, which use the media to expose lower-level bureaucracies to facilitate work, and other media reports.

32. The chance of a public-initiated complaint being investigated and reported by the media is very small, and even if it is reported, the agendas of the initial complainant and that of the media may not be the same.

33. For detailed description of these strategies, see Liang Jianzeng, *Jiaodian fangtan hongpishu.*

34. Ibid., pp. 66–67.

35. Guo Zhenzhi, *Cong "Jiaodian fangtan,"* p. 12. In fact, there have been criticisms of the media's overwhelming "killing power" by China's legal community. Such criticisms point out that the phenomenon of "trial by the media" undermines judicial authority and due process.

36. See Sun Wusan, "Piping baodao zhouwei zhili jishu," for a more detailed discussion of this case.

37. See, for example, "Heizoufang baowei Baigou, dagongzhe jiankang kanyou" (Underground Factories Surround Baigou, Health of Workers Worrisome), *Dahe bao* (Dahe Daily), March 15, 2002, p. 1.

38. Du Wenyu, "Zhengfu qiantou xiang duice, quanli yuanzhu dagongzhe" (Government Took the Lead in Thinking about Strategies, Fully Mobilized to Assist Workers), *Dahe bao* (Dahe Daily), March 16, 2002, p. 1.

39. Liang Jianzeng, *Jiaodian fangtan hongpishu,* p. 61.

40. The perspective from Baigou, of course, is quite different. Locals lamented the devastating impact of the media exposure and the subsequent governmental actions on the local economy. They saw the entire event as a case of overkill, whereby the media and central authorities oversimplified a complicated situation and dramatized the problem in order to claim the moral high ground. Some even felt that the local officials, who had been entrepreneurial and instrumental in developing the industry and promoting the local economy, were unfortunate victims. They claimed that the responsibility first of all lay with the manufacturers of the cheap and substandard glues, not with the local businesses and officials. They charged that the media's simplistic reporting and subsequent central government intervention worsened the local investment environment and led to a flow of capital and customers to competing townships that carried on business as usual. Although the different perspectives of the central and local governments demonstrate on the surface a disjuncture in the central-local relationship, at a deeper level the case underscores a more profound conflictual relationship between business and labor interests, as well as the role of the state in regulating this relationship.

41. Enacted in 1982, this detention policy aimed at controlling entry of rural migrants into the cities and became a means by which urban law-and-order authorities extorted money from rural migrants in the cities; they would detain people who did not have work permits or temporary residence permits, releasing them only after they had paid fines.

42. For a brief account of the case, see Shanghai shehui kexue yuan, *Zhongguo zhengzhi fazhan jincheng 2004* (The Trajectory of Chinese Political Development in 2004) (Beijing: Shishi chubanshe, 2004), pp. 292–309; see also Xu

Wenzhong, "Nanfang dushibao zhengsu guocheng jiemi" (Revelations Concerning the Suppression of Southern Metropolis News), *Zhonghua tansuo* (China Explorations), supplement to *Ming Pao* (Vancouver Edition), May 3, 2004, pp. 1–4.

43. Xu Wenzhong, "Nanfang dushibao"; Philip P. Pan, "In China, an Editor Triumphs, and Fails," *Washington Post*, August 1, 2004, p. A01, at http://www.washingtonpost.com/wp-dyn/articles/A30835–2004Jul31.html (accessed March 24, 2006); Leu Siew Ying, "Outrage Prompted Editor's Release," *South China Morning Post*, August 31, 2004.

44. Guo Zhenzhi, *Cong "Jiaodian fangtan."*

45. Chen Chongshan, "Sheiwei nongmin shuohua? Nongcun shouzhong diwei fenxi" (Who Speaks for Farmers? An Analysis of the Status of Rural Audiences), *Xiandai chuanbo* (Modern Communication), no. 3 (2003): 35–37; Zhao, *Media, Market, and Democracy in China.*

46. Guo Zhenzhi, *Cong "Jiaodian fangtan."*

47. Liang Jianzeng, *Jiaodian fangtan hongpishu.*

48. Qiao Yunxia, Hu Lianli, and Wang Junjie, "Zhongguo xinwen yulun jiandu xianzhuang diaocha fenxi"(A Survey and Analysis of Public Opinion Supervision in China), *Xinwen yu chuanbo yanjiu* (Journalism and Communication Research), no. 4 (2002): 21–28.

49. Xu Xiao, "Weihe difang baodao bushou zhongshi" (Why Are Local Media Reports Ignored?), at http://news.rednet.com.cn/Articles/2004/04/554283.HTM (accessed September 15, 2004).

50. Since 2002 a series of state policies has sought to close county-level party organs and transform full-fledged county-level television stations into relay stations with only limited time for local news broadcasts. These policies, however, especially those regarding broadcasting, face strong resistance from local authorities.

51. Zhao, "Watchdogs on Party Leashes?" p. 590.

52. Guo Zhenzhi, *Cong "Jiaodian fangtan,"* appendix 2, document category 4, interview no. 15, p. 5.

53. Su Xueshan, "Jiaodian fangtan de yulun jiandu neirong weihe jianshao" (Why Has Public Opinion Supervision Content Decreased at Focus Interviews?), at http://news.sina.com.cn/c/2003–12–08/10512314972.shtml (accessed March 24, 2006).

54. Lei Weizheng, "Shinian yijian" (Ten Years to Make One Sword), *Zhongguo jizhe* (The Chinese Journalist), no. 6 (2004), at www.woxie.com/article/list.asp?id=20547 (accessed March 24, 2006).

55. Ji Shuoming, "Xia jingji yi zizhong, difang xiang zhongyang shuobu" (Localities Say No to the Center, Asserting Economic Prowess), at http://www5.chinesenewsnet.com/MainNews/Forums/BackStage/2005_9_17_9_6_14_730.html (accessed April 4, 2006). Although we are unable to verify

Ji's report independently, interviews with media insiders in Beijing confirmed the existence of new guidelines aimed at curbing the media's practice of "[public opinion] supervision in a different jurisdiction."

56. Ibid.

57. On Cheng Yizhong, see Leu Siew Ying, "Outrage Prompted Editor's Release." On *Xinjing bao,* see Geoffrey A. Fowler and Juying Qin, "Editors at *Beijing News* Protest Efforts to Tone Down Coverage," *Wall Street Journal,* December 31, 2005, p. A3.

58. Joseph Kahn, "China Shuts Down Influential Weekly Newspaper in Crackdown on Media," *New York Times,* January 25, 2006, p. A13.

59. Edward Cody, "China Puts Journalist on Trial," *Washington Post,* January 20, 2006, p. A12.

60. Liu Binlu, "Jiaojing duizhang buman piping baodao, shuaizhong baoshe zishi bei tingzhi" (Traffic Police Chief Who Was Unhappy with Critical News Report and Led an Attack at a Newspaper Office Was Suspended), at www.southcn.com/news/china/focuspic/200510210206.htm (accessed March 24, 2006).

61. Wang and Wei, *Yulun jiandu yu xinwen jiufen;* Sun Xupei, *Dangdai Zhongguo xinwen gaige.*

62. Xiaoming Hao and Kewen Zhang, "The Chinese Press and Libel: Political and Legal Implications," *Gazette* (Leiden), no. 55 (1995): 77–91.

63. Yu Jianrong, "Nongmin youzuzhi kangzheng jiqi zhengzhi fengxian" (Organized Resistance by Farmers and Its Political Risks), *Zhanlüe yu guanli* (Strategy and Management), no. 3 (2003): 1–16; Yu Jianrong, "Nongcun"; Tian, "Agrarian Crisis"; Sun Liping, *Duanlie.*

64. Tian, "Agrarian Crisis," p. 72.

65. Alex Chan, "From Propaganda to Hegemony: Jiaodian Fangtan and China's Media Policy," *Journal of Contemporary China,* 11, no. 30 (February 2002): 35–51; Zhao, "Watchdogs on Party Leashes?" See also Ian Weber, "Reconfiguring Chinese Propaganda and Control Modalities: A Case Study of Shanghai's Television System," *Journal of Contemporary China,* 11, no. 30 (2002): 53–75.

66. Hua Xu, "Morality Discourse in the Marketplace: Narratives in the Chinese Television News Magazine *Oriental Horizon,*" *Journalism Studies,* 1, no. 4 (November 2000): 646.

67. Public lecture, September 13, 2004, University of British Columbia, Vancouver.

68. Relevant domestic media reports are posted by the network itself. See www.chinacomplaint.com/shownews.asp?art_id=226&cat_id=30 (accessed September 16, 2004). This Web site was no longer accessible, however, when this chapter was finalized on March 24, 2006. It is possible that it has been blocked.

69. Cited in Tian Jing and Feng Liang, "Hu-Jiang Power Struggles Enter Cyberspace," *Asia Times Online,* at www.atimes.com/atimes/China/FG20Ad04.html (accessed August 28, 2004).

70. Sun Zhan and Zhang Shuang, "Minjian jiandu wang: Di'er xinfang" (A Nonstate Supervision Network: A Second Ombudsman), *Zhongguo xinwen zhoukan* (China Newsweek), August 2, 2004, pp. 36–38.

71. By September 2004, however, Li's Web site reportedly had been shut down four times. See Sun and Zhang, "Minjian"; Zhang Kun and Zhang Yuzheng, "Yu Li Xinde mian dui mian" (Face-to-Face with Li Xinde), *Xin'an wanbao* (Xin'an Evening News), September 15, 2004, at www.yuluncn.com/Article_Show.asp?ArticleID=1106 (accessed September 16, 2004).

72. Zhao Dagong, "Zhongguo minjian fanfubai wangzhan yijing xingcheng lianmeng" (China's Independent Anti-corruption Web Sites Have Formed an Alliance), May 20, 2005, at www.peacehall.com/news/gb/pubvp/2005/05/200505200147.shtml (accessed January 26, 2006).

73. Jean C. Oi, "Two Decades of Rural Reform in China: An Overview and Assessment," *China Quarterly,* no. 159 (September 1999): 626.

74. A widely exposed form of power abuse by the media is to use the threat of writing a critical report to extort cash or advertising contracts from potential targets.

Contributors

YONGSHUN CAI is Assistant Professor in the Division of Social Science at Hong Kong University of Science and Technology.

XI CHEN is Assistant Professor in the Department of Political Science at Louisiana State University.

MARY E. GALLAGHER is Assistant Professor in the Department of Political Science at the University of Michigan.

MERLE GOLDMAN is Professor Emerita in the Department of History at Boston University.

JOHN JAMES KENNEDY is Assistant Professor in the Department of Political Science at the University of Kansas.

CHING KWAN LEE is Associate Professor in the Department of Sociology at the University of Michigan.

RICHARD LEVY is Professor in the Department of Political Science at Salem State College, Massachusetts.

LIANJIANG LI is Associate Professor in the Department of Government and International Studies at Hong Kong Baptist University.

RALPH LITZINGER is Associate Professor in the Department of Anthropology and Director of the Asian/Pacific Studies Institute at Duke University.

JEAN C. OI is Walter Haas Professor in the Department of Political Science at Stanford University.

ELIZABETH J. PERRY is Henry Rosovsky Professor in the Department of Government at Harvard University.

BENJAMIN L. READ is Assistant Professor in the Department of Political Science at the University of Iowa.

SUN WUSAN is Associate Professor in the Institute of Journalism at the Chinese Academy of Social Sciences.

LILY L. TSAI is Assistant Professor in the Department of Political Science at MIT.

ZHAO SHUKAI is Senior Researcher in the Development Research Center of the State Council of the PRC.

YUEZHI ZHAO is Associate Professor in the School of Communication at Simon Fraser University, British Columbia.

Harvard Contemporary China Series

Edited and with an Introduction by
William A. Joseph, Christine P. W. Wong, and David Zweig

From May Fourth to June Fourth: Fiction and Film in Twentieth-Century China
Edited by Ellen Widmer and David Der-Wei Wang

Engendering China: Women, Culture, and the State
Edited by Christina K. Gilmartin, Gail Hershatter,
Lisa Rofel, and Tyrene White

Zouping in Transition:
The Process of Reform in Rural North China
Edited by Andrew G. Walder

The Paradox of China's Post-Mao Reforms
Edited by Merle Goldman and Roderick MacFarquhar

Changing Meanings of Citizenship in Modern China
Edited by Merle Goldman and Elizabeth J. Perry